Examining the HEALTH DISPARITIES RESEARCH PLAN of the NATIONAL INSTITUTES OF HEALTH

Unfinished Business

Committee on the Review and Assessment of the NIH's Strategic Research Plan and Budget to Reduce and Ultimately Eliminate Health Disparities

Board on Health Sciences Policy

Gerald E. Thomson, Faith Mitchell, Monique B. Williams, *Editors*

INSTITUTE OF MEDICINE
OF THE NATIONAL ACADEMIES

THE NATIONAL ACADEMIES PRESS
Washington, D.C.
www.nap.edu

THE NATIONAL ACADEMIES PRESS • 500 Fifth Street, N.W. • Washington, DC 20001

NOTICE: The project that is the subject of this report was approved by the Governing Board of the National Research Council, whose members are drawn from the councils of the National Academy of Sciences, the National Academy of Engineering, and the Institute of Medicine. The members of the committee responsible for the report were chosen for their special competences and with regard for appropriate balance.

This study was supported by Contract No. NO1-OD-4-2139 between the National Academy of Sciences and National Center on Minority Health and Health Disparities, U.S. Department of Health & Human Services. Any opinions, findings, conclusions, or recommendations expressed in this publication are those of the author(s) and do not necessarily reflect the view of the organizations or agencies that provided support for this project.

Library of Congress Cataloging-in-Publication Data

Examining the health disparities research plan of the National Institutes of Health : unfinished business / Committee on the Review and Assessment of the NIH's Strategic Research Plan And Budget to Reduce and Ultimately Eliminate Health Disparities, Board on Health Sciences Policy ; Gerald E. Thomson, Faith Mitchell, Monique Williams, editors.
p. ; cm.
Includes bibliographical references and index.
ISBN 0-309-10121-2 (hardback) — ISBN 0-309-65775-X (PDFs)
1. Health services accessibility—United States. 2. Social medicine—United States. 3. Medical policy—United States. 4. Medical care—United States—Evaluation. I. Thomson, Gerald E. II. Mitchell, Faith, 1952- . III. Williams, Monique. IV. National Research Council (U.S.). Committee on the Review and Assessment of the NIH's Strategic Research Plan And Budget to Reduce and Ultimately Eliminate Health Disparities.
[DNLM: 1. National Institutes of Health (U.S.) 2. Health Services Research—United States. 3. Cultural Diversity—United States. 4. Health Services Accessibility—United States. 5. Program Development—United States. 6. Research Design—United States. 7. Socioeconomic Factors—United States. W 84 AA1 E96 2006]
RA418.3.U6E93 2006
362.1′0425—dc22
2006011067

Additional copies of this report are available for sale from the National Academy Press, 500 Fifth Street, N.W., Lockbox 285, Washington, D.C. 20055; (800) 624-6242 or (202) 334-3313 (in the Washington metropolitan area), Internet, http://www.nap.edu.

For more information about the Institute of Medicine, visit the IOM home page at: **www.iom.edu.**

Printed in the United States of America.

The serpent has been a symbol of long life, healing, and knowledge among almost all cultures and religions since the beginning of recorded history. The serpent adopted as a logotype by the Institute of Medicine is a relief carving from ancient Greece, now held by the Staatliche Museen in Berlin.

"Knowing is not enough; we must apply.
Willing is not enough; we must do."
—Goethe

INSTITUTE OF MEDICINE
OF THE NATIONAL ACADEMIES

Advising the Nation. Improving Health.

THE NATIONAL ACADEMIES

Advisers to the Nation on Science, Engineering, and Medicine

The **National Academy of Sciences** is a private, nonprofit, self-perpetuating society of distinguished scholars engaged in scientific and engineering research, dedicated to the furtherance of science and technology and to their use for the general welfare. Upon the authority of the charter granted to it by the Congress in 1863, the Academy has a mandate that requires it to advise the federal government on scientific and technical matters. Dr. Ralph J. Cicerone is president of the National Academy of Sciences.

The **National Academy of Engineering** was established in 1964, under the charter of the National Academy of Sciences, as a parallel organization of outstanding engineers. It is autonomous in its administration and in the selection of its members, sharing with the National Academy of Sciences the responsibility for advising the federal government. The National Academy of Engineering also sponsors engineering programs aimed at meeting national needs, encourages education and research, and recognizes the superior achievements of engineers. Dr. Wm. A. Wulf is president of the National Academy of Engineering.

The **Institute of Medicine** was established in 1970 by the National Academy of Sciences to secure the services of eminent members of appropriate professions in the examination of policy matters pertaining to the health of the public. The Institute acts under the responsibility given to the National Academy of Sciences by its congressional charter to be an adviser to the federal government and, upon its own initiative, to identify issues of medical care, research, and education. Dr. Harvey V. Fineberg is president of the Institute of Medicine.

The **National Research Council** was organized by the National Academy of Sciences in 1916 to associate the broad community of science and technology with the Academy's purposes of furthering knowledge and advising the federal government. Functioning in accordance with general policies determined by the Academy, the Council has become the principal operating agency of both the National Academy of Sciences and the National Academy of Engineering in providing services to the government, the public, and the scientific and engineering communities. The Council is administered jointly by both Academies and the Institute of Medicine. Dr. Ralph J. Cicerone and Dr. Wm. A. Wulf are chair and vice chair, respectively, of the National Research Council.

www.national-academies.org

COMMITTEE ON THE REVIEW AND ASSESSMENT OF THE NIH'S STRATEGIC RESEARCH PLAN AND BUDGET TO REDUCE AND ULTIMATELY ELIMINATE HEALTH DISPARITIES

GERALD E. THOMSON *(Chair)*, Lambert & Sonneborn Professor of Medicine, Emeritus, Senior Associate Dean, Emeritus, Columbia University College of Physicians and Surgeons, New York, NY

JOHN F. ALDERETE, Professor, Department of Microbiology, University of Texas Health Science Center at San Antonio, San Antonio, TX

MOON CHEN, JR., Professor, Department of Epidemiology and Preventive Medicine, University of California, Davis, School of Medicine, Associate Director for Cancer Prevention and Control (Population Sciences), University of California, Davis, CA

HARVEY R. COLTEN, Vice President & Senior Associate Dean, Academic Affairs, Columbia University, Health Sciences and College of Physicians & Surgeons, New York, NY

ROBERT A. HIATT, Professor, Epidemiology and Biostatistics, UCSF Comprehensive Cancer Center, Population Sciences, San Francisco, CA

SHERMAN JAMES, Susan B. King Professor of Public Policy, Duke University, Durham, NC

ICHIRO KAWACHI, Professor of Social Epidemiology, Director, Harvard Center for Society and Health, Harvard School of Public Health, Boston, MA

CLAUDE LENFANT, President, World Hypertension League, Gaithersburg, MD

SPERO M. MANSON, Professor of Psychiatry, Head, American Indian and Alaska Native Programs, University of Colorado at Denver and Health Sciences Center, Denver, CO

JEANNE MIRANDA, Professor in Residence, University of California, Department of Psychiatry and Biobehavioral Science, Los Angeles, CA

KYU RHEE, Medical Director, Upper Cardozo Community Health Center, Washington, DC

LYNNE D. RICHARDSON, Associate Professor, Emergency Medicine, Director, Emergency Medicine Residency, Mount Sinai School of Medicine, Department of Emergency Medicine, New York, NY

ANTONIA M. VILLARRUEL, Professor, Director, Center for Health Promotion, University of Michigan, School of Nursing, Ann Arbor, MI

DAVID WILLIAMS, Harold Cruse Collegiate Professor of Sociology, Senior Research Scientist, Institute for Social Research, University of Michigan, Ann Arbor, MI

HEALTH SCIENCES POLICY BOARD LIAISON

MARTHA N. HILL, Dean and Professor, The Johns Hopkins University, School of Nursing, Baltimore, MD

IOM PROJECT STAFF

FAITH MITCHELL, Senior Program Officer
MONIQUE B. WILLIAMS, Program Officer
THELMA L. COX, Senior Program Assistant

IOM Staff

ANDREW M. POPE, Director, Board on Health Sciences Policy
AMY HAAS, Administrative Assistant
CARLOS GABRIEL, Financial Associate (until May 2005)
DAVID CODREA, Financial Associate

Reviewers

This report has been reviewed in draft form by individuals chosen for their diverse perspectives and technical expertise, in accordance with procedures approved by the National Research Council's (NRC's) Report Review Committee. The purpose of this independent review is to provide candid and critical comments that will assist the institution in making its published report as sound as possible and to ensure that the report meets institutional standards for objectivity, evidence, and responsiveness to the study charge. The review comments and draft manuscript remain confidential to protect the integrity of the deliberative process. We wish to thank the following individuals for their review of this report:

PAULA A. BRAVEMAN, University of California, San Francisco
H. JACK GEIGER, City University of New York Medical School
BRADFORD GRAY, The Milbank Quarterly, The Urban Institute
RUTH HANFT, James Madison University
ROBERT A. LOWE, Oregon Health & Science University
NICOLE LURIE, The RAND Corporation
JOHN E. MAUPIN, Meharry Medical College
RUBENS J. PAMIES, University of Nebraska Medical Center
TIMOTHY SIZE, Rural Wisconsin Health Cooperative

Although the reviewers listed above have provided many constructive comments and suggestions, they were not asked to endorse the conclusions or recommendations nor did they see the final draft of the report before its release. The review of this report was overseen by **NEAL VANSELOW,** Tulane University,

Professor Emeritus, and **DAVID KINDIG,** Wisconsin Public Health and Health Policy Institute, University of Wisconsin-Madison.

Appointed by the NRC and Institute of Medicine, they were responsible for making certain that an independent examination of this report was carried out in accordance with institutional procedures and that all review comments were carefully considered. Responsibility for the final content of this report rests entirely with the authoring committee and the institution.

Preface

Although the overall health of Americans has improved considerably over the past several decades, the health of racial and ethnic minorities and other populations continues to lag behind that of whites. For decades, there have been declarations identifying correction of health disparities as a national priority but progress has been slow, and the suffering, disability, and death continue. If the gaps between populations persist and some minority populations continue to grow disproportionately, within several decades most Americans will be members of populations at risk for disparate health.

Improving the situation requires much better understanding of health disparities. The National Institutes of Health (NIH) has supported and conducted extensive research related to minority health and health disparities. The NIH health disparities research effort was addressed by Congress with the "Minority Health and Health Disparities Research and Education Act of 2000." Among its provisions, the legislation called for establishing the National Center on Minority Health and Health Disparities (NCMHD) with two broad areas of responsibility: first, administration of extensive grants and awards aimed at strengthening the country's personnel and institutional capacities to conduct research on minority health and health disparities; and second, coordination of all health disparities research across NIH together with oversight of the development and implementation of an NIH-wide strategic plan for health disparities research. NCMHD was established in 2000 and, in 2004, asked the Institute of Medicine to assess the adequacy and coordination of the Strategic Plan that had been developed. The study committee began the review late in 2004 with completion targeted for late 2005.

The extensive Strategic Plan features three broad research, research capacity, and outreach goals along with detailed objectives. Included are the individual plans of 25 of the 27 Institutes and Centers, as well as 2 Offices within the Office of the Director. As a catalogue of ongoing and intended health disparities research activity across NIH, it is impressive. As a strategy in a health disparities research campaign, it is a beginning.

To be sure, the effort faces strong challenges. The first is the nature of the research itself. The range of diseases and conditions for which there are differences spans virtually all biomedical disciplines. There are complex, interrelated social, economic, behavioral, health care, and other environmental aspects—and the differences, their features, and the roles of contributing factors vary among affected populations and subpopulations.

The review committee sees the opportunity and need for NIH to focus even more on health disparities as a research entity and move knowledge and understanding forward as no other agency or setting can. Along with understanding the biomedical aspects of diseases and conditions that are the manifestations of health disparities, there is need to know more about the contributions and interactions of core conditions and factors that may be common to the genesis of disparate health. The NIH should take leadership in helping to understand, further define, and develop methodology regarding health disparities research. As well, given the particular importance of the translation of new information into best practices in the care of patients, there is opportunity to better understand, design, and assess communication of health disparities information to health professionals and the public as a core NIH effort with much to be learned and applied.

A second challenge has to do with coordination and management of such an extensive plan and program across NIH where the Institutes and Centers have a degree of autonomy that can make it difficult to effect concerted programs. The challenge is an example of other efforts to achieve trans-NIH coordination of broad interdisciplinary programs, such as those organized for AIDS, obesity, and neuroscience. The extensive nature of the health disparities research effort requires that there be a well-structured effort with ongoing, continuous improvement of the plan and program that is the result of extensive involvement from within and from outside of NIH contributing to identification of research needs, assessments, evaluation and priority determinations. Along with central oversight and attention to the detailed aspects of the programs, there must be a broader view and vision and assurance that needed research areas are not neglected. Also, there is the opportunity to bring together and involve much expertise from across NIH and from across the nation to inform the NIH program, its planning, evaluation and priorities.

The Strategic Plan and its strategy for health disparities research can be strengthened as part of an integrated, cohesive, coordinated trans-NIH program, developed with the best available thought, addressing relevant, prioritized questions and issues with clearly initiated and evaluated programs, and with the production of information which allows the NIH, and the nation, to be assured that needed research on health disparities is being addressed as effectively and expeditiously as possible.

Throughout the review, the Committee felt the implications and urgency of the task and brought to the review the utmost devotion and commitment. We are grateful for the expertise and efforts of the staff, including Faith Mitchell, the Project Director, Monique Williams, Program Officer, and Thelma Cox, Senior Program Assistant.

Dr. Elias Zerhouni, the Director of NIH, Dr. Raynard Kington, Deputy Director of NIH, and the NIH Office of Budget were forthcoming and most helpful. We are particularly grateful to the NCMHD and its Director, John Ruffin, and the staff for their intense devotion, cooperation and assistance and to the Institutes and Centers which provided valuable information and insights. We are thankful for the cooperation, responses, testimony and other information provided by the Institutes and Centers and Offices within the Office of the Director and those provided by the many distinguished individuals and devoted organizations.

Gerald E. Thomson, M.D., *Chair*
Committee on the Review and Assessment of the
NIH's Strategic Research Plan and Budget
to Reduce and Ultimately Eliminate Health Disparities

Acknowledgments

The editors would like to thank several people for their testimony to the Committee: Lawrence Agodoa, Duane Alexander, Barbara Alving, Victoria A. Cargill, Francis D. Chesley, Jr., Gail C. Christopher, Mark Clanton, Gem Daus, Adolph Falcon, Charles Francis, René González, Garth Graham, Doug Hussey, Carolyn M. Kane, Raynard Kington, Ronny B. Lancaster, Yvonne Maddox, John J. McGowan, Vivian W. Pinn, Winston Price, Griffin Rodgers, Leonard S. Rubenstein, John Ruffin, David Satcher, Allen M. Spiegel, Louis W. Sullivan, Walter W. Williams, Jerome Wilson, and Elias A. Zerhouni.

We thank Nancy Adler, Neil R. Powe, Kasisomayajula Viswanath, and Edwina H. Yeung for their background papers that informed the committee's deliberations.

Among the IOM staff, special thanks are due to Thelma Cox and Andy Pope.

Contents

Executive Summary

ABSTRACT

This report is an assessment of the National Institutes of Health (NIH) Strategic Research Plan and Budget to Reduce and Ultimately Eliminate Health Disparities and the adequacy of coordination of the development and implementation of the Strategic Plan across NIH Institutes and Centers.

Congressional legislation in 2000 called for the establishment of the NIH National Center on Minority Health and Health Disparities and a Strategic Plan to address the continuing poor health states of minorities, those with low income, and people living in rural areas. The plan includes the strategic plans of 25 Institutes and Centers and 2 Offices within the Office of the Director. Goals and objectives in research, research capacity, and communication are expected to form the foundation for the NIH health disparities research program.

The study committee viewed the Strategic Plan in the context of the need for NIH health disparities research to be conducted as an integrated and inclusive field of study rather than an aggregate of independent research plans and activities occurring in separate research domains. Such an approach, for example, would help to further needed study of social, behavioral, environmental and other root factors interactive across diseases, conditions and affected populations. As well, there would be more assurance that needed areas of research are not neglected.

A concerted minority health and health disparities research program and its Strategic Plan is a challenging trans-NIH effort because of the scope and complexity of the research, and the NIH organizational and functional setting that makes it difficult to manage initiatives across NIH. Development and implementation of the Strategic Plan presently lack the central management and coordination necessary to meet the challenge. Development and revision of the Strategic Plan has been delayed and incomplete. The Committee did not find organized, collective involvement of the Institutes and Centers and expertise from outside of NIH in overall planning. The Plan includes extensive programs in the Institutes and Centers, without evidence that these efforts are centrally coordinated, appropriately assessed regarding priorities and outcomes, or otherwise viewed as part of an overall NIH strategy. Continuous, effective, and demonstrable trans-NIH coordination and management with clearly established responsibility and authority should be assured by the Director of NIH through the Director of the National Center on Minority Health and Health Disparities, including timely updates of the Strategic Plan and collective involvement of the Institutes and Centers in overall planning and implementation, monitoring, and evaluation of the Strategic Plan and the health disparities research program.

Needed additions to the Strategic Plan include attention to the integration of research on the multifactorial nature of health disparities; population research; targeted and timed objectives; collaborative, integrated research on disparate health care; identification of additional affected populations; access to a registry of conditions for which differences between populations exist; assessments and evaluations of programs intended to increase institutional and research-personnel capacities to conduct health disparities research; and attention to public and professional communication regarding health disparities as a specific, trans-NIH program.

The health of racial and ethnic minorities, poor people, and other disadvantaged groups in the United States is worse than the health of the overall population. National concerns for these differences, termed health disparities, and the associated excess mortality and morbidity have been expressed as a high priority in national health status reviews, including *Healthy People 2000* and *Healthy People 2010*. The National Institutes of Health (NIH) ranks this issue third among its top five priorities.

Research is fundamental to the understanding and ultimate correction of health disparities. The needed research is as far-ranging and complex as the disparities. Involved are biomedical factors that span the entire range of medical specialties and research domains—and these factors are strongly intertwined with vital social, behavioral, and population research issues, as well as disparate health care.

As the nation's foremost research agency, NIH plays a leading role in health disparities research. Although NIH has accomplished much important research related to health disparities, there has been concern that NIH ensure that research efforts are optimally marshaled to address health disparities. The Minority Health and Health Disparities Research and Education Act of 2000 (P.L. 106-525) delineated NIH's role in improving minority health and reducing health disparities. The legislation called for the establishment of the National Center on Minority Health and Health Disparities (NCMHD) to administer special grant programs, coordinate minority health and health disparities research across NIH and lead the development of an NIH-wide strategic plan on health disparities. Detailed descriptions of NCMHD's responsibilities and mandates are included in the legislation (see Appendix A). Established in 2000, NCMHD directed development of the NIH Strategic Research Plan and Budget to Reduce and Ultimately Eliminate Health Disparities, which was completed in 2003.

CHARGE TO THE COMMITTEE

In 2004, the 4th year of the NIH minority health and health disparities initiative, NCMHD asked the Institute of Medicine to:

- Assess the adequacy of the trans-NIH minority health and health disparities Strategic Plan in achieving the NIH's goals and objectives. Specifically, the Committee was to evaluate the Strategic Plan with respect to:
  - Research (e.g., How well does the Strategic Plan advance scientific understanding of the causes and means to reduce and ultimately eliminate the disproportionate burden of disease among health disparity groups?),
  - Research Infrastructure (e.g., Does the Strategic Plan adequately expand opportunities and the institutional capacity—such as the environment, leadership, and commitment to health disparities research—for research on health disparities?),
  - Public Information and Community Outreach (e.g., How adequately does the plan address needs for the dissemination and application of research findings to reduce and ultimately eliminate health disparities?);
- Assess the adequacy of coordination across NIH ICs in helping to develop and carry out the Strategic Plan and avoid duplication of administrative resources among ICs and divisions; and
- Identify means, including potential legislative modifications, to help NIH achieve its minority health and health disparity Strategic Plan objectives.

In its approach, the Committee reviewed the challenges and needs of health disparities research and analyzed (a) the adequacy of the Strategic Plan as a document and plan of action, including the ICs' individual strategic plans; (b) budget information; (c) trans-NIH organization of the efforts; and (d) experiences with implementation, coordination, and monitoring. The process included open meeting sessions with the directors of NIH and NCMHD, directors and leaders of several large ICs and Offices within the Office of the Director, and individuals and representatives of numerous government agencies and private organizations concerned with health disparities. Commissioned papers and a commissioned survey were used to further inform the Committee.

HEALTH DISPARITIES: DEFINITIONS, MEASUREMENT, AND UNDERSTANDING

Understanding and correcting the poorer health of populations in the United States is complicated by the need for more consensus on definitions, the wide range of diseases and conditions, a variety of causal factors, and varying measurements of factors and their interactions. Even as research and attention to correction move ahead, core questions and issues need more focus. NIH should take leadership in helping to further define, measure, and better understand health disparities, and also help to guide attention to research needs and opportunities.

Findings:

- **Lack of consensus regarding conceptual and operational definitions of disparities and the complexity of measuring health and health determinants pose challenges for the identification, understanding, monitoring and elimination of health disparities.**
- **There is a continuing need for NIH-funded research to develop, test, and refine measures and conceptual approaches for assessing and monitoring health disparities. Research is required to answer fundamental questions: Which factors are most critical to monitor? How can they best be measured?**
- **Currently available information does not provide a full and accurate description of disparities between, and within, racial and ethnic groups and across the full spectrum of socioeconomic status. Detailed, accurate data on Hispanic, Asian/Pacific Islander, African American, and American Indian/Alaska Native subgroups are needed, including data on income, education, and occupation. Such data will provide an important source for research on disparities and for monitoring progress toward reducing and eliminating disparities across the nation.**
- **Sophisticated and creative approaches to studying the processes that cause health disparities are needed. Coordinated, collaborative trans-NIH initiatives, with the active involvement of multiple ICs, will be needed to understand common backgrounds for multiple diseases. Coordinated, collaborative trans-agency approaches will be required to successfully investigate the complex relation-**

ships and interactions among race, ethnicity, gender, income, education, occupation, immigrant generation, and area of residence.

Recommendation: NIH, through NCMHD and the ICs and, when appropriate, collaborating agencies, should undertake research to further refine and develop the conceptual, definitional, and methodological issues involved in health disparities research and to further the understanding of the causes of disparities.

For such research, priority areas should include, first, the development and refinement of valid measures of exposures relevant to understanding and evaluating health disparities. For example:

- Interagency disparity research initiatives to develop valid and reliable measures of health effects of social factors; genetic risk; stress; racial/ethnic discrimination; and health care access and quality.
- Disparities research embedded into large studies (molecular, clinical, and epidemiological), national data sets, and public health monitoring measures through the greater inclusion of appropriate measures of race, ethnicity, socioeconomic status, and residential characteristics, and of the psychosocial and environmental factors that are likely to shape health disparities in the population being studied at each time point of data collection.
- In population-based studies, the inclusion of information on racial and ethnic subpopulations and other relevant characteristics, such as immigrant status, language preference, and detailed socioeconomic data, should be encouraged. Investigators funded by the ICs should be encouraged to gather information on socioeconomic status and other dimensions of social stratification.

Second, priority areas should include initiatives to further enhance understanding of the etiology of health disparities. For example:

- Multidisciplinary initiatives to advance the study of disparities, including gene-environment interactions and biological mechanisms mediating disparities.
- Trans-NIH disparity research initiatives to elucidate the pathways and mechanisms by which health disparities occur, including the identification of common backgrounds for multiple diseases and disease-specific mechanisms that may facilitate the development of strategies for intervention.

DEVELOPMENT OF THE STRATEGIC PLAN

Creation of the extensive Strategic Plan included the development of individual strategic plans by 25 of the 27 ICs and 2 Offices within NIH's Office of the Director, followed by reviews and approvals, including those of NCMHD and the director of NIH. Although development of the Strategic Plan began before the legislation and the establishment of NCMHD, the first Strategic Plan, that for 2002–2006, was not available until 2003. It was expected, both by the legislation and as described in the initial Strategic Plan, that the Strategic Plan would be revised and updated annually. The only updated Strategic Plan, that for 2004–2008, was available to the review committee late in Fiscal Year 2005 as an incomplete, unapproved draft without a budget.

Finding: NIH has not updated the Strategic Plan as intended by the legislation and the NIH.

Recommendation: The NIH director should assure that the Strategic Plan is reviewed and revised annually using an established, trans-NIH process subject to timely review, approval, and dissemination.

THE STRATEGIC RESEARCH PLAN AND BUDGET

Although the only complete and approved Strategic Plan available for review was the 2002–2006 Strategic Plan, the Committee felt that it would be most helpful to include a review and assessment of the unapproved Strategic Plan for 2004–2008.

The Strategic Plan has three goal areas: research, research capacity, and outreach and communication (see Box 3-1 and Table 3-3 in Chapter 3).

The **research goal** forms the basis for substantial objectives that properly address the understanding of diseases and disabilities, detection and diagnosis, prevention, treatment, and, in the 2004 Strategic Plan, attention to the multifactorial causes of health disparities. Additional research objectives warrant emphasis and inclusion.

Minority health and health disparities research should include attention to the nonbiological and biological multifactorial background of disease and disability. Integration of such aspects of research with activities related to the Strategic Plan objective dealing with "understanding . . . the development and progression of diseases and disabilities that contribute to minority health and other disparities" should be encouraged. The need for information on health disparity populations should also be an objective of the Strategic Plan. Recognition of the relationship between health care disparities and disparities in health status is not currently described in the Strategic Plan. Opportunities for collaborative, interagency research in health care disparities should be fostered by a specific objective.

Finding: The Strategic Plan has placed inadequate emphasis on understanding social and behavioral determinants of health and their interaction with biological factors; better understanding of the characteristics of populations affected by poor health and the characteristics of diseases

and conditions for which disparities exist in those populations; the relationship between population disparities in health care and differences in health status; and research opportunities regarding disparities in health care.

Recommendation: The Strategic Plan research objectives should promote more integration of research on the multifactorial nature of health disparities, including nonbiological factors; population research to further the understanding of the presence, prevalence, trends, and other elements of health disparity conditions; and, when opportunity exists, an understanding of the causes of disparities in health care.

The **research capacity** goal and the listed objectives were found to be appropriate by the Committee. The Committee emphasized the importance and potentials of certain aspects of the objectives—specifically, diversity in the scientific workforce, the participation of minority individuals in clinical trials, community-based participatory research, and the need for assessments of programs.

Diversity in the scientific workforce, and an increase in the numbers of researchers who will engage in health disparities research, are important objectives. During the minority health and health disparities research program and the implementation of the Strategic Plan (2000–2004), successes and trends in providing support for the development of researchers so far have varied with the type of career-support mechanisms. Minority Research Fellow and Research Career Awards increased, but Research Training Grants for minorities changed little. Participation of minority individuals in clinical trials did increase during this period.

The Strategic Plan's objectives should include assessments of the results and impacts of research infrastructure programs (including institutional awards) on the capacity to conduct minority health and health disparities research. This information is needed to evaluate the effectiveness of programs, identify approaches in need of modification, set priorities, and make evaluations available for internal and external reviews.

Community-based participatory research can be a valuable, if challenging, research approach. The Strategic Plan and the health disparities research program provide an opportunity to analyze and evaluate community-based participatory research in health disparities research and to generate experience-based guidance on its use in future health disparities research efforts. NCMHD can play a central role in fostering the understanding and application of community-based participatory research in health disparities.

Findings:

- **The Strategic Plan does not provide for assessments of the results of the research capacity and infrastructure programs included as**

objectives. Such information is needed to evaluate the effectiveness of these programs, identify approaches in need of modification, set priorities, and make evaluations available for internal and external reviews.

- **The inclusion of community-based participatory research as an objective of the Strategic Plan is appropriate. There is a need for development of metrics, analysis, assessment and evaluation of community-based participatory research for a better sense of the issues and settings for which it is most promising.**

Recommendation: The Strategic Plan should include measurable targets and time periods for the research capacity objectives. NIH, through NCMHD's oversight, should develop methods of measuring, analyzing and monitoring the results of programs that address research capacity, including workforce, institutional, infrastructure, and community-based participatory health disparity research objectives.

The objectives listed in support of the **community outreach, information dissemination, and public health education goal** are reasonable. There are important areas in which more information is needed to improve public information and outreach strategies related to health disparities, including attention to the complexity, difficulties, and challenges of communication and the need for an organized, coordinated, trans-NIH approach to the communication effort.

Finding: The current objectives for outreach and public information identify target audiences, but attention is needed to issues of inequalities in public communication, including those related to access and use of, and ability to act on, information. Additional understanding is needed regarding effective communication with those who provide care to groups with poor health. Coordination of communication programs across NIH could help with examination of specific audience needs and evaluations of programs.

Recommendation: The Strategic Plan's communication programs should be organized as a specific trans-NIH effort with centralized coordination with particular attention to the strategic planning, design, prioritization, implementation, and evaluation of efforts across NIH. The initiative should: be informed by advisory expertise; develop a surveillance system to identify information needs and availability, sources, behaviors, and use patterns; and promote attention to the issue of inequalities in health communication.

THE STRATEGIC PLANS OF THE ICS

The Strategic Plan's goals and objectives cannot be achieved unless they are adopted by the ICs and reflected in their objectives and activities. The individual strategic plans of the ICs contain an impressive array of planned activities related to the overall Strategic Plan objectives, but some overall objectives appear infrequently as intended IC activities. Time-based, targeted research activities would help with assessments of the results of research programs.

Finding: There is no evidence that the strategic plans of the ICs were developed as part of a concerted, trans-NIH strategic planning process. Planned IC activities are not time-based or targeted.

Recommendation:

- **The development of updated Strategic Plans should include assessments of the appropriateness of the individual strategic plans of the ICs, including whether they adequately reflect the overall goals and objectives of the NIH Strategic Plan.**
- **Objectives should be time-based and targeted with measurable outcomes.**

HEALTH DISPARITIES AS DEFINED BY THE STRATEGIC PLAN

Although defining health disparities is difficult (see Chapter 2), the Strategic Plan and the minority health and health disparities research program required working definitions. The legislation and the Strategic Plan indicate that in addition to racial and ethnic minorities and low socioeconomic and rural populations there may be other population groups that warrant inclusion in health disparities research and the Strategic Plan. As described by the legislation, it is expected that the director of NCMHD, consulting with the director of the Agency for Healthcare Research and Quality, will, when appropriate, designate additional groups experiencing diseases and conditions for which there are disparities. Such designations should be the result of a well-informed process with specific criteria.

Findings:

- **Beyond the basic definitions of health disparities indicated by Congress and used by NIH, there are no further criteria for deciding what constitutes a health disparity group. Understanding the health impacts of social stratification (e.g., in the education system or the labor market) presents an additional approach to health disparities research.**
- **There is need for a resource that provides updated listings of: diseases and conditions for which differences exist; affected popu-**

lations; prevalence data; and other information that would provide a knowledge base on the scope and impact of disparity conditions. This resource would help in planning health disparity studies, setting priorities, and assessing research activities.

Recommendation: NCMHD should consider the designation of additional health disparity groups based on an informed process and developed criteria. It should promote development of, and access to, a registry of diseases and conditions for which disparities exist with regard to race, ethnicity, socioeconomic status, geographic locale, and other designated health disparity populations.

THE STRATEGIC PLAN BUDGET

The first Strategic Plan, for 2002–2006, and the 2001 Annual Report included budgets developed without uniform accounting, coding definitions, and methodologies for attributing research activities to minority health and health disparities efforts. The second Strategic Plan (2004–2008) was available for review as an unapproved draft that did not include a budget. The two subsequent Annual Reports, for 2002 and 2003, were also incomplete and unapproved.

The enabling legislation recognized the need for incremental funding to be provided to the NIH and authorized up to $100 million in additional annual funding for minority health and health disparities research to be added to separate appropriations for the conduct and support of the health disparities research program, but the incremental funds were not allocated to the NIH. The committee expressed concern that the absence of such funding might have impeded the establishment of new health disparities research programs, which would reasonably incur additional research and management costs.

Regarding the ways in which budget information is reported, it would be helpful to have budget information categorized by funding for each goal area, along with the funds allocated for each objective under each goal, and individually for each involved IC and office. Such information would facilitate monitoring and review.

Findings:

- **Incremental funding was not provided to NIH for the minority health and health disparities research program.**
- **As of July 2005, during the 5th year of the program period, no complete, standardized, approved budget information was available from the Strategic Plan or the Annual Reports. The absence of such information calls into question the validity and efficacy of the Strategic Plan and Annual Reports as tools for planning and coordination.**

- **For more accurate evaluation, detailed information on specific categories and aspects of the minority health and health disparities research program and the Strategic Plan would be helpful.**

Recommendation: Within NIH, a clear and timely budget process should be linked to the Strategic Plan, and it should be updated in a timely manner. Annual budgets should include information for NIH as a whole, and for each involved IC and Office, and should detail allocations for the Strategic Plan goal areas and each objective. Trans-NIH budget information on efforts made in the major categories of research, research capacity, and communication also should be made available.

Based on information provided by the NIH Budget Office, the Committee attempted to compare funding for minority health research (involving minority populations) and health disparities research (minority health plus groups with low socioeconomic status and rural populations) for the years 1998 through 2004, though (except for 2003 and 2004) the data were not standardized. The application of new, standardized definitions of minority health and health disparities in Fiscal Year 2003 apparently changed the reported NIH funding for minority health research, from $2.13 billion to $2.09 billion, and changed the estimate of funding for health disparities research from $3.16 billion to $2.43 billion. Using the old methodology, the percentage of the NIH total budget attributed to health disparities research was calculated to be 11 percent in 1999, and 12 percent each year from 2001 to 2003. With the new methodology it was 9 percent for 2003 and 2004. In comparison, the proportion for minority health research held at around 8 percent from 1999 to 2004, reflecting the fact that during the period in which the NIH budget doubled (1998–2003), spending on minority health research kept pace.

THE NCMHD

The Office of Research on Minority Health, established in 1990, became NCMHD in 2000 as a result of the legislation (P.L. 106-525). The legislation also prescribed NCMHD's dual responsibilities: (a) the administration of large, legislatively mandated grant programs dealing with research infrastructure and capacity; and (b) service as the hub of responsibility for coordinating and managing the Strategic Plan. The Committee questioned NCMHD's current resources and capacity to deal with these responsibilities.

Findings:

- **The dual roles of NCMHD as a granting center and as a coordinator of major trans-NIH efforts are unique. The leadership of NCMHD and its Advisory Council call attention to the need for increased administrative staffing for NCMHD.**

- **There is a need for increased science leadership and presence in NCMHD, particularly for proper management of the trans-NIH initiative.**

Recommendation:

- **The NIH director should review and assess the administrative staffing of NCMHD to ensure that it is sufficient to attend to the Center's responsibilities.**
- **Increasing the science leadership and presence within NCMHD should be pursued by the NIH and NCMHD directors. This entails the appointment of additional eminent scientists, recognized in the areas of minority health and health disparities, and the establishment by NCMHD of committees and panels with relevant expertise from within and outside NIH.**

MANAGEMENT AND COORDINATION OF THE STRATEGIC PLAN AND MINORITY AND HEALTH DISPARITIES RESEARCH

The breadth and complexity of the health disparities research agenda and the Strategic Plan present an extraordinary challenge for trans-NIH management. To best manage these efforts, NIH needs to:

- Ensure concerted involvement of the ICs and Offices to develop and regularly update the Strategic Plan;
- Ensure that all ICs and pertinent Offices are attentive to the Strategic Plan's mission, goals, and objectives;
- Avoid gaps, such as populations, conditions, needs, and approaches, that would otherwise not be identified or addressed by the independent operation of the ICs;
- Involve the best expertise from across the NIH and from the external scientific community;
- Avoid duplicating administrative and research efforts;
- Facilitate collaboration and coordinated research approaches;
- Coordinate outreach and communication;
- Create an organized program structure for effective monitoring and research articulation with other government agencies; and
- Devote attention to research and budget priorities.

The potential for conflicting priorities is real. The ICs' budgets reflect commitments, mandates, and priorities resulting from budget presentations to, and authorizations from, Congress. If there is truly a concerted trans-NIH priority for minority health and health disparities research, which is stated to be third among the agency's top five priorities, then this concern should be active in priority formulations and decisions within the ICs.

Development of the Strategic Plan does not involve the coordinated, concerted, and collective participation of the ICs. There is no ongoing, continuous update process with an established trans-NIH structure involving the ICs and others to produce planning improvements and results in periodic, meaningful updates and revisions of the Strategic Plan. There is no evidence of trans-NIH planning of priorities regarding minority health and health disparities research activities and resources for the NIH as a whole or with respect to the ICs. In discussions with the Committee, directors and other leading members of several large ICs with extensive minority health and health disparities programs expressed a very high level of commitment to and enthusiasm for these activities. However, it was evident that there had been little to no contact with the NCMHD during the development or implementation of these projects and programs. Activities and programs were pursued independently of NCMHD, except that some, particularly in the past, had been co-funded, or sometimes totally funded, by NCMHD.

There is no manifest organizational structure for the trans-NIH Strategic Plan and health disparities program. Advisory and coordinating committees are not described or apparent. Experts from scientific, health care, and affected communities are not involved in advising and participating in ongoing planning in established, structured, predictable ways. The result is a gaping lack of opportunity to properly inform and contribute to the identification of research and related needs, plans, and strategy.

No results summarizing the monitoring and assessment of minority health and health disparities research, and related activities for the NIH, or with respect to the ICs, are evident. Annual reports are late, languish incomplete and unapproved, and do not contain evidence of central NIH assessments of research and program activities. Moreover, budget and finance issues are not addressed by a centralized entity responsible for the minority health and health disparities research program and the Strategic Plan.

The Committee saw the need to be certain that there is clearly designated authority to coordinate and manage the Strategic Plan and health disparities research program. Although the legislation indicates that the NCMHD director is responsible for coordinating all NIH minority health and health disparities research, the responsibility for monitoring and managing the Strategic Plan and the program falls on the NIH director, the NCMHD director, and the IC directors. The text of the approved initial Strategic Plan (2002–2006) indicates that NCMHD is responsible for such functions, but it was unclear to the Committee whether this authority is widely understood.

Finding: The level of trans-NIH coordination needed to effectively implement the Strategic Plan has not been evident. Instead, the Committee

concluded that an uncoordinated, unmonitored, loosely administered trans-NIH program existed, with substantial commitments and activities of largely independent ICs, but without the coordinated, concerted program needed. Clarity regarding the responsibilities and authority may be a factor in achieving more effective management. The mandates of the NIH director are key elements in structuring and assuring effective management.

Recommendation: The NIH director, through the established authority of the NCMHD director, should ensure continuous, effective coordination of the health disparities research program across NIH, including:

- **Timely development of Strategic Plan revisions;**
- **Effective, ongoing participation of the ICs in the Strategic Plan and the health disparities research program;**
- **Establishment of appropriate committees involving the directors of the ICs and others to facilitate collaboration and coordinated approaches to health disparities research and the setting of priorities;**
- **Fostering of conferences and the use of committees and panels involving the NIH, extramural scientific communities, and others to inform and advise on initiatives and directions; and**
- **Monitoring of the execution of the Strategic Plan to ensure that its elements are implemented.**

1

Introduction

In the United States, health varies considerably. Racial and ethnic minorities, poor people, and other groups experience worse health in a variety of circumstances. Called health disparities, these differences are reflected by indices such as excess mortality and morbidity and shorter life expectancy. Beyond the statistics, the suffering, disability, and death among large and growing segments of the population tear at the nation's conscience.

National concern over health disparities has been expressed for several decades. Examples include the 1979 U.S. Department of Health, Education, and Welfare report, *The Health Status of Minorities and Low-Income Groups* (Health Resources Administration, 1979); the 1979 *Healthy People* report (U.S. Public Health Administration, 1979); the 1986 *Report of the Secretary's Task Force on Black and Minority Health* (U.S. DHHS, 1985); the *Healthy People 2000* report (U.S. DHHS, 1991), which listed the reduction of health disparities as one of three goals; and the *Healthy People 2010* report (U.S. DHHS, 2000), which had the elimination of health disparities as one of its two goals.

The causes of disparities in health status are complicated and only partly understood. Research is a fundamental aspect of the national strategy to understand, reduce, and eliminate disparities in health status. The research is complex, involving a broad range of biomedical, social, economic, and behavioral issues. The scope of the research extends across research domains and medical specialties. Widespread in the general population, the relevant diseases and conditions occur with increased prevalence or severity, or have worse outcomes, in minorities, those with low income, and certain other groups, such as some rural populations (Eberhardt and Pamuk, 2004; Hartley, 2004). The biomedical aspects range from molecular, genetic, and pathophysiological factors to aspects of diagnosis, detection, progression, treatment, and prevention. Also, there is need to understand the overarching social, economic, educational, behavioral, and environmental factors that predispose groups to specific diseases and conditions. Finally, along with the changing knowledge base, there is the need for rapid and effective translation of existing and new information into best care practices. This entails communicating this information to affected populations and communities, their health care providers, individuals within educational settings, and those involved with health care policy. These challenges require the understanding, design, development, and assessment of specific intervention programs.

The National Institutes of Health (NIH) plays the nation's leading role in minority health and health disparities research. NIH has conducted extensive research related to minority health and health disparities for some time. An NIH Office of Minority Health Research was established in 1990. More recently, NIH declared health disparities to be third among its top five priorities (Morton, 2005; Zerhouni, 2004). NIH's vision of newer approaches to health research involves planning for and conducting health disparities research, with an emphasis on cross-disciplinary team research efforts and a focus on the predominance of chronic diseases (Zerhouni, 2005a, b).

Disparities in health care are separate from, but often contribute to, health status disparities (Smedley et al., 2003). These inequities in the quality of medical care are also independently and specifically related to race, ethnicity, and socioeconomic status. Excess morbidity, mortality, and disability are likely consequences of disparities in health care and undoubtedly contribute to the poorer health among affected groups. Inequities in standards of care related to group characteristics and circumstances raise issues of injustice.

An extensive and growing research effort is directed toward disparate health care. This research includes many issues related to the investigation of differences in health states that call for effective collaboration among NIH, private research entities, and other government agencies, such as the Agency for Healthcare Research and Quality (AHRQ), the Centers for Disease Control and Prevention (CDC), the Office of the Secretary of Health and Human Services (HHS), the Office of Rural Health Policy in the Health Resources and Services Administration, and perhaps other government departments such as Education and Justice. HHS is addressing the need for coordinated government efforts. Similarly, NIH should seek overlapping, collaborative research opportunities.

Although much national research in health disparities is under way, there has been concern for assurance that the NIH research program is effectively marshaled.

CONGRESSIONAL LEGISLATION: THE MINORITY HEALTH AND HEALTH DISPARITIES RESEARCH AND EDUCATION ACT OF 2000

In 2000, Congress enacted Title I of Public Law 106-525, The Minority Health and Health Disparities Research and Education Act of 2000 (Appendix A). This legislation delineated the role of the NIH in improving minority health and reducing health disparities by calling for the establishment of the National Center on Minority Health and Health Disparities (NCMHD) and by detailing many other NIH-related responsibilities and activities.

NCMHD's stated purpose is "the conduct and support of research, training, dissemination of information, and other programs with respect to minority health conditions and other populations with health disparities." The legislation used the definition of minorities that was used in previous legislation—specifically, that found in Section 1707(g) of the Public Health Service Act—as follows:

> (1) The term "racial and ethnic minority group" means American Indians (including Alaska Natives, Eskimos, and Aleuts), Asian Americans, Native Hawaiians and other Pacific Islanders, Blacks, and Hispanics.
>
> (2) The term "Hispanic" means individuals whose origin is Mexican, Puerto Rican, Cuban, Central or South American, or any other Spanish-speaking country.

The director of the newly established NCMHD was given the responsibility to determine which health disparity populations were to be added to existing groups—which include minorities, individuals with low socioeconomic status, and those living in rural areas—to comprise the overall focus group for health disparities research. In addition, the legislation called for the NCMHD director to be responsible for coordinating all minority health research and other health disparity research conducted or supported by NIH.

To further the initiative, a comprehensive plan and budget for NIH's minority health and health disparities research program was to be developed by the NIH director, the NCMHD director, and the directors of the NIH's Institutes and Centers (ICs). The Strategic Plan, to be developed no later than 12 months after November 22, 2000, the date of enactment of the legislation, was to include objectives and priorities. Moreover, the directors of NIH, NCMHD, and the ICs were to: (a) promote coordination and collaboration among the ICs; (b) ensure that priority is given to conducting and supporting minority health disparities research with regard to the expenditure of funds appropriated for NCMHD activities; (c) ensure that the amounts appropriated are expended in accordance with the plan and budget; and (d) review the plan and budget no less than annually, revising both as appropriate.

The legislation called for authorization of the NCMHD director to grant research endowments to Centers of Excellence (as defined under Section 736 of the Public Health Service Act (42 U.S.C. 293)) and to assist the director of NIH's Center for Research Resources in committing resources for construction at Institutions of Emerging Excellence. In addition, the NCMHD director was to establish loan repayment programs for health professionals who agreed to engage in minority health disparities research.

The NCMHD director was to prepare an annual report on NCMHD activities that was to include the progress made in NIH health disparities research, a summary and analysis of expenditures made for NIH health disparities research activities, a separate statement on minority health/health disparities research, and appropriate recommendations from the director.

Following enactment of the legislation, NCMHD was created and undertook responsibilities for the Centers of Excellence Program, the Loan Repayment Program, and the Endowment Program, as well as for the NIH-wide minority health and health disparities research program and the Strategic Plan. The NIH Strategic Research Plan and Budget to Reduce and Ultimately Eliminate Health Disparities was produced in 2003.

CHARGE TO THE COMMITTEE

In 2004, the 4th year of the NIH Minority Health and Health Disparities Research legislation, NCMHD asked the Institute of Medicine to:

- Assess the adequacy of the trans-NIH minority health and health disparities Strategic Plan in achieving the NIH's goals and objectives. Specifically, the Committee was to evaluate the Strategic Plan with respect to:
  - Research (e.g., How well does the Strategic Plan advance scientific understanding of the causes and means to reduce and ultimately eliminate the disproportionate burden of disease among health disparity groups?),
  - Research Infrastructure (e.g., Does the Strategic Plan adequately expand opportunities and the institutional capacity—such as the environment, leadership, and commitment to health disparities research—for research on health disparities?),
  - Public Information and Community Outreach (e.g., How adequately does the plan address needs for the dissemination and application of research findings to reduce and ultimately eliminate health disparities?);
- Assess the adequacy of coordination across NIH ICs in helping to develop and carry out the Strategic Plan and avoid duplication of administrative resources among ICs and divisions; and
- Identify means, including potential legislative modifications, to help NIH achieve its minority health and health disparity Strategic Plan objectives.

The Committee viewed the charge as including a review and analysis of the Strategic Plan budget. In its approach, the Committee analyzed the adequacy of the Strategic Plan as a document and plan of action, including in this review the individual strategic plans of the ICs. The Committee recognized that the adequacy of the Strategic Plan, and the potential for its success, depend on the meaningful inclusion of the overall NIH goals and objectives in the individual plans and actions of the ICs. The Strategic Plan's success also depends on the trans-NIH organizational setting and means of coordinated development, implementation, and monitoring. To assess the Strategic Plan's feasibility and to recommend improvements, the Committee considered early experiences with implementing and coordinating the program to be important.

COMMITTEE PROCESS

The Committee was given less than a year to complete its task—a time constraint that necessarily shaped its approach to information and data collection. The Committee held five 2.5-day meetings during the 10 months between October 2004 and July 2005. In open, public sessions (see Appendix B), the panel heard presentations from and held discussions with six ICs with considerable responsibility for and activity in health disparities research, including the National Cancer Institute; NCMHD; National Heart, Lung, and Blood Institute; National Institute of Allergy and Infectious Diseases; National Institute of Child Health and Human Development; and National Institute of Diabetes and Digestive and Kidney Diseases. Two Offices from the Office of the Director involved in or with responsibility for coordinating trans-NIH programs—the Office of AIDS Research and the Office of Research on Women's Health—were also part of discussions. During open sessions, the panel also heard from and held discussions with: the NIH director; the NCMHD director; members of NCMHD's National Advisory Council; AHRQ's Director of the Office of Extramural Research, Education, and Priority Populations; HHS's Acting Deputy Assistant Secretary for Minority Health; CDC's Director of the Office of Minority Health; representatives of several organizations concerned with health disparities; and concerned individuals. In addition, numerous organizations provided written commentary (see Appendix C).

The Committee reviewed the contents of the NIH Strategic Plan and the individual strategic plans of the 25 participating ICs and 2 Offices. The Committee conducted a commissioned survey of all 27 ICs, the Office of AIDS Research, and the Office of Research on Women's Health to compile information on the implementation of, experience with, and recommendations for the Strategic Plan. Included were inquiries about research funding distributions, training grants, the recruitment of minority research subjects, the career development of investigators studying minority and health disparity groups,[1] public communication activities and products, and perceived barriers to implementation. Background papers were commissioned on aspects of health disparities, research infrastructure, and outreach and communication.

Through these information sources and a literature review, the Committee developed recommendations that address the charge. The report does not assess

[1]"Health disparity groups," an awkward term, is used in this report because it is the terminology used in the Strategic Plan.

the extent to which NIH met the research objectives stated in the Strategic Plan. Such an assessment was not included in the charge to the Committee and would have required considerably more time than the Committee was given. Furthermore, the report does not tell NIH how to conduct its work by making suggestions about decisions or program directions. Rather, it responds to the broad areas of concern outlined in the charge.

ORGANIZATION OF THE REPORT

The report continues in Chapter 2 with a review of health disparities and the complexity of the problem with respect to definitions, measurement, and understanding. In Chapter 3, the NIH Strategic Research Plan and Budget to Reduce and Ultimately Eliminate Health Disparities is described and examined, including the overall NIH plan and those of the 27 ICs and the 2 Offices within the NIH Office of the Director. The development, and updates, of the Strategic Plan are examined, along with the appropriateness and promise of their content. Chapter 4 reviews the Strategic Plan's budget and financial aspects, which can be used as monitoring indexes of the Plan's commitments and activities. Budget analysis also lends insight into the influence of the resource setting on the Plan's feasibility. In Chapter 5, NCMHD is reviewed as a keystone center and coordinator of the Strategic Plan and the health disparities research effort. Chapter 6 reviews experiences with the coordination, monitoring, and management of the Strategic Plan and its health disparities program after 4 years, with the intent to examine the organizational setting in which the Plan is developed and implemented, particularly with respect to trans-NIH coordination.

2

Health Disparities: Concepts, Measurements, and Understanding

Significant and persistent differences in disease rates and health outcomes between people of differing race, ethnicity, socioeconomic status, and area of residence have been well documented (Eberhardt and Pamuk, 2004; Hartley, 2004). The National Institutes of Health (NIH) Strategic Plan presents data on health among several selected populations that show marked differences in such diverse health indicators as infant mortality, cancer mortality, coronary heart disease mortality, and the prevalence of diabetes, end-stage renal disease, and stroke (see Table D-4, Appendix D). Not only do certain racial and ethnic minority groups have a lower life expectancy, but these groups also bear a disproportionate disease burden from diabetes, hypertension, AIDS, low birth weight, and very low birth weight, when compared to the white majority population. More recent data reveal differences in all-cause and cause-specific mortality as a function of socioeconomic characteristics and area of residence (Tables D-8 and D-9, Appendix D).

The patterns are complex, and some groups (e.g., Asian Americans, Hispanics) appear to have better health outcomes than white Americans. However, these data must be viewed with a clear understanding of several important methodological limitations including variation of age distribution within different racial/ethnic groups, differences in cause-specific death rates for different racial/ethnic groups, racial/ethnic misclassification, and intra-ethnic variation among subgroups.

Age adjustment is a routine statistical method used to compare rates of health events for populations or groups that differ in age structure. An age-adjusted rate is a weighted average of age-specific rates, where the weights are determined by the age structure of the age standard. (The current age standard used by the National Center for Health Statistics is the year 2000 standard population, which reflects the age distribution of the U.S. population in the year 2000.) Racial/ethnic populations in the United States vary considerably in age structure, with the median age for whites being older than that of all other major racial/ethnic groups. For this reason, the National Center for Health Statistics (NCHS, 2004) indicates that age-adjusted rates are relative indexes for comparison but not actual measures of risk—a distinction often overlooked.

With use of age-specific, rather than age-adjusted, data different patterns between racial and ethnic groups emerge (Table 2-1). These data document continuing racial and ethnic differences in death rates from heart disease, malignant neoplasms, cerebrovascular disease, chronic respiratory diseases, diabetes, HIV, and homicide. In contrast to an all-cause age-adjusted death rate that is about 30 percent higher than that of whites, age-specific rates reveal that African Americans have all-cause mortality rates that are about 75 percent higher than those of whites after age 45. With age-specific data, American Indian mortality rates at certain ages for cerebrovascular diseases, diabetes, and homicide are higher than those of the white population, a finding that is masked in the age-adjusted data. The all-cause age-adjusted mortality data for Hispanics indicate that this population has a lower death rate than that of whites, but a more complex pattern emerges with age-specific data with, depending on age, higher Hispanic death rates for cerebrovascular diseases, diabetes, HIV, and homicide.

Mortality data are usually presented as all-cause and cause-specific; causes are selected for reporting based upon frequency in the general population. A review of cause-specific, age-specific mortality rates for various racial/ethnic populations reveals large differences (Table 2-1). For certain conditions, Hispanics have higher age-specific cause-specific mortality rates than whites, despite the lower all-cause mortality of these groups. Data gathering that is guided by leading causes of death in the majority population may miss important causes of morbidity and mortality in other racial/ethnic groups. For the purpose of identifying disparities, use of age-specific and cause-specific rates, in addition to all-cause data, provides a more accurate comparison of relative health status between groups.

When reviewing racial/ethnic health data, another important issue to consider is misclassification, particularly among American Indians. Unfavorable and widening disparities in cardiovascular disease mortality for American Indians/Native Alaskans have been largely unrecognized because of errors in national data that disproportionately affect this group (Rhoades, 2005). National mortality event data for the past several decades suggest that cardiovascular mortality for American Indians is lower than in the general U.S. population; such data are reflected in Table 2-1 (Lee et al., 1998). In contrast, the Strong Heart Study, a longitudinal epidemiological study of a diverse group of American Indians, found that incidence and mortality rates for cardiovascular disease are equal to, or higher than, those in comparable general populations (Howard et al., 1999). These discrepancies may be

TABLE 2-1 Age-Adjusted and Age-Specific Death Rates by Race/Ethnicity, 2002

	Race/Ethnicity Deaths per 100,000				
Cause of Death	Non-Hispanic White	African American	American Indian	Asian/Pacific Islander	Hispanic
Age-adjusted all causes	837.5	1083.3	677.4	474.4	629.3
Ages 5 to 44					
All causes	197.58	161.29	122.22	43.89	143.67
Heart disease	21.33	19.51	7.87	4.70	9.25
Malignant neoplasm	28.60	16.47	8.07	9.43	16.42
Cerebrovascular diseases	3.18	4.02	2.03	1.49	2.77
Chronic lower respiratory diseases	1.70	2.30	0.48	0.26	0.90
Diabetes	3.41	3.41	1.84	0.28	1.93
HIV-related	4.15	17.85	2.42	0.66	7.46
Homicide	6.17	28.37	9.47	3.53	18.29
Ages 45 to 64					
All causes	610.91	1,055.33	597.72	297.98	461.13
Heart disease	144.93	275.75	112.76	61.78	97.91
Malignant neoplasm	217.14	291.74	133.32	122.86	126.22
Cerebrovascular diseases	19.18	57.83	21.42	21.84	22.52
Chronic lower respiratory diseases	24.47	22.97	16.62	4.37	7.12
Diabetes	19.25	49.68	46.44	10.22	27.39
HIV-related	3.59	43.84	2.40	1.70	12.88
Homicide	2.74	12.89	6.51	2.74	5.38
Ages 65 and over					
All causes	5,234.71	5,494.18	3,278.05	2,581.92	3,293.72
Heart disease	1,663.84	1,759.47	899.17	793.86	1,067.70
Malignant neoplasm	1,124.41	1,246.71	674.65	590.60	692.77
Cerebrovascular diseases	410.97	455.60	219.56	281.99	242.42
Chronic lower respiratory diseases	333.74	185.84	189.30	99.82	128.27
Diabetes	138.03	275.55	239.37	106.45	208.76
HIV-related	0.52	10.04	0.00	0.70	2.55
Homicide	1.84	6.19	5.50	1.71	2.60

NOTE: Rates based on fewer than 20 deaths are considered unreliable and are not shown.

SOURCE: NCHS, 2006.

explained by racial misclassification in national vital event data. The National Center for Health Statistics found that death rates for American Indians/Native Alaskans were underestimated by nearly 21 percent, compared with an overestimation of 1 percent among white populations (Rosenberg et al., 1999). Research based on vital event data that does not account for racial misclassification is at risk of grossly underestimating mortality in these populations (Rhoades, 2005).

Data that incorporate large groupings by race and ethnicity fail to distinguish substantial differences in health status within some racial groups. For example, Asian/Pacific Islanders as a group have lower rates of infant deaths (4.8 per 1,000 live births) than whites (5.7), African Americans (13.6), American Indians (8.9), or Hispanics (5.5). However, the overall Asian/Pacific Islander rate masks substantial variation among Asians and Pacific Islanders: the rate for Hawaiians (8.7) is more than double that of Chinese (3.2), with intermediate rates shown by Japanese (4.5) and Filipinos (5.7). Similarly, among Hispanics, while the overall infant death rate is 5.5 per 1,000 births, Puerto Ricans experience a relatively high rate of 8.3 deaths, Cubans experience a low of 4.2 deaths per 1,000, and Mexicans and Central and South Americans experience intermediate rates (See Table D-6, Appendix D). Subgroup-specific data, if available, might clearly identify persistently disadvantaged Hispanic and Asian subpopulations.

These differences may reflect within-group and between-group variations in susceptibility to disease due to biological and genetic factors, as well as differences in social and environmental conditions. The study of disparities is the study of the multiple, complex, and sometimes subtle relationships among genetic susceptibility, individual behavior, social environment, physical surroundings, disease prevention, and treatment interventions that lead to the observed differences in health status and health outcomes. The science of disparities involves elucidating the individual mechanisms that are responsible for diseases and disabilities that contribute to health disparities, understanding the interactions among these individual mechanisms, and explaining the differential impact of these mechanisms and interactions on various population subgroups. Successful development of the science will require the full range of research approaches: basic, translational, clinical, epidemiological, behavioral, and health services research.

Creating scientific knowledge to reduce and ultimately eliminate health disparities involves significant definitional and methodological challenges. Proper review of the NIH Strategic Plan requires consideration of the current scientific context within which the goals and objectives are being established and pursued. The Committee identified several key conceptual and methodological issues central to the study of health disparities.[1]

DEFINING HEALTH DISPARITIES

The Distinction Between Difference and Disparity

Health disparities are not simply differences in health. The term *disparity* may connote a difference that is inequitable, unjust, or unacceptable (Krieger, 2005; Whitehead, 1992). Characterization of a *difference* as unjust has been

[1] A detailed discussion of several of these issues is presented in *Overview of Health Disparities* by Nancy E. Adler, Appendix D.

discussed at length in the scientific literature (see discussion in Braveman and Gruskin, 2003). Such characterization requires a detailed understanding of the nature and etiology of the difference and is likely to involve multiple criteria such as avoidability, mutability, and detriment to groups that are disadvantaged in terms of opportunities and access to resources. For example, the 2003 Institute of Medicine report *Unequal Treatment* cites a model of the distinction between difference and disparity for health care quality (Appendix E). The term "health disparities" is, however, widely used to describe differences in health status without necessarily implying the presence of injustice (see Adler, Appendix D). Thus the term "health disparities" is used in the legislation establishing the NIH health disparities program, by NIH in its definitions, and by the NIH Strategic Plan.

Lack of Consensus Definition

Research on health disparities has already yielded substantial information about the magnitude of the problem, as well as preliminary understanding of etiologies and mechanisms. These insights suggest possible interventions to improve the nation's health. Although previous research demonstrates the feasibility and importance of studying health disparities, further research is needed to maximize our ability to identify, measure, reduce, and eliminate disparities.

There is not complete agreement on how to define or measure health disparities because observed differences vary depending on which groups are observed and what is measured. Numerous approaches have been taken, including comparing the health of minorities to that of nonminorities, comparing the health of specific groups with that of the overall population, and comparing specific groups to each other. Still another approach is to start with an observed difference in health and then establish whether this difference constitutes a disparity (i.e., whether it is inequitable or unjust). Groups may be described by gender, race, ethnicity, education, occupation, income, place of residence, or other characteristics chosen by the observer. The choice of group characteristics may be based on a conceptual model, observed empirical differences, or beliefs regarding what is just.

Lack of Appropriate Measures of Health Status

Unlike inequities in health care, which are relatively straightforward to identify and characterize, disparities in health status may be difficult to discern. The pattern and extent of health disparities vary depending on what measures of health are used. Although disparities in mortality are well documented, mortality is a significantly limited end point for studies. For that reason, intermediate indicators of health may be more useful in identifying the underlying mechanisms of disparities. Both mortality and morbidity are functions of multiple factors including biological vulnerability, exposure/resistance to disease, behavioral risk/protective factors, quality of diagnosis and treatment, and availability and accessibility of services, each of which may show different patterns of inequality. Furthermore, measuring health should not solely consist of counting adverse outcomes. Health services researchers have developed several quality-of-life measures, but there is no single, summative measure of the overall health and functioning of individuals that can be aggregated to assess the comparative health of groups. Adequate understanding of health disparities will require valid and consistent measurement of disparities as well as the variables that shape them.

MEASURING HEALTH DISPARITIES

Data on Racial and Ethnic Health Disparities

Existing data on inequalities in health status, health care access and quality, and health outcomes for certain racial and ethnic minority groups are subject to several limitations. As previously mentioned, much of the available data is based on large groupings by race and ethnicity. This frequently omits some groups. For example, many studies report only black/white differences, resulting in a relative paucity of data on Hispanics, Asians/Pacific Islanders, and American Indians/Alaska Natives. Furthermore, as previously discussed, these broad categories serve to mask substantial variation in health within some of the groups.

Members of the same ethnic group from different countries and areas of origin show different patterns of health and disease. This has been demonstrated repeatedly among subgroups of Hispanics and Asians/Pacific Islanders; substantial variation by subgroup also exists among African Americans and American Indians. Further complicating the examination of racial/ethnic group differences, the health status of immigrants appears to vary by their length of time in the United States. Understanding and addressing racial/ethnic health disparities will clearly require looking at subgroups within large ethnic categories, despite the difficulty in obtaining adequate data.

Data on Socioeconomic Health Disparities

Many health outcomes vary with socioeconomic status—though again, the patterns of disparity vary depending on the measures of health used and socioeconomic variables studied. Researchers and public health agencies often fail to collect empirical data on income, education, and occupation. Studies that do measure socioeconomic status often do so in an incomplete or inconsistent manner. Experts agree that poverty is causally related to poor health status; however, there is continuing debate about whether relative inequality in income—i.e., the shape of income distribution in a population—matters in itself, apart from the effects of absolute income levels and particularly poverty.

Currently, the empirical data reveal a discontinuous association between mortality and education, thus suggesting that education confers benefits due to a credentialing function rather than simply due to knowledge accumulation. Moreover, the same level of schooling results in differences in other dimensions of socioeconomic status for women and racial/ethnic minorities—for instance, income. Much of the data from other countries use occupation as a principal determinant of social class, but the association between occupational class and health is less consistently described in the United States.

Data on Rural Health Disparities

People living in rural areas seem to have worse health outcomes than people living in metropolitan areas, but this pattern does not hold across all racial and ethnic groups (Committee on the Future of Rural Health Care, 2005; NCHS, 2004). For some indicators, suburban counties show better health status than either rural areas or urban centers, thus suggesting the need for finer differentiations than simply urban and rural (Eberhardt and Pamuk, 2004). In addition to determining differences by the degree of urban or rural locale, health status differs by geographic region (Hartley, 2004). It is unclear whether this is explained by the fact that some areas of the country are more rural than others, by regional differences in socioeconomic levels, or by other relevant differences in living conditions in various parts of the country.

Interactions Among Sociodemographic Factors Associated with Disparities

Characteristics such as minority racial/ethnic status, low socioeconomic position, and rural residence frequently coexist within populations, reflecting exposures and vulnerabilities that may interact to produce health disparities. Education and income are nonrandomly distributed across racial and ethnic groups. Both African Americans and Hispanics are overrepresented in lower categories of socioeconomic status. For some health outcomes, the differences between racial/ethnic minorities and whites become nonsignificant, once income is controlled. For many health outcomes, the gap between races diminishes with higher income, though a difference remains at each income level. Whether this residual effect reflects poor measurement of economic status or the importance of other factors (e.g., discrimination) warrants further investigation.

The meaning of specific indicators of socioeconomic status may differ across groups (Williams, 1999). At each level of income, for example, African Americans and Hispanics have lower net worth and live in poorer neighborhoods than whites (Williams and Jackson, 2005). The meaning of educational attainment also varies across groups (Farmer and Ferraro, 2005). Higher education confers fewer health benefits on minorities and women, consistent with lower social and economic returns on education. Special problems arise for groups that have received their education in other countries with different educational systems and accreditation levels. The data suggest that one cannot adequately study racial and ethnic disparities in health without considering socioeconomic factors and vice versa (Kawachi et al., 2005; Lillie-Blanton and LaVeist, 1996). Therefore, it may be fruitful to examine the effects of socioeconomic status within racial/ethnic groups (Adler, Appendix D). Similarly, evaluations of disparities in rural and urban health need to consider race/ethnicity and socioeconomic status (Probst et al., 2004).

As Adler points out, "whites make up 84 percent of rural populations, African Americans comprise 8 percent, non-black Hispanics comprise 5 percent, and Asians/Pacific Islanders and American Indians/Native Alaskans comprise less than 2 percent each. There are differences in racial/ethnic composition of rural populations in different regions of the country. Rural African Americans are predominantly in the South . . . and rural Hispanics are living primarily in the West" (Adler, Appendix D). As shown in Table D-15, Appendix D, there are substantial differences in educational attainment by both race/ethnicity and area of residence. "Of working-age adults, 40 percent of African Americans in rural areas lack a high school diploma, compared to 19 percent in urban areas; comparable figures are 50 percent to 42 percent for Hispanics and 15 percent to 9 percent for whites, in rural versus urban areas. Differences are less marked among older adults for whom a lack of high school graduation was more common and show smaller discrepancies by either race/ethnicity or rural/urban residence. Rural residence is also associated with an increased likelihood of being in a low-paying job. The increased likelihood holds for all three ethnic groups, although the difference between urban and rural rates is less for Hispanics than for whites or African Americans" (Adler, Appendix D).

Recent Progress

In July 2005, as part of the Healthy People 2010 monitoring process, the Centers for Disease Control and Prevention's National Center for Health Statistics issued a report titled *Methodological Issues in Measuring Health Disparities* (Keppel et al., 2005). This report contains 11 specific guidelines intended to "bring greater consistency to the measurement of differences in quantifiable indicators of health." Although the report represents an important step, it deals with just a limited number of technical issues in the definition and measurement of disparities. The guidelines standardize the reference group to be used in documenting disparities. If midpoint assessments of the Healthy People 2010 indicators are performed using these guidelines, the resulting body of empirical data will be a useful resource for researchers studying disparities. Regarding health care disparities, the Agency for Healthcare Research and Quality has, since 2003, issued an annual *National Healthcare Disparities Report*. This report summarizes disparities in health care access and quality for racial and ethnic minorities.

The annual data, presented in a consistent format, will allow indicators of health care access and quality to be monitored over time.

UNDERSTANDING HEALTH DISPARITIES

One striking finding about health disparities is their occurrence across a wide range of diseases with differing etiologic risk factors. Elucidating the mechanisms by which health disparities occur will require identifying both common backgrounds for multiple diseases and disease-specific mechanisms. Known determinants of health, such as genetic vulnerabilities, access to and the quality of health care, the physical environment, the social environment, health-related behaviors, and exposure to stress, should be considered in the investigation of the causes of disparities (Bulatao and Anderson, 2004; Singer and Ryff, 2001).

Biological Factors

Recent scientific advances have resulted in unprecedented opportunities to explore the biological determinants of disease. New technologies allow for rapid accumulation of vast amounts of biological data, and new techniques involving bioinformatics and biomathematics provide new tools to analyze these data. These advances provide an opportunity to study pathophysiologic processes at the cellular and molecular levels, making it possible to understand how differences in genetic variation and metabolic processes contribute to health disparities and how genetic susceptibility interacts with behavioral, nutritional, pharmacological, and environmental variables.

Health Care Access and Quality

Health care deficiencies involve both poor access to care and poor quality of care. Access to care is a concept that has been extensively studied and for which reliable measures exist. The report *Unequal Treatment: Confronting Racial and Ethnic Disparities in Healthcare* provides extensive documentation of the differences in the appropriateness and quality of care received by members of racial and ethnic minority groups (Smedley et al., 2003). Disparities in access and quality also impact the poor and, although not well studied, likely affect those in rural locations, and residents of disadvantaged neighborhoods.

Physical Environment

Physical locations vary with respect to exposures to toxins, pathogens, and carcinogens. The built, or manmade, environment may present differential risks from chemical substances, such as lead paint, crowding, and noise. The built environment can also constrain exercise, reduce access to healthy foods, facilitate risky behaviors, and discourage health-promoting activities.

Social Environment

At the individual level, the social environment is described by factors such as social connectedness and social support. These factors may benefit health in diverse ways: providing the ability to mobilize resources when needed to deal with problems and threats, buffering the effects of stress exposure, and facilitating access to information from others about health issues. At the aggregate level, lower morbidity and mortality are evident in communities with greater social capital, which may be defined as the resources available to individuals and groups within communities as a result of their social network of connections. Social capital can be measured by indicators such as levels of interpersonal trust, norms of reciprocity, and patterns of social engagement. A related concept to social capital is collective efficacy, which refers to the ability of community residents to undertake collective action for mutual benefit. Collective efficacy and social capital have been shown to contribute to health even when the socioeconomic status of a neighborhood is controlled for—although greater social capital and collective efficacy are generally associated with more advantaged communities.

Behavioral Factors

Health behaviors and lifestyle contribute significantly to morbidity and premature mortality. Both health-promoting and risky behaviors may be rooted in cultural norms and also be influenced by family socialization early in life. Behavior patterns are often formed during childhood or adolescence, with lasting impacts on adult health. Behaviors are also influenced by education, both formal and experiential. Behaviors that impair or support good health may also be facilitated or discouraged by environmental factors, for example, the influence of the built environment on patterns of physical activity.

Stress

Exposure to stress and the resulting behavioral and biological responses put individuals at risk for a range of diseases. Studies documenting greater stress exposure for groups disadvantaged by race, ethnicity, or socioeconomic status suggest that differential stress exposure, which can include perceived discrimination, may be an important mechanism by which social disadvantage gets "into the body" to affect health. The concept of allostatic load refers to the overburdening of the normal functioning of allostasis, which is the process of maintaining physiological stability in response to stress, through metabolic change. It was developed to describe the damage to physiological systems caused by exposure to chronic stress. Allostatic load provides a summative measure of the cumulative effects of stress and may reflect the multiple biological pathways by which social disadvantage can affect a range of health outcomes (McEwen, 1998; McEwen and Stellar, 1993).

Discrimination

In addition to the indirect effects of discrimination on health through social and economic pathways, associated community exposure, increased barriers to quality health care, institutional racism and other forms of discrimination, some research suggests that the experience of discrimination may itself be detrimental to health (Williams, 1999). The associations are complex and appear to demonstrate that not only exposure, but also responses to that exposure, have health consequences. Current research on how to best measure experiences of discrimination has added to our understanding of this type of risk factor for African Americans, but less is known about the discrimination experiences of other groups (Seeman, 2004).

Conceptual Models

As illustrated in the Adler paper (Appendix D), several conceptual models have been developed to explain the complex pathways by which biological, medical, behavioral, and environmental determinants of health differentially affect individuals and groups (Baum et al., 1999; Brunner and Marmot, 1999; Hertzman, 1999; House, 2002; House and Williams, 2000; Kaplan, 1999; Kuh and Ben-Shlomo, 1997; Kuh et al., 1997). Some models focus on a single determinant, while others provide unifying contexts of multiple determinants. Still other models suggest additional pathways and approaches to identifying the mechanisms by which health disparities occur. These conceptual models generate important considerations for disparities research: (a) that race, ethnicity, socioeconomic status, and other demographic variables have direct, indirect, and interactive effects on health; (b) the importance of considering individual, family, and community levels of influence on health; and (c) the temporal continuity throughout life. Adequate understanding of health disparities will require measurement of the potential variables that shape differences in health. The choice of variables examined should be explicitly linked to models or theories of disparities, which can provide principles for selecting the variables with the greatest research yield for reducing health disparities.

IMPLICATIONS FOR THE NIH RESEARCH AGENDA

We have described the scientific context within which the NIH health disparities research program should develop the scientific knowledge base about the biological, genetic, behavioral, social, and environmental determinants of health disparities. NIH's research agenda is impacted by the nature and extent of health disparities; the conceptual and methodological issues involved in defining and measuring them; the complex nature of the relationships between race, ethnicity, gender, income, education, occupation, and area of residence; and the challenge of identifying the complicated, multifaceted, interrelated causes of health disparities. There is a clear need for continued theoretical and empirical work to develop, refine, and evaluate measures of health, health outcomes, and health disparities. There is also a need for creative and sophisticated research to understand the biological, behavioral, and environmental pathways by which health disparities are created. The need to examine common pathways to multiple diseases will require the sustained attention of multiple Institutes and Centers (ICs) as well as true collaboration across NIH. The design and conduct of research to eliminate health disparities will require trans-NIH initiatives, as well as engaging other agencies within the Department of Health and Human Services and other departments within the federal government.

Findings:

(1) **Lack of consensus regarding conceptual and operational definitions of disparities and the complexity of measuring health and health determinants pose challenges for the identification, understanding, monitoring and elimination of health disparities.**

(2) **There is a continuing need for NIH-funded research to develop, test, and refine measures and conceptual approaches for assessing and monitoring health disparities. Research is required to answer fundamental questions: Which factors are most critical to monitor? How can they best be measured?**

(3) **Currently available information does not provide a full and accurate description of disparities between, and within, racial and ethnic groups and across the full spectrum of socioeconomic status. Detailed, accurate data on Hispanic, Asian/Pacific Islander, African American, and American Indian/Alaska Native subgroups are needed, including data on income, education, and occupation. Such data will provide an important source for research on disparities and for monitoring progress toward reducing and eliminating disparities across the nation.**

(4) **Sophisticated and creative approaches to studying the processes that cause health disparities are needed. Coordinated, collaborative trans-NIH initiatives, with the active involvement of multiple ICs, will be needed to understand common backgrounds for multiple diseases. Coordinated, collaborative trans-agency approaches will be required to successfully investigate the complex relationships and interactions among race, ethnicity, gender,**

income, education, occupation, immigrant generation, and area of residence.

Recommendation 1: NIH, through the National Center on Minority Health and Health Disparities and the ICs and, when appropriate, collaborating agencies, should undertake research to further refine and develop the conceptual, definitional, and methodological issues involved in health disparities research and to further the understanding of the causes of disparities.

For such research, priority areas should include, first, the development and refinement of valid measures of exposures relevant to understanding and evaluating health disparities. For example:

- Interagency disparity research initiatives to develop valid and reliable measures of health effects of social factors; genetic risk; stress; racial/ethnic discrimination; and health care access and quality.
- Disparities research embedded into large studies (molecular, clinical, and epidemiological), national data sets, and public health monitoring measures through the greater inclusion of appropriate measures of race, ethnicity, socioeconomic status, and residential characteristics, and of the psychosocial and environmental factors that are likely to shape health disparities in the population being studied at each time point of data collection.
- In population-based studies, the inclusion of information on racial and ethnic subpopulations and other relevant characteristics, such as immigrant status, language preference, and detailed socioeconomic data, should be encouraged. Investigators funded by the ICs should be encouraged to gather information on socioeconomic status and other dimensions of social stratification.

Second, priority areas should include initiatives to further enhance understanding of the etiology of health disparities. For example:

- Multidisciplinary initiatives to advance the study of disparities, including gene-environment interactions and biological mechanisms mediating disparities.
- Trans-NIH disparity research initiatives to elucidate the pathways and mechanisms by which health disparities occur, including the identification of common backgrounds for multiple diseases and disease-specific mechanisms that may facilitate the development of strategies for intervention.

3

Development and Availability of the Strategic Plan

The initial Strategic Plan grew out of a process that began in 1999, when a National Institutes of Health (NIH) Working Group was established to examine health disparities research. In 2000, legislation created NIH's National Center on Minority Health and Health Disparities (NCMHD). The trans-NIH Working Group on Health Disparities was co-chaired by the acting deputy director of NIH and the director of the National Institute of Allergy and Infectious Diseases. The Working Group included the directors and representatives of NIH Institutes and Centers (ICs) and the directors of the Office of AIDS Research, the Office of Behavioral and Social Sciences Research, the Office of Disease Prevention, and the Office of Research on Women's Health. The acting NIH director and the director of the Office of Research on Minority Health also served as ex officio members (NIH, 2000).

The Working Group recommended that NIH develop a strategic plan dealing with minority health and health disparities. The group was also charged with developing that plan, which was to include individual strategic plans from ICs and Offices. The plans were developed in consultation with professional and patient advocacy groups, the public, the ICs' respective advisory councils, and the scientific community.

A draft plan was published in October 2000 for technical and public review. This early version of the Strategic Plan established goals for research, research infrastructure, and public information and community outreach that are used in the 2002 and 2004 Strategic Plans (NIH, 2000).

In 2000, the newly created NCMHD assumed responsibility for the Strategic Plan. By December 2001, the ICs had submitted completed plans, and in March

2002, NCMHD submitted the NIH Strategic Research Plan and Budget to Reduce and Ultimately Eliminate Health Disparities for 2002–2004 to the NIH director for review. During 2002, the ICs and Offices provided comments to NCMHD on the draft. The Strategic Plan was resubmitted to the NIH director in July 2002. In March 2003, the Strategic Plan was submitted to Congress, thus becoming official and publicly available roughly a year behind the legislation's target date (Table 3-1).

From October 30, 2003, to January 5, 2004, the 2002 Strategic Plan was posted for public comment. Several sources suggested that the definition of health disparities populations be broadened to include additional groups, such as people

TABLE 3-1 Strategic Plan Time Line

Fiscal Year (FY) 2002 Strategic Plan	
September 1999	Harold Varmus establishes a working group to examine health disparities research. The working group recommends the development of a strategic plan.
January 2000	Ruth Kirschstein reestablishes the Working Group on Health Disparities. It is co-chaired by Yvonne Maddox and Anthony Fauci. Members include the directors of the NIH ICs and Offices.
October 6, 2000	The draft Strategic Plan is published for technical and public review.
November 22, 2000	The Minority Health and Health Disparities Research and Education Act of 2000 (P.L. 106-525) creates the NCMHD.
December 2001	The draft 2002 Strategic Plan is completed after submission and revision of IC plans.
March 11, 2002	The 2002 Strategic Plan is submitted to the NIH Office of the Director for clearance.
July 2002	The 2002 Strategic Plan is resubmitted to the Director's Office after comments have been received from the ICs and Offices.
March 2003	The 2002 Strategic Plan is submitted to Congress.
FY 2004 Strategic Plan	
November 2003–January 2004	The 2002 Strategic Plan is posted for public comment on the NCMHD website.
May 2004	NCMHD requests submissions from the ICs and Offices for the updated Strategic Plan.
October 2004	The draft 2004 Strategic Plan is submitted to the NCMHD Advisory Council for comments.

SOURCE: NIH, 2000, 2003; Ruffin, 2004.

suffering from orphan diseases, the mentally and physically disabled, prisoners, specific racial subpopulations, and lesbian, gay, bisexual, and transgender communities. Other suggestions included: expanding the scope of inquiry to include access to health care and the quality of health care; improving data collection and data quality; producing an accurate definition of health disparities; developing additional programs to improve research infrastructure at minority academic institutions; and developing racially and culturally sensitive outreach and public communication programs (Table 3-2).

The legislation called for annual reviews and "appropriate revisions" of the Strategic Plan. The Plan itself stipulates that it "will be updated and reviewed on a yearly basis." However, as of July 2005, the Strategic Plan for 2004–2008—which should have officially updated the previous Strategic Plan—had not yet been approved by NCMHD or its advisory council, nor had it been submitted to the director of NIH. Compared with the 2002 Strategic Plan, the draft of the 2004

TABLE 3-2 Public Comment Themes

Theme	Illustrative Example
General	• Include among health disparities populations: lesbian, gay, bisexual, and transgender communities; Haitians; individuals suffering from orphan diseases; underrepresented Asian subpopulations; the mentally ill; men; prisoners; the handicapped
Research	• Increase the scope of research to include cultural, psychological, behavioral, social, racial, and gender-based influences on health • Study racial/ethnic disparities in access to health care • Produce accurate, uniform definitions of health disparities and improve data collection and the quality of data on health disparities
Research infrastructure	• Sponsor programs to mentor, educate, and provide grant support to minorities who pursue health career opportunities • Promote partnerships between minority-serving and research-intensive institutions • Support and expand community outreach efforts and community participation • Broaden partnerships and leverage resources available from professional associations, health care organizations, academic institutions, and other community members that serve minority communities • Identify and make available successful community-based intervention strategies
Outreach and public communication	• Ensure that all communications with health disparities populations and their subgroups address their needs and perspectives

SOURCE: Adapted from NCMHD, 2004.

Strategic Plan included significant changes in the description of research goals and objectives. The ICs' individual strategic plans had also been updated. No budget was provided.

The timing and rate of production of the Strategic Plans were disappointing. There had been just two Strategic Plans in the 5-year period of the program—the first produced in the 3rd year and the second, as yet incomplete, near the end of the 5th year.

Finding: NIH has not updated the Strategic Plan as intended by the legislation and the NIH.

Recommendation 2: The NIH director should assure that the Strategic Plan is reviewed and revised annually using an established, trans-NIH process subject to timely review, approval, and dissemination.

THE 2002 AND 2004 STRATEGIC PLANS

As of March 2005, even with the preceding developmental efforts, the Committee found it difficult to identify the Strategic Plan. Although the 2004 Strategic Plan had not yet been fully approved, it did include significant updates in the overall goals and objectives as well as updates in the ICs' individual strategic plans, which had been approved by the respective IC directors. The Committee felt that it would be more helpful, retrospectively and prospectively, to review and assess the 2004 Strategic Plan as the most recently available intended Strategic Plan, rather than to limit its review to the original 2002 Strategic Plan.

The 2002 and 2004 Strategic Plans describe the scope of the problem of health disparities among minorities and other populations, specific objectives for research and related programs, and the means for advancing those objectives. They present a broad range of research and related activities that the NIH intended to undertake.

Each Strategic Plan includes two volumes. The Executive Summary, goals, objectives, and budget of the NIH-wide Strategic Plan, along with other background material, are included in Volume I, and the strategic plans for each NIH IC and Office involved in the program comprise Volume II (see Appendix F of this report for Volume I of the 2004 Strategic Plan).

The first two sections of Volume I describe the development of the Strategic Plan and summarize the magnitude of the health disparities problem. The text emphasizes the need for a coordinated, trans-NIH approach in order to achieve the Strategic Plan's goals. For instance, the Strategic Plan identifies the need for ICs to integrate nonbiological factors in health disparities research.

The text describes the overall Strategic Plan as "not merely a compilation of all the activities of the NIH entities, but an aggregation of primary areas of emphasis and activities conducted across the NIH." What is not described is an overall vision of health disparities, including a research strategy that addresses a timed and targeted trajectory, the research agenda's link to other government and nongovernment efforts, and a sense of NIH's priority.

The Strategic Plan calls attention to the need to enhance the infrastructure and capacity for health disparities research by supporting the research infrastructure of minority and minority-serving institutions that may have inadequate resources, increasing the number of minority researchers, and increasing the overall number of researchers conducting health disparities research. Additionally, the Strategic Plan urges the development of new and innovative ways to reach populations coping with health disparities and their care givers, so that research findings benefit target populations. Finally, the Strategic Plan calls for the establishment of interim goals and objectives with quantifiable outcomes, whenever possible.

Goals and Objectives

The Strategic Plan has three goal areas: (1) research; (2) research capacity; and (3) community outreach, information dissemination, and public health education (Box 3-1). These goal areas are appropriate for the broad challenges addressed by the Strategic Plan. They reflect NIH's attention to research, as well as the need to develop and support the extramural infrastructure and capacity to conduct the research. The goal areas also address the need for efficient translation of information into better care for patients by informing health professionals, patients, and communities. The 2004 Strategic Plan expands upon the 2002 Plan's objectives for each goal, as indicated by italics in Boxes 3-1 to 3-4 and shading in Table 3-3.

Research

The 2004 Strategic Plan research goal "to advance the understanding of the development and progression of diseases and disabilities that contribute to health disparities in racial and ethnic minority populations and other health disparity populations, including the medically underserved, by increasing and diversifying biomedical, behavioral, social science, and health services research, as well as cultural, linguistic, and social epidemiology research conducted and supported by the NIH" reflects significant changes from the 2002 Strategic Plan goal. The new goal includes wording addressing health disparity populations other than racial and ethnic minorities (with specific mention of the medically underserved) and the diversification of research to include behavioral, social science, social epidemiology, and health services research. These are important, highly appropriate additions that recognize the broad, multifactorial, and multidisciplinary issues that the Strategic Plan should include (Box 3-2).

BOX 3-1
Strategic Plan Goals, Fiscal Years 2002 and 2004
(Italic indicates new or updated text since the Fiscal Year 2002 Strategic Plan)

Research (2002): To advance the understanding of the development and progression of diseases and disabilities that contribute to minority health and other health disparities.

Research (2004): To advance the understanding of the development and progression of diseases and disabilities that contribute to health disparities in *racial and ethnic minority populations and other health disparity populations, including the medically underserved, by increasing and diversifying biomedical, behavioral, social science, and health services research, as well as cultural, linguistic, and social epidemiology research conducted and supported by the NIH.*

Research Infrastructure (2002): To increase minority health and health disparity research training, career development, and institutional capacity.

Research *Capacity* (2004): To increase minority health and health disparity research training, career development, and institutional *research* capacity and *infrastructure.*

Public Information and Community Outreach (2002): To ensure that the public, health care professionals, and research communities are informed and educated concerning the latest advances in minority health and health disparities research.

Community Outreach, Information *Dissemination, and Public Health Education* (2004): To ensure that the public, health care professionals, and research communities are informed and educated concerning the latest advances in minority health and health disparities research.

Consideration of Additional Research Objectives

Three additional research areas warrant consideration as enhanced or additional objectives: (a) social factors; (b) population research; and (c) medical care disparities.

Social Factors

Social factors contribute to health disparities (see Chapter 2 and Appendix D), and more attention is needed to understand the multifactorial background of health disparities. To that end, research should include the behavioral and social aspects of diseases and disabilities. The 2004 Strategic Plan research objectives include a new objective that calls for conducting such research in partnership

TABLE 3-3 Objectives for the Fiscal Year 2004 Strategic Plan

Research Objectives	Research Capacity Objectives	Outreach Objectives
• Advance understanding of the development and progression of diseases and disabilities that contribute to health disparities	• Increase the number of participants in clinical trials from racial and ethnic minority populations and other health disparity populations	• Provide the latest research-based information to health care providers to enhance the care provided to individuals within racial and ethnic minority populations and other health disparity populations
• Develop new or improved approaches for detecting or diagnosing the onset or progression of diseases and disabilities that contribute to health disparities	• Expand opportunities in research training and career development for, and provide research supplements to, research investigators from racial and ethnic minority populations and other health disparity populations	• Facilitate the incorporation of science-based information into the curricula of medical and allied health professions schools, theological education institutions, public health schools, and into continuing education activities of health professionals
• Develop new or improved approaches for preventing or delaying the onset or progression of diseases and disabilities that contribute to health disparities	• Increase the number of researchers conducting health disparities research	• Maintain ongoing communication linkages and partnerships with community-based and faith-based organizations, health care associations, foundations, and academic institutions, and foster dialogue with racial and ethnic minority populations and other health disparity populations, including the underserved
• Develop new or improved approaches for treating diseases and disabilities that contribute to health disparities	• Increase funding support for thė construction and renovation of research facilities across the nation aimed at enhancing the ability of these institutions to conduct health disparities research	• Develop computer databases and Internet resources to disseminate current information about scientific research and discovered and other activities regarding heath disparities
• In partnership with other agencies of the Department of Health and Human Services, advance understanding of the multifactorial causes of health disparities, including nonbiological bases of disease incidence and progression	• Provide increased funding at institutions across the country for resources, new equipment, and shared equipment programs for use in health disparities research	
	• Increase the peer review representation in peer review of individuals from racial and ethnic minority populations and other health disparity populations	

TABLE 3-3 continued

Research Objectives	Research Capacity Objectives	Outreach Objectives
	• Promote the development of inter-institutional partnerships between historically research-intensive and historically minority-serving institutions that seek to build a research infrastructure • Improve research data collection systems, and enhance data quality regarding health disparities, and develop uniform data systems that facilitate strategies for the elimination of health disparities • In collaboration with schools and programs of public health, state and local health departments, and academic health departments, support and promote community-based participatory research	• Develop targeted public health education programs focused on particular disease areas in order to reach those individuals within racial and ethnic minority populations and other health disparity populations who experience health disparities within these disease areas • Facilitate, document, and disseminate practical strategies responsive to the health care needs, and appropriate to the cultural and linguistic needs, of communities throughout the United States • Collaborate with public health and other health-oriented policy centers to translate research findings into policy documents that can be used by policy groups and other stakeholders to explain new discoveries from a policy perspective to decision makers

SOURCE: Adapted from NCMHD, 2004.

with other agencies within Health and Human Services. This new objective will need to be translated into more attention to interdisciplinary, transdisciplinary, and transprofessional science that will advance the understanding of health disparities by working across the spectrum of biological, behavioral, and social determinants. Also, research on the multifactorial nature of health disparities should be integrated as part of the first objective on "understanding the development and progression of diseases and disabilities that contribute to health disparities" rather than only taking place in partnership with other agencies.

BOX 3-2
Fiscal Year 2004 Strategic Plan Research Objectives
(Italic indicates new text)

Goal: To advance the understanding of the development and progression of diseases and disabilities that contribute to health disparities in *racial and ethnic minority populations and other health disparity populations, including the medically underserved, by increasing and diversifying biomedical, behavioral, social science, and health services research, as well as cultural, linguistic, and social epidemiology research conducted and supported by the NIH.*

- Advance understanding of the development and progression of diseases and disabilities that contribute to health disparities
- Develop new or improved approaches for detecting or diagnosing the onset or progression of diseases and disabilities that contribute to health disparities
- Develop new or improved approaches for preventing or delaying the onset or progression of diseases and disabilities that contribute to health disparities
- Develop new or improved approaches for treating diseases and disabilities that contribute to health disparities
- *In partnership with other agencies of the Department of Health and Human Services, advance the understanding of the multifactorial causes of health disparities, including nonbiological bases of disease incidence and progression*

Population Research

There is a continuing need to identify and understand the presence and extent of dissimilar health conditions in populations and groups identified as having worse health situations. Such analyses can serve as bases for recognizing research and interventional needs and opportunities, as well as for assessing effects of intervention. Moreover, current definitions and designations of minority and health disparity groups do not identify important subgroups with specific health disparities, such as those within the Asian American and Pacific Islander population. To plan research and to properly identify groups and their health disparities, population information for subgroups is needed. Consequently, the Strategic Plan should address this issue.

Disparities in Health Care

Disparities in health care associated with race, ethnicity, and socioeconomic status are pervasive and well documented (Smedley et al., 2003). A lack of access to care and poor-quality care contribute to poor health outcomes and an avoidably worse health status. Research on disparities in the quality of care includes: (a) the continued compilation of information on the scope and nature of disparate care, with respect to the affected populations and groups as well as the settings in which it occurs; (b) contributing factors, including the possible role of bias; (c) the design and assessment of interventions, including linkages to quality initiatives; and (d) education and policy issues. Many such projects deal with medical procedures and care in clinical settings in which there are important interfaces with issues and problems of interest to, or investigated by, NIH-supported research. Although federally supported research on disparities in medical care has largely been seen as within the purview of the Agency for Healthcare Research and Quality (AHRQ) and not NIH, in the area of minority health and health disparities such strict separation of research domains may result in lost opportunities to pursue particular disparity issues. Depending on the opportunity, these issues could be included as part of the research objectives and actions of ICs directed at detection, diagnosis, treatment, and prevention of specific diseases and disabilities, either independently or collaboratively with other agencies such as AHRQ and the Centers for Disease Control and Prevention. Such research should be recognized as part of the Strategic Plan's stated objectives.

Finding: The Strategic Plan has placed inadequate emphasis on understanding social and behavioral determinants of health and their interaction with biological factors; better understanding of the characteristics of populations affected by poor health and the characteristics of diseases and conditions for which disparities exist in those populations; the relationship between population disparities in health care and differences in health status; and research opportunities regarding disparities in health care.

Recommendation 3: The Strategic Plan research objectives should promote more integration of research on the multifactorial nature of health disparities, including nonbiological factors; population research to further the understanding of the presence, prevalence, trends, and other elements of health disparity conditions; and when opportunity exists, an understanding of the causes of disparities in health care.

Research Capacity

The research capacity goal is "to increase minority health and health disparity research training, career development, and institutional research capacity and infrastructure." Objectives for this goal in the 2002 Strategic Plan addressed several appropriate aspects of research infrastructure and capacity, including: increased representation of racial and ethnic minorities and other health disparity populations in clinical trials; support for biomedical career development of underrepresented minorities; increased minority representation in peer review; and improvement of physical research capacity to enhance the ability of institutions to conduct health disparities research. The 2004 Strategic Plan includes additional objectives for building research capacity. These objectives call for increasing the number of researchers conducting health disparities research, improving data collection related to health disparities, increasing partnerships between research-intensive institutions and minority-serving institutions, and increasing community-based participatory research (Box 3-3). The Committee found the research capacity objectives to be appropriate and commented on the importance, potential, and early experience with certain aspects—diversity in the scientific workforce, the participation of minority subjects in clinical trials, community-based participatory research, the importance of reliable data, and the need for the assessment of programs—which are explored in further detail below.

Increasing the participation of underrepresented minorities in the **scientific workforce** is an important element of building the country's research capacity

BOX 3-3
Fiscal Year 2004 Strategic Plan Research Capacity Objectives
(Italic indicates new text)

Goal: To increase minority health and health disparity research training, career development, and institutional *research* capacity and *infrastructure*.

- Increase the number of participants in clinical trials from racial and ethnic minority populations and other health disparity populations
- Expand opportunities in research training and career development for, and provide research supplements to, research investigators from racial and ethnic minority populations and other health disparity populations
- *Increase the number of researchers conducting health disparities research*
- Increase funding support for the construction and renovation of research facilities across the nation aimed at enhancing the ability of these institutions to conduct health disparities research
- Provide increased funding at institutions across the country for resources, new equipment, and shared equipment programs for use in health disparities research
- Increase the peer review representation in peer review of individuals from racial and ethnic minority populations and other health disparity populations
- *Promote the development of inter-institutional partnerships between historically research-intensive and historically minority-serving institutions that seek to build research infrastructure*
- *Improve research data collection systems, and enhance data quality regarding health disparities, and develop uniform data systems that facilitate strategies for the elimination of health disparities*
- *In collaboration with schools and programs of public health, state and local health departments, and academic health departments, support and promote community-based participatory research*

(Building Engineering and Science Talent, 2004; Committee for the Assessment of NIH Minority Health Research Training Programs, 2005; Committee on National Needs for Biomedical and Behavioral Scientists, 2000; Congressional Commission on the Advancement of Women and Minorities in Science, Engineering and Technology Development, 2000; George et al., 2001; Jackson, 2003; National Science Board, 2003; National Science and Technology Council, 2000). Although there has been some increase in the number of underrepresented minorities in the scientific workforce, the number is still disproportionately low (Committee on National Needs for Biomedical and Behavioral Scientists, 2000). Many argue that society's complex scientific problems are best addressed by a diverse scientific workforce with vested interest in these issues (Kington et al., 2001). Minority scientists' general knowledge and understanding of their communities can facilitate health disparities research and ultimately inform the solution of medical problems in both minority and nonminority communities (Committee for the Assessment of NIH Minority Health Research Training Programs, 2005; Smedley et al., 2004).

As stated in the Strategic Plan, the principles underlying the support of research capacity include the understanding that NIH's ability to reduce health disparities through research proposed in the Strategic Plan requires "a strong commitment to training and supporting investigators in these areas," along with the understanding that NIH's "ability to sustain and even increase the momentum of recent scientific progress and our international leadership in medical research depends upon recruitment, training, support, and retention of biomedical investigators from diverse population groups." Moreover, it has been observed that NIH's ability to sustain or increase scientific progress in medical research can be enhanced by recruitment, training, support, and retention of biomedical investigators from diverse population groups and the development of relevant facilities and institutions (Committee on National Needs for Biomedical and Behavioral Scientists, 2000; Smedley et al., 2004).

At NIH, the success of minority training has varied by the type of career support mechanism. Total funding for Research Fellowship (F) Awards increased from $95 million in 2001 to $113 million in 2004, and the proportion of grants awarded per year to underrepresented minorities increased from 12 percent to 16 percent (Figure 3-1). For these NIH data, underrepresented minorities comprise those groups that are underrepresented in medicine, reported as Hispanics, American Indians or Alaska Natives, blacks or African Americans, and Native Hawaiians or Pacific Islanders.

In FY 2004, Research Career (K) Awards to underrepresented minority scientists totaled 7.9 percent of all awards (Figure 3-2). From 2001 to 2004, the total number of Research Career Awards increased, while the proportion given to minority scientists remained at approximately 8 percent. The distribution of Research Career Awards across ICs for 2004 is seen in Figure 3-3. Between 2001 and 2003, funding for Research Training Grant (T) Awards increased 13 percent

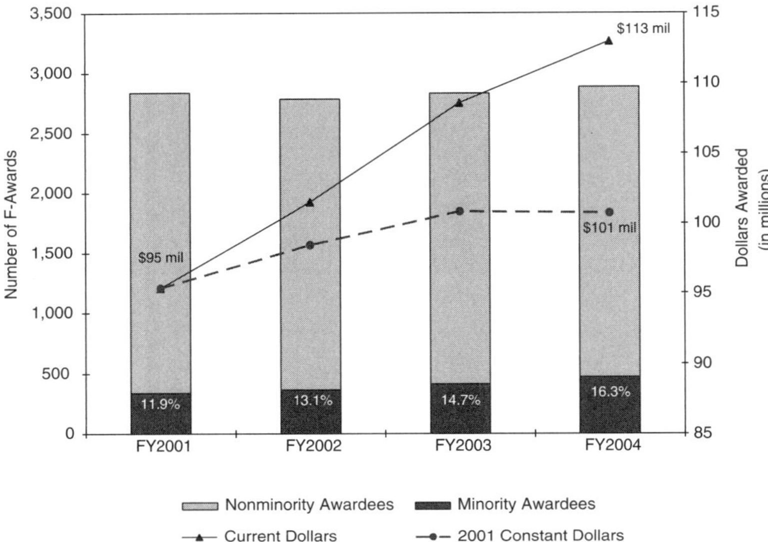

FIGURE 3-1 Amount of funding for NIH Research Fellowship Program, distribution of NIH Research Fellowship (F) Awards, and proportion awarded to underrepresented minority scientists. Amounts adjusted for inflation using the Biomedical Research and Development Price Index (BRDPI). SOURCE: Powe and Yeung, 2005.

after adjusting for inflation, but the proportion of appointments reportedly given to underrepresented minority scientists declined slightly, from 16.7 percent to 15.8 percent (Figure 3-4).

The participation of minority individuals in **clinical trials** has been a concern. Identified barriers to participation include: mistrust of physicians, scientists, and the government; concerns about exploitation; and socioeconomic status. Problems related to the research process also can act as barriers. These problems include misunderstanding the purpose of a clinical trial, misunderstanding the purpose of informed consent (Ard et al., 2005; Brooks et al., 2001; Corbie-Smith et al., 1999; Harris et al., 1996; Harrison, 2001; Shavers-Hornaday et al., 1997), and researchers' perception that minorities are uninterested or unwilling to participate or are unlikely to adhere to the treatment schedule (Noah, 2003). Interventions to improve minority participation in clinical trials typically concentrate on community education, elevating levels of trust in the health care system, and cultural strategies (Ard et al., 2003; CDC, 1998; Corbie-Smith et al., 1999; Partridge et al., 2005; Spruill, 2004).

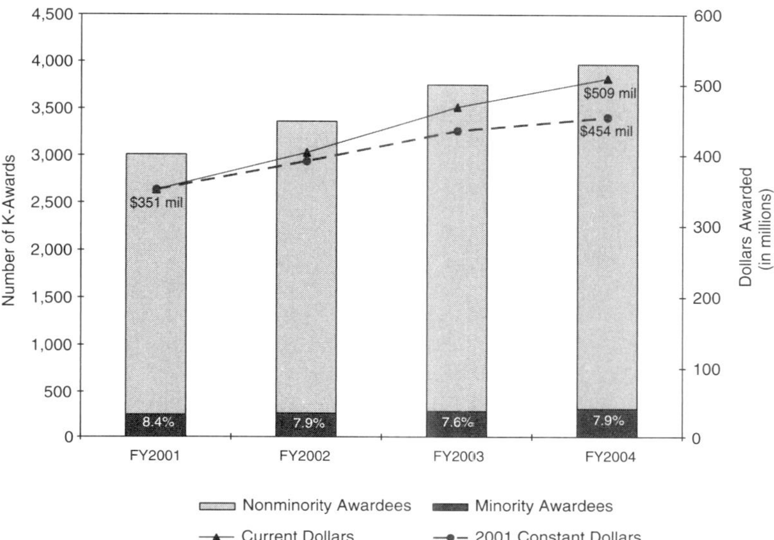

FIGURE 3-2 Amount of funding for NIH Research Career program, distribution of Research Career (K) Awards, and proportion awarded to underrepresented minority scientists. Amounts adjusted for inflation using the BRDPI. SOURCE: Powe and Yeung, 2005.

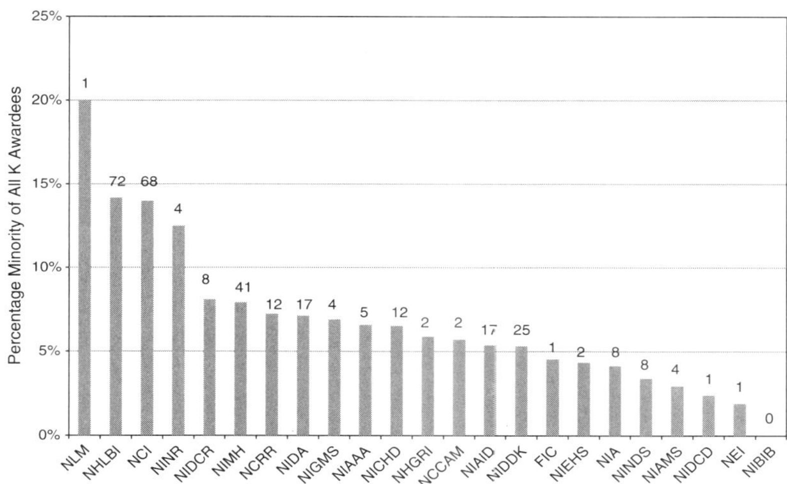

FIGURE 3-3 Proportion of Research Career (K) Awards given to underrepresented minority scientists by Institute/Center in Fiscal Year 2004. Institutes/Centers are labeled with the number of Career Research Awards granted to underrepresented minorities. Acronyms: see Appendix I. SOURCE: Powe and Yeung, 2005.

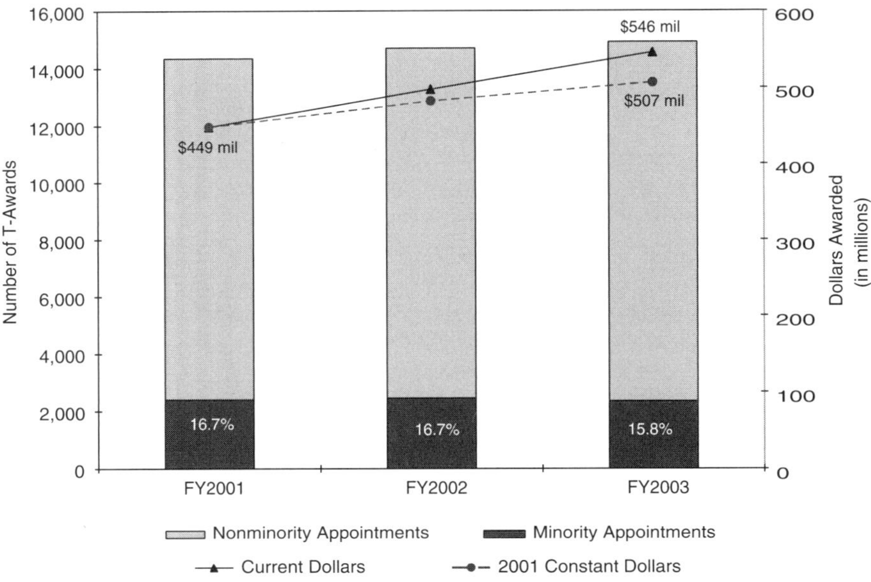

FIGURE 3-4 NIH Training Grant (T) appointments, proportion awarded to underrepresented minority scientists, and amount of funding for the Training Grant Program. Amounts adjusted for inflation using the BRDPI. SOURCE: Powe and Yeung, 2005.

NIH's role in improving the participation of minority groups in clinical trials was underscored by the 1999 Institute of Medicine (IOM) report *The Unequal Burden of Cancer* (Haynes and Smedley, 1999), which concluded that "without a concerted effort to enhance this process, ethnic minority and medically underserved communities will continue to lag behind the American majority in benefiting from . . . scientific advancements and medical breakthroughs." That report recommended that NIH—and specifically the National Cancer Institute—explore creative approaches to (1) encourage members of minority groups to participate in research and (2) report on the results of these efforts.[1] From 2001 to 2003, the number of Phase III clinical trial participants increased, but the proportion of minority participants decreased to 26.6 percent (Figure 3-5).

Presenting statistics by both race and ethnicity would facilitate the analysis of clinical trial participation by individuals from minority groups. Currently, assessment of the number of minorities participating in clinical trials is hindered by the report of race statistics in accord with the 1997 and 1977 Office of Man-

[1] See http://www.crchd.nci.nih.gov/ for National Cancer Institute programs that address this issue.

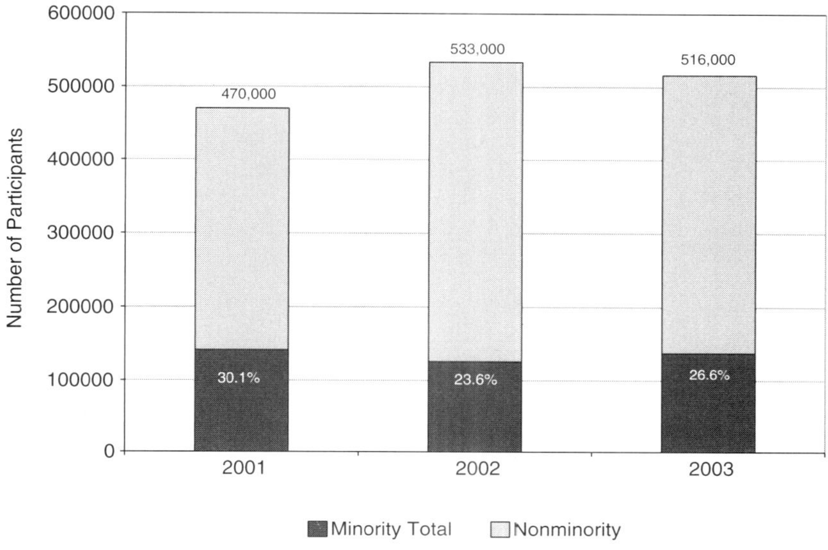

FIGURE 3-5 NIH total recruitment in Phase III clinical trials for Fiscal Years 2001–2003. SOURCE: Powe and Yeung, 2005. Updated using ORWH, 2005.

agement and Budget (OMB) Standards. The number of minority enrollees is determined by using data from two forms. The "old" form has five race categories following the OMB 1977 Standards, and the "new" form has seven race categories and Hispanic ethnicity, following the OMB 1997 Standards. All Hispanics are classified as minorities on the old form, but only nonwhite Hispanics are counted as minorities on the new form. Individuals classified as two or more races are not counted as minorities, no matter which two races they report. Data collected on the new form, then, could potentially undercount the total number of minorities.

The Kellogg Foundation (Kellogg Community Health Scholars Program, 2005) defines **community-based participatory research** as a "collaborative approach to research that equitably involves all partners in the research process and recognizes the unique strengths that each brings. [Community-based participatory research] begins with a research topic of importance to the community [and] has the aim of combining knowledge with action and achieving social change to improve health outcomes and eliminate health disparities." Proponents of community-based participatory research see it as a way to incorporate historical and structural factors, such as poverty, discrimination, and culture, into the study of health issues in the community while drawing on partnerships among investigators, respondents, and other community members and stakeholders (Gebbie et al., 2003).

This approach to community research could bring benefits, including the equitable participation of community members and researchers, which creates an environment of trust and knowledge sharing that traditional research structures lack. Furthermore, the sense of seeking "knowledge for action" as well as "knowledge for understanding" empowers community members and fosters their investment in the research agenda by engendering stronger research and high-quality results (Israel et al., 1998; O'Fallon and Dearry, 2002). Moreover, this research potentially yields results relevant to the interests, circumstances, and needs of the involved communities that apply them, results that are more immediately actionable in local situations for patients and/or practitioners, and findings that are more credible to practitioners and policy makers elsewhere because they were generated in partnership with people like themselves (Aungst et al., 2003).

Conducting community-based participatory research is challenging. Significant groundwork (outreach, education, identification of partners, development of infrastructure) needs to be done before communities are ready to participate in these projects. Because research funding is typically provided for individual studies rather than for building community capacity, sustainability is a major factor in the success of these projects. Concerns about sustainability can undermine initial partnership efforts. In this respect, NCMHD support for building the infrastructure for community-based research is particularly important. In another challenge, community-based participatory research takes more time than traditional research—sometimes frustrating both community members and investigators anticipating results. Also, lack of trust or mutual respect can undermine the principles of the research, while funding conflicts may weaken relationships. The research's scientific rigor may be questioned and the research design may complicate data analysis, resulting in further challenges that can negatively affect investigators' careers. According to some (Holkup et al., 2004; Lantz et al., 2001), however, community-based participatory research can be productive when solutions for facilitating the process are implemented.

At NIH, 17 of 26 ICs queried indicated that in general they had supported community-based participatory research projects (Powe and Yeung, 2005), though a review of the ICs' strategic plans revealed that only 6 ICs and Offices had included community-based participatory health disparities research projects in their strategic plans.

There is an unmet need for **valid and reliable data** on health disparities to (a) identify and survey disparities and (b) explore and explain disparities (Fremont and Lurie, 2004). The inadequacy of current data, discussed in Chapter 2 as a concern for the NIH research program, ranges from basic information, such as annual race/ethnicity-specific measures of health status, to more detailed items, such as geocoded individual-level health status and sociodemographic data sets. In *Healthy People 2010*, for example, which lists diseases and conditions for which racial disparities might exist, baseline race/ethnicity-specific measures were missing for some race and ethnicity groups for many of the disorders on the list. Moreover, further surveillance data were not available for all race and ethnic groups (Ver Ploeg and Perrin, 2004).

Lacking appropriately collected and coded data, researchers may be unable to link individual-level health survey data to structural data that describe the social, economic, and political environments that might be factors in particular health outcomes—a linkage that is particularly important in the investigation of health disparities. Additional problems include a lack of standardization in ethnic and racial categories, inaccuracy in the reporting of racial statistics, and sample sizes that are too small to allow statistically meaningful comparisons (Ver Ploeg and Perrin, 2004).

It is difficult to get information on the **effects of the various research infrastructure and capacity programs** supported by NIH. Given the importance of these programs, information on program outcomes and impacts is needed for assessments of the programs' effectiveness. Information should be continuously gathered and analyzed for those programs included in the Strategic Plan's objectives, such as programs directed at minorities to address research training and career development, and those aimed at increasing the number of researchers conducting health disparities research. For these programs, it would be particularly useful to know what works, which training environments are most successful, and which factors facilitate or limit career success (Committee on National Needs for Biomedical and Behavioral Scientists, 2000; George et al., 2001).

Also, the Strategic Plan should include assessments of programs that support: the construction and renovation of research facilities aimed at enhancing the ability of institutions to conduct health disparities research; the provision of equipment and shared equipment programs for use in health disparities research; the promotion of inter-institutional partnerships between historically research-intensive and historically minority-serving institutions; and the improvement of data collection and attempts to develop uniform data systems. Although the Office on Research in Women's Health regularly compiles and reports data on minorities enrolled in clinical research studies, analysis and assessment of these data is needed with respect to the minority health and health disparities program and the Strategic Plan.

A recent National Academies report on minority training programs at NIH raised similar concerns regarding the need for information and assessment (Committee for the Assessment of NIH Minority Research Training Programs, 2005). That report recommended that a set of clear and measurable training objectives, specific to minority training, be set forth; that NIH commit to the continued funding of these programs; and that appropriate guidelines and measures for evaluating these programs be established.

Findings:

- **The Strategic Plan does not provide for assessments of the results of the research capacity and infrastructure programs included as objectives. Such information is needed to evaluate the effectiveness of these programs, identify approaches in need of modification, set priorities, and make evaluations available for internal and external reviews.**
- **The inclusion of community-based participatory research as an objective of the Strategic Plan is appropriate. There is a need for development of metrics, analysis, assessment and evaluation of community-based participatory research for a better sense of the issues and settings for which it is most promising.**

Recommendation 4: The Strategic Plan should include measurable targets and time periods for the research capacity objectives. NIH, through NCMHD's oversight, should develop methods of measuring, analyzing and monitoring the results of programs that address research capacity, including workforce, institutional, infrastructure, and community-based participatory health disparity research objectives.

Community Outreach, Information Dissemination, and Public Health Education

In the Strategic Plan, the community outreach, information dissemination, and public health education goal is "to ensure [that] the public, health-care professionals, and research communities are informed and educated concerning the latest advances in minority health and health disparities research." The communication goal encourages efforts that "extend beyond dissemination of the results of research to other scientists and include the transmission of all information that may improve the health of racial and ethnic minorities and other health disparity populations to the general public, patients, advocacy groups, health-care providers, media, and policy makers." The Strategic Plan proposes "a comprehensive and aggressive outreach to those groups whom the research is intended to help and their health-care providers. These messages must be tailored to the communities at highest risk for the adverse consequences of the health disparity in question. The efforts must also include producing health information that is culturally applicable, ensuring that it is disseminated to the appropriate communities, and assessing the effectiveness of these communication efforts."

Several new objectives in the 2004 Strategic Plan call for the dissemination of practical strategies related to health disparities and collaborations to translate research findings into policy documents. In addition, the 2002 Strategic Plan's objective for communication and dialogue was expanded to include several types of community organizations—community-based and faith-based organizations,

BOX 3-4
Fiscal Year 2004 Strategic Plan Community Outreach, Information Dissemination, and Public Health Education Objectives
(Italic indicates new text)

Goal: To ensure that the public, health-care professionals, and research communities are informed and educated concerning the latest advances in minority health and health disparities research.

- Provide the latest research-based information to health-care providers to enhance the care provided to individuals within racial and ethnic minority populations and other health disparity populations
- Facilitate the incorporation of science-based information into the curricula of medical and allied health professions schools, theological education institutions, public health schools, and into the continuing education activities of health professionals
- *Maintain ongoing communication linkages and partnerships with community-based and faith-based organizations, health-care associations, foundations, and academic institutions and foster dialogue with racial and ethnic minority populations and other health disparity populations, including the underserved*
- Develop computer databases and Internet resources to disseminate current information about scientific research and discoveries and other activities regarding heath disparities
- Develop targeted public health education programs focused on particular disease areas in order to reach those individuals within racial and ethnic minority populations and other health disparity populations who experience health disparities within these disease areas
- *Facilitate, document, and disseminate practical strategies responsive to the health-care needs, and appropriate to the cultural and linguistic needs, of communities throughout the United States*
- *Collaborate with public health and other health-oriented policy centers to translate research findings into policy documents that can be used by policy groups and other stakeholders to explain new discoveries from a policy perspective to decision makers*

health care associations, foundations, and academic institutions—in addition to population groups that experience health disparities. These are relevant and significant additions to the Strategic Plan (Box 3-4).

Translating research information with clinical implications and derived best practices to the direct care of patients poses a serious challenge (Lenfant, 2003; Sehgal, 2003). The important recognition that disparities in communication may play a role in health disparities prompts concern for a more organized and concerted effort in this area (see Viswanath, Appendix G). Like health disparities, communication disparities are complex. The Strategic Plan addresses two major areas: (a) the dissemination of research-derived information to practitioners and institutions providing care to those affected by disparities in health, including public hospitals and community health centers, and (b) the provision of information to people and communities. For communication with providers of care, problems include sponsor incentives and commitment, the origin and nature of the information, the appropriate patient care and educational settings in which the information should be disseminated, and the lack of organized approaches. For NIH, approaches should include increased sensitivity to these challenges, the promotion of effective information systems, the assessment of existing models, the involvement of audiences in the design and assessment of what is needed and effective, and the promotion of research on such communication (Viswanath, Appendix G). As more reliable and effective methods are sought, opportunities to design, implement, assess, and improve the particularly demanding and important problems of translating minority health and health disparities information will be developed for the benefit of communication programs other than those focused on minority health and health disparities research.

An even greater challenge is disseminating information to the public. As Viswanath (Appendix G) points out, there are three problem areas, all varying with race, ethnicity, culture, and other group characteristics: (a) access to information, including such factors as the availability of information, differences in media channels, and the affordability of access (including problems related to the digital divide); (b) the attention to and processing of information; and (c) the ability and capacity of individuals and groups to use the information as it relates to such factors as language, health literacy, and culture as well as the environment and the availability of opportunities. These problems create inequities in communication of health information which may contribute to health status inequities.

Outreach and communication are so challenging and important that these issues warrant particular attention as a further organized, concerted trans-NIH effort within the Strategic Plan—well beyond that described in the sporadic objective areas of individual IC strategic plans. Such a core effort could be informed and assisted by communication scholars, as well as by representatives from the audiences being served.

Finding: The current objectives for outreach and public information identify target audiences, but attention is needed to issues of inequalities in public communication, including those related to access and use of, and ability to act on, information. Additional understanding is needed regarding effective communication with those who provide care to groups with poor health. Coordination of communication programs across NIH could help with examination of specific audience needs and evaluations of programs.

Recommendation 5: The Strategic Plan's communication programs should be organized as a specific trans-NIH effort with centralized coordination with particular attention to the strategic planning, design, prioritization, implementation, and evaluation of efforts across NIH. The initiative should: be informed by advisory expertise; develop a surveillance system to identify information needs and availability, sources, behaviors, and use patterns; and promote attention to the issue of inequalities in health communication.

THE STRATEGIC PLANS OF THE ICS

The Strategic Plan's goals and objectives cannot be achieved unless they are translated into objectives and actions by the ICs. Twenty-five ICs, the Office of AIDS Research, and the Office of Behavioral and Social Sciences Research are part of the 2002 and 2004 Strategic Plans. The ICs and Offices used various methods to identify objectives and programs for their individual strategic plans within the overall framework of the Strategic Plan goals and objectives. This resulted in a variety of objectives, reflected in initiatives that address a broad range of diseases, disabilities, and strategies.

The Committee reviewed the plans outlined by the ICs in Volume II of the 2002 and 2004 Strategic Plans. In addition, it commissioned a survey of the ICs to review their experience in addressing and implementing the Strategic Plan. The survey included achievements, barriers encountered, and recommendations for improving the process. Patterns of similarity to, and difference from, the overall Strategic Plan were noted.

Some objectives from the overall Strategic Plan appear prominently in the ICs' objectives and planned actions. For example, in the research area, the most frequent IC objectives are those focused on advancing the understanding of the development and progression of diseases and disabilities that contribute to health disparities. In the area of research capacity, the ICs have numerous planned actions, including minority-targeted and untargeted awards, programs for students ranging in age from elementary school to professional school, and collaboration with minority-serving institutions. In communication, the numerous planned actions also vary in content, target audience, and methods for disseminating information. Outreach messages range from disease and coping information to behavior recommendations and treatment options (Powe and Yeung, 2005).

The ICs' plans infrequently mention some Strategic Plan objectives, including those addressing data collection systems and community-based research. Similarly, outreach objectives dealing with the provision of information directed at professional school curricula, the use of computer databases, and involvement in policy development were not widely adopted. In addition, the ICs' plans give little attention to the provision of information to health care providers, despite widespread awareness of the need for rapid and effective translation of research findings into the direct care of patients. Even some research objectives considered relevant to the domains of many ICs are unclearly identified as objectives or intended activities in their strategic plans—for example, those addressing the detection, prevention, or understanding of multifactorial causes of disparities in health. Gaps between the overall objectives of the Strategic Plan and those of the ICs for which the objectives are relevant predict a lack of significant activity and achievement in these areas.

It is noted that some ICs have planned activities in epidemiology and collaboration with, or involvement in, research on disparities in health care, areas that are relevant but were not included in the overall objectives of the Strategic Plan. This report recommends that they be included (see Recommendation 3).

The draft 2004 Strategic Plan included individual strategic plans for each IC, but there was no evidence that these plans were developed as part of a coordinated trans-NIH plan. Hence, it is unclear whether the 2004 Strategic Plan's revised objectives guided the ICs' updated plans. Because it lacks a budget, the draft 2004 Strategic Plan's value as a planning and management tool is diminished.

The Committee was most concerned about the need to coordinate the ICs' strategic plans as part of a truly concerted trans-NIH plan. The ICs' individual strategic plans are the ultimate implementation of the NIH Strategic Plan, and so they should appropriately reflect the Strategic Plan's overall goals and objectives. This requires a central, coordinated assessment of the ICs' strategic plans, considering both the relevance to the purview of the ICs and NIH-wide and IC program priorities. Such a review should be a documented part of updating and revising the IC strategic plans to ensure they are complete and relevant. In addition, ongoing review and monitoring of the overall Strategic Plan should include assessments of whether, and to what extent, the ICs' objectives and activities have been carried out, as well as any results. Such information, including central analysis and evaluation by NCMHD, should be part of an effective annual reporting system. At the time of review by the Committee, just one approved annual report (2001) was available.

Finding: There is no evidence that the Strategic Plans of the ICs were developed as part of a concerted, trans-NIH strategic planning process. Planned IC activities are not time-based or targeted.

Recommendation 6:

- **The development of updated Strategic Plans should include assessments of the appropriateness of the individual strategic plans of the ICs, including whether they adequately reflect the overall goals and objectives of the NIH Strategic Plan.**

- **Objectives should be time-based and targeted with measurable outcomes.**

HEALTH DISPARITIES AS DEFINED BY THE STRATEGIC PLAN

As discussed in Chapter 2, the term "health disparities" may connote inequitable or unjust differences in health, but the term also has been increasingly used over the past several years to describe differences in health without necessarily implying the presence of injustice. Thus, "health disparities" is used in the enabling legislation establishing the NCMHD, in NIH definitions, and by the Strategic Plan.

Also, as noted in Chapter 2, complete agreement does not exist on the best or most valid way to identify disparity groups (Carter-Pokras and Banquet, 2002; Weitz et al., 2001). The Strategic Plan defines health disparities in terms of the disproportionate burden of illness and disease experienced by racial and ethnic groups, resulting from the interaction of biological factors, the environment, and specific health behaviors. As primary causes of health disparities, it identifies factors that have been widely discussed—i.e., socioeconomic status, education, biological factors, access and quality of health care, racial and ethnic discrimination, and cultural issues.

For reporting purposes, the 2004 Strategic Plan used the methodological guidelines developed by the NIH Committee on Minority Health and Health Disparities Research Definitions and Application Methodology, effective January 2004 (see Chapter 4 and Appendix H). When finalized, the budget of the 2004 Strategic Plan will also use these guidelines, which were an important advance in NIH's use of established criteria to define groups experiencing health disparities and track related expenditures. Prior to this guidance, NIH had neither uniform definitions of health disparity groups nor a system for tracking expenditures that were specifically directed at health disparities. The 1999 IOM report, *The Unequal Burden of Cancer,* recommended that NIH "improve the accuracy of its assessment of research that is relevant to ethnic minority and medically underserved groups by replacing the current 'percent relevancy' accounting method with one that identifies studies whose purpose is to address a priori research questions uniquely affecting ethnic minority and medically underserved groups."

The NIH Committee was convened in response to language in P.L. 106-525 that called for a report recommending a methodology to "determine the extent of the resources of the National Institutes of Health that are dedicated to minority health disparities research and other health disparities research." The methodological guidelines in the Committee's report established operational definitions of minority health and health disparities research, provided a methodology for applying these definitions, contained criteria for identifying minority health and health disparity groups and diseases, and served as the foundation for identifying, coding, tracking, and reporting NIH activities and resources.

In accordance with the methodological guidelines, the 2004 Strategic Plan defined health disparity populations as comprising those minority groups delineated within Section 1707(g) of the Public Health Service Act, in addition to low socioeconomic status populations and rural populations.[2]

In addition to racial and ethnic minorities, low socioeconomic status groups, and rural populations, other groups may warrant such a designation—including, for example, the uninsured, the urban underserved, certain immigrant groups, or those for whom language is a barrier. It is thus expected, as described by the enabling legislation, that NCMHD, in consultation with AHRQ, will designate additional groups. As such, the development of more specific criteria, presumably by a process established by NCMHD, will be needed.

As processes are developed, it should be recognized that identifying multiple disparity groups may cause efforts to reduce and eliminate disparities to become fragmented, duplicative, or even zero sum (i.e., one disparity group competing with another for scarce resources). It has been argued (see Adler, Appendix D) that the strategy of identifying multiple disparity populations may ultimately be less fruitful than a strategy focused on identifying and intervening in disparity *processes*. For example, low socioeconomic status is not a homogeneous disparity group or population. Rather, low socioeconomic status is a description of the end result of a social stratification *process* in which some individuals end up with less access to opportunities, such as quality schooling, adequate income, or safe jobs.

In addition to continued attention to the definition of health disparities, there is a need for a registry or clearinghouse of health disparity diseases and conditions, including regularly updated information on the prevalence of diseases and conditions and the populations affected. Such a registry would help with evaluation of the appropriateness and adequacy of the targets and activities of the overall Strategic Plan and those of specific ICs, and provide guidance for planning, priority setting, and policy decisions for the NIH and others. This registry would also provide key information to those involved or interested in health disparities research, which could track prevalence and trends across multiple indicators, health outcomes, and population subgroups. Among other functions, the registry would also help to prioritize research and interventions aimed at eliminating disparities. In addition, a registry would facilitate collaboration and allow the needs of subpopulations to be identified.

[2]Section 1707(g) defines minority groups as American Indians (including Alaska Natives, Eskimos, and Aleuts), Asian Americans, Native Hawaiians and other Pacific Islanders, Blacks, and Hispanics, where Hispanic means individuals whose origin is Mexican, Puerto Rican, Cuban, Central or South American, or any other Spanish-speaking country.

Findings:

- **Beyond the basic definitions of health disparities indicated by Congress and used by NIH, there are no further criteria for deciding what constitutes a health disparity group. Understanding the health impacts of social stratification (e.g., in the education system or the labor market) presents an additional approach to health disparities research.**
- **There is need for a resource that provides updated listings of: diseases and conditions for which differences exist; affected populations; prevalence data; and other information that would provide a knowledge base on the scope and impact of disparity conditions. This resource would help in planning health disparity studies, setting priorities, and assessing research activities.**

Recommendation 7: NCMHD should consider the designation of additional health disparity groups based on an informed process and developed criteria. It should promote development of, and access to, a registry of diseases and conditions for which disparities exist with regard to race, ethnicity, socioeconomic status, geographic locale, and other designated health disparity populations.

4

Budget and Finances

The Committee assessed the Strategic Plan budgets, recognizing their importance in planning, monitoring, and assessment. Review of the budgets and financial information was limited because the Strategic Plans and Annual Reports were not sources of complete, up-to-date budget information and because interpreting the information proved difficult.

AVAILABILITY OF BUDGET INFORMATION

The availability of accurate, approved budget information was limited during the period of Committee review, from October 2004 through July 2005. Budget information should have been available from the Strategic Plan and the Annual Reports. However, the initial Strategic Plan budget (2002) had been approved but had not been developed with uniform definitions and methodology standards, and the draft of the unapproved 2004 Strategic Plan did not include budgets. Likewise, the first Annual Report (Fiscal Year [FY] 2001) detailing implementation of the Strategic Plan included a budget developed without uniform methodology, as did the unapproved Annual Report for FY 2002. The unapproved Annual Report for FY 2003 used the newly developed methodology.

INTERPRETATION OF BUDGET INFORMATION: DEFINITIONS AND METHODS

The interpretation of budget information for National Institutes of Health (NIH) minority health and health disparities research for periods before FY 2003 is difficult because the definitions and methodology for coding across the NIH were not uniform. Before the initiation of the health disparities research program and the Strategic Plan, NIH Institutes and Centers (ICs) were already conducting extensive research related to minority health and health disparities. Most of this research involved the study of diseases, conditions, and circumstances that were important to the general population and that constituted major factors contributing to disparate health statuses affecting minorities and other groups due to greater prevalence, increased severity, and worse outcomes. However, there were no standardized accounting methods for budget allocations to what was considered to be minority health and health disparities research. Comparisons and trend assessments were less certain. Hence, the trans-NIH organization of the health disparities research initiative and the Strategic Plan emphasized the need for a uniform methodology and budget definitions.

The NIH Research Definitions and Application Methodology (Boxes 4-1, 4-2, and Appendix H), the origins of which were described in Chapter 3, provided guidelines for reporting the two components of minority health and health disparities research: the Minority Health Report and the Health Disparities Report. The Health Disparities Report combines information from the Minority Health Report with data on activities addressing two additional health disparity populations: low socioeconomic status and rural populations. Section 485(d)(1) of the enabling minority health and health disparities legislation defines a health disparity population as one for which "if, as determined by the Director of the Center [NCMHD] after consultation with the Director of the Agency for Healthcare Research and Quality, there is a significant disparity in the overall rate of disease incidence, prevalence, morbidity, mortality, or survival rates in the population as compared to the health status of the general population."

The definitions of applicable research activities for basic research, infrastructure, and outreach projects include only projects targeted at minority health and health disparity issues. For clinical research, both targeted and nontargeted projects qualify, with nontargeted projects defined as those with rates of minority participants to total participants of 25 percent or greater. For low socioeconomic and rural groups, activity is reported based on emphasis levels assigned by the NIH's Computer Retrieval of Information on Scientific Projects (CRISP).

Although adopted halfway through the 4th year of the 5-year program, the New Definitions and Methodology are useful standards created by a collective NIH effort. The new standards, applied in early 2004 and retroactively applied to FY 2003 NIH expenditures, promise to provide more reliable and useful data.

INCREMENTAL FUNDING FOR THE NIH MINORITY HEALTH AND HEALTH DISPARITIES RESEARCH PROGRAM

It is reasonable to expect that the health disparities research and Strategic Plan initiative would bring about additional NIH programs and other financial

BOX 4-1
Minority Health Report

Minorities are defined by statute as American Indians/Alaskan Natives (including Eskimos and Aleuts), Asian Americans, Native Hawaiians and other Pacific Islanders, blacks, and Hispanics (i.e., individuals whose origin is Mexican, Puerto Rican, Cuban, Central or South American, or any other Spanish-speaking country).

Targeted research (report at 100 percent) includes:

- basic research on a disease, condition, or biological process that affects **exclusively or almost exclusively** one or more minority populations;
- basic research on a behavior that is found **exclusively or almost exclusively** in one or more minority populations;
- basic research on whether and/or how the mechanisms of disease or basic biological processes differ in minority populations, or how behaviors differ in minority populations;
- clinical research conducted **exclusively or almost exclusively** in one or more minority populations;
- clinical research investigating whether and/or how the manifestations, consequences, or responses to treatment of diseases or other conditions differ in minority populations; and
- clinical research investigating how behaviors differ in minority populations.

Nontargeted research (report at the percent minority participation, as long as it exceeds the threshold of 25 percent) includes:

- clinical research focused on prevention, diagnosis, or treatment of diseases or other conditions that affect minority populations.

Targeted infrastructure (report at 100 percent) includes:

- solicited programs that are focused exclusively on developing the research capabilities of historically black colleges and universities and minority medical schools and
- solicited programs designed to enhance the research resources specifically available to underrepresented minorities at other institutions educating or training high numbers of one or more minority populations that are underrepresented in biomedical or behavioral research.

Targeted research training and career development (report at 100 percent) includes:

- programs that focus **exclusively** on supporting research training or career development of underrepresented minorities.

Nontargeted research training and career development (report only dollars received by underrepresented minority individuals) includes:

- activities that support research training or career development of underrepresented minority investigators, but that are not focused exclusively on these population groups.

Targeted outreach (report at 100 percent) includes:

- programs that focus **exclusively** on providing health-related information to minority populations and
- programs that focus **exclusively** on providing information to health care providers about preventing, diagnosing, or treating diseases or other conditions in minority populations.

SOURCE: NIH Committee on Minority Health and Health Disparities Research Definitions and Application Methodology (Appendix H).

BOX 4-2
Health Disparities Report

Health disparities populations are minority populations, low socioeconomic status (low-SES) populations, and rural populations.

Minority health issues are considered to be a subset of health disparities issues. The Health Disparities Report includes all activities in the Minority Health Report plus activities related to low-SES and rural populations. An activity that addresses minority health **as well as** low SES or rural health is included in the Health Disparities Report based on either its percent relevance to minority health or its percent relevance to low SES and rural health—whichever is higher.

Targeted research (report at 100 percent) includes:

- basic research on a disease, condition, or biological process that affects **exclusively or almost exclusively** low-SES or rural populations;
- basic research on a behavior that is found **exclusively or almost exclusively** in low-SES or rural populations;
- basic research on whether and/or how the mechanisms of disease or basic biological processes differ in low-SES or rural populations, or how behaviors differ in minority populations;
- clinical research on whether and/or how the manifestations, consequences, or responses to treatment of diseases or other conditions differ in low-SES or rural populations; and
- clinical research conducted **exclusively or almost exclusively** in low-SES or rural populations.

Nontargeted research (report at 50/25 percent if coded in the NIH CRISP as secondary/tertiary for low SES or rural health, or at the minority participation percent, if higher) includes:

- clinical research related to the manifestations, consequences, or responses to treatment of diseases or other conditions in low-SES or rural populations and
- clinical research conducted in populations that include low-SES or rural populations.

Infrastructure is equal to the minority health figure for this category (due to difficulties in identifying institutions that educate large numbers of people from low-SES or rural populations).

Research training and career development is equal to the minority health figure for this category (due to difficulties in identifying trainees of low-SES or rural backgrounds and institutions that educate large numbers of people from low-SES or rural populations).

Targeted outreach (report at 100 percent) includes:

- programs that focus **exclusively** on providing health-related information to low-SES or rural populations and
- programs that focus **exclusively** on providing information to health care providers about preventing, diagnosing, or treating diseases or other conditions in low-SES or rural populations.

SOURCE: NIH Committee on Minority Health and Health Disparities Research Definitions and Application Methodology (Appendix H).

needs beyond those existing prior to 2000. Without incremental funding to NIH, progress in implementing the program could have been impeded by priority decisions with respect to other commitments.

The reality that additional funding would be needed for funding for the NIH health disparities initiative was addressed in Section 485E(l) of P.L. 106-525: "For the purpose of carrying out this subpart, there are authorized to be appropriated $100,000,000 for fiscal year 2001, and such sums as may be necessary for each of the fiscal years 2002 through 2005. Such authorization of appropriations is in addition to other authorizations of appropriations that are available for the conduct and support of minority health disparities research or other health disparities research by the agencies of the National Institutes of Health."

The authorized additional funds were not appropriated to NIH. It appears that the NIH director added $74.5 million of NIH funds to the health disparities initiative in FY 2001, of which $20 million was allocated to the National Center on Minority Health and Health Disparities and $54 million was distributed among the ICs, presumably increasing their base budgets. No such additional funding was appropriated in subsequent years. Thus, incremental funding to the NIH as specified by the legislation was not provided.

NIH BUDGET ALLOCATIONS FOR HEALTH DISPARITIES

The Committee attempted to compare appropriated funds and expenditures on minority health and health disparities activities within the ICs from FY 1998 to FY 2004 using published data and data provided by the Budget Office of the NIH Director, recognizing, as noted above, that except for 2003 and 2004, the data were not standardized in accordance with the new definitions and methodology. For all years, health disparities expenditures, as reported, include those for minority health, although they are discussed separately here.

In 2000, at the onset of the health disparities research program, two of the 25 participating ICs (National Institute of Child Health and Human Development [NICHD] and National Institute of Nursing Research [NINR]) and the Office of the Director reported spending more than 20 percent of their budgets on minority health activities, and almost half of ICs reported spending more than 5 percent (Tables 4-1 and 4-2). Overall, NIH used approximately 8 percent of its budget for minority health programs in FY 2000. In FY 2002, total NIH funding for health disparities increased by 16.9 percent over FY 2001 levels, from $23.7 billion to $27.7 billion; in FY 2003, it increased another 14.2 percent to $31.6 billion, according to the original accounting methodology for estimating spending (figures for health disparities were not reported in 2000; Table 4-3).[1] With the application of the new definitions and methodology, the adjusted 2003 funding for health disparities was reported to be $24.3 billion, $734.5 million less than origi-

[1]Amounts are not adjusted for inflation.

TABLE 4-1 Percentage of Total Appropriation Used for Minority Health Research Activities by the NIH Institutes and Centers (ICs), Fiscal Years 1999–2004

Participating ICs	1998 %	1999[a] %	2000[a] %	2001[a] %	2002[a] %	2003[a] %	2003[b] %	2004[b] %
NCI	2.97	2.62	2.75	2.76	2.91	2.87	3.06	4.61
NHLBI	8.73	9.25	10.23	9.43	9.40	9.54	9.76	10.07
NIDCR	7.95	6.75	5.12	5.95	5.59	6.48	8.81	10.05
NIDDK	8.98	8.64	9.45	9.00	8.53	11.06	11.06	10.17
NINDS	1.95	2.40	2.42	2.86	3.71	3.93	5.16	4.81
NIAID	0.60	14.52	14.08	13.87	14.14	7.84	7.79	8.05
NIGMS	6.69	7.39	8.32	8.47	8.21	8.24	8.24	8.53
NICHD	14.05	22.69	23.73	24.65	24.94	25.22	13.33	13.38
NEI	3.24	3.57	4.06	4.05	3.99	3.63	2.47	2.60
NIEHS	3.89	3.44	4.58	3.99	3.62	1.02	2.18	2.66
NIA	9.18	8.80	8.67	8.38	8.51	8.72	10.58	11.41
NIAMS	11.11	10.03	9.61	9.80	10.96	10.94	7.11	6.15
NIDCD	1.94	1.81	1.16	1.07	1.71	2.29	5.02	5.68
NIMH	2.26	1.95	2.20	2.02	2.14	13.14	13.14	13.33
NIDA	8.36	8.00	8.08	8.29	8.43	8.98	10.14	9.61
NIAAA	14.70	16.22	9.23	9.81	9.36	0.84	8.74	8.31
NINR	18.05	20.77	22.27	21.44	23.34	21.07	21.06	22.35
NHGRI	1.29	1.65	1.33	2.03	2.51	2.61	2.29	3.61
NIBIB	—	—	—	—	0.28	0.36	3.82	3.17
NCRR	7.33	6.05	5.77	4.89	4.81	5.45	5.18	5.06
NCCAM	—	—	5.67	14.04	7.07	9.94	9.94	10.81
NCMHD	—	—	—	96.17	93.45	83.36	83.36	83.37
FIC	0.00	2.84	2.73	2.21	1.78	0.74	0.74	2.08
NLM	0.92	1.30	1.11	1.55	3.17	1.07	1.07	1.26
OD	25.62	28.10	33.74	0.00	2.52	3.08	3.15	1.88
NIH	6.02	7.79	7.96	8.00	8.11	7.89	7.72	8.21

NOTE: Acronyms: see Appendix I.
— Not applicable.

[a]Calculation is based on the prior methodology for defining minority health.
[b]Calculation is based on the new definition of minority health.

SOURCE: NIH, 2005.

nally estimated for 2003. In 2004, the annual increment represented a 6.6 percent increase, which was lower than before the application of the new methodology but still greater than the total NIH budget increase of 3.0 percent.

The change in methodology revealed that NIH was spending approximately 3 percent less of its total budget on health disparities activities than originally reported in FY 2003. The percentage of the total NIH budget allocated to health disparities research was reported to be 11 percent in 1999 and 12 percent each year from 2001 to 2003 (old methodology; Figure 4-1 and Table 4-4). After application of the new methodology to the 2003 data, NIH allocated 9 percent in

TABLE 4-2 Annual Expenditures on Minority Health Research Activities by the NIH Institutes and Centers (ICs), Fiscal Years 1998–2004 (Dollars in Millions)

Participating ICs	1998[a]	1999[a]	2000[a]	2001[a]	2002[a]	2003[a]	2003[b]	2004[b]
NCI	$75.6	$76.6	$91.3	$103.5	$121.9	$131.7	$140.4	$218.3
NHLBI	133.7	165.9	207.7	216.7	241.7	266.5	272.7	289.7
NIDCR	16.7	15.8	13.8	18.2	19.1	24.1	32.7	38.5
NIDDK	80.9	88.2	110.5	126.0	133.2	190.5	190.5	185.2
NINDS	15.3	21.7	24.9	33.7	49.2	57.2	75.1	72.2
NIAID	8.1	227.8	250.3	283.1	331.3	282.9	281.0	334.3
NIGMS	71.3	88.5	112.7	130.1	141.7	152.2	152.2	162.5
NICHD	94.8	170.3	203.6	240.6	277.2	304.1	160.8	166.3
NEI	11.5	14.1	18.3	20.7	23.2	23.0	15.6	17.0
NIEHS	12.8	12.9	20.3	22.5	23.4	7.1	15.2	18.9
NIA	47.7	52.4	59.5	65.8	75.9	86.6	105.1	116.9
NIAMS	30.5	30.9	33.6	38.9	49.1	53.2	34.6	30.8
NIDCD	3.9	4.2	3.1	3.2	5.8	8.5	18.6	21.7
NIMH	16.9	16.8	21.4	22.3	26.7	176.3	176.3	184.2
NIDA	44.1	48.2	55.4	64.7	74.7	86.3	97.5	95.2
NIAAA	33.4	42.1	27.0	33.4	35.9	3.5	36.4	35.6
NINR	11.5	14.5	19.9	22.4	28.1	27.5	27.5	30.1
NHGRI	2.8	4.4	4.5	7.8	10.8	12.1	10.6	17.3
NIBIB	—	—	—	—	0.3	1.0	10.6	9.1
NCRR	33.3	33.6	39.0	40.0	48.7	62.1	59.0	59.7
NCCAM	—	—	3.9	12.5	7.4	11.3	11.3	12.6
NCMHD	—	—	—	125.1	147.2	154.8	154.8	159.6
FIC	0.0	1.0	1.2	1.1	1.0	0.5	0.5	1.4
NLM	1.5	2.4	2.4	3.8	8.8	3.2	3.2	4.0
OD	75.9	86.1	95.2	0.0	5.9	8.2	8.4	6.1
NIH	822.2	1,218.2	1,419.3	1,636.1	1,888.4	2,134.3	2,090.5	2,287.4

NOTE: Acronyms: see Appendix I.
— Not applicable.

[a]Calculation is based on the prior methodology for defining minority health.
[b]Calculation is based on the new definition of minority health.

SOURCE: NIH, 2005.

both 2003 and 2004. For minority health research, NIH spent approximately 8 percent of its total funding annually from 1999 through 2004 (Table 4-1). Even after application of the new methodology, the percentage did not change much, as seen in Figure 4-1. The new methodology seemed mostly to affect the health disparities component.

An NIH view of the adjusted allocations report (Zerhouni, 2004) noted large changes in three ICs: the National Institute of Allergy and Infectious Diseases (NIAID), with a change of $451 million in the health disparities portion of the 2003 budget; the National Cancer Institute (NCI), with a change of $157 million;

TABLE 4-3 Annual Expenditures on Health Disparities Research Activities by the NIH Institutes and Centers (ICs), Fiscal Years 1999, 2001–2004[a] (Dollars in Millions)

Participating ICs	1999[b]	2001[b]	2002[b]	2003[b]	2003[c]	2004[c]
NCI	$197.0	$350.3	$383.1	$414.0	$256.6	$264.8
NHLBI	177.1	218.2	255.1	279.0	276.9	295.3
NIDCR	13.7	19.0	24.4	27.1	36.9	42.3
NIDDK	88.2	126.0	133.2	237.9	196.4	197.7
NINDS	89.7	33.7	49.2	57.2	77.9	73.8
NIAID	460.8	579.5	663.3	734.7	282.9	338.1
NIGMS	89.6	149.8	150.9	162.0	174.6	202.4
NICHD	173.1	242.9	280.7	307.0	180.1	184.5
NEI	24.1	36.3	39.8	40.7	16.6	18.4
NIEHS	22.4	30.4	32.5	33.7	29.1	31.2
NIA	58.4	73.3	84.6	91.5	142.3	158.8
NIAMS	31.6	38.8	48.7	54.3	36.1	32.3
NIDCD	4.2	4.5	5.8	8.5	19.9	22.8
NIMH	124.7	160.0	182.9	202.9	202.9	213.2
NIDA	89.7	26.9	95.8	120.4	119.0	127.3
NIAAA	30.1	33.4	35.9	34.6	39.8	39.3
NINR	26.2	28.9	29.4	32.2	34.8	36.9
NHGRI	6.1	10.2	10.9	13.7	12.2	19.1
NIBIB	—	—	0.3	1.7	12.3	11.5
NCRR	51.6	64.9	89.1	100.5	74.5	66.6
NCCAM	—	12.5	7.8	11.5	11.5	12.8
NCMHD	—	125.1	154.2	181.7	181.7	186.4
FIC	1.0	1.1	1.0	2.3	0.6	1.4
NLM	2.8	3.0	6.6	6.1	3.6	5.6
OD	4.7	2.8	6.4	9.2	10.9	6.2
NIH	1,766.8	2,371.5	2,771.6	3,164.4	2,429.9	2,588.6

NOTE: Fiscal Year 2000 funding information was not collected. Acronyms: see Appendix I.
— Not applicable.

[a]Includes minority health expenditures reported in Table 4-2.
[b]Calculation is based on the prior methodology for defining minority health.
[c]Calculation is based on the new definition of minority health.

SOURCE: NIH, 2005.

and NICHD, with a $127 million change. All these changes were ascribed to heavy clinical trial activity supported by those ICs and the impact of the new methodology on accounting for clinical trials.

The revised methodology had varying effects on the ICs' reported allocations. The proportions of budgets allocated to health disparities research were adjusted downward for NCI, the National Eye Institute, NIAID, the National Institute of Diabetes and Digestive and Kidney Diseases, and NICHD. The largest change was for NICHD, which demonstrated a 40 percent drop in the previously reported allocation to health disparities research and almost a 50 percent

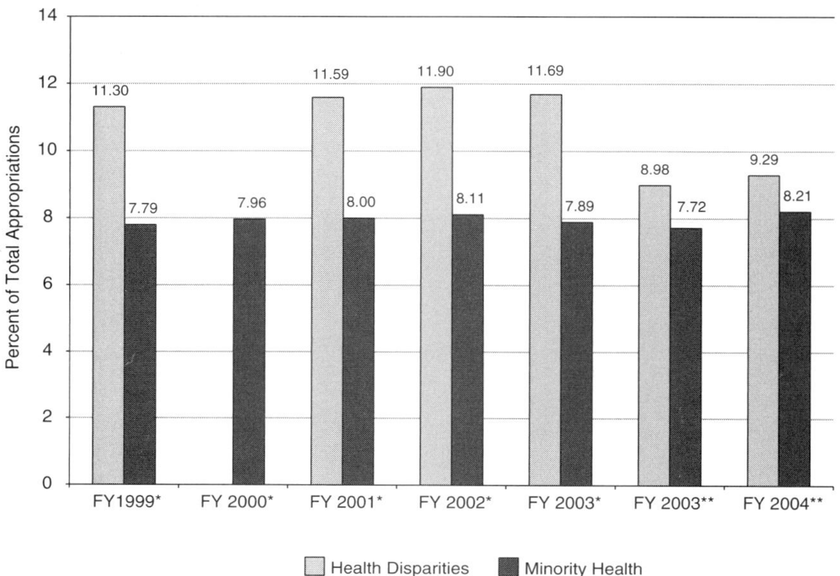

FIGURE 4-1 Percentage of total NIH budget funding minority health and health disparities research activities between 1999 and 2004. SOURCE: NIH Office of Budget, 2005.

NOTE: Health disparities includes minority health expenditures plus low SES and rural health research expenditures.

* Estimates derived from old accounting methodology.

** Estimates derived from new accounting methodology.

drop for minority health research. Increases were seen for the National Institute on Aging, the National Institute on Deafness and Other Communication Disorders, and the National Institute of Dental and Craniofacial Research. Even after the application of the new methods, NICHD channeled comparatively large allocations to health disparities research (15 percent). Likewise, NINR allocated 25 percent of its budget to such research.

The NIH budget approximately doubled from $13.6 billion in 1998 to $27.1 billion in 2003 (Table 4-5).[2] Funding for projects related to minority health increased during that period from $0.8 billion to $2.1 billion (Table 4-2). Even when measured against the adjusted 2003 minority health budget figures, spending on minority health research kept pace with the doubling of the NIH budget that occurred between 1998 and 2003.

---

[2]Budgets are compared in current dollars.

TABLE 4-4 Percentage of Total Appropriation Used for Health Disparities Research Activities by the NIH Institutes and Centers (ICs), Fiscal Years 1999, 2001–2004[a]

Participating ICs	1999[b] %	2001[b] %	2002[b] %	2003[b] %	2003[c] %	2004[c] %
NCI	6.73	9.33	9.15	9.01	5.59	5.59
NHLBI	9.88	9.49	9.91	9.99	9.91	10.26
NIDCR	5.85	6.20	7.13	7.29	9.92	11.04
NIDDK	8.64	9.00	8.53	13.81	11.40	10.85
NINDS	9.94	2.86	3.71	3.93	5.35	4.92
NIAID	29.37	28.38	28.32	20.37	7.84	8.14
NIGMS	7.49	9.76	8.75	8.77	9.45	10.63
NICHD	23.07	24.89	25.25	25.46	14.93	14.85
NEI	6.09	7.11	6.86	6.42	2.62	2.82
NIEHS	5.96	5.38	5.04	4.83	4.16	4.40
NIA	9.79	9.33	9.48	9.21	14.32	15.49
NIAMS	10.27	9.80	10.87	11.17	7.42	6.45
NIDCD	1.81	1.49	1.71	2.29	5.38	5.97
NIMH	14.49	14.47	14.67	15.13	15.13	15.43
NIDA	14.88	3.44	10.81	12.51	12.37	12.85
NIAAA	11.59	9.81	9.36	8.33	9.57	9.17
NINR	37.57	27.70	24.39	24.68	26.65	27.37
NHGRI	2.31	2.67	2.55	2.94	2.62	3.99
NIBIB	—	—	0.28	0.61	4.44	4.01
NCRR	9.31	7.94	8.81	8.82	6.54	5.65
NCCAM	—	14.04	7.49	10.12	10.12	10.96
NCMHD	—	96.17	97.85	97.81	97.81	97.36
FIC	2.82	2.21	1.78	3.58	0.94	2.08
NLM	1.55	1.22	2.41	2.04	1.19	1.77
OD	1.54	1.32	2.70	3.47	4.10	1.88
NIH	11.30	11.59	11.90	11.69	8.98	9.29

NOTE: Fiscal Year 2000 funding information was not collected. Acronyms: see Appendix I.
— Not applicable.

[a]Includes minority health expenditures reported in Table 4-1.
[b]Calculation is based on the prior definition of health disparities research.
[c]Calculation is based on the new definition of health disparities research.

SOURCE: NIH, 2005.

During the period of budget doubling, most ICs witnessed a budget increase of at least 75 percent (Table 4-5). The available information suggests that for most ICs, the portion of their budgets attributed to minority health and health disparities research increased proportionally to, or at a greater rate, than their budget change—though for some, reported increments were far less.

Currently, the proportion of expenditures on health disparities varies by IC, with the mean being about 9 percent (Table 4-4). Over the short period that the Strategic Plan has been in effect, there is no indication that this proportion has increased.

TABLE 4-5 Annual Appropriations of the NIH Institutes and Centers (ICs), Fiscal Years 1998–2004 (Dollars in Millions)

Participating ICs	1998	1999	2000	2001	2002	2003	2004
NCI	$2,547	$2,925	$3,315	$3,754	$4,181	$4,592	$4,739
NHLBI	1,531	1,793	2,029	2,299	2,573	2,794	2,879
NIDCR	209	234	269	306	343	372	383
NIDDK	901	1,021	1,168	1,400	1,562	1,723	1,822
NINDS	781	903	1,029	1,176	1,327	1,456	1,501
NIAID	1,352	1,569	1,778	2,042	2,342	3,607	4,155
NIGMS	1,066	1,197	1,354	1,535	1,725	1,847	1,905
NICHD	675	750	858	976	1,112	1,206	1,242
NEI	356	396	450	510	581	633	653
NIEHS	330	375	442	565	645	698	711
NIA	519	596	686	786	892	994	1,025
NIAMS	275	308	350	396	448	486	501
NIDCD	201	230	264	300	342	370	382
NIMH	750	861	973	1,106	1,247	1,341	1,382
NIDA	527	603	686	781	887	962	991
NIAAA	227	260	292	340	384	416	429
NINR	64	70	90	104	120	131	135
NHGRI	218	265	336	382	429	465	479
NIBIB	—	—	—	—	112	278	287
NCRR	454	554	677	817	1,011	1,139	1,179
NCCAM	—	—	68	89	104	113	117
NCMHD	—	—	—	130	158	186	191
FIC	28	35	43	50	57	63	65
NLM	161	181	214	246	276	300	317
OD	296	306	282	212	235	266	328
NIH	13,648	15,629	17,821	20,458	23,296	27,067	27,888

NOTE: Acronyms: see Appendix I.
— Not applicable.

SOURCE: NIH, 2005.

The amount of funds that NIH should allocate to minority health and health disparities research remains an open question. It could be said that with the proper assessment of needs, careful planning, and appropriate priority setting, the budget will reflect the importance of addressing health disparities and the commitment expressed by Congress and NIH to face this challenge. However, little evidence to date suggests that such analyses, projections, and decisions have been coordinated across the NIH-wide program.

The proportions reported likely represent budget priorities made within ICs, which were not available for review for the overall health disparities research program and the Strategic Plan. NIH ICs have budget commitments and priorities dependent on budget presentations to, and funding authorizations by, Congress. The NIH's overall agency priority for health disparities research, third among the agency's top five priorities (Morton, 2005; Zerhouni, 2004), should be a factor in the ICs' priority processes. The ICs' processes for establishing such priorities should be of concern to those responsible for the overall health disparities research and Strategic Plan program, as well as to other reviewers. Furthermore, information from such considerations could be the bases of arguments for additional categorical funds to NIH or to the respective ICs.

Other concerns arise from the use of budget and financing information for proper planning, monitoring, and decisions about the Strategic Plan. For example, the general public, Congress, other government agencies, and organizations with a special interest in the Strategic Plan should know what resources are being expended in specific categories related to the health disparities research efforts and the Strategic Plan. It would be helpful to have the budget information categorized by funding for each goal area—along with the funds allocated for each objective under each goal—for future monitoring of the program and the Strategic Plan as a whole and individually for each IC and Office involved. In addition, trans-NIH funding information could be available for specific entities and problems (e.g., minority health/health disparities-related programs in obesity, diabetes, AIDS, infant health) as well as for the support allocated to research faculty development, educational institutions, minority-serving institutions, community-based research, and specific outreach endeavors, such as communication with providers and communities.

Findings:

- **Incremental funding was not provided to NIH for the minority health and health disparities research program.**
- **As of July 2005, during the 5th year of the program period, no complete, standardized, approved budget information was available from the Strategic Plan or the Annual Reports. The absence of such information calls into question the validity and efficacy of the Strategic Plan and Annual Reports as tools for planning and coordination.**
- **For more accurate evaluation, detailed information on specific categories and aspects of the minority health and health disparities research program and the Strategic Plan would be helpful.**

Recommendation 8: Within NIH, a clear and timely budget process should be linked to the Strategic Plan, and it should be updated in a timely manner. Annual budgets should include information for NIH as a whole, and for each involved IC and office, and should detail allocations for the Strategic Plan goal areas and each objective. Trans-NIH budget information on efforts made in the major categories of research, research capacity, and communication also should be made available.

5

The National Center on Minority Health and Health Disparities

The origins of the National Center on Minority Health and Health Disparities (NCMHD) can be traced back to the 1990 creation of the Office of Research on Minority Health (ORMH) within the Office of the Director of the National Institutes of Health (NIH). This office emerged from the strong interest among Congress and the community in seeing NIH focus on research on minority health and health disparities. The office was expected to stimulate and coordinate research programs by NIH ICs. During the existence of ORMH, resources were allocated from the appropriation of NIH's Office of the Director. In November 2000, P.L. 106-525 established NCMHD. Dr. John Ruffin was named acting director, a position he held until 2001, at which time he was sworn in as the first director of NCMHD.

NCMHD plays two key roles within the NIH minority health and health disparities program and Strategic Plan. First, as a newly created center, NCMHD oversees extensive funding programs directed at research infrastructure and capacity, including institutional endowment awards, the Centers of Excellence Program, and the Loan Repayment Programs. Second, in an unusual role for an NIH center, NCMHD has the responsibility for coordinating minority health and health disparities research and the Strategic Plan across NIH.

THE NCMHD AS A CENTER

NCMHD administers three programs mandated by the legislation: the Centers of Excellence (Project EXPORT) Program, the Research Endowment Program, and the Loan Repayment Program.

Centers of Excellence (Project EXPORT)

NCMHD's Centers of Excellence Program supports the training of researchers from minority and health disparity populations and the construction of facilities for conducting health disparities research at minority and majority academic institutions and organizations. Priority research focus areas include cancer, cardiovascular disease, stroke, diabetes, and the health of mothers and their infants. Eligibility to compete for the awards is determined by the size of an institution or consortium's student population from minority health disparities groups and evidence of its commitment to recruit, retain, and graduate minority students from its educational programs (NCMHD, 2005a).

In Fiscal Year (FY) 2005, 74 Centers of Excellence were being supported in 29 states and the District of Columbia, Puerto Rico, and the U.S. Virgin Islands (see Appendix J).

Research Endowment Program

This program is designed to compensate for past educational and financial policies that had a disparate impact on the ability of schools serving racial and ethnic minority and low-income students by providing support for program development, making capital improvements, and access to emerging technology (NCMHD, 2005c). The endowments are awarded according to a formula based on the size of the school's corporate endowment and its status as a currently funded Section 736 institution. (Section 736 of the Public Health Service Act refers to health professions institutions and graduate programs with enrollments of underrepresented minorities that exceed the national average for such institutions.) The endowments can be broadly used to support infrastructure for both research and training.

The distinction between the goals of the Research Endowment Program and those of the Centers of Excellence Program is not readily apparent. However, in its FY 2006 budget justification, NCMHD states that it "will continue to explore opportunities where this program can be linked to the Centers of Excellence" (Ruffin, 2005). In FY 2005, 11 institutions received Research Endowment funding (see Appendix K).

Loan Repayment Programs

This important program seeks to alleviate the financial barriers that may discourage health professionals from minority and underserved communities from pursing a research career. NCMHD has established two distinct programs: the Health Disparities Research Loan Repayment Program and the Extramural Clinical Research Loan Repayment Program for Individuals from Disadvantaged Backgrounds. Both programs repay up to $35,000 per year for education loan debts in exchange for a commitment to conduct at least 2 years of basic, clinical, or behavioral research (NCMHD, 2005b).

The goal of the Health Disparities Research Loan Repayment Program is to attract interest in research careers that focus on minority health disparities research or research related to the medically underserved. As a means of building the diversity of the biomedical workforce, and in keeping with P.L. 106-525, 50 percent of the awards are made to individuals from health disparity populations.

The Extramural Clinical Research Loan Repayment Program for Individuals from Disadvantaged Backgrounds is designed to attract health professionals from low-income families into clinical research (including, but not limited to, health disparities research).

In FY 2001, there were just 32 Loan Repayment Awards, but the number increased almost 10-fold to 304 awards in FY 2004 (Figure 5-1). The total number of awards going to both underrepresented minorities and to nonminorities conducting health disparities research increased from 2001 to 2004.

Since 2001, NCMHD has distributed 625 Loan Repayment Awards, or approximately 75 percent of the total awarded. The distribution among other Institutes and Centers (ICs) is seen in Figure 5-2.

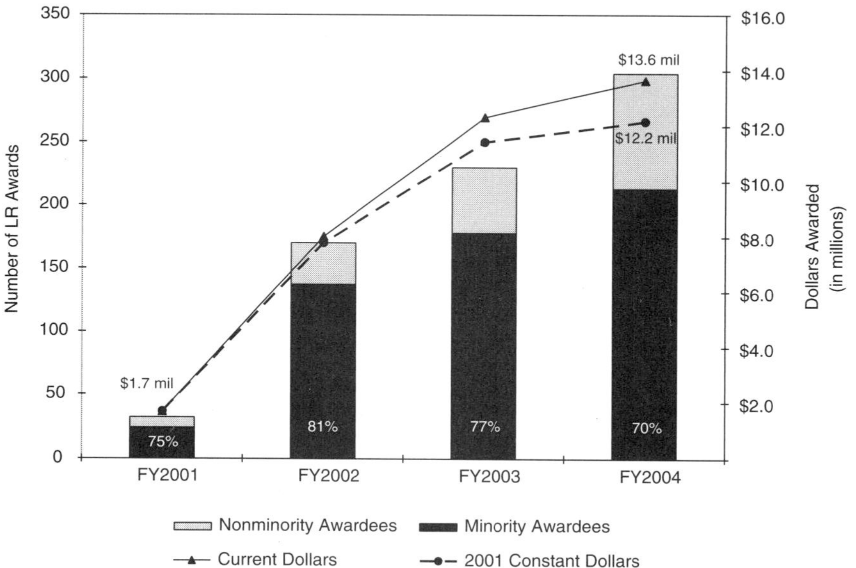

FIGURE 5-1 Total NIH Loan Repayment Awards distributed for Fiscal Years 2001–2004 and total award amount for disparities research. SOURCE: Powe and Yeung, 2005.

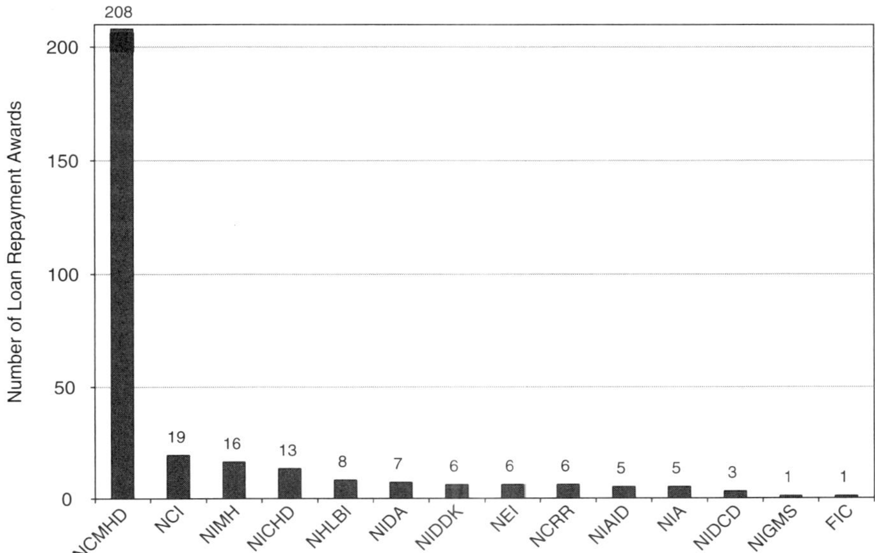

FIGURE 5-2 Loan Repayment Awards for minority health research in Fiscal Year 2004. Acronyms: see Appendix I. SOURCE: Powe and Yeung, 2005.

Research Capacity Building

The goal of this program is to develop a cadre of researchers who will contribute to reducing and eliminating health disparities. Two specific programs are in place to meet this objective: the Research Infrastructure in Minority Institutions (RIMI) Program and the Minority Health and Health Disparities International Research Training (MHIRT) Program.

The NCMHD RIMI Program originally developed as a partnership between the NIH National Center for Research Resources and ORMH. RIMI's primary goal is to strengthen the integration of teaching and research at predominantly minority-serving academic institutions, through support of faculty training, especially as it relates to research in areas that address the elimination of health disparities, student training, educational experiences that will encourage students and faculty to conduct health disparities research, and academic infrastructure.

The MHIRT Program, formerly the Minority International Research Training Program, provides opportunities for approximately 300 U.S. minority undergraduate, graduate, and medical students to gain 10 to 12 weeks of research experience abroad each year. The program is managed by NCMHD, but the NIH's Fogarty International Center provides co-funding and program staff support for the international aspects of the supported programs. Research efforts include cancer epidemiology, reproductive biology, parasitology, malaria, ethnopharmacology, and neurobiology.

Community-Based Research and Outreach

NCMHD recently established an Office of Community-Based Participatory Research and Outreach, which launched a new program that will support collaborative partnerships between academic institutions and community-based organizations. These partnerships will support several activities, including: (a) research studies examining the interface of physical and psychological environments and their health impacts on communities of color and the medically underserved, (b) methodological research looking at effective methods of measuring racism and community-level outcomes, (c) the evaluation of outcomes, and (d) research impact. This program is intended to build on NCMHD's existing community-based research and outreach initiatives through its Project EXPORT program (Ruffin, 2005).

Collaborations with Other ICs

In addition to the core programs described above, NCMHD co-funds a number of collaborations with NIH's other ICs. NCMHD reports that over the last 3 years, it has provided roughly $180 million to support more than 500 collaborative projects, thus representing an average NCMHD contribution of $360,000 per project (Ruffin, 2005).

RESPONSIBILITIES FOR THE MINORITY HEALTH AND HEALTH DISPARITIES RESEARCH PROGRAM AND THE STRATEGIC PLAN

NCMHD has responsibilities for the NIH-wide minority health and health disparities research program and the Strategic Plan. The extent and definition of the responsibilities, and the nature of the authority that manages the responsibilities, are important organizational questions and issues (see Chapter 6). NCMHD currently functions in a de facto manner, with the responsibilities treated as mandates.

Resources and Capacity of the NCMHD

Given its dual missions as a grant-making center and as an apparent coordinator and manager of the trans-NIH minority health and health disparities program and the Strategic Plan, NCMHD considers its financial base and staffing resources to be inadequate. Although NCMHD's budget and staffing have increased since its creation, its leadership and Advisory Council still regard these resources as inadequate for managing the dual responsibilities with which NCMHD has been tasked (Kane, 2004; Ruffin, 2004; Sullivan, 2004).

Science Leadership and Presence Within the NCMHD

A critical need for the coordination and management of the minority health and health disparities research program and the Strategic Plan involves the presence of distinguished science leadership and expertise in minority health and health disparities within, and available to, NCMHD for the trans-NIH research program and the Strategic Plan. Such leadership and presence is important for advice about and assistance with the planning, coordination, monitoring, assessment, and meaningful articulation of health disparities research issues with the ICs, as well as with other agencies and the nation's relevant science community. This broad and challenging need can be satisfied by the presence of eminent science leadership within NCMHD, and, importantly, by assembling and having access to expertise from across NIH and from the scientific, provider, and other relevant communities. This may be accomplished by including these individuals in committees and panels, either standing or ad hoc, to contribute to the science base, presence, and resources of NCMHD, the ICs, and other agencies.

Findings:

- **The dual roles of NCMHD as a granting center and as a coordinator of major trans-NIH efforts are unique. The leadership of NCMHD and its Advisory Council call attention to the need for increased administrative staffing for NCMHD.**
- **There is a need for increased science leadership and presence in NCMHD, particularly for proper management of the trans-NIH initiative.**

Recommendation 9:

- **The NIH director should review and assess the administrative staffing of NCMHD to ensure that it is sufficient to attend to the Center's responsibilities.**
- **Increasing the science leadership and presence within NCMHD should be pursued by the NIH and NCMHD directors. This entails the appointment of additional eminent scientists, recognized in the areas of minority health and health disparities, and the establishment by NCMHD of committees and panels with relevant expertise from within and outside NIH.**

6

Management of the Strategic Plan and the Health Disparities Research Program

To achieve the Strategic Plan's goals and objectives, activities must be coordinated among the Institutes and Centers (ICs) and Offices within the National Institutes of Health (NIH). Effective coordination presents a major challenge, first because of the research's scope and complexity and second because of the NIH organizational and functional setting.

THE CHALLENGE OF STRUCTURING A TRANS-NIH HEALTH DISPARITIES RESEARCH PROGRAM AND STRATEGIC PLAN

Biomedical **research on health disparities** spans almost every research discipline and area, as reflected by the participation of almost all NIH ICs in the Strategic Plan (the National Library of Medicine and the National Center for Research Resources are not involved). Beyond the research itself, another challenge is providing adequate attention to the infrastructure and the capacity for extramural health disparities research, including the enhancement of research facilities and development of scientists involved in health disparities research. Finally, communication of research findings and best practices to providers, the medical education system, patients, and communities represent important research-to-care translation components.

These biomedical research, research capacity, and communication factors should be addressed by the programs of the ICs involved in the Strategic Plan. Indeed, many of these factors were already addressed within the programs of the

ICs. But the Strategic Plan should have generated a coordinated organization with more creativity, collaboration, effectiveness, and productivity across the entire minority health and health disparities program.

NIH's organization and function is a major factor in the success of the Strategic Plan and the minority health and health disparities research program. Increases in the number of ICs and their organizational relationships to NIH as an entity have increased this complexity in recent decades (Committee on the Organizational Structure of the National Institutes of Health, 2003). Emerging fields of biomedical information, technology, and research have been accompanied by a parallel multiplication of medical specialties and academic departments, and increases in the number of NIH ICs. From 1986 through 2000, 8 new Institutes and 4 new Centers were established, many as a result of congressional action. NIH currently includes 19 Institutes, 7 Centers, and the National Library of Medicine.

The NIH Institutes (Figure 6-1) have been described (McGeary and Smith, 2002) as organized in relation to five categories: diseases (cancer, mental health, diabetes, digestive and kidney disease, drug and alcohol abuse); organ systems (heart, lung, and blood; the eye); stage of life (child and human development, aging); scientific field (general medical sciences, environmental health services, the human genome); and profession or technology (nursing, dental, imaging, bioengineering). Some Centers have missions that are supported throughout the NIH, while others conduct and support intramural and extramural research. Within the Office of the Director, four Offices have specific coordinating and support functions: the Office of AIDS Research (OAR), the Office of Research on Women's Health (ORWH), the Office of Behavioral and Social Sciences Research, and the Office of Disease Prevention.

NIH's success and immense contribution to progress in biomedical science and health care can partly be attributed to: (a) its adaptation to the need for specialized centers of research capable of focusing highly specialized expertise and (b) the articulation of the ICs with similar concentrations of science and scientists in medicine and academia. At the same time, some have been concerned about whether the growth of ICs has been entirely necessary and how much this proliferation may contribute to increased difficulty in managing NIH as a cohesive agency. This is particularly germane when NIH addresses an extensive, cross-cutting research endeavor that requires coordination among several ICs, as well as collaborations with other government agencies.

Although the number of ICs has been the subject of continued analysis—and even recommendations that there be some consolidation (Committee on the Organizational Structure of the National Institutes of Health, National Research Council, 2003)—there has been even more concern about the organization of the ICs across NIH and their functional relationships with NIH as an entity. Those relation-

FIGURE 6-1 Current organization of the National Institutes of Health Institutes and Centers. SOURCE: Committee on the Organizational Structure of the National Institutes of Health, 2003.

ships have been described as a loose confederacy of somewhat independent entities with decentralized control. The ICs have considerable independence and autonomy with respect to research programs and a lesser degree of independence regarding budgeting.

Trans-NIH Initiatives

Although much collaborative research is conducted between and among the ICs, broader NIH-wide initiatives have been organized in a number of ways to achieve important centralized, trans-NIH organization and coordination. The Committee reviewed examples and experiences as it assessed the organization of the health disparities research program and the Strategic Plan. Some examples follow.[1]

OAR. NIH AIDS research, involving several institutes, is overseen by the OAR, which coordinates scientific, budgetary, legislative, and policy elements of the NIH AIDS research program. OAR was established in 1988 as an office within the Office of the NIH Director. Its role and responsibilities were set forth in P.L. 103-43, the National Institutes of Health Revitalization Act of 1993.

OAR reviews and approves all NIH-conducted and NIH-supported AIDS research, as well as the related budgets. It also produces a comprehensive trans-NIH annual strategic plan (the Plan for HIV-Related Research) and evaluates all AIDS activities of NIH ICs. The Plan for HIV-Related Research is developed with a consensus on scientific priorities set with the assistance of several planning groups, including IC directors and staff, researchers from academia and industry, foundations, community representatives, representatives from other government agencies, and the OAR Advisory Council. Each involved IC comments on the final plan. The ICs' budgets for AIDS-related research are submitted to OAR and reviewed in relation to the overall Plan for HIV-Related Research, OAR priorities, and the plans of other ICs. The NIH director and the OAR determine the overall NIH budgetary allocation for AIDS research, and the OAR then allocates research budgets to each IC.

As an office within the Office of the Director, OAR does not have grant-making authority but does exercise control and coordination over all NIH AIDS research. OAR is responsible for representing, implementing, coordinating, and monitoring NIH AIDS research. Keys to OAR's ability to coordinate and manage the trans-NIH AIDS program effectively include clear authority over the budgets for AIDS research, presence in the Office of the NIH director, and extensive use of trans-NIH coordinating committees and advisory groups as resources of scientific expertise.

ORWH. The ORWH was established in 1990. Its responsibilities were described in the NIH Revitalization Act of 1993. While serving to advise the NIH director on women's health issues, ORWH has a great deal of influence over NIH research in this area. ORWH does not have budgetary authority over such research, but it does provide funding to ICs for projects on women's health while working across NIH to ensure the development of opportunities for women in biomedical careers and women's health research. ORWH is also responsible for ensuring the inclusion of women and minorities as subjects in biomedical re-

---

[1] See the following websites for information on trans-NIH research programs at the NIH: http://www.obesityresearch.nih.gov/about/about.htm, http://nihroadmap.nih.gov/index.asp, http://www4.od.nih.gov/orwh/, http://www.nih.gov/od/oar/index.htm, http://www.niddk.nih.gov/fund/diabetes specialfunds/funding.htm, and http://neuroscienceblueprint.nih.gov/.

search including Phase III clinical trials—a role that it manages with great attention to detail and completeness. ORWH issues comprehensive reports that track the participation of individuals as subjects in clinical research (U.S. DHHS, 2005). This central function of ORWH has been a factor in its trans-NIH influence. Reportedly, from its beginning ORWH leadership has been seen as scientifically credible and well integrated into the fabric of NIH activities. Success in ORWH's trans-NIH roles is attributed to its establishment by legislation, strong support from the Office of the Director of the NIH, responsibility for a trans-NIH reporting function, and the scientific credibility of, and respect for, its leadership.

NIH Obesity Research Task Force. The NIH director established the NIH Obesity Research Task Force in April 2003 "to accelerate progress in obesity research across NIH." It is co-chaired by the Director of the National Institute of Diabetes and Digestive and Kidney Diseases (NIDDK) and the Director of the National Heart, Lung, and Blood Institute (NHLBI). The Task Force, which includes representatives from the NIDDK, the NHLBI, and other NIH ICs, was charged with the development of the Strategic Plan for NIH Obesity Research, published in August 2004, with the purpose of providing "a guide for coordinating obesity research activities across NIH and for enhancing the development of new research efforts based on identification of areas of greatest scientific opportunity and challenge." The planning process involved contributions from external experts at scientific and other meetings, interactions with scientific and advocacy organizations, and review of the draft document by selected individuals.

The Strategic Plan for NIH Obesity Research includes theme areas that are analogous to the goal areas of the health disparities Strategic Plan. Implementation of these theme areas will involve interdisciplinary research teams, a focus on children and racial and ethnic minorities, special attention to translational research, and the dissemination of research results to the public. Beyond development of the Strategic Plan for NIH Obesity Research, the Task Force's responsibilities and its involvement in coordination are unclear. The success of this trans-NIH planning effort reflects its establishment and support by the NIH director, the leadership of the Task Force, the effective involvement of the ICs, and the extensive involvement of experts from NIH and from the extramural scientific community.

NIH Neuroscience Blueprint. The NIH Neuroscience Blueprint, announced in October 2004, is a new interagency partnership intended to reinforce ongoing NIH efforts to increase collaborative research and information sharing among 14 ICs that conduct or support research on the brain and nervous system. The ICs will carry out independent research but collaborate and share resources on research challenges and training that can be addressed collectively. The Neuroscience Blueprint builds on an existing cooperative relationship established through initiatives and working groups on specific disorders. It will target neuroscience challenges that will benefit from a collaborative approach beginning with three unifying themes: development of the nervous system throughout the life span, neurodegeneration from disease and aging, and nervous system plasticity (changes in response to the environment, experience, injury, and disease). How the Neuroscience Blueprint will be managed and coordinated is not specified.

Two additional trans-NIH initiatives instituted by the director of NIH are aimed at facilitating cohesive, integrated NIH core efforts: the NIH Roadmap and the Office of Portfolio Analysis and Strategic Initiatives (OPASI).

NIH Roadmap. The NIH Roadmap is an initiative spearheaded by the director of NIH with the purpose of identifying major opportunities and gaps in biomedical research, in order to enhance the progress of medical research. Development of the Roadmap involved broad consultation with representatives of the scientific community and public constituencies and the extensive participation of NIH working groups, the NIH Council of Public Representatives, and the Advisory Committee to the Director.

From 2004 to 2005, the first Roadmap initiatives were begun. They reflect the themes of: (a) New Pathways, which seeks to advance understanding of biological systems; (b) Research Teams of the Future, which explores new organizational models for team sciences; and (c) Re-engineering the Clinical Research Enterprise, which will develop new approaches to discovery and clinical validation of research results. The Roadmap, initiated and guided by the director of the NIH, forms the basis for the overarching planning of NIH's strategies for research for the coming years.

OPASI. In FY 2006, the NIH plans to create a new office within the Office of the Director, OPASI, which is intended to provide tools to facilitate the planning and management of trans-NIH initiatives, including an improved process for collecting IC data on expenditures on various diseases, conditions, and research fields, and improvements in data about the burden of disease. OPASI will also develop, with input from the ICs, common processes and formats, where necessary, for the conduct of NIH-wide planning and evaluation. For its trans-NIH planning efforts, OPASI will seek broad public input—from the public, health care providers, policy makers, and scientists—in addition to soliciting advice from within the NIH. The office will also coordinate and make more effective use of the NIH-wide evaluation process (Kington, 2005). The ultimate structure, responsibilities, and authorities of OPASI with respect to the trans-NIH initiatives are not yet clear, but OPASI could exert far-reaching effects on the management and coordination of the minority health and health disparities program and the Strategic Plan.

The Committee's review of trans-NIH programs and efforts noted that apparent success of trans-NIH coordination and management is related to several factors, including:

- Legislative authority
- Budget authority
- A clear science agenda/focus
- Clear support from the director of the NIH
- Responsibility and accountability within ICs
- Strong, structured articulation of ICs with a central coordinating entity, including trans-NIH committees and other groups led by the coordinating entity

COORDINATION OF THE STRATEGIC PLAN AND MINORITY HEALTH AND HEALTH DISPARITIES RESEARCH

It could be said that there is no trans-NIH research effort more challenging than the health disparities research program and its Strategic Plan. Although most similar, the AIDS research program differs in scope because it is developed around a single disease, complicated and challenging as it is. By contrast, the minority health and health disparities research includes a broader scope of diseases and conditions.

Coordination of the minority health and health disparities program and the Strategic Plan across NIH should address needs for:

- Concerted involvement of ICs and Offices in the development of the Strategic Plan, including continuous review and annual updates, which are a collective result of experiences, assessments, new inclusions, and other changes.
- Ensuring that all ICs and pertinent offices are attentive to the mission, goals, and objectives of the Strategic Plan.
- Avoiding gaps, such as populations, conditions, needs, and approaches, that would otherwise not be identified and addressed by the independent operation of the ICs.
- Bringing the best expertise from across NIH and from the external scientific community as a resource for the program and for strategic planning.
- Avoiding duplication of administrative and research efforts.
- Facilitating collaborative and coordinated approaches to minority and health disparity research areas that affect and involve more that one institute or center.
- Coordinating approaches to those aspects of outreach and communication that, rather than being addressed individually by the ICs, would benefit from collectively planned and coordinated trans-NIH efforts, including evaluations of project results and identification and further trials of promising methods.
- Creating an NIH coordination structure and mechanism that will articulate with other government agencies (e.g., the Centers for Disease Control and

Prevention, the Agency for Healthcare Research and Quality, the Department of Health and Human Services) on minority health and health disparities, particularly with respect to the relation between research on disparities in health status and disparities in access to health care and its quality.

- Monitoring such a broad NIH activity. This includes avoiding duplication of efforts and use of resources, ensuring that funds committed in Strategic Plans are expended as described, and regularly assessing progress and outcomes.
- Addressing research and budget priorities.

Particularly important is recognizing, and attending to, the interface between fundamental priorities. IC programs and budgets are the products of commitments, mandates, and priorities resulting from presentations and requests to, and authorizations from, Congress. If there is truly a concerted trans-NIH priority for minority health and health disparities research, that prioritization should be demonstrably active in the program priority decisions of the ICs.

The Committee saw little evidence of integration, coordination, or monitoring of health disparities research and the Strategic Plan across NIH. Several observations, as detailed below, led to this conclusion.

Review and revision of the Strategic Plan does not involve the coordinated, concerted, and collective participation of the ICs. There is no ongoing, continuous update process with an established trans-NIH structure involving ICs and others that produces planning improvements and results in periodic, meaningful updates and revisions of the Strategic Plan. There is no evidence of trans-NIH planning of priorities regarding minority health and health disparities research activities and resources for the NIH as a whole or with respect to the ICs. In discussions with the Committee, directors and other leading members of several large ICs with extensive minority health and health disparities programs expressed a very high level of commitment to and enthusiasm for these activities. However, it was evident that there had been little to no contact with the National Center for Minority Health and Health Disparities (NCMHD) during the development or implementation of the projects and programs. Activities and programs were pursued independently of NCMHD, except that some, particularly in the past, had been co-funded or totally funded by NCMHD.

There is no manifest organizational structure for the trans-NIH Strategic Plan and health disparities program. Advisory and coordinating committees are not described or apparent. Experts from scientific, health care, and affected communities are not involved in advising and participating in ongoing planning in established, structured, predictable ways. Thus, there is a great loss of opportunity to properly inform and contribute to the identification of research and related needs, planning, and strategizing.

No results summarizing the monitoring and assessment of minority health and health disparities research and related activities for NIH or the ICs are evident. Annual reports are late, languish incomplete and unapproved, and do not contain evidence of central NIH assessments of research and program activities. Moreover, budget and finance issues are not addressed by a centralized entity responsible for the minority health and health disparities research program and the Strategic Plan.

Recognizing this need for leadership and management, the Committee found it difficult to be certain of an established, clear responsibility and authority for coordinating and monitoring the Strategic Plan and health disparities research. The enabling legislation, P.L. 106-525, expects NCMHD to have and to be involved with such responsibilities, as indicated in Section 485E(e):

> The director of the Center shall act as the primary Federal official with responsibility for coordinating all minority health disparities research and other health disparities research conducted or supported by the National Institutes of Health.

Also, Section 485E(f) indicates that "the Director of NIH, the Director of the Center, and the directors of the other agencies of the National Institutes of Health in collaboration (and in consultation with the advisory council for the Center)" together are responsible for establishing the Strategic Plan and budget and reviewing its progress. These responsibilities include ensuring that the Strategic Plan and budget establish priorities, verifying that the amounts appropriated are expended in accord with the Strategic Plan and budget, and reviewing and revising the Strategic Plan and budget annually.

These monitoring responsibilities are described in the legislation as the joint responsibilities of the director of NIH, the director of NCMHD, and the directors of the ICs. To avoid misunderstanding of the authority to manage and monitor the program across NIH, it is important to clarify how such an arrangement of responsibilities is achieved in practice. That is, it must be made clear whether specific authority is delegated to the director of NCMHD by the director of NIH and understood to exist by the directors of the ICs—or, alternatively, whether there are truly joint responsibilities and operational authorities (a situation that would be confusing). When the Committee requested clarification, it was told by the NIH director that the responsibilities and authority were shared between the director of NIH and the director of NCMHD. Moreover, reviews and discussions with leaders and representatives of the ICs and Offices within the Office of the Director suggested that the responsibilities and authorities were not uniformly clear. This situation differs from other trans-NIH initiatives.

The Executive Summaries of the 2002 Strategic Plan and the 2004 draft indicate the following: "Within the NIH, the National Center on Minority Health and Health Disparities (NCMHD) serves as the focal point for planning and coordinating minority health and other health disparities research." Also, in the approved Strategic Plan for 2002–2006 and the draft of the 2004–2008 Strategic Plan, NCMHD's responsibility for establishing and updating the Strategic Plan and budget and coordinating health disparities research is set forth. This is appropriate and in accord with the legislation. However, whether NCMHD's authority is understood and acted upon throughout NIH is unclear.

Finding: The level of trans-NIH coordination needed to effectively implement the Strategic Plan has not been evident. Instead, the Committee concluded that an uncoordinated, unmonitored, loosely administered trans-NIH program existed, with substantial commitments and activities of largely independent ICs, but without the coordinated, concerted program needed. Clarity regarding the responsibilities and authority may be a factor in achieving more effective management. The mandates of the NIH director are key elements in structuring and assuring effective management.

Recommendation 10: The NIH director, through the established authority of the NCMHD director, should ensure continuous, effective coordination of the health disparities research program across NIH, including:

- **Timely development of Strategic Plan revisions;**
- **Effective, ongoing participation of the ICs in the Strategic Plan and the health disparities research program;**
- **Establishment of appropriate committees involving the directors of the ICs and others to facilitate collaboration and coordinated approaches to health disparities research and the setting of priorities;**
- **Fostering of conferences and the use of committees and panels involving the NIH, extramural scientific communities, and others to inform and advise on initiatives and directions; and**
- **Monitoring of the execution of the Strategic Plan to ensure that its elements are implemented.**

References

Ard JD, Carter-Edwards L, Svetkey LP. 2003. A new model for developing and executing culturally appropriate behavior modification clinical trials for African Americans. *Ethnicity and Disease* 13(2):279–285.

Ard JD, Durant RW, Edwards LC, Svetkey LP. 2005. Perceptions of African-American culture and implications for clinical trial design. *Ethnicity and Disease* 15(2):292–299.

Aungst J, Haas A, Ommaya A, Green LW, eds. 2003. *Exploring Challenges, Progress, and New Models for Engaging the Public in the Clinical Research Enterprise: Clinical Research Roundtable Workshop Summary*. Washington, DC: The National Academies Press.

Baum A, Garofalo JP, Yali AM. 1999. Socioeconomic status and chronic stress: Does stress account for SES effects on health? In, Adler N, Marmot M, McEwen BS, Stewart J, eds. *Socioeconomic Status and Health in Industrial Nations*. New York: Annals of the New York Academy of Sciences. Pp. 131–144.

Braveman P, Gruskin S. 2003. Defining equity in health. *Journal of Epidemiology and Community Health* 57:254-258.

Brooks K, Fessler BJ, Bastian H, Alarcón GS. 2001. Sociocultural issues in clinical research. *Arthritis Care and Research* 45(2):203–207.

Brunner E, Marmot M. 1999. Social organization, stress and health. In, Marmot M, Wilkinson RG, eds. *Social Determinants of Health*. Oxford, UK: Oxford University Press. Pp. 17–43.

Building Engineering and Science Talent. 2004. *A Bridge for All: Higher Education Design Principles to Broaden Participation in Science, Technology, Engineering and Mathematics*. San Diego, CA: Building Engineering and Science Talent.

Bulatao RA, Anderson NB, eds. 2004. *Understanding Racial Differences in Health in Late Life: A Research Agenda*. Washington, DC: The National Academies Press.

Carter-Pokras O, Banquet C. 2002. What is a "health disparity"? *Public Health Reports* 117: 426–434.

CDC (Centers for Disease Control and Prevention). 1998. Recruiting black men to a clinical trial to evaluate prostate cancer screening Detroit, Michigan, 1998. *Morbidity and Mortality Weekly Report* 47(33):964–966.

Committee for the Assessment of NIH Minority Research Training Programs, Oversight Committee for the Assessment of NIH Minority Research Training Programs, Board on Higher Education and Workforce, National Research Council. 2005. *Assessment of NIH Minority and Research Training Programs*. Washington, DC: The National Academies Press.

Committee on National Needs for Biomedical and Behavioral Scientists, Education and Career Studies Unit, National Research Council. 2000. *Addressing the Nation's Changing Needs for Biomedical and Behavior Scientists, Phase 3*. Washington, DC: National Academy Press.

Committee on the Future of Rural Health Care, Institute of Medicine. 2005. *Quality Through Collaboration: The Future of Rural Health Care*. Washington, DC: The National Academies Press.

Committee on the Organizational Structure of the National Institutes of Health, National Research Council. 2003. *Enhancing the Vitality of the National Institutes of Health: Organizational Change to Meet New Challenges*. Washington, DC: The National Academies Press.

Congressional Commission on the Advancement of Women and Minorities in Science, Engineering and Technology Development. 2000. *Land of Plenty: Diversity as America's Competitive Edge in Science, Engineering, and Technology* [Online]. Available: http://www.nsf.gov/od/cawmset/ [accessed November 14, 2005].

Corbie-Smith G, Thomas SB, Williams MV, Moody-Ayers S. 1999. Attitudes and beliefs of African Americans toward participation in medical research. *Journal of General Internal Medicine* 14(9):537–546.

Eberhardt MS, Pamuk ER. 2004. The importance of place of residence: Examining health in rural and nonrural areas. *American Journal of Public Health* 94(10):1682–1686.

Farmer MM, Ferraro KF. 2005. Are racial disparities in health conditional on socioeconomic status? *Social Science and Medicine* 60(1):191–204.

Fremont A, Lurie N. 2004. The role of racial and ethnic data collection in eliminating disparities in health care. In, Ver Ploeg M, Perrin E, eds. *Eliminating Health Disparities: Measurement and Data Needs*. Washington, DC: The National Academies Press. Pp. 202–231.

Gebbie K, Rosenstock L, Hernandez LM, eds. 2003. Committee on Educating Public Health Professionals for the 21st Century. *Who Will Keep the Public Healthy? Educating Public Health Professionals for the 21st Century*. Washington, DC: The National Academies Press.

George YS, Neale DS, Van Horne V, Malcom SM. 2001. *In Pursuit of a Diverse Science, Technology, Engineering, and Mathematics Workforce: Recommended Research Priorities to Enhance Participation by Underrepresented Minorities*. Washington, DC: American Association for the Advancement of Science.

Harris Y, Gorelick PB, Samuels P, Bempong I. 1996. Why African Americans may not be participating in clinical trials. *Journal of the National Medical Association* 88(10):630–634.

Harrison RW III. 2001. Impact of biomedical research on African Americans. *Journal of the National Medical Association* 93(3 Supplement):6S–7S.

Hartley D. 2004. Rural health disparities, population health, and rural culture. *American Journal of Public Health* 94(10):1675–1678.

Haynes MA, Smedley BD, eds. 1999. *The Unequal Burden of Cancer: An Assessment of NIH Research and Programs for Ethnic Minorities and the Medically Underserved*. Washington, DC: National Academy Press.

Health Resources Administration. 1979. *Health Status of Minorities and Low Income Groups* [HRA 79-627]. Washington, DC: U.S. Department of Health, Education, and Welfare.

Hertzman C. 1999. Population health and human development. In, Keating DP, Hertzman C, eds. *Developmental Health and the Wealth of Nations: Social, Biological, and Educational Dynamics*. New York: Guildford Press. Pp. 21–40.

Holkup P, Tripp-Reimer T, Salois E, Weinert C. 2004. Community-based participatory research: An approach to intervention research with a Native American community. *Advances in Nursing Science* 27:162–175.

House JS. 2002. Understanding social factors and inequalities in health: 20th century progress and 21st century prospects. *Journal of Health and Social Behavior* 43:125–142.

House JS, Williams D. 2000. Understanding and reducing socioeconomic and racial/ethnic disparities in health. In, Smedley BD, Syme SL, eds. *Promoting Health: Intervention Strategies from Social and Behavioral Research.* Washington, DC: National Academy Press. Pp. 81–124.

Howard BV, Lee ET, Cowan LD, Devereux RB, Galloway JM, Go OT, Howard WJ, Rhoades ER, Robbins DC, Sievers ML, Welty TK. 1999. Rising tide of cardiovascular disease in American Indians. The Strong Heart Study. *Circulation* 99:2389–2395.

Israel BA, Schulz EP, Becker A. 1998. Review of community-based research: Assessing partnership approaches to improve public health. *Annual Review of Public Health* 19:173–202.

Jackson SA. 2003. *Envisioning a 21st Century Science and Engineering Workforce for the United States.* Washington, DC: The National Academies Press.

Kane C. 2004. *Testimony to the Committee on the Review and Assessment of the NIH's Strategic Research Plan and Budget to Reduce and Ultimately Eliminate Health Disparities.* Washington, DC: December 10, 2004.

Kaplan GA. 1999. Part III summary: What is the role of the social environment in understanding inequalities in health? In, Adler NE, Marmot M, McEwen B, Stewart J, eds. *Socioeconomic Status and Health in Industrialized Nations.* New York: Annals of the New York Academy of Sciences. Pp. 116–119.

Kawachi I, Daniels N, Robinson DE. 2005. Health disparities by race and class: Why both matter. *Health Affairs* 24(2):343–352.

Kellogg Community Health Scholars Program. 2005. *Community Health Scholars Program.* [Online]. Available: http://www.sph.umich.edu/chsp/program/index.shtml [accessed September 2, 2005].

Keppel K, Pamuk E, Lynch J, Carter-Pokras O, Kim I, Mays VM, et al. 2005. Methodological issues in measuring health disparities. National Center for Health Statistics. *Vital Health Statistics* 2(141):1–16.

Kington R. 2005. *Fiscal Year 2006 Budget Request: Congressional Justification.* [Online]. Available: http://odeo.od.nih.gov/pubs/FY2006BudgetRequest.pdf [accessed November 15, 2005].

Kington R, Tisnado D, Carlisle DM. 2001. Increasing racial and ethnic diversity among physicians: An intervention to address health disparities? In, Smedley BD, Stith AY, Colburn L, Evans C, eds. *Summary of the Symposium on Diversity in Health Professions and in Honor of Herbert W. Nickens, M.D. The Right Thing to Do, the Smart Thing to Do: Enhancing Diversity in the Health Professions.* Washington, DC: National Academy Press. Pp. 57–90.

Kreiger N. 2005. Defining and investigating social disparities in cancer: Critical issues. *Cancer Causes and Control* 16(1):5–14.

Kuh D, Ben-Shlomo Y. 1997. *A Life Course Approach to Chronic Disease Epidemiology.* Oxford, UK: Oxford University Press.

Kuh D, Power C, Blane D, Bartley M. 1997. Social pathways between childhood and adult health. In, Kuh D, Ben-Shlomo Y, eds. *A Life Course Approach to Chronic Disease Epidemiology.* Oxford, UK: Oxford University Press. Pp. 169–200.

Lantz P, Viruell-Fuentes E, Israel B, Softley D, Guzman R. 2001. Can communities and academia work together on public health research? Evaluation results from a community-based participatory research partnership in Detroit. *Journal of Urban Health: Bulletin of the New York Academy of Medicine* 78:495–507.

Lee ET, Cowan LD, Welty TK, Sievers M, Howard WJ, Oopik A, Wang W, Yeh J, Devereux RB, Rhoades ER, Fabsitz RR, Go O, Howard BV. 1998. All-cause mortality and cardiovascular disease mortality in three American Indian populations, aged 45-74 years, 1984–1988. The Strong Heart Study. *American Journal of Epidemiology* 147:995–1008.

Lenfant C, 2003. Clinical research to clinical practice—lost in translation? *New England Journal of Medicine* 349:868–874.

Lillie-Blanton M, LaVeist T. 1996. Race/ethnicity, the social environment, and health. *Social Science and Medicine* 43(1):83–91.

McEwen BS. 1998. Stress, adaptation, and disease: Allostasis and allostatic load. *Annals of the New York Academy of Sciences* 840:33–44.

McEwen BS, Stellar E. 1993. Stress and the individual: Mechanisms leading to disease. *Archives of Internal Medicine* 153:2093–2101.

McGeary M, Smith PM. 2002. *Organizational Structure of the National Institutes of Health. Background Paper for the National Academies Committee on the Organizational Structure of the NIH*. Washington, DC: National Academy Press.

Morton CC. 2005, April 29. Health disparities a top NIH priority, says Director Zerhouni. *Harvard Public Health NOW* [Online]. Available: http://www.hsph.harvard.edu/now/apr29/disparities.html [accessed November 14, 2005].

National Science and Technology Council. 2000. *Ensuring a Strong U.S. Scientific, Technical, and Engineering Workforce in the 21st Century* [Online]. Available: http://www.ostp.gov/html/workforcerpt.pdf [accessed November 28, 2005].

National Science Board. 2003. *The Science and Engineering Workforce; Realizing America's Potential*. Washington, DC: National Science Foundation.

NCHS (National Center for Health Statistics). 2004. *Health, United States, 2004 Edition with Chartbook on Trends in the Health of Americans*. Hyattsville, MD: Government Printing Office.

NCHS. 2006. Special Tabulation for the Committee on the Review and Assessment of the NIH's Strategic Research Plan and Budget to Reduce and Ultimately Eliminate Health Disparities.

NCMHD (National Center on Minority Health and Health Disparities). 2004. *NIH Strategic Research Plan and Budget to Reduce and Ultimately Eliminate Health Disparities, Fiscal Years 2002–2006; Public Comments 2004*. Bethesda, MD: NCMHD.

NCMHD. 2005a. *About NCMHD Centers of Excellence*. [Online]. Available: http://www.ncmhd.nih.gov/our_programs/excellence/index.asp [accessed August 13, 2005].

NCMHD. 2005b. *Loan Repayment Program*. [Online]. Available: http://www.ncmhd.nih.gov/our_programs/loan/index.asp [accessed August 13, 2005].

NCMHD. 2005c. *NCMHD Research Endowment Program*. [Online]. Available: http://www.ncmhd.nih.gov/our_programs/endowment/index.asp [accessed August 13, 2005].

NIH (National Institutes of Health). 2000. *National Institutes of Health Strategic Research Plan to Reduce and Ultimately Eliminate Health Disparities, Fiscal Years 2002–2006*. DRAFT: October 6, 2000. [Online]. Available: http://www.nih.gov/about/hd/strategicplan.pdf [accessed September 2, 2005].

NIH. 2003. *National Institutes of Health Strategic Plan to Reduce and Ultimately Eliminate Health Disparities 2002–2006*. [Online]. Available: http://ncmhd.nih.gov/our_programs/strategic/volumes.asp [accessed November 28, 2005].

NIH. 2005. Data provided to the Committee on the Review and Assessment of the NIH's Strategic Research Plan and Budget to Reduce and Ultimately Eliminate Health Disparities by the NIH Office of Budget, Office of the Director.

NIH Office of Budget. 2005. *National Institutes of Health Appropriations History by Institute and Center*. [Online]. Available: http://officeofbudget.od.nih.gov/UI/AppropriationsHistoryByIC.htm [accessed November 28, 2005].

Noah BA. 2003. The participation of underrepresented minorities in clinical research. *American Journal of Law, Medicine, and Ethics* 29:221–245.

O'Fallon L, Dearry A. 2002. Community-based participatory research as a tool to advance environmental health sciences. *Environmental Health Perspectives* 110:155–159.

ORWH (Office of Research on Women's Health). 2005. *Monitoring Adherence to the NIH Policy on the Inclusion of Women and Minorities as Subjects in Clinical Research. Comprehensive Report: Tracking of Human Subjects Research as Reported in Fiscal Year 2003 and Fiscal Year 2004*. Bethesda, MD: NIH.

Partridge EE, Fouad MN, Hinton AW, Hardy CM, Liscovicz N, White-Johnson F, et al. 2005. The Deep South Network for Cancer Control: Eliminating cancer disparities through community-academic collaboration. *Family and Community Health. Decreasing Health Disparities* 28(1): 6–19.

Powe NR, Yeung EH. 2005. *Results of a Questionnaire to Assess Progress on NIH Research and Programs on Minority Health and Health Disparities.* Unpublished background paper for the National Academies IOM Committee on the Review and Assessment of the NIH's Strategic Research Plan and Budget to Reduce and Ultimately Eliminate Health Disparities.

Probst JC, Moore CG, Glover SH, Samuels ME. 2004. Person and place: The compounding effects of race/ethnicity and rurality on health. *American Journal of Public Health* 94:1695–1703.

Rhoades DA. 2005. Racial misclassification and disparities in cardiovascular disease among American Indians and Alaska Natives. *Circulation* 111:1250–1256.

Rosenberg HM, Maurer JD, Sorlie PD, Johnson NJ, MacDorman MF, Hoyert DL, Spitler JF, Scott C. 1999. Quality of death rates by race and Hispanic-origin, a summary of current research. *Vital Health Statistics* 2:1–13.

Ruffin J. 2004. *Testimony to the Committee on the Review and Assessment of the NIH's Strategic Research Plan and Budget to Reduce and Ultimately Eliminate Health Disparities.* Washington, DC: October 6, 2004.

Ruffin J. 2005. *Fiscal Year 2006 Budget Request: Congressional Justification.* Washington, DC: Department of Health and Human Services, National Institutes of Health. [Online]. Available: http://ncmhd.nih.gov/about_ncmhd/JRuffinTestimonyAppropsMarch2005.pdf [accessed November 28, 2005].

Seeman TS. 2004. *Racial/Ethnic and Socioeconomic Disparities in Health: How Socioeconomic Status Gets "Under the Skin."* Washington, DC: National Press Club.

Sehgal AR. 2003. Impact of quality improvement efforts on race and sex disparities in hemodialysis. *Journal of the American Medical Association* 289(8):996–1000.

Shavers-Hornaday VL, Lynch CF, Burmeister LF, Torner JC. 1997. Why are African Americans under-represented in medical research studies? Impediments to participation. *Ethnicity and Health* 2(1/2):31–45.

Singer B, Ryff C, eds. 2001. *New Horizons in Health: An Integrative Approach.* Washington, DC: National Academy Press.

Smedley BD, Stith AY, Nelson AR, eds. 2003. *Unequal Treatment: Confronting Racial and Ethnic Disparities in Healthcare.* Washington, DC: The National Academies Press.

Smedley BD, Stith Butler A, Bristow LR, eds. 2004. *In the Nation's Compelling Interest: Ensuring Diversity in the Health-Care Workforce.* Washington, DC: The National Academies Press.

Spruill I. 2004. Project Sugar: A recruitment model for successful African-American participation in health research. *Journal of the National Black Nurses Association* 15(2):48–53.

Sullivan L. 2004. *Testimony to the Committee on the Review and Assessment of the NIH's Strategic Research Plan and Budget to Reduce and Ultimately Eliminate Health Disparities.* Washington, DC: December 10, 2004.

U.S. DHHS (U.S. Department of Health and Human Services). 1985. *Report of the Secretary's Task Force on Black and Minority Health.* Washington, DC: U.S. Government Printing Office.

U.S. DHHS. 1991. *Healthy People 2000: National Health Promotion and Disease Prevention Objectives.* Washington, DC: Public Health Service.

U.S. DHHS. 2000. *Healthy People 2010. 2nd ed. With Understanding and Improving Health and Objectives for Improving Health.* Washington, DC: U.S. Government Printing Office.

U.S. DHHS. 2005. *NIH Tracking/Inclusion Committee: Comprehensive Report: Tracking of Human Subjects Research as Reported in Fiscal Year 2003 and Fiscal Year 2004. Monitoring Adherence to the NIH Policy on the Inclusion of Women and Minorities as Subjects in Clinical Research.* Bethesda, MD: National Institutes of Health.

U.S. Public Health Administration. 1979. *Healthy People: The Surgeon General's Report on Health Promotion and Disease Prevention* [PHS 79-55071]. Washington, DC: U.S. Department of Health, Education, and Welfare.

Ver Ploeg M, Perrin E, eds. 2004. *Eliminating Health Disparities: Measurement and Data Needs. Panel on DHHS Collection of Race and Ethnic Data* Washington, DC: The National Academies Press.

Weitz TA, Freund KM, Wright L. 2001. Identifying and caring for underserved populations: Experience of the National Centers of Excellence in Women's Health. *Journal of Women's Health and Gender-Based Medicine* 10(10):937–952.

Whitehead M. 1992. The concepts and principles of equity and health. *International Journal of Health Services* 22(3):429–445.

Williams DR. 1999. Race, socioeconomic status, and health; the added effects of racism and discrimination. *Annals of the New York Academy of Sciences* 896:173–188.

Williams DR, Jackson PB. 2005. Social sources of racial disparities in health. *Health Affairs* 24(2): 325–334.

Zerhouni E. 2004. *Testimony to the Committee on the Review and Assessment of the NIH's Strategic Research Plan and Budget to Reduce and Ultimately Eliminate Health Disparities*. Washington, DC: December 9, 2004.

Zerhouni E. 2005a. U.S. biomedical research; basic, translational, and clinical studies. *Journal of the American Medical Association* 294(11):1352–1358.

Zerhouni E. 2005b. Translational and clinical science—time for a new vision. *New England Journal of Medicine* 353(15):1621–1623.

A

Public Law 106–525
106th Congress

An Act

To amend the Public Health Service Act to improve the health of minority individuals.

Nov. 22, 2000
[S. 1880]

Be it enacted by the Senate and House of Representatives of the United States of America in Congress assembled,

SECTION 1. SHORT TITLE; TABLE OF CONTENTS.

Minority Health and Health Disparities Research and Education Act of 2000. 42 USC 202 note.

(a) SHORT TITLE.—This Act may be cited as the "Minority Health and Health Disparities Research and Education Act of 2000".

(b) TABLE OF CONTENTS.—The table of contents of this Act is as follows:

SEC. 2. FINDINGS.

42 USC 287c–31 note.

The Congress finds as follows:

(1) Despite notable progress in the overall health of the Nation, there are continuing disparities in the burden of illness and death experienced by African Americans, Hispanics, Native Americans, Alaska Natives, and Asian Pacific Islanders, compared to the United States population as a whole.

(2) The largest numbers of the medically underserved are white individuals, and many of them have the same health care access problems as do members of minority groups. Nearly 20,000,000 white individuals live below the poverty line with many living in nonmetropolitan, rural areas such as Appalachia, where the high percentage of counties designated as health professional shortage areas (47 percent) and the high rate of poverty contribute to disparity outcomes. However, there is a higher proportion of racial and ethnic minorities in the United States represented among the medically underserved.

(3) There is a national need for minority scientists in the fields of biomedical, clinical, behavioral, and health services research. Ninety percent of minority physicians educated at Historically Black Medical Colleges live and serve in minority communities.

(4) Demographic trends inspire concern about the Nation's ability to meet its future scientific, technological, and engineering workforce needs. Historically, non-Hispanic white males have made up the majority of the United States scientific, technological, and engineering workers.

(5) The Hispanic and Black population will increase significantly in the next 50 years. The scientific, technological, and engineering workforce may decrease if participation by underrepresented minorities remains the same.

(6) Increasing rates of Black and Hispanic workers can help ensure a strong scientific, technological, and engineering workforce.

(7) Individuals such as underrepresented minorities and women in the scientific, technological, and engineering workforce enable society to address its diverse needs.

(8) If there had not been a substantial increase in the number of science and engineering degrees awarded to women and underrepresented minorities over the past few decades, the United States would be facing even greater shortages in scientific, technological, and engineering workers.

(9) In order to effectively promote a diverse and strong 21st century scientific, technological, and engineering workforce, Federal agencies should expand or add programs that effectively overcome barriers such as educational transition from one level to the next and student requirements for financial resources.

(10) Federal agencies should work in concert with the private nonprofit sector to emphasize the recruitment and retention of qualified individuals from ethnic and gender groups that are currently underrepresented in the scientific, technological, and engineering workforce.

(11) Behavioral and social sciences research has increased awareness and understanding of factors associated with health care utilization and access, patient attitudes toward health services, and risk and protective behaviors that affect health and illness. These factors have the potential to then be modified

to help close the health disparities gap among ethnic minority populations. In addition, there is a shortage of minority behavioral science researchers and behavioral health care professionals. According to the National Science Foundation, only 15.5 percent of behavioral research-oriented psychology doctorate degrees were awarded to minority students in 1997. In addition, only 17.9 percent of practice-oriented psychology doctorate degrees were awarded to ethnic minorities.

TITLE I—IMPROVING MINORITY HEALTH AND REDUCING HEALTH DISPARITIES THROUGH NATIONAL INSTITUTES OF HEALTH; ESTABLISHMENT OF NATIONAL CENTER

SEC. 101. ESTABLISHMENT OF NATIONAL CENTER ON MINORITY HEALTH AND HEALTH DISPARITIES.

(a) IN GENERAL.—Part E of title IV of the Public Health Service Act (42 U.S.C. 287 et seq.) is amended by adding at the end the following subpart:

"Subpart 6—National Center on Minority Health and Health Disparities

"SEC. 485E. PURPOSE OF CENTER. 42 USC 287c–31.

"(a) IN GENERAL.—The general purpose of the National Center on Minority Health and Health Disparities (in this subpart referred to as the 'Center') is the conduct and support of research, training, dissemination of information, and other programs with respect to minority health conditions and other populations with health disparities.

"(b) PRIORITIES.—The Director of the Center shall in expending amounts appropriated under this subpart give priority to conducting and supporting minority health disparities research.

"(c) MINORITY HEALTH DISPARITIES RESEARCH.—For purposes of this subpart:

"(1) The term 'minority health disparities research' means basic, clinical, and behavioral research on minority health conditions (as defined in paragraph (2)), including research to prevent, diagnose, and treat such conditions.

"(2) The term 'minority health conditions', with respect to individuals who are members of minority groups, means all diseases, disorders, and conditions (including with respect to mental health and substance abuse)—

"(A) unique to, more serious, or more prevalent in such individuals;

"(B) for which the factors of medical risk or types of medical intervention may be different for such individuals, or for which it is unknown whether such factors or types are different for such individuals, or

"(C) with respect to which there has been insufficient research involving such individuals as subjects or insufficient data on such individuals.

"(3) The term 'minority group' has the meaning given the term 'racial and ethnic minority group' in section 1707.

"(4) The terms 'minority' and 'minorities' refer to individuals from a minority group.

"(d) HEALTH DISPARITY POPULATIONS.—For purposes of this subpart:

"(1) A population is a health disparity population if, as determined by the Director of the Center after consultation with the Director of the Agency for Healthcare Research and Quality, there is a significant disparity in the overall rate of disease incidence, prevalence, morbidity, mortality, or survival rates in the population as compared to the health status of the general population.

"(2) The Director shall give priority consideration to determining whether minority groups qualify as health disparity populations under paragraph (1).

"(3) The term 'health disparities research' means basic, clinical, and behavioral research on health disparity populations (including individual members and communities of such populations) that relates to health disparities as defined under paragraph (1), including the causes of such disparities and methods to prevent, diagnose, and treat such disparities.

"(e) COORDINATION OF ACTIVITIES.—The Director of the Center shall act as the primary Federal official with responsibility for coordinating all minority health disparities research and other health disparities research conducted or supported by the National Institutes of Health, and—

"(1) shall represent the health disparities research program of the National Institutes of Health, including the minority health disparities research program, at all relevant Executive branch task forces, committees and planning activities; and

"(2) shall maintain communications with all relevant Public Health Service agencies, including the Indian Health Service, and various other departments of the Federal Government to ensure the timely transmission of information concerning advances in minority health disparities research and other health disparities research between these various agencies for dissemination to affected communities and health care providers.

"(f) COLLABORATIVE COMPREHENSIVE PLAN AND BUDGET.—

"(1) IN GENERAL.—Subject to the provisions of this section and other applicable law, the Director of NIH, the Director of the Center, and the directors of the other agencies of the National Institutes of Health in collaboration (and in consultation with the advisory council for the Center) shall—

Deadline.

"(A) establish a comprehensive plan and budget for the conduct and support of all minority health disparities research and other health disparities research activities of the agencies of the National Institutes of Health (which plan and budget shall be first established under this subsection not later than 12 months after the date of the enactment of this subpart);

"(B) ensure that the plan and budget establish priorities among the health disparities research activities that such agencies are authorized to carry out;

"(C) ensure that the plan and budget establish objectives regarding such activities, describes the means for achieving the objectives, and designates the date by which the objectives are expected to be achieved;

"(D) ensure that, with respect to amounts appropriated for activities of the Center, the plan and budget give priority in the expenditure of funds to conducting and supporting minority health disparities research;

"(E) ensure that all amounts appropriated for such activities are expended in accordance with the plan and budget;

"(F) review the plan and budget not less than annually, and revise the plan and budget as appropriate;

"(G) ensure that the plan and budget serve as a broad, binding statement of policies regarding minority health disparities research and other health disparities research activities of the agencies, but do not remove the responsibility of the heads of the agencies for the approval of specific programs or projects, or for other details of the daily administration of such activities, in accordance with the plan and budget; and

"(H) promote coordination and collaboration among the agencies conducting or supporting minority health or other health disparities research.

"(2) CERTAIN COMPONENTS OF PLAN AND BUDGET.—With respect to health disparities research activities of the agencies of the National Institutes of Health, the Director of the Center shall ensure that the plan and budget under paragraph (1) provide for—

"(A) basic research and applied research, including research and development with respect to products;

"(B) research that is conducted by the agencies;

"(C) research that is supported by the agencies;

"(D) proposals developed pursuant to solicitations by the agencies and for proposals developed independently of such solicitations; and

"(E) behavioral research and social sciences research, which may include cultural and linguistic research in each of the agencies.

"(3) MINORITY HEALTH DISPARITIES RESEARCH.—The plan and budget under paragraph (1) shall include a separate statement of the plan and budget for minority health disparities research.

"(g) PARTICIPATION IN CLINICAL RESEARCH.—The Director of the Center shall work with the Director of NIH and the directors of the agencies of the National Institutes of Health to carry out the provisions of section 492B that relate to minority groups.

"(h) RESEARCH ENDOWMENTS.—

"(1) IN GENERAL.—The Director of the Center may carry out a program to facilitate minority health disparities research and other health disparities research by providing for research endowments at centers of excellence under section 736.

"(2) ELIGIBILITY.—The Director of the Center may provide for a research endowment under paragraph (1) only if the institution involved meets the following conditions:

"(A) The institution does not have an endowment that is worth in excess of an amount equal to 50 percent of the national average of endowment funds at institutions that conduct similar biomedical research or training of health professionals.

"(B) The application of the institution under paragraph (1) regarding a research endowment has been recommended pursuant to technical and scientific peer review and has been approved by the advisory council under subsection (j).

"(i) CERTAIN ACTIVITIES.—In carrying out subsection (a), the Director of the Center—

"(1) shall assist the Director of the National Center for Research Resources in carrying out section 481(c)(3) and in committing resources for construction at Institutions of Emerging Excellence;

"(2) shall establish projects to promote cooperation among Federal agencies, State, local, tribal, and regional public health agencies, and private entities in health disparities research; and

"(3) may utilize information from previous health initiatives concerning minorities and other health disparity populations.

"(j) ADVISORY COUNCIL.—

"(1) IN GENERAL.—The Secretary shall, in accordance with section 406, establish an advisory council to advise, assist, consult with, and make recommendations to the Director of the Center on matters relating to the activities described in subsection (a), and with respect to such activities to carry out any other functions described in section 406 for advisory councils under such section. Functions under the preceding sentence shall include making recommendations on budgetary allocations made in the plan under subsection (f), and shall include reviewing reports under subsection (k) before the reports are submitted under such subsection.

"(2) MEMBERSHIP.—With respect to the membership of the advisory council under paragraph (1), a majority of the members shall be individuals with demonstrated expertise regarding minority health disparity and other health disparity issues; representatives of communities impacted by minority and other health disparities shall be included; and a diversity of health professionals shall be represented. The membership shall in addition include a representative of the Office of Behavioral and Social Sciences Research under section 404A.

"(k) ANNUAL REPORT.—The Director of the Center shall prepare an annual report on the activities carried out or to be carried out by the Center, and shall submit each such report to the Committee on Health, Education, Labor, and Pensions of the Senate, the Committee on Commerce of the House of Representatives, the Secretary, and the Director of NIH. With respect to the fiscal year involved, the report shall—

"(1) describe and evaluate the progress made in health disparities research conducted or supported by the national research institutes;

"(2) summarize and analyze expenditures made for activities with respect to health disparities research conducted or supported by the National Institutes of Health;

"(3) include a separate statement applying the requirements of paragraphs (1) and (2) specifically to minority health disparities research; and

"(4) contain such recommendations as the Director considers appropriate.

"(l) AUTHORIZATION OF APPROPRIATIONS.—For the purpose of carrying out this subpart, there are authorized to be appropriated $100,000,000 for fiscal year 2001, and such sums as may be necessary for each of the fiscal years 2002 through 2005. Such authorization of appropriations is in addition to other authorizations of appropriations that are available for the conduct and support of minority health disparities research or other health disparities research by the agencies of the National Institutes of Health.".

(b) CONFORMING AMENDMENT.—Part A of title IV of the Public Health Service Act (42 U.S.C. 281 et seq.) is amended—

(1) in section 401(b)(2)— 42 USC 281.

(A) in subparagraph (F), by moving the subparagraph two ems to the left; and

(B) by adding at the end the following subparagraph:

"(G) The National Center on Minority Health and Health Disparities."; and

(2) by striking section 404.

SEC. 102. CENTERS OF EXCELLENCE FOR RESEARCH EDUCATION AND TRAINING. 42 USC 283b.

Subpart 6 of part E of title IV of the Public Health Service Act, as added by section 101(a) of this Act, is amended by adding at the end the following section:

"SEC. 485F. CENTERS OF EXCELLENCE FOR RESEARCH EDUCATION AND TRAINING. 42 USC 287c–32.

"(a) IN GENERAL.—The Director of the Center shall make awards of grants or contracts to designated biomedical and behavioral research institutions under paragraph (1) of subsection (c), or to consortia under paragraph (2) of such subsection, for the purpose of assisting the institutions in supporting programs of excellence in biomedical and behavioral research training for individuals who are members of minority health disparity populations or other health disparity populations. Grants. Contracts.

"(b) REQUIRED USE OF FUNDS.—An award may be made under subsection (a) only if the applicant involved agrees that the grant will be expended—

"(1) to train members of minority health disparity populations or other health disparity populations as professionals in the area of biomedical or behavioral research or both; or

"(2) to expand, remodel, renovate, or alter existing research facilities or construct new research facilities for the purpose of conducting minority health disparities research and other health disparities research.

"(c) CENTERS OF EXCELLENCE.—

"(1) IN GENERAL.—For purposes of this section, a designated biomedical and behavioral research institution is a biomedical and behavioral research institution that—

"(A) has a significant number of members of minority health disparity populations or other health disparity populations enrolled as students in the institution (including individuals accepted for enrollment in the institution);

"(B) has been effective in assisting such students of the institution to complete the program of education or training and receive the degree involved;

"(C) has made significant efforts to recruit minority students to enroll in and graduate from the institution, which may include providing means-tested scholarships and other financial assistance as appropriate; and

"(D) has made significant recruitment efforts to increase the number of minority or other members of health disparity populations serving in faculty or administrative positions at the institution.

"(2) CONSORTIUM.—Any designated biomedical and behavioral research institution involved may, with other biomedical and behavioral institutions (designated or otherwise), including tribal health programs, form a consortium to receive an award under subsection (a).

"(3) APPLICATION OF CRITERIA TO OTHER PROGRAMS.—In the case of any criteria established by the Director of the Center for purposes of determining whether institutions meet the conditions described in paragraph (1), this section may not, with respect to minority health disparity populations or other health disparity populations, be construed to authorize, require, or prohibit the use of such criteria in any program other than the program established in this section.

"(d) DURATION OF GRANT.—The period during which payments are made under a grant under subsection (a) may not exceed 5 years. Such payments shall be subject to annual approval by the Director of the Center and to the availability of appropriations for the fiscal year involved to make the payments.

"(e) MAINTENANCE OF EFFORT.—

"(1) IN GENERAL.—With respect to activities for which an award under subsection (a) is authorized to be expended, the Director of the Center may not make such an award to a designated research institution or consortium for any fiscal year unless the institution, or institutions in the consortium, as the case may be, agree to maintain expenditures of non-Federal amounts for such activities at a level that is not less than the level of such expenditures maintained by the institutions involved for the fiscal year preceding the fiscal year for which such institutions receive such an award.

"(2) USE OF FEDERAL FUNDS.—With respect to any Federal amounts received by a designated research institution or consortium and available for carrying out activities for which an award under subsection (a) is authorized to be expended, the Director of the Center may make such an award only if the institutions involved agree that the institutions will, before expending the award, expend the Federal amounts obtained from sources other than the award.

"(f) CERTAIN EXPENDITURES.—The Director of the Center may authorize a designated biomedical and behavioral research institution to expend a portion of an award under subsection (a) for research endowments.

"(g) DEFINITIONS.—For purposes of this section:

"(1) The term 'designated biomedical and behavioral research institution' has the meaning indicated for such term in subsection (c)(1). Such term includes any health professions school receiving an award of a grant or contract under section 736.

"(2) The term 'program of excellence' means any program carried out by a designated biomedical and behavioral research institution with an award under subsection (a), if the program is for purposes for which the institution involved is authorized in subsection (b) to expend the grant.

"(h) AUTHORIZATION OF APPROPRIATIONS.—For the purpose of making grants under subsection (a), there are authorized to be appropriated such sums as may be necessary for each of the fiscal years 2001 through 2005.".

SEC. 103. EXTRAMURAL LOAN REPAYMENT PROGRAM FOR MINORITY HEALTH DISPARITIES RESEARCH.

Subpart 6 of part E of title IV of the Public Health Service Act, as amended by section 102 of this Act, is amended by adding at the end the following section:

"SEC. 485G. LOAN REPAYMENT PROGRAM FOR MINORITY HEALTH DISPARITIES RESEARCH. 42 USC 287c–33.

"(a) IN GENERAL.—The Director of the Center shall establish a program of entering into contracts with qualified health professionals under which such health professionals agree to engage in minority health disparities research or other health disparities research in consideration of the Federal Government agreeing to repay, for each year of engaging in such research, not more than $35,000 of the principal and interest of the educational loans of such health professionals. Contracts.

"(b) SERVICE PROVISIONS.—The provisions of sections 338B, 338C, and 338E shall, except as inconsistent with subsection (a), apply to the program established in such subsection to the same extent and in the same manner as such provisions apply to the National Health Service Corps Loan Repayment Program established in subpart III of part D of title III.

"(c) REQUIREMENT REGARDING HEALTH DISPARITY POPULATIONS.—The Director of the Center shall ensure that not fewer than 50 percent of the contracts entered into under subsection (a) are for appropriately qualified health professionals who are members of a health disparity population.

"(d) PRIORITY.—With respect to minority health disparities research and other health disparities research under subsection (a), the Secretary shall ensure that priority is given to conducting projects of biomedical research.

"(e) FUNDING.—

"(1) AUTHORIZATION OF APPROPRIATIONS.—For the purpose of carrying out this section, there are authorized to be appropriated such sums as may be necessary for each of the fiscal years 2001 through 2005.

"(2) AVAILABILITY OF APPROPRIATIONS.—Amounts available for carrying out this section shall remain available until the expiration of the second fiscal year beginning after the fiscal year for which the amounts were made available.".

SEC. 104. GENERAL PROVISIONS REGARDING THE CENTER.

Subpart 6 of part E of title IV of the Public Health Service Act, as amended by section 103 of this Act, is amended by adding at the end the following section:

"SEC. 485H. GENERAL PROVISIONS REGARDING THE CENTER. 42 USC 287c–34.

"(a) ADMINISTRATIVE SUPPORT FOR CENTER.—The Secretary, acting through the Director of the National Institutes of Health, shall provide administrative support and support services to the

Director of the Center and shall ensure that such support takes maximum advantage of existing administrative structures at the agencies of the National Institutes of Health.

"(b) EVALUATION AND REPORT.—

Deadline. "(1) EVALUATION.—Not later than 5 years after the date of the enactment of this subpart, the Secretary shall conduct an evaluation to—

"(A) determine the effect of this subpart on the planning and coordination of health disparities research programs at the agencies of the National Institutes of Health;

"(B) evaluate the extent to which this subpart has eliminated the duplication of administrative resources among such Institutes, centers and divisions; and

"(C) provide, to the extent determined by the Secretary to be appropriate, recommendations concerning future legislative modifications with respect to this subpart, for both minority health disparities research and other health disparities research.

"(2) MINORITY HEALTH DISPARITIES RESEARCH.—The evaluation under paragraph (1) shall include a separate statement that applies subparagraphs (A) and (B) of such paragraph to minority health disparities research.

Deadline. "(3) REPORT.—Not later than 1 year after the date on which the evaluation is commenced under paragraph (1), the Secretary shall prepare and submit to the Committee on Health, Education, Labor, and Pensions of the Senate, and the Committee on Commerce of the House of Representatives, a report concerning the results of such evaluation.".

42 USC 287c–31 note.

SEC. 105. REPORT REGARDING RESOURCES OF NATIONAL INSTITUTES OF HEALTH DEDICATED TO MINORITY AND OTHER HEALTH DISPARITIES RESEARCH.

Deadline. Not later than December 1, 2003, the Director of the National Center on Minority Health and Health Disparities (established by the amendment made by section 101(a)), after consultation with the advisory council for such Center, shall submit to the Congress, the Secretary of Health and Human Services, and the Director of the National Institutes of Health a report that provides the following:

(1) Recommendations for the methodology that should be used to determine the extent of the resources of the National Institutes of Health that are dedicated to minority health disparities research and other health disparities research, including determining the amount of funds that are used to conduct and support such research. With respect to such methodology, the report shall address any discrepancies between the methodology used by such Institutes as of the date of the enactment of this Act and the methodology used by the Institute of Medicine as of such date.

(2) A determination of whether and to what extent, relative to fiscal year 1999, there has been an increase in the level of resources of the National Institutes of Health that are dedicated to minority health disparities research, including the amount of funds used to conduct and support such research. The report shall include provisions describing whether and to what extent there have been increases in the number and amount of awards to minority serving institutions.

TITLE II—HEALTH DISPARITIES RESEARCH BY AGENCY FOR HEALTHCARE RESEARCH AND QUALITY

SEC. 201. HEALTH DISPARITIES RESEARCH BY AGENCY FOR HEALTHCARE RESEARCH AND QUALITY.

(a) IN GENERAL.—Part A of title IX of the Public Health Service Act (42 U.S.C. 299 et seq.) is amended—

(1) in section 902, by striking subsection (g); and 42 USC 299a.

(2) by adding at the end the following:

"SEC. 903. RESEARCH ON HEALTH DISPARITIES. 42 USC 299a–1.

"(a) IN GENERAL.—The Director shall—

"(1) conduct and support research to identify populations for which there is a significant disparity in the quality, outcomes, cost, or use of health care services or access to and satisfaction with such services, as compared to the general population;

"(2) conduct and support research on the causes of and barriers to reducing the health disparities identified in paragraph (1), taking into account such factors as socioeconomic status, attitudes toward health, the language spoken, the extent of formal education, the area or community in which the population resides, and other factors the Director determines to be appropriate;

"(3) conduct and support research and support demonstration projects to identify, test, and evaluate strategies for reducing or eliminating health disparities, including development or identification of effective service delivery models, and disseminate effective strategies and models;

"(4) develop measures and tools for the assessment and improvement of the outcomes, quality, and appropriateness of health care services provided to health disparity populations;

"(5) in carrying out section 902(c), provide support to increase the number of researchers who are members of health disparity populations, and the health services research capacity of institutions that train such researchers; and

"(6) beginning with fiscal year 2003, annually submit to the Congress a report regarding prevailing disparities in health care delivery as it relates to racial factors and socioeconomic factors in priority populations. Reports.

"(b) RESEARCH AND DEMONSTRATION PROJECTS.—

"(1) IN GENERAL.—In carrying out subsection (a), the Director shall conduct and support research and support demonstrations to—

"(A) identify the clinical, cultural, socioeconomic, geographic, and organizational factors that contribute to health disparities, including minority health disparity populations, which research shall include behavioral research, such as examination of patterns of clinical decisionmaking, and research on access, outreach, and the availability of related support services (such as cultural and linguistic services);

"(B) identify and evaluate clinical and organizational strategies to improve the quality, outcomes, and access to care for health disparity populations, including minority health disparity populations;

"(C) test such strategies and widely disseminate those strategies for which there is scientific evidence of effectiveness; and

"(D) determine the most effective approaches for disseminating research findings to health disparity populations, including minority populations.

"(2) USE OF CERTAIN STRATEGIES.—In carrying out this section, the Director shall implement research strategies and mechanisms that will enhance the involvement of individuals who are members of minority health disparity populations or other health disparity populations, health services researchers who are such individuals, institutions that train such individuals as researchers, members of minority health disparity populations or other health disparity populations for whom the Agency is attempting to improve the quality and outcomes of care, and representatives of appropriate tribal or other community-based organizations with respect to health disparity populations. Such research strategies and mechanisms may include the use of—

"(A) centers of excellence that can demonstrate, either individually or through consortia, a combination of multidisciplinary expertise in outcomes or quality improvement research, linkages to relevant sites of care, and a demonstrated capacity to involve members and communities of health disparity populations, including minority health disparity populations, in the planning, conduct, dissemination, and translation of research;

"(B) provider-based research networks, including health plans, facilities, or delivery system sites of care (especially primary care), that make extensive use of health care providers who are members of health disparity populations or who serve patients in such populations and have the capacity to evaluate and promote quality improvement;

"(C) service delivery models (such as health centers under section 330 and the Indian Health Service) to reduce health disparities; and

"(D) innovative mechanisms or strategies that will facilitate the translation of past research investments into clinical practices that can reasonably be expected to benefit these populations.

"(c) QUALITY MEASUREMENT DEVELOPMENT.—

"(1) IN GENERAL.—To ensure that health disparity populations, including minority health disparity populations, benefit from the progress made in the ability of individuals to measure the quality of health care delivery, the Director shall support the development of quality of health care measures that assess the experience of such populations with health care systems, such as measures that assess the access of such populations to health care, the cultural competence of the care provided, the quality of the care provided, the outcomes of care, or other aspects of health care practice that the Director determines to be important.

"(2) EXAMINATION OF CERTAIN PRACTICES.—The Director shall examine the practices of providers that have a record of reducing health disparities or have experience in providing culturally competent health services to minority health disparity populations or other health disparity populations. In examining such practices of providers funded under the authorities of this Act, the Director shall consult with the heads of the relevant agencies of the Public Health Service.

"(3) REPORT.—Not later than 36 months after the date of the enactment of this section, the Secretary, acting through the Director, shall prepare and submit to the appropriate committees of Congress a report describing the state-of-the-art of quality measurement for minority and other health disparity populations that will identify critical unmet needs, the current activities of the Department to address those needs, and a description of related activities in the private sector. Deadline.

"(d) DEFINITION.—For purposes of this section:

"(1) The term 'health disparity population' has the meaning given such term in section 485E, except that in addition to the meaning so given, the Director may determine that such term includes populations for which there is a significant disparity in the quality, outcomes, cost, or use of health care services or access to or satisfaction with such services as compared to the general population.

"(2) The term 'minority', with respect to populations, refers to racial and ethnic minority groups as defined in section 1707.".

(b) FUNDING.—Section 927 of the Public Health Service Act (42 U.S.C. 299c–6) is amended by adding at the end the following:

"(d) HEALTH DISPARITIES RESEARCH.—For the purpose of carrying out the activities under section 903, there are authorized to be appropriated $50,000,000 for fiscal year 2001, and such sums as may be necessary for each of the fiscal years 2002 through 2005.".

TITLE III—DATA COLLECTION RELATING TO RACE OR ETHNICITY

SEC. 301. STUDY AND REPORT BY NATIONAL ACADEMY OF SCIENCES. 42 USC 3501 note.

(a) STUDY.—The National Academy of Sciences shall conduct a comprehensive study of the Department of Health and Human Services' data collection systems and practices, and any data collection or reporting systems required under any of the programs or activities of the Department, relating to the collection of data on race or ethnicity, including other Federal data collection systems (such as the Social Security Administration) with which the Department interacts to collect relevant data on race and ethnicity.

(b) REPORT.—Not later than 1 year after the date of enactment of this Act, the National Academy of Sciences shall prepare and submit to the Committee on Health, Education, Labor, and Pensions of the Senate and the Committee on Commerce of the House of Representatives, a report that— Deadline.

(1) identifies the data needed to support efforts to evaluate the effects of socioeconomic status, race and ethnicity on access to health care and other services and on disparity in health and other social outcomes and the data needed to enforce existing protections for equal access to health care;

(2) examines the effectiveness of the systems and practices of the Department of Health and Human Services described in subsection (a), including pilot and demonstration projects

of the Department, and the effectiveness of selected systems and practices of other Federal, State, and tribal agencies and the private sector, in collecting and analyzing such data;

(3) contains recommendations for ensuring that the Department of Health and Human Services, in administering its entire array of programs and activities, collects, or causes to be collected, reliable and complete information relating to race and ethnicity; and

(4) includes projections about the costs associated with the implementation of the recommendations described in paragraph (3), and the possible effects of the costs on program operations.

(c) AUTHORIZATION OF APPROPRIATIONS.—For the purpose of carrying out this section, there are authorized to be appropriated such sums as may be necessary for fiscal year 2001.

TITLE IV—HEALTH PROFESSIONS EDUCATION

SEC. 401. HEALTH PROFESSIONS EDUCATION IN HEALTH DISPARITIES.

(a) IN GENERAL.—Part B of title VII of the Public Health Service Act (42 U.S.C. 293 et seq.) is amended by inserting after section 740 the following:

42 USC 293e. **"SEC. 741. GRANTS FOR HEALTH PROFESSIONS EDUCATION.**

"(a) GRANTS FOR HEALTH PROFESSIONS EDUCATION IN HEALTH DISPARITIES AND CULTURAL COMPETENCY.—

"(1) IN GENERAL.—The Secretary, acting through the Administrator of the Health Resources and Services Administration, may make awards of grants, contracts, or cooperative agreements to public and nonprofit private entities (including tribal entities) for the purpose of carrying out research and demonstration projects (including research and demonstration projects for continuing health professions education) for training and education of health professionals for the reduction of disparities in health care outcomes and the provision of culturally competent health care.

"(2) ELIGIBLE ENTITIES.—Unless specifically required otherwise in this title, the Secretary shall accept applications for grants or contracts under this section from health professions schools, academic health centers, State or local governments, or other appropriate public or private nonprofit entities (or consortia of entities, including entities promoting multidisciplinary approaches) for funding and participation in health professions training activities. The Secretary may accept applications from for-profit private entities as determined appropriate by the Secretary.

"(b) AUTHORIZATION OF APPROPRIATIONS.—There are authorized to be appropriated to carry out subsection (a), $3,500,000 for fiscal year 2001, $7,000,000 for fiscal year 2002, $7,000,000 for fiscal year 2003, and $3,500,000 for fiscal year 2004.".

(b) NURSING EDUCATION.—Part A of title VIII of the Public Health Service Act (42 U.S.C. 296 et seq.) is amended—

42 USC 296f. (1) by redesignating section 807 as section 808; and

42 USC 296e–1. (2) by inserting after section 806 the following:

"SEC. 807. GRANTS FOR HEALTH PROFESSIONS EDUCATION.

"(a) GRANTS FOR HEALTH PROFESSIONS EDUCATION IN HEALTH DISPARITIES AND CULTURAL COMPETENCY.—The Secretary, acting through the Administrator of the Health Resources and Services Administration, may make awards of grants, contracts, or cooperative agreements to eligible entities for the purpose of carrying out research and demonstration projects (including research and demonstration projects for continuing health professions education) for training and education for the reduction of disparities in health care outcomes and the provision of culturally competent health care. Grants under this section shall be the same as provided in section 741.".

"(b) AUTHORIZATION OF APPROPRIATIONS.—There are to be appropriated to carry out subsection (a) such sums as may be necessary for each of the fiscal years 2001 through 2004.".

SEC. 402. NATIONAL CONFERENCE ON HEALTH PROFESSIONS EDUCATION AND HEALTH DISPARITIES. 42 USC 293e note.

(a) IN GENERAL.—Not later than 1 year after the date of enactment of this Act, the Secretary of Health and Human Services (in this section referred to as the "Secretary"), acting through the Administrator of the Health Resources and Services Administration, shall convene a national conference on health professions education as a method for reducing disparities in health outcomes. Deadline.

(b) PARTICIPANTS.—The Secretary shall include in the national conference convened under subsection (a) advocacy groups and educational entities as described in section 741 of the Public Health Service Act (as added by section 401), tribal health programs, health centers under section 330 of such Act, and other interested parties.

(c) ISSUES.—The national conference convened under subsection (a) shall include, but is not limited to, issues that address the role and impact of health professions education on the reduction of disparities in health outcomes, including the role of education on cultural competency. The conference shall focus on methods to achieve reductions in disparities in health outcomes through health professions education (including continuing education programs) and strategies for outcomes measurement to assess the effectiveness of education in reducing disparities.

(d) PUBLICATION OF FINDINGS.—Not later than 6 months after the national conference under subsection (a) has convened, the Secretary shall publish in the Federal Register a summary of the proceedings and findings of the conference. Deadline. Federal Register, publication.

(e) AUTHORIZATION OF APPROPRIATIONS.—There is authorized to be appropriated such sums as may be necessary to carry out this section.

SEC. 403. ADVISORY RESPONSIBILITIES IN HEALTH PROFESSIONS EDUCATION IN HEALTH DISPARITIES AND CULTURAL COMPETENCY.

Section 1707 of the Public Health Service Act (42 U.S.C. 300u–6) is amended—

(1) in subsection (b), by adding at the end the following paragraph:

"(10) Advise in matters related to the development, implementation, and evaluation of health professions education in decreasing disparities in health care outcomes, including cultural competency as a method of eliminating health disparities.";

(2) in subsection (c)(2), by striking "paragraphs (1) through (9)" and inserting "paragraphs (1) through (10)"; and

(3) in subsection (d), by amending paragraph (1) to read as follows:

"(1) RECOMMENDATIONS REGARDING LANGUAGE.—

"(A) PROFICIENCY IN SPEAKING ENGLISH.—The Deputy Assistant Secretary shall consult with the Director of the Office of International and Refugee Health, the Director of the Office of Civil Rights, and the Directors of other appropriate departmental entities regarding recommendations for carrying out activities under subsection (b)(9).

"(B) HEALTH PROFESSIONS EDUCATION REGARDING HEALTH DISPARITIES.—The Deputy Assistant Secretary shall carry out the duties under subsection (b)(10) in collaboration with appropriate personnel of the Department of Health and Human Services, other Federal agencies, and other offices, centers, and institutions, as appropriate, that have responsibilities under the Minority Health and Health Disparities Research and Education Act of 2000.".

TITLE V—PUBLIC AWARENESS AND DISSEMINATION OF INFORMATION ON HEALTH DISPARITIES

42 USC 287c–31 note.

SEC. 501. PUBLIC AWARENESS AND INFORMATION DISSEMINATION.

(a) PUBLIC AWARENESS ON HEALTH DISPARITIES.—The Secretary of Health and Human Services (in this section referred to as the "Secretary") shall conduct a national campaign to inform the public and health care professionals about health disparities in minority and other underserved populations by disseminating information and materials available on specific diseases affecting these populations and programs and activities to address these disparities. The campaign shall—

(1) have a specific focus on minority and other underserved communities with health disparities; and

(2) include an evaluation component to assess the impact of the national campaign in raising awareness of health disparities and information on available resources.

(b) DISSEMINATION OF INFORMATION ON HEALTH DISPARITIES.—The Secretary shall develop and implement a plan for the dissemination of information and findings with respect to health disparities under titles I, II, III, and IV of this Act. The plan shall—

(1) include the participation of all agencies of the Department of Health and Human Services that are responsible for serving populations included in the health disparities research; and

(2) have agency-specific strategies for disseminating relevant findings and information on health disparities and improving health care services to affected communities.

TITLE VI—MISCELLANEOUS PROVISIONS

SEC. 601. DEPARTMENTAL DEFINITION REGARDING MINORITY INDIVIDUALS.

Section 1707(g)(1) of the Public Health Service Act (42 U.S.C. 300u–6) is amended—

(1) by striking "Asian Americans and" and inserting "Asian Americans;"; and

(2) by inserting "Native Hawaiians and other" before "Pacific Islanders;".

SEC. 602. CONFORMING PROVISION REGARDING DEFINITIONS.

For purposes of this Act, the term "racial and ethnic minority group" has the meaning given such term in section 1707 of the Public Health Service Act.

SEC. 603. EFFECTIVE DATE. 42 USC 281 note.

This Act and the amendments made by this Act take effect October 1, 2000, or upon the date of the enactment of this Act, whichever occurs later.

Approved November 22, 2000.

LEGISLATIVE HISTORY—S. 1880 (H.R. 3250):

HOUSE REPORTS: No. 106–986 accompanying H.R. 3250 (Comm. on Commerce).
CONGRESSIONAL RECORD, Vol. 146 (2000):
Oct. 26, considered and passed Senate.
Oct. 31, considered and passed House.
WEEKLY COMPILATION OF PRESIDENTIAL DOCUMENTS, Vol. 36 (2000):
Nov. 22, Presidential statement.

B

Agendas of Open Meetings

INSTITUTE OF MEDICINE

Committee on the Review and Assessment of the National Institutes of Health's Strategic Research Plan to Reduce and Ultimately Eliminate Health Disparities

Marriott Bethesda Hotel
5151 Pooks Hill Road
Bethesda, Maryland 20814

Agenda (Meeting #1)

Wednesday, October 6

OPEN SESSION

1:30 p.m. **WELCOME AND INTRODUCTIONS**
Gerald Thomson, M.D.

OVERVIEW AND SPONSOR'S CHARGE TO THE COMMITTEE

The Strategic Plan of the National Institutes of Health—Conceptual Framework, Goals, and Objectives

Elias A. Zerhouni, M.D.
Director, National Institutes of Health

John Ruffin, Ph.D.
Director, National Center for Minority Health and Health Disparities, NIH

2:30 p.m. **DISCUSSION OF STUDY CHARGE WITH SPONSOR**

John Ruffin, Ph.D.

4:00 p.m. **ADJOURN**

INSTITUTE OF MEDICINE

Committee on the Review and Assessment of NIH's Strategic Research Plan to Reduce and Ultimately Eliminate Health Disparities

The National Academies Building (Room 150)
2101 Constitution Avenue, NW
Washington, D.C. 20418

Agenda (Meeting #2)

Thursday, December 9

OPEN SESSION

11:30 a.m. WELCOME AND INTRODUCTIONS
Gerald E. Thomson, M.D.
Chair, Committee on the Review and Assessment of NIH's Strategic Research Plan to Reduce and Ultimately Eliminate Health Disparities

11:40 a.m. NATIONAL INSTITUTE OF CHILD HEALTH AND HUMAN DEVELOPMENT, NIH

Duane Alexander, M.D.
Director

Yvonne Maddox, Ph.D.
Deputy Director

1:00 p.m. WORKING LUNCH (provided in meeting room)

1:30 p.m. NATIONAL INSTITUTES OF HEALTH

Elias A. Zerhouni, M.D.
Director

2:30 p.m. NATIONAL CENTER ON MINORITY HEALTH AND HEALTH DISPARITIES, NIH

John Ruffin, Ph.D.
Director

Jerome Wilson, Ph.D.
Associate Director for Scientific Programs Operation

Doug Hussey
Director Division of Scientific Planning and Policy Analysis

Angela Vincent (invited)
Former Program Director for the Endowment Program

Friday, December 10

OPEN SESSION

8:30 a.m. WELCOME AND INTRODUCTIONS

Gerald Thomson, M.D.
Chair, Committee on the Review and Assessment of NIH's Strategic Research Plan to Reduce and Ultimately Eliminate Health Disparities

9:00 a.m. NATIONAL ADVISORY COUNCIL ON MINORITY HEALTH AND HEALTH DISPARITIES, NIH

Carolyn M. Kane, Ph.D.
Advisory Council Member

Louis W. Sullivan, M.D,
Advisory Council Member

INSTITUTE OF MEDICINE

Committee on the Review and Assessment of NIH's Strategic Research Plan to Reduce and Ultimately Eliminate Health Disparities

The National Academies' Keck Building
500 Fifth Street, NW, Washington, D.C. 20001

Agenda (Meeting #3)

Monday, March 7, 2005

OPEN SESSION

10:00 a.m.	*Charles Francis, M.D.* President, American College of Physicians Director, Office of Health Disparities, New York Academy of Medicine
11:00 a.m.	National Institute of Allergy and Infectious Diseases, NIH *John J. McGowan, Ph.D.* Director, Division of Extramural Activities Associate Director for Management and Operations
12:30 a.m.	LUNCH
1:30 p.m.	Agency for Healthcare Research and Quality, HSS *Francis D. Chesley, Jr., M.D.* Director, Office of Extramural Research, Education, and Priority Populations
2:30 pm.	Office of AIDS Research, NIH *Victoria A. Cargill, M.D., M.S.C.E.* Director of Minority Research, Director of Clinical Studies
4:00 p.m.	Centers for Disease Control and Prevention *George Mensah, M.D.* (invited) Chief, Cardiovascular Branch National Center for Chronic Disease Prevention and Health Promotion
5:00 p.m.	ADJOURN
6:00 p.m.	COMMITTEE DINNER

Tuesday, March 8, 2005

OPEN SESSION

9:30 a.m.	PANEL DISCUSSION
	Joint Center for Political and Economic Studies *Gail C. Christopher, D.N.,* Director, Health Policy Institute
	National Medical Association *Winston Price, M.D.,* President
11:00 a.m.	National Heart, Lung, and Blood Institute, NIH *Barbara Alving, M.D., MACP,* Deputy Director
12:30 p.m.	LUNCH
1:30 p.m.	Department of Health and Human Services *Garth Graham, M.D., M.P.H.* Head, Office of Minority Health
2:30 p.m.	Association of Minority Health Professions Schools *John Maupin, M.D.,* President President, Meharry Medical College, Nashville, TN
	Minority Health Professions Foundation *Ronny B. Lancaster,* President Chief Operating Officer, Morehouse School of Medicine, Atlanta, GA
3:30 p.m.	Physicians for Human Rights *Leonard S. Rubenstein, J.D.,* Executive Director

INSTITUTE OF MEDICINE

Committee on the Review and Assessment of NIH's Strategic Research Plan to Reduce and Ultimately Eliminate Health Disparities

The National Academies Building
2101 Constitution Avenue, NW, Washington, D.C. 20418

Agenda (Meeting #4)

Tuesday, May 10, 2005

OPEN SESSION

10:00 a.m.	National Cancer Institute, NIH *Mark Clanton, M.D.* Deputy Director, Office of the Director Cancer Care Delivery System
11:00 a.m.	Office of Research on Women's Health, NIH *Vivian W. Pinn, M.D.* Associate Director for Research on Women's Health Director, Office of Research on Women's Health
12:00 a.m.	LUNCH
1:00 pm.	National Institute of Diabetes and Digestive and Kidney Diseases, NIH *Allen M. Spiegel, M.D.,* Director *Dr. Lawrence Agodoa* Director, Office of Minority Health Research Coordination *Dr. Griffin Rodgers;* Deputy Director
2:15 p.m.	Centers for Disease Control and Prevention *Captain Walter W. Williams, M.D., M.P.H.* Associate Director for Minority Health Director, Office of Minority Health
3:15 p.m.	Hispanic Association of Colleges and Universities *René González*
4:00 p.m.	*David Satcher, M.D.* President, Morehouse School of Medicine

Wednesday, May 11, 2005

OPEN SESSION

11:00 a.m. Asian and Pacific Islander American Health Forum
Gem Daus, Policy Director

12:00 p.m. LUNCH

1:00 p.m. National Alliance for Hispanic Health
Adolph Falcon, Director of Policy

C

List of Participants Providing Testimony or Written Commentary to the Committee

TESTIMONY TO THE COMMITTEE

Lawrence Agodoa, M.D., Director, Office of Minority Health Research Coordination, National Institutes of Diabetes and Digestive and Kidney Diseases, National Institutes of Health

Duane Alexander, M.D., Director, National Institute of Child Health and Human Development

Barbara Alving, M.D., MACP, Deputy Director, National Heart, Lung, and Blood Institute, National Institutes of Health

Victoria A. Cargill, M.D., M.S.C.E., Director of Minority Research, Director of Clinical Studies, Office of AIDS Research, National Institutes of Health

Francis D. Chesley, Jr., M.D., Director, Office of Extramural Research, Education, and Priority Populations, Agency for Healthcare Research and Quality, Department of Health and Human Services

Gail C. Christopher, D.N., Director, Health Policy Institute, Joint Center for Political and Economic Studies

Mark Clanton, M.D., Deputy Director, Office of the Director, National Cancer Institute, National Institutes of Health

Gem Daus, M.A., Policy Director Asian and Pacific Islander American Health Forum

Adolph Falcon, Director of Policy, National Alliance for Hispanic Health

Charles Francis, M.D., Office of Health Disparities, New York Academy of Medicine

René González, Hispanic Association of Colleges and Universities

Garth Graham, M.D., M.P.H., Acting Deputy Assistant Secretary for Minority Health, Department of Health and Human Services

Doug Hussey, Director, Division of Scientific Planning and Policy Analysis, National Center for Minority Health and Health Disparities
Carolyn M. Kane, Ph.D., National Center on Minority Health and Health Disparities Advisory Council
Raynard Kington, M.D., Ph.D., Deputy Director, National Institutes of Health
Ronny B. Lancaster, President, Minority Health Professions Foundation; Chief Operating Officer, Morehouse School of Medicine, Atlanta, GA
Yvonne Maddox, Ph.D., Deputy Director, National Institute of Child Health and Human Development
John J. McGowan, Ph.D., Director, Division of Extramural Activities, Associate Director for Management and Operations National Institute of Allergy and Infectious Diseases, National Institutes of Health
Vivian W. Pinn, M.D., Associate Director for Research on Women's Health; Director, Office of Research on Women's Health Office of Research on Women's Health, National Institutes of Health
Winston Price, M.D., President, National Medical Association
Griffin Rodgers, M.D., Deputy Director, National Institute of Diabetes and Digestive and Kidney Diseases, National Institutes of Health
Leonard S. Rubenstein, J.D., Executive Director, Physicians for Human Rights
John Ruffin, Ph.D., Director, National Center on Minority Health and Health Disparities
David Satcher, M.D., President, Morehouse School of Medicine
Allen M. Spiegel, M.D., Director, National Institute of Diabetes and Digestive and Kidney Diseases, National Institutes of Health
Louis W. Sullivan, M.D., National Center on Minority Health and Health Disparities Advisory Council
Captain Walter W. Williams, M.D., M.P.H., Associate Director for Minority Health; Director, Office of Minority Health, Centers for Disease Control and Prevention, Department of Health and Human Services
Jerome Wilson, Ph.D., Associate Director for Scientific Programs Operation, National Center for Minority Health and Health Disparities
Elias A. Zerhouni, M.D., Director, National Institutes of Health

Written Commentary to the Committee

American Lung Association
American Psychological Association
American Public Health Association
Susan G. Komen Breast Cancer Foundation
National Association of Public Hospitals and Health Systems
National Hispanic Medical Association
Physicians for Human Rights

D

Overview of Health Disparities

Nancy E. Adler, Ph.D.
University of California, San Francisco

This paper examines conceptual approaches and current data on health disparities in the United States. The concept of health disparities requires some discussion before looking at the data. Health disparities are more than simply differences in health. The fact that some individuals or groups die sooner, or experience a disease more severely, than others is a necessary yet insufficient condition to establish a disparity. As Braveman and Gruskin (2003) noted, the fact that young people are healthier than the elderly is not an unfair difference. A disparity implies that the difference is inequitable and unjust (Carter-Pokras and Baquet, 2002). To determine whether a difference is unjust, one criterion is to question whether that difference is avoidable or immutable. Some definitions question whether the difference is detrimental to groups that are already disadvantaged, in opportunity or resources.

No consensus exists on the definition of health disparities (which are also referred to as health inequalities) or how to measure them. Carter-Pokras and Baquet (2002) noted that definitions of health disparities depend on "who is deciding what is avoidable and unjust and how it is decided." They identified 11 current definitions of disparities and categorized them into three general approaches. Some compare populations based on minority status, asking whether the health of minorities differs from nonminorities. Others compare the health of specific groups with that of the overall population, asking whether a given group

---

Background paper prepared for the Institute of Medicine's Committee on the Review and Assessment of the National Institute of Health's (NIH's) Strategic Research Plan to Reduce and Ultimately Eliminate Health Disparities.

has poorer health than the population at large. The third approach is to compare specific groups, asking whether Group X has poorer health than Group Y. Three of the 11 definitions address differences in both health and health care.

A markedly different approach to health disparities is to start with an observed difference on health indicators and then establish whether this difference constitutes a disparity (i.e., whether it is inequitable or unjust). For example, Murray, Michaud, McKenna, and Marks (1998) reported marked differences in life expectancy within the United States. They identified more than a 40-year gap in life expectancy between the shortest-lived group (Native American and Alaskan Native males in six counties in South Dakota) and the longest-lived group (Asian American females in Bergen County, New Jersey). At first glance, this approach appears to be purely empirical. However, researchers choose which demographic or spatial characteristics to monitor based on either available data or pre-existing theories or expectations of which groups or places may experience poorer health. Braveman, Starfield, and Geiger (2001) were critical of an approach that simply examined health extremes, without including a comparison of social groups that experience social disadvantage. They argued that although examining extremes in health may provide a good starting point, these additional analyses will be key to understanding disparities.

To adequately understand health disparities, researchers need valid and consistent measurement of disparities and the variables that shape them. Researchers located in different regions of the world have different traditions in choosing a metric to measure disparities. Occupational level is the most common independent variable in the United Kingdom, while education or occupation dominates in other European countries, and race/ethnicity is the most common variable in the United States (Murray et al., 1999). The choice of variables examined must be explicitly linked to models or theories of disparities. For example, although the shortest- and longest-lived groups described above differ by gender, ethnicity, and place of residence, they also are likely to differ in education, income, and other factors. The difference in longevity may be due to particular variables and/or their interactions; some variables also may be markers for other factors that have a more direct causal link. The choice of variables to examine may also be affected by what is considered to be unjust.

Just as a consensual definition of disparities remains elusive, so does a shared definition of health. There is no single, summative measure of the state of an individual's health, other than longevity. Length of life is clearly quantifiable. However, even mortality has its limitations as a measure. First, although people would generally prefer to live as long as possible, quality of life also matters. As a result, many researchers use lifespan weighted by quality or disability (quality-adjusted life years or disability-adjusted life years), particularly in doing cost-benefit analyses of various health policies or treatments. These measures, too, are limited. No summative measure is currently available that captures the World

Health Organization (1948) definition of health as "a state of complete physical, mental and social well-being and not merely the absence of disease or infirmity."

Second, mortality as the end point poses challenges to conducting research that can identify the mechanisms by which disparities operate. Some experiences associated with disadvantages that affect longevity occur in early life. To establish causal effects on mortality, one needs prospective cohort studies such as the British cohort studies of children born in 1946 and in 1958 or the planned U.S. birth cohort study. Even with such cohorts, no single study can capture all the processes involved in health disparities. To conduct more timely research, intermediate indicators of health are needed.

Third, mortality is a function of multiple factors, including vulnerability and exposure to disease or injury and the quality of diagnosis and treatment, each of which may show different patterns of inequality. For example, the incidence of breast cancer is higher among women with more education and income. However, among women with breast cancer, survival is longer for patients of higher socioeconomic status (SES). Mortality from breast cancer will reflect both of these associations. Studying only disparities in overall mortality will mask the two components of mortality (incidence and survival).

Fourth, different diseases, and causes of death, have distinct patterns of disparities. Some diseases (e.g., sickle cell anemia in African Americans) have a strong genetic component, whereas differences in the prevalence of other diseases are likely due more directly to social disadvantage. A variety of diseases may share a common pathway. One striking finding is that health disparities can be observed across a wide range of diseases that have different etiologic risk factors. However, specific aspects of disadvantage, and associated mechanisms, have been implicated in some diseases but not others. Adequately addressing health disparities will require identifying both common pathways to multiple diseases and disease-specific mechanisms.

An Empirical View

Some insight into how researchers are approaching and defining health disparities can be gained by examining the types of published studies that use relevant terms. The term *health disparity* has only recently come into common use. Table D-1 shows the increase in the number of articles published on *health disparities* as a key term. While only 1 article with this term emerged from a PubMed search of articles from 1985 to 1989 and only 11 and 18 articles in the next two 5-year time periods, respectively, 439 such articles were published from 2000 to 2004. The term *health inequalities* came into usage slightly earlier (3 articles for 1980–1984, 11 for 1985–1989, 34 for 1990–1994, and 86 for 1995–1999), but in the past 5 years, use of the term *health disparities* appears to have become more popular. This may partly reflect growing research in the United

TABLE D-1 Number of Articles Appearing in Medical Literature with Key Term *Health Disparity* or *Health Inequality*

	1980–1984	1985–1989	1990–1994	1995–1999	2000–2004
Health disparity	0	1	11	18	439
Health inequality	3	11	34	86	380

States, where *health disparities* is more commonly used; researchers in Europe and Great Britain more frequently report on *health inequalities*. The increase may also reflect the adoption of the term *health disparities* by the National Institutes of Health (NIH) for this domain of work.

The kinds of disparities or inequalities that are being examined can be seen in other key words associated with *health disparities*. As discussed earlier, there are many definitions for health disparities and the groups or variables being compared. The term *health disparities* is sometimes used synonymously with *racial and ethnic disparities*, though most definitions of health disparities include education, income, and geographic location. Table D-2 presents the number of papers published from 2000 to 2004 that use the term *health disparities* as a key word, along with the terms *race, ethnicity, SES*, or components of these (e.g., African American or black, Asian, Hispanic or Latino, occupation, education, income) as well as *gender* or *sex* and *rural*. This provides a rough indicator of which aspect of health disparities researchers are examining.

As can be seen in Table D-2, relatively few papers use the term *SES* in relation to health disparities (n = 25), but substantially more report on the specific components of SES, for example, income (n = 56) and education (n = 104). Fifty-seven articles during this time period report on health disparities in conjunction

TABLE D-2 Number of Articles Published from 2000–2004 on Health Disparities and Specific Variables

Health Disparities and:	
Socioeconomic status	25
Income	56
Education	104
Occupation	3
Race	57
Ethnicity	35
African American or black	61
Asian	22
Hispanic or Latino	69
Native American or American Indian	17
Rural	21
Gender/sex	50

with race and 35 with ethnicity, with comparable numbers reporting health disparities associated with specific groups: African Americans (n = 61), Asians (n = 22), Hispanics or Latinos (n = 69), and Native Americans or American Indians (n = 17). A small number of articles report on health disparities and rural health (n = 21) and somewhat more on sex or gender and health disparities (n = 50). There may be some overlap among these categories, but these data provide a rough order of magnitude of the studies and trends in using the term *health disparity*. Importantly, the data suggest no single category dominates the empirical work being reported on health disparities. This snapshot of key words reveals a spread of papers reporting on disparities associated with SES and its components, race/ethnicity, gender, and rural health.

The parallel snapshot looking at health inequalities is a bit different. As noted earlier, studies using this term are more likely to come from Europe, particularly Great Britain, where researchers have focused more on health differences associated with socioeconomic factors, rather than with racial and ethnic factors. As a result, relatively more papers report on health inequalities in conjunction with SES, rather than with race or ethnicity.

Table D-2 reports only on the number of papers using the term *health disparities* in relation to SES and race/ethnicity. A much larger literature on the association of these sociodemographic factors and health exists, though it does not explicitly identify these factors in key words as a health disparity.

Paralleling the marked increase in research on health disparities, the number of articles reporting on sociodemographic factors and health (without using *health disparities* as a key word) has increased exponentially, as seen in Table D-3.

Articles on SES and health increased from 337 in 1975–1979 to nearly 1900 in 2000–2004. Articles on race and health, or ethnicity and health, increased from 182 and 35, respectively, in 1975–1979, to 4172 and 2913, respectively, in 2000–2004. The largest category by far is education and health, but a number of these articles may be reporting on health education and not necessarily on the association of educational attainment and health. The pattern of increase, however, is similar to the other categories, and some part of the growth in publications reflects increasing research on the health effects of education, outside of specific health education. There is also a substantial literature on sex/gender and health and on rural health.

Defining Health Disparity Groups

The Minority Health and Health Disparities Research and Education Act of 2000 defines health disparity populations (or groups) as those for which "there is a significant disparity in the overall rate of disease incidence, prevalence, morbidity, mortality or survival rates." As discussed earlier, which group is identified as being a disparity group will differ depending on which of the above health indicators is used. For example, men could be viewed as a disparity group relative

TABLE D-3 Number of Articles Appearing in Medical Literature on Sociodemographic Factors and Health (Without Using *Health Disparities* as a Key Word)

Topic	1975–1979	1980–1984	1985–1989	1990–1994	1995–1999	2000–2004
Socioeconomic status and health	337	734	1189	1657	1801	1898
Race and health	182	316	678	1661	2750	4172
Ethnicity and health	35	82	167	594	1468	2913
Income and health	850	1148	1946	3351	5149	6491
Education and health	13,333	12,971	17,658	27,733	37,827	44,989
Occupation and health	116	211	446	777	989	1263
African American or black and health	322	498	1105	2746	4284	6290
Asian and health	76	178	373	766	1482	2674
Hispanic or Latino and health	86	207	448	1205	1885	2994
Native American and health	5	10	31	99	224	265
American Indian and health	25	6	48	124	225	345
Rural and health	3067	3186	3822	6723	8340	9892
Sex or gender and health	2199	2935	5836	12,840	21,117	30,201

to women if mortality rates are used, but women would be seen as a disparity group if some measures of morbidity are used. Similarly, differences in disease incidence or prevalence depend on the disease examined. Some differences between men and women derive from biology: There is a greater prevalence of breast cancer among women than men. Only women experience cervical or ovarian cancer; only men experience prostate cancer. Differences in these disease rates do not fit the definition of a disparity because they are unavoidable.

When examining other diseases, the question of whether a difference in prevalence represents a disparity becomes more complex. For example, women have a lower prevalence of cardiovascular disease than men. It can be debated whether this difference represents a disparity. The female advantage may reflect the protective effects of female hormones—a biological difference that is not modifiable by social policy. However, the extent of the male-female difference could also be due to modifiable conditions that reflect social disadvantage. It is possible that greater hardships faced by women as the result of discrimination in the workplace, exposure to sexual harassment and abuse, and so forth lessen the biological advantage they might otherwise enjoy. To the extent that this is the case, the disparity is the reduction in the "natural" female advantage. Others might argue that men face greater lifetime stresses than women and that the difference in cardiovascular diseases represents some combination of an unavoidable biological difference and a modifiable difference. However, given that, on average, men have greater social advantages than women, this would not fit the definition of a health disparity, if one assumes that only avoidable differences experienced by disadvantaged groups qualify as a disparity.

Lung cancer is an example of a disease whose patterns have grown more similar between women and men, but one would not see this as a reduction in disparities. Men once had a relatively greater prevalence of lung cancer, compared with women, than they do today. The change in the relative prevalence reflects changes in rates of smoking among men and women: Over time, as women's rate of smoking has increased, so has their rate of lung cancer. The difference in the prevalence of smoking, and the resulting difference in lung cancer rates, meet the criterion of an avoidable difference. However, the perceived fairness of this change depends upon one's explanation for the greater rates of smoking among men than women in the 20th century. Ironically, the greater social equality of women may have provided more opportunity for women to take on male risk factors, such as smoking.

The example of gender suggests that a further definition of health disparities may be useful. Even under ideal social and environmental conditions, there will be differences in rates of some diseases and in longevity due to genetic, and other biological, factors. Both individuals and groups may differ in vulnerability to specific diseases, due to this variation. Eventually, medical treatments for genetic risk may equalize individuals' capacities for a healthy lifespan. If so, failures to reach the same end point could be considered a disparity because anything less would be potentially avoidable and inequitable. Thus, disparities could be defined as the extent to which individuals, or segments of the population, fail to achieve their highest potential state of health, at a given age, given currently available medical treatments.

Current Approaches to Disparity Groups: Race/Ethnicity

Several definitions of health disparities equate disparities with differences among racial and ethnic groups. The NIH Strategic Plan Volume 1 (2002, pp. 19–20) presents data on health among several selected populations. These data are reproduced in Table D-4. They show marked differences in such diverse health indicators as infant mortality, cancer mortality, coronary heart disease mortality, and the prevalence of diabetes, end-stage renal disease, and stroke. More recent data are available from *Health, United States, 2004* (National Center for Health Statistics, 2004), recently released by the Centers for Disease Control and Prevention (CDC). Table D-5 presents the overall death rate, as well as death rates for the two leading causes of death—heart disease and malignant neoplasms. Table D-6 presents data on infant deaths.

There are two clear observations that can be made about the data presented in both of these tables. One is that African Americans show more adverse health outcomes on each one of the indicators. They have the greatest morbidity and mortality on every reported indicator, and the gap is often substantial. For example, compared with Asians or Pacific Islanders who experience 4.8 deaths for every 1,000 live births, African Americans experi-

TABLE D-4 Health Disparities of Certain Conditions in Selected Populations

	Index in Selected Populations				
Health Condition and Specific Example	White	African American	Hispanic or Latino	Asian or Pacific Islander	American Indian or Alaska Native
Infant mortality rate, per 1,000 live births	5.9	13.9	5.8	5.1	9.1
Cancer mortality rate, per 100,000	199.3	255.1	123.7	124.2	129.3
Lung cancer, age-adjusted death rate	38.3	46.0	13.6	17.2	25.1
Female breast cancer, age-adjusted death rate	18.7	26.1	12.1	9.8	10.3
Coronary heart disease mortality, rate per 100,000	206	252	145	123	126
Stroke mortality, rate per 100,000	58	80	39	51	38
Diabetes diagnosed, rate per 100,000	36	74	61	DSU	DSU
End-stage renal disease, rate per 1,000,000	218	873	DNA	344	589

NOTE: DSU, data are statistically unreliable; DNA, data have not been analyzed.
SOURCE: National Institutes of Health, 2002.

TABLE D-5 Death Rates per 100,000 by Race/Ethnicity, 2002

	White	African American	American Indian	Asian	Hispanic	Non-Hispanic White
All causes	829	1083.3	677.4	474.4	629.3	837.5
Heart disease	236.7	308.4	157.4	134.6	180.5	239.2
Malignant neoplasm	191.7	238.8	125.4	113.6	128.4	195.6

SOURCE: National Center for Health Statistics, 2004.

ence 13.6 deaths. The next highest group, American Indians or Alaskan Natives, have a rate of 8.9 deaths.

The second observation is that no other group shows consistently poor health outcomes across indicators. Whites show poorer outcomes than groups other than African Americans on most of the reported health indicators (e.g., overall cancer

TABLE D-6 Infant Deaths per 1,000 Live Births, 2000–2002, Overall by Education

Race/Ethnicity	Overall
White	5.7
Non-Hispanic white	5.7
Black	13.5
Non-Hispanic black	13.6
American Indian/Alaskan Native	8.9
Asian/Pacific Islander	4.8
Chinese	3.2
Japanese	4.5
Filipino	5.7
Hawaiian	8.7
Other	4.8
Hispanic or Latino	5.5
Mexican	5.4
Puerto Rican	8.3
Cuban	4.2
Central/South American	4.9
Other	6.7

SOURCE: National Center for Health Statistics, 2004, Tables 19 and 20.

mortality as well as death rate for breast and lung cancer, coronary heart disease and stroke mortality, and prevalence of AIDS). American Indians or Alaskan Natives have the second highest rates of infant mortality, and Hispanics or Latinos have the second highest prevalence of diabetes. Asian Americans or Pacific Islanders show the most favorable profile. They experience the lowest rates of infant mortality, overall cancer mortality and death from lung and breast cancer, and coronary heart disease mortality. They have a markedly lower prevalence of AIDS than any group other than Native Americans/Alaskan Natives. They show intermediate rates of stroke mortality and end-stage renal disease.

One problem with the conclusions reached above is that they are based on large groupings by race and ethnicity. These broad categories may mask substantial variation in health within some of the groups. Members of the same ethnic group from different countries and areas of origin have different degrees of disadvantage and health risk. For example, as shown in Table D-6, Asians/Pacific Islanders as a group have the lowest rate of infant deaths (4.8 per 1,000 births) compared with other groups. However, this masks substantial variation among Asians and Pacific Islanders. The rate for Hawaiians (8.7) is more than double that of Chinese (3.2), with intermediate rates shown by Japanese (4.5) and Filipinos (5.7). A similarly large span in outcomes is shown among Hispanics and Latinos. As a group, they show the second lowest rates of infant deaths (5.5 per

1,000 births). Within this category, however, Puerto Ricans experience 8.3 deaths, whereas Cubans experience 4.2 deaths per 1,000, with intermediate rates shown by Central and South Americans and by Mexicans. Within both whites and blacks, removal of Hispanics has little impact on rates, probably because Hispanics make up a relatively small proportion of the larger group. Recent analyses reported by Zsembik and Fennell (2005) using National Health Interview data from 1997 to 2001 compared a number of medical conditions, functional impairment, and overall self-rated health for Mexicans, Puerto Ricans, Cubans, and Dominicans in the United States along with blacks and whites. The pattern of health advantage depended, in part, on the health outcome examined; however, overall, Mexicans reported better health outcomes than others, while Puerto Ricans reported poorer outcomes. The relative position of Cubans and Dominicans differed by outcome.

Data from Palaniappan, Wang, and Fortmann (2004) also show variation in disparities when examining subgroups in relation to specific diseases. They examined rates of death from coronary heart disease and from all causes broken down into more precise subgroups of Asians. Although Asian Indians had the lowest rates of all-cause mortality, as can be seen in Table D-7, they had relatively high rates of coronary heart disease compared with other Asian groups. Among blacks as well, subgroups vary substantially. Fang, Madhavan and Alderman (1996) reported significant differences in the rates of mortality from cardiovascular disease among blacks born in different parts of the United States or in the Caribbean. Mortality rates among blacks residing in New York City were markedly higher than among those residing in the South, intermediate among those born in the Northeast, and lowest among those born in the Caribbean.

These data illustrate the importance of looking at subgroups within large ethnic categories. However, it is often difficult to obtain adequate data to evaluate health disparities in these subgroups because of their relatively small numbers. This becomes even more acute when studying smaller populations, such as those from specific countries or ethnic groups. For example, Yang, Mills, and Riordan

TABLE D-7 Mortality Ratios for Coronary Heart Disease (CHD) and All-Cause Mortality in California, 1996–2000

	Men		Women	
	All Causes	CHD	All Causes	CHD
Non-Hispanic white	107	111	109	107
Non-Hispanic black	156	124	155	160
Hispanic	75	67	70	74
Chinese	58	48	56	47
Japanese	64	60	59	46
Asian Indian	53	92	59	97

SOURCE: Palaniappan et al., 2004.

(2004) reported markedly higher incidence rates and mortality from cervical cancer among Hmong women than among other Asians/Pacific Islanders, and Cho and Hummer (2001) reported substantial variations in disability status among subpopulations of Asians/Pacific Islanders, with the Hmong, Laotians, and Cambodians showing the poorest outcomes. These groups differ by SES, as well. For example, within the Asian immigrant group, more than 60 percent of those from India or Taiwan are college graduates, compared with roughly 5 percent of those from Cambodia or Laos (Rumbaut, 1996). Even within a given group, subpopulations may experience greater disadvantage and poorer health (e.g., Native Americans living on reservations versus other Native Americans).

Further complicating ethnic group differences in health, health status appears to vary by length of time in the United States. First-generation immigrants appear to have a health advantage across virtually every group (Singh and Miller, 2004). This may be due, in part, to the *healthy immigrant* effect, in which there is differential selection for those who have the characteristics (including better health) that allows them to immigrate to the United States (Thomas and Karagas, 1996). It may also reflect protective effects of traditional diets, supportive social networks, or other health practices of first-generation immigrants. Supporting this view, Eschbach, Ostir, Patel, Markides, and Goodwin (2004) report lower mortality among older Mexican Americans living in neighborhoods with a high density of Mexican Americans. They attributed this difference to the protective effects of the concentration, which may buffer Mexican Americans from "unhealthful aspects of U.S. culture" (Eschbach et al., 2004, p. 1810).

Finally, as shown in recent analyses by Williams (2005), the extent of disparities also varies depending on the measure used. Disparities will differ not only between different diseases, but also within mortality rates, depending on the measure. For example, Williams showed greater disparities between African Americans and whites when age-specific comparisons were made, rather than age-adjusted comparisons. Looking at age-specific rates also shows differences that occur only at some points across the lifespan.

The approach to disparities suggested earlier—which frames disparity as the gap between current health status and biologically feasible health—suggests a strategy of using the group with the best health outcome as the comparison group. This group presumably represents the highest achievable outcome under current social and health care conditions, though one would need to evaluate potential genetic factors. Research could then be directed to understanding the other factors responsible for the gap between the optimal outcome and the groups with the poorest outcomes. These may be disease-specific mechanisms. At the same time, the large, persistent, and consistent disadvantage suffered by African Americans across diseases suggests that some common mechanisms systematically affect this group's health. It also suggests that more attention should be paid to cross-cutting factors that systematically affect African Americans' health. Potential factors are described below.

Current Approaches to Disparity Groups: SES

Early research on socioeconomic factors and health tended to report health outcomes of those in poverty versus those above the poverty line. In the past two decades, research has increasingly examined health differences across the full socioeconomic spectrum. The shift in perspective was stimulated by data from the Whitehall Study of British civil servants (Marmot et al., 1978). These data demonstrated a *graded* association of occupational grade and 10-year mortality. Even within this relatively homogenous group of individuals, all of whom were employed, higher occupational grade conferred a lower risk for a range of diseases and for subsequent mortality.

Challenged by findings from the Whitehall Study, researchers began to evaluate the patterning of health disparities by socioeconomic variables beyond the bivariate association with poverty or nonpoverty (and even beyond the categorization into poor, near poor, and nonpoor). Data to evaluate whether a similar SES-health gradient occurred in the United States were difficult to find, as most public health monitoring and epidemiologic surveys provide data on race and ethnicity but not on income; many sources do not even include education. Those that collected or reported data on income were often coded only in terms of being above or below the poverty line.

The research that has been done on a broader SES spectrum has generally shown a graded, but nonlinear, association between income and mortality. Data on income and mortality from the National Longitudinal Mortality Study reported by Backlund, Sorlie, and Johnson (1999) were best characterized by a two-slope model, with a sharp drop in mortality as income increased from $2,500 a year to $22,500 (in 1980 dollars) and a continued but more gradual drop above that income level up to $57,500—the highest income level reported. The graphic representation of the association of income and mortality provided by Wolfson, Kaplan, Lynch, Ross, and Backlund (1999) shown in Figure D-1 similarly shows a steeper drop in the relative risk of mortality as income increases at the lower part of the income distribution. Superimposed on the graph of the relative risk of mortality is a graph showing the population distribution. A relatively small proportion of the U.S. population is at the very bottom of the income distribution, where the steepest drop occurs. Most of the population resides in the distribution between about $15,000 and $40,000 of income, which is above the poverty line. Thus, if one limited research to those below the poverty line as a disparity group, such research would not incorporate an understanding of the largest segment of the population in which disparities occur. There is a continued drop in the relative risk of mortality even above $50,000, but it is much shallower and encompasses a smaller portion of the population.

These data suggest the difficulty in defining a disparity group by income. In terms of individual need and alleviating the most extreme disparity, those in poverty should be the focus. At the same time, a much higher proportion of the

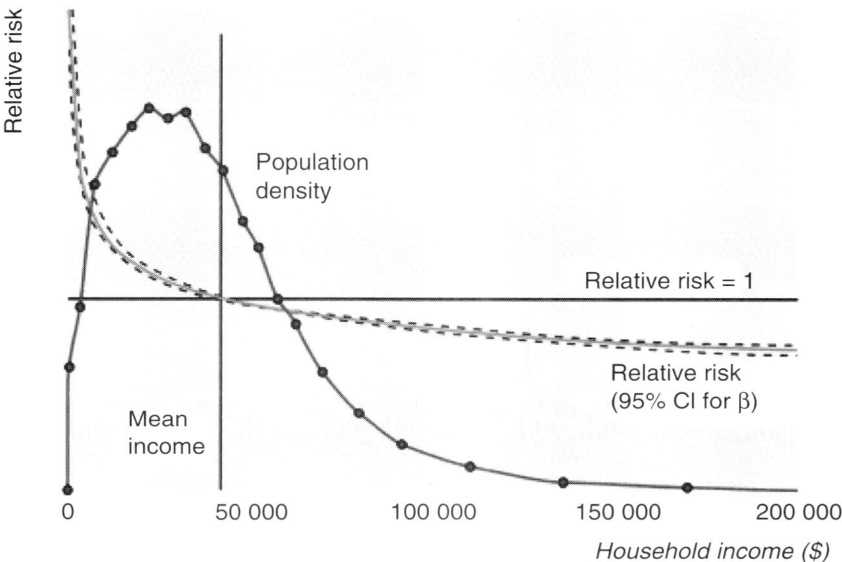

FIGURE D-1 Relative risk of dying and population distribution for U.S. individuals by household income ($). SOURCE: Wolfson et al., 1999.

population is above the poverty line, yet experiences higher mortality than those who are relatively more affluent, and attention must also be paid to this broader segment. Given that the increased burden is greatest among those in the bottom 30 to 40 percent of the income distribution, this segment of the population should be of particular concern.

One caveat about these data is that they were collected more than 15 years ago, so the absolute levels of income will have a different meaning. In addition, the distribution of income has changed over time, with increasing income inequality. There is debate in the field regarding whether absolute versus relative income is more important for health and whether the distribution of income across the population has an additional impact. Studies have shown that greater income inequality at the level of states (Kaplan et al., 1996; Kennedy et al., 1996) and countries (Wilkinson, 1996) is associated with higher mortality. These data are at the population level, and it may be that such inequality adversely affects the health of the entire population. It may also be that greater income inequality has a proportionately greater impact on those at the bottom of the income hierarchy, though the empirical work on this is inconclusive. More recent data suggest that the association between income inequality and health may occur in the United States, but to a lesser extent in other countries, and may vary by time period.

TABLE D-8 Age-Adjusted Death Rates per 100,000 by Educational Level (Age 25–64), 2002

	< 12	12	13+
All causes	575.1	490.9	211.3
Chronic/noncommunicable diseases	432.0	374.4	168.6
Injuries	99.2	84.9	32.1
Communicable diseases	42.7	30.5	10.2
HIV	18.2	12.6	3.8
Other	24.5	17.9	6.4

SOURCE: National Center for Health Statistics, 2004, Table 34.

In contrast with income, which shows a continued drop in mortality as income increases (though with a much sharper drop in the lower portion of the distribution), the associations of mortality with education are less continuous. Table D-8 provides information on death rates for those who did not graduate from high school (< 12 years), high school graduates (12 years), and those with some post-secondary education (13+ years). For all-cause mortality and for each of the specific causes, the death rates are lower for those with more education. The gap is larger between high school graduates and those with some post-secondary education. The latter are a mixed group, as some have a college and/or advanced degree and others have either some post-secondary education but no degree or have earned an associate's degree. Other research shows differences between those with some post-secondary education versus those with a bachelor's degree and also, for white men, between those with a bachelor's degree versus those with advanced degrees. The health benefit of an advanced degree versus a college degree, however, may be less for African American men and women and for white women, consistent with lower social and economic returns on education.

Education provides a mixture of resources. To the extent that education provides information, knowledge, and skills that improve health, each additional year of education should contribute somewhat equally to improved health. However, educational attainment also serves as a credentialing function. As a result, there will be a greater benefit for achieving years of schooling that result in a degree or credential than for additional years that do not. Thus, the benefits of completing the 12th year of schooling that results in a high school degree is greater than the benefit of the 10th or 11th year of schooling. This is referred to as the sheepskin effect.

There may also be some effect due to the personality traits of those who complete their schooling. Conscientiousness, for example, has been linked to greater longevity (e.g., Friedman et al., 1995). Those who are more conscientious may exhibit this trait both in relation to their schooling (leading to greater attainment) and in relation to their health. Similarly, as Victor Fuchs has suggested, those who are willing to delay gratification to invest in their schooling to obtain a degree may do the same in relation to their health. These are not mutually exclusive explanations to the sheepskin effect, as both may be operating and contribute to the discontinuous effect of education at credentialing milestones. Yet another explanation for the association of education and health is that social networking (and associated social norms) change as one moves on to the next level of education.

The empirical data are consistent with the hypothesis that education confers benefits due to credentialing and/or due to the related characteristics associated with completion, rather than simply due to knowledge accumulation or social norms. Figure D-2 from Backlund et al. (1999) shows that for both men and

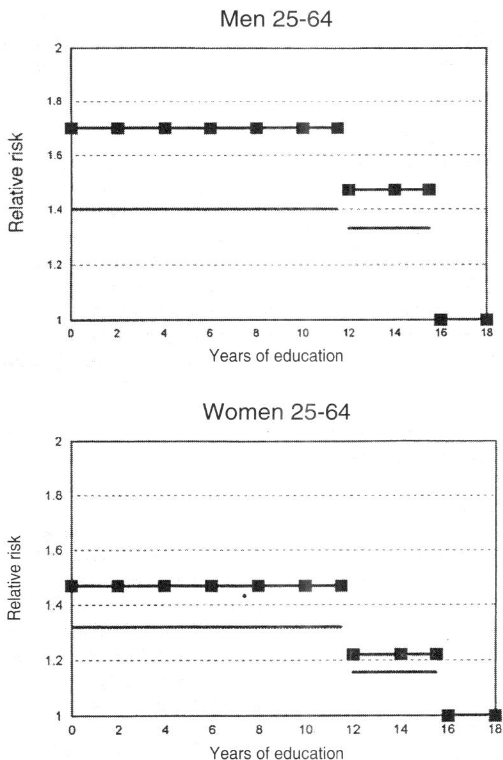

FIGURE D-2 Predicted relative risks using the best-fitting models for education and income for men and women aged 25–64. Solid line with squares adjusted for demographic variables. Solid line adjusted for socioeconomic status and demographic variables. SOURCE: Backlund et al., 1999.

women, the relative risk of mortality is essentially flat for those with 11 years or less of education, drops for those who are high school graduates, and remains unchanged until 16 years of schooling, which indicates college graduation, at which point there is another drop in mortality.

Current Approaches to Disparity Groups: Rural Health

Those who live in rural areas show more adverse health outcomes than those in metropolitan areas. Hartley (2004) noted that in the *Urban and Rural Health Chartbook* (National Center for Health Statistics, 2001), populations in rural areas showed poorer outcomes on 21 of the 23 health indicators, including mortality. *Health, United States, 2004* (National Center for Health Statistics, 2004) provides more recent data on mortality by level of urbanization, as well as by region. As can be seen in Table D-9, the age-adjusted death rate increases as urbanization decreases. The highest death rate (914.3) is in nonmetropolitan areas, while the lowest (833.1) is in large metropolitan areas. When broken down by race, this pattern holds for whites. For African Americans, however, death rates are less different across levels of urbanization, although they are still higher in non-metropolitan than in medium or large metropolitan areas. There are differences in health indicators such as self-rated health and limitation of activity by residence area. In relation to the former, 8.7 percent of those residing within a metropolitan area report being in fair or poor health compared with 11.7 percent of those outside a metropolitan area. Similarly, 11.4 percent of those in metropolitan areas report experiencing a limitation of activity due to a chronic condition, compared with 15.9 percent of those outside a metropolitan area.

Death from injury and suicide are more common in rural areas. Figure D-3, taken from Peek-Asa, Zwerling, and Stallones (2004), shows the mortality rate from unintentional injuries for three types of metropolitan areas and two types of nonmetropolitan areas. The highest rate occurs in the most rural settings (i.e., nonmetropolitan areas without a city). The next highest rate occurs in non-

TABLE D-9 Age-Adjusted Death Rates by Region and Level of Urbanization, 2000–2002

	All	White	Black
Metropolitan			
Large	833.1	813.0	1079.3
Medium	844.6	829.1	1114.9
Small	875.1	856.4	1153.4
Nonmetropolitan			
Micropolitan	897.7	880.7	1158.7
Nonmicropolitan	914.3	894.2	1149.4

SOURCE: National Center for Health Statistics, 2004, Table 33.

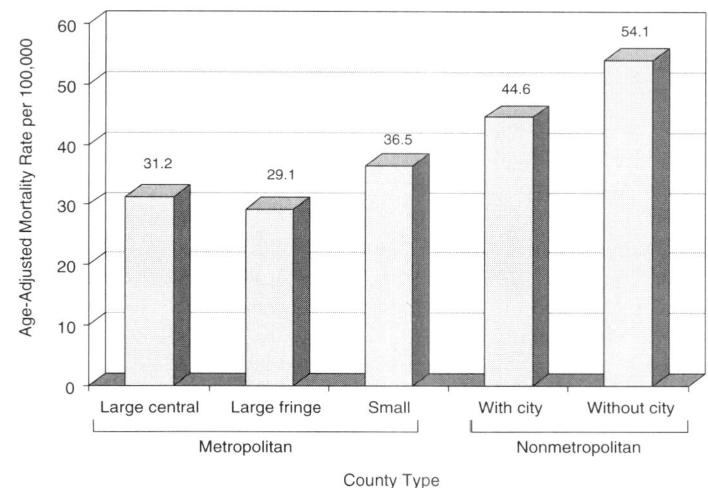

FIGURE D-3 Unintentional traumatic injury death rates, by urbanization level: United States, 1996–1998. SOURCE: Peek-Asa et al., 2004.

metropolitan areas with a city, followed by small metropolitan areas. Importantly, the death rate in large fringe areas is somewhat lower than in large central cities. A similar pattern was reported by Eberhardt and Pamuk (2004) for mortality rates for suicide and for a range of risk factors (e.g., smoking, limitation of activity, and obesity). The difference between the central city and the large fringe was particularly great for sedentary activity during leisure, with rates in the central city second only to the most rural area.

Consistent with the data presented above, Hartley (2004) noted that because suburban counties show the most positive health profiles, with better health status than either the rural areas or urban centers, finer differentiations than simply urban and rural should be made. This is the case for some indicators but not for others. On some health indicators, suburban areas show an intermediate level of health between urban and rural (e.g., Weeks et al., 2004).

In addition to differences by degree of urbanicity or rurality, health status differs by geographic region. Tables D-10 and D-11 show rates of poor/fair self-rated health and limitations of activity, respectively, for different groups. As described above, there are differences between those within or outside a metropolitan area, but there are also regional differences. A greater proportion of those living in the South than in other regions report poor or fair health, whereas more in the Midwest report a limitation of activity due to chronic conditions, compared with other regions. There is no cross-reference for rural/urban status by geographic area. One confounding factor is that some areas of the country are

TABLE D-10 Self-Rated Health: Percent Reporting Fair or Poor Health, 2002, by Race/Ethnicity and Geographic Locale

	All	Poor	Near Poor	Nonpoor
White, all	8.6			
Non-Hispanic white	8.2	19.1	14.3	6.0
African American	14.1			
Non-Hispanic African American	14.0	24.5	17.4	8.8
American Indian/Alaskan Native	13.1			
Asian	6.7			
Hispanic, Latino	13.1	20.9	15.4	8.7
All	9.3	20.4	14.6	6.4

Residence	Within MSA	Outside MSA
Urban/rural	8.7	11.7
Area of country		
Northeast	8.1	
Midwest	8.3	
South	10.9	
West	8.7	

NOTE: MSA, metropolitan statistical area.

SOURCE: National Center for Health Statistics, 2004, Table 57.

TABLE D-11 Limitation of Activity Due to Chronic Conditions, 2002, by Race/Ethnicity and Geographic Locale

	Percent with Any Activity Limited			
	All	Poor	Near Poor	Nonpoor
White, all	12.1			
Non-Hispanic white	12.4	25.3	19.5	9.7
African American	14.9			
Non-Hispanic African American	15.0	25.0	17.9	10.0
American Indian	19.4			
Asian	6.4			
Hispanic, Latino	10.7	16.4	12.2	7.7
Total	12.4	22.9	17.5	9.5

Residence	Within MSA	Outside MSA
Urban/rural	11.4	15.9
Area of country		
Northeast	11.8	
Midwest	13.1	
South	12.7	
West	11.5	

NOTE: MSA, metropolitan statistical area.

SOURCE: National Center for Health Statistics, 2004.

more rural than others, so geographic differences may, in part, be due to the degree of rural residence. Additionally, the conditions of rural life may differ in various parts of the country. Rural areas may differ in terms of physical environments such as water quality, the type of agriculture, and even the built environment. Rural residents also vary in sociodemographic characteristics.

Interaction Among Factors Associated with Disparities

The sections above present data showing health disparities by race and ethnicity, education, income, and rural/urban residence. However, these characteristics of individuals and groups do not exist in isolation. Groups that are disadvantaged in one domain of life are often disadvantaged in others.

The interconnections among different factors associated with health disparities are clearest in the overlap of race/ethnicity with SES. Both African Americans and Hispanics are overrepresented in lower-SES categories. Data from the 2000 census summarized in Table D-12 show that 49 to 50 percent of Hispanics and 26 to 30 percent of African Americans have less than a high school education, compared with 13 to 14 percent of whites. Differences by gender in education are greater for Asians than for the other groups. Table D-13 shows the differences in median income, ranging from $29,645 for African Americans to $47,777 for whites; the differences in wealth are even more dramatic.

For some health outcomes, differences between African Americans and whites become insignificant once income is controlled for (Haan and Kaplan, 1985). For other health outcomes, although the difference between groups is substantially reduced, a residual effect associated with race/ethnicity remains. Whether this residual effect reflects poor measurement of economic status or the importance of other factors is unknown. The residual effect is particularly strong for birth outcomes. Data presented in Table D-14 show life expectancy at age 25 for U.S. males by race and income (Lin et al., 2003). The data show that the overall difference in life expectancy is greater by SES than by race: There is a 4.4-year difference between blacks and whites, compared with a 7.9-year and 8.6-year difference between those earning less than $10,000 and those earning more than $25,000 within whites and blacks, respectively. Although the data show that the gap between races diminishes slightly with higher incomes, a difference between whites and blacks remains at each income level. Some part of this difference may have to do with other socioeconomic differences between blacks and whites not captured by household income. At each level of income, for example, African Americans and Hispanics have lower net worth and live in worse neighborhoods than whites. For example, among the lowest quintile of income, whites have a net worth of almost $50,000, whereas the net worth of African Americans and Hispanics is a little more than $7000. Thus, controlling for income will not adequately control for differences in wealth.

TABLE D-12 Education by Gender and Race/Ethnicity

Level of Education	Men				Women			
	White	African American	Asian	Hispanic	White	African American	Asian	Hispanic
< HS	14%	30%	18%	50%	13%	26%	26%	49%
HS	27%	30%	15%	19%	32%	30%	19%	22%
Some/all AA	28%	26%	21%	19%	30%	28%	19%	19%
BA	17%	8%	25%	7%	14%	9%	25%	6%
Grad	14%	6%	21%	5%	11%	7%	11%	4%

NOTE: HS, high school; AA, associate's degree; BS, bachelor's degree; Grad, graduate school.

SOURCE: U.S. Census Bureau, 2000, Summary File 4.

TABLE D-13 Median Income by Racial/Ethnic Group

Households	Median Income (Dollars)
Non-Hispanic white	47,777
Non-Hispanic black	29,645
Asian	55,699
Hispanic	32,997

SOURCE: DeNavas-Walt et al., 2004.

The meaning of specific indicators of SES may differ across groups, and it may be fruitful to examine SES effects within groups. In addition to the problems of equating the implications of a given income across groups as discussed above, the meaning of educational attainment may vary as well. This is most problematic for groups that have received their education in other countries, with different educational systems and levels of accreditation. Even within the United States, a given level of educational attainment may not confer the same resources and advantages, due to differences in the quality of the schooling. High school graduates from underfunded inner-city schools do not have the same opportunities as graduates of more affluent suburban schools or private schools. Due to residential segregation and local funding of schools, African Americans are especially likely to experience poor-quality schooling. As a result, the economic and health benefits of high school graduation may be diminished.

The data presented above suggest that one cannot adequately study racial and ethnic disparities in health without considering socioeconomic factors and vice versa. Similarly, race/ethnicity and SES need to be considered in evaluating disparities in rural and urban health. Probst, Moore, Glover, and Samuels (2004) noted that generalizations about rural health largely capture the experience and outcomes of whites, because whites make up 84 percent of rural populations, African Americans comprise 8 percent, nonblack Hispanics comprise 5 percent, and Asians/Pacific Islanders and American Indians/Native Alaskans comprise less than 2 percent each. There are differences in racial/ethnic composition of

TABLE D-14 Life Expectancy at Age 25, U.S. Men: Race and Income Differences

Income in 1980	White	Black	Race Difference
All	50.1	45.7	4.4
Less than $10,000	45.0	41.6	3.4
$10,000–$24,999	50.2	47.4	2.8
$25,000 or more	52.9	50.2	2.7
Socioeconomic status difference	7.9	8.6	

SOURCE: Lin et al., 2003.

rural populations in different regions of the country. Rural African Americans are predominantly in the South, and of these, half are living in Mississippi, Georgia, and North and South Carolina. In contrast, rural Hispanics are living primarily in the West, with over one quarter of rural Hispanics in Texas alone (Probst et al., 2004).

Conclusions about the nature of disparities may differ if one looks at characteristics individually rather than in conjunction with associated factors. For example, Coughlin (2002) presented a deeper analysis of a finding of lower rates of cancer screening for African Americans versus whites in the overall population. They broke down the overall rates to look at rates in three different types of counties: black counties in the South, other counties in South, and all other counties in United States. In this analysis, they found no differences by race within each of those categories; the differences by race were due to the different distribution of populations across the three types of counties.

Similarly, Probst et al. (2004) noted that "health issues among rural racial/ethnic minorities cannot be separated from educational and economic issues" (p. 1697). As shown in Table D-15, there are substantial differences in educational attainment by both race/ethnicity and area of residence. Of working-age adults, 40 percent of African Americans in rural areas lack a high school diploma, compared with 19 percent in urban areas; comparable figures are 50 percent and 42 percent for Hispanics and 15 percent and 9 percent for whites in rural versus urban areas. Differences are less marked among older adults, for whom a lack of high school graduation was more common, and show smaller discrepancies by

TABLE D-15 Socioeconomic Profile of Urban and Rural African Americans, Hispanics, and Whites

		Group		
	Geographic Locale	African American	Hispanic	White
Percentage of working-age[a] adults lacking a high school diploma (1999–2000)	Rural	40	50	15
	Urban	19	42	9
Percentage of older[b] adults lacking a high school diploma (1997–1998)	Rural	76	81	39
	Urban	54	67	28
Percentage in low-paying occupations[c]	Rural	68	62	43
	Urban	47	57	28

SOURCE: Probst et al., 2004.

[a]Persons between the ages of 18 and 64.

[b]Persons aged 65 and over.

[c]These are occupations in which the worker has a relatively high likelihood of remaining in poverty.

either race/ethnicity or rural/urban residence. Rural residence is also associated with an increased likelihood of being in a low-paying job. The increased likelihood holds for all three ethnic groups, although the difference between urban and rural rates is less for Hispanics than for whites or African Americans. Given the predominance of whites in rural areas, the data suggest that to understand the relatively poorer health outcomes of whites compared with other groups on some health indicators, area of residence should be examined.

Gender

Considerable literature exists on gender and health. As discussed earlier, the comparisons by gender are complex, reflecting both biological and social differences. A review of this area is beyond the scope of this review. However, it is important to note that health disparities associated with race/ethnicity, SES, and rural residence may differ by gender. As with race and ethnicity, the actual meaning of these variables may differ for men and women. Women's status may be determined more by a husband's socioeconomic characteristics than vice versa so that household, rather than personal, income may be particularly salient for women. Women's roles differ in various ethnic groups, so gender differences may vary by ethnicity, as well. As will be seen in the section on conceptual models below, most portray gender as a modifying factor in the pathways linking socioeconomic factors with health.

MOVING BEYOND DOCUMENTATION TO UNDERSTANDING HEALTH DISPARITIES

Healthy People 2010 (U.S. Department of Health and Human Services, 2000) defined two goals: (a) to increase the quality and years of healthy life and (b) to eliminate health disparities. The analysis presented above suggests that these two goals are closely linked. Perhaps the most effective way, on a population level, to increase quality and years of healthy life is to improve these among the groups who are farthest away from maximal health and longevity (though this will also depend on the relative size of the group). The data discussed above provide evidence for how far society must go to achieve the second goal. As a public health function, it will be important to continue to monitor the nature and degree of disparities. Such monitoring is essential to evaluating how well we are doing in achieving the *Healthy People 2010* goals.

One important role for NIH-funded research in this domain is to develop the best measures and approaches for assessing and monitoring disparities for public health monitoring activities, as well as ongoing surveys. This requires research on: what needs to be monitored (e.g., socioeconomic factors, gender, race/ethnicity, and area of residence), how these can best be measured (e.g., meaningful measures of SES for specific populations, diseases, and questions), and which factors are most critical to monitor (e.g., the importance of measuring race/ethnicity and SES together). Such data will, in turn, be an important source for research on disparities.

A second important domain of NIH-funded research is to move beyond monitoring disparities to understanding their cause. If we hope to eliminate disparities, this knowledge is crucial. We need to understand the pathways and mechanisms by which health disparities occur. The current literature in health disparities has moved from the initial work that largely documented the existence of disparities to research that attempts to understand underlying mechanisms. Below, I discuss approaches and conceptual models that guide this work and the variables that are commonly identified as important pathways.

Approaches to Understanding Causes of Health Disparities

One approach to understanding health disparities is to examine them in light of what is known more generally about determinants of health. It is logical to assume that health disparities operate through factors that determine health. The following discussion is organized around the categories of determinants first discussed by Lee and Paxman (1997) and updated by McGinnis, Williams-Russo, and Knickman (2002). Based on analyses from the CDC, they present the relative contribution of a range of factors to premature mortality. Sociodemographic factors including SES, race/ethnicity, gender, and area of residence were not evaluated. Rather, they represent more proximal determinants that may mediate the impact of the sociodemographic variables on health. The factors are health care deficiencies, genetic vulnerabilities, social environment, physical environment, and behavior and lifestyle.

Health Care

Health care is not the most important determinant of either health or health disparities, but it is the most salient. In the United States today, virtually all the discussion about health is linked to health care. The problems of the uninsured and lack of access to quality care are serious. More than 45 million Americans lack health insurance. African Americans and other disadvantaged racial and ethnic groups; individuals with less education, income, and in low-wage occupations; and those in rural areas are less likely to have health insurance, have poorer access to health care, and receive poorer quality of care. Recent reports such as *Unequal Treatment: Confronting Racial and Ethnic Disparities in Healthcare* (Smedley et al., 2003) and the *National Healthcare Disparities Report* (U.S. Department of Health and Human Services, 2003) document the existence of disparities in health care that result in differences in the effectiveness and quality of care received by members of racial and ethnic minority groups, even when they do have access to care. Although not studied as extensively, disparities in access and care are also likely important for the poor and residents of both rural locations and disadvantaged neighborhoods.

The recommendations provided in *Unequal Treatment* (Smedley et al., 2003), if implemented, would contribute to reducing health disparities, but they would be insufficient to eliminate them. While crucial, health care is estimated to account for only 10 percent of premature mortality. Health disparities exist in countries in which there is universal coverage (though actual use and quality may differ for the more and less advantaged). Moreover, disparities in mortality occur both from diseases lacking effective treatment and those with more effective treatment. Perhaps most importantly, disparities emerge in the incidence of disease and not simply in the associated mortality. For diseases in which early detection significantly slows disease progression and mortality, differential access and the quality of secondary prevention will account for some degree of health disparities. However, given that most health care systems do relatively little in terms of primary prevention, differences associated with health care may have little impact on the onset of disease. In this case, other determinants play a relatively larger role.

Genetic Factors

Although relatively few disorders are due solely to genetic factors, many diseases have a genetic component. It is unlikely that genetic factors themselves account for health disparities (other than those associated with sex differences). In some instances, differences between racial or ethnic groups have been attributed to genetic differences, but there is little data documenting such differences. For example, in the United States, African Americans are more likely to be hypertensive than are European Americans—a difference that has sometimes been thought to reflect a genetic predisposition to hypertension among African Americans. If this were the case, one would expect to find a greater prevalence of hypertension among populations for blacks compared with European Americans wherever they lived. Given the greater homogeneity of the gene pool in Africa than among African Americans in the United States, one might also expect a higher prevalence of hypertension in Africa than among African Americans. However, Cooper et al. (1997) showed that the opposite is true. The prevalence of hypertension was 16 percent in West Africa, 26 percent among blacks in the Caribbean, and 33 percent among blacks in the United States. These data suggest that social, more than genetic, factors are responsible for the elevated rates in the United States.

Rather than simply search for genes that can explain disparities between groups, it will be important to consider how genetic predispositions interact with environmental factors associated with sociodemographic factors to influence health. Those who experience a greater disadvantage, whether due to their race and ethnicity, SES, sex, or area of residence, are exposed to different physical and social environments. These environments can, in turn, affect gene expression and subsequent vulnerability to disease. The difference in this approach can be seen by taking the example of obesity. A risk factor for a variety of diseases and for premature mortality, obesity is more common in more disadvantaged groups. Genetic factors play a role in obesity, but it is unlikely that the genetic predisposition to obesity is the sole explanation for these differences. Only about 6 percent of obesity is attributable to a single gene. The rest is likely to be due to polygenomic factors, environmental factors, and/or the interaction of genetic and environmental factors. The explosion in the prevalence of obesity has occurred in a relatively short amount of time, during which time genes in the population cannot have changed by a substantial amount. Rather, as we know for other genetic factors, the interaction between genes and environment is crucial. With regard to obesity, it is likely that the interaction of the genes with environments that encourage overconsumption of energy-dense foods and discourage energy expenditure, in the form of exercise, will result in obesity. These environments vary by social disadvantage, as discussed below.

Environmental Factors

There are several types of environmental factors that affect health risk. One is exposure to traditional sources of health risks, including toxins, pathogens, and carcinogens. The second is the built environment. The third is the social environment. Each is discussed below.

Environmental exposures. Exposure to toxins, pathogens, and carcinogens, as well as physical hazards, is not randomly determined. As has been documented by those in the environmental justice movement, minority communities and poor communities are disproportionately exposed to health-damaging environments. Such communities are in closer proximity to toxic dumpsites and industrial plants as well as highways with their resultant car emissions. Low-skill occupations in which less-educated people and people of color are overrepresented often involve more physical risk and exposure to chemicals, heat, and noise. In rural areas, farm workers are exposed to pesticides in their work, and the children of these families also have a higher risk of exposure.

Some environmental exposures result from the built environment. In urban areas, residential segregation has resulted in African Americans being concentrated in high-poverty areas with substandard housing. Rates of exposure to lead in paint are higher, thereby leading to dramatic differences in blood lead levels. For example, individuals (both children and adults) from poor families have a 6-fold higher rate of blood lead levels than those from high-income families. Middle-income families also show an elevated rate (about double) compared with high-income families but substantially less than low-income families (Pamuk et al., 1998).

Environmental exposures probably do not account for a substantial degree of premature mortality, but they may contribute more to morbidity. The increasing rate of childhood asthma among poor children in the inner cities may, in part, be due to environmental exposure related to the deterioration of housing stock in areas of concentrated poverty (Claudio et al., 1999). The morbidity associated with asthma may reduce later socioeconomic attainment. To the extent that children with asthma miss school, school achievement may be adversely affected, and opportunities for higher education that can lead to higher income jobs may be reduced. This may be especially true for children from less-advantaged families who may find the management of asthma more challenging.

Built environment. In addition to a differential risk of direct exposure to chemical and other substances, disadvantaged individuals and groups also have greater exposure to crowding and noise. These factors may also not be major causes of mortality, but they may increase risk factors such as hypertension (Evans, 2001) as well as adversely affect children's cognitive performance, which, in turn, affects academic achievement (Evans and Lepore, 1992). Perhaps more importantly, the built environment can constrain exercise and reduce access to healthy foods and health-promoting behaviors. Low-income neighborhoods are less likely to have recreational facilities, safe places to walk, and access to well-stocked grocery stores, and they provide easier access to fast-food outlets and liquor stores (Morland et al., 2002). This will be discussed in more detail below.

Social environment. Two aspects of the social environment are relevant for understanding health disparities. The first is social connectedness. Studied in a variety of ways, social cohesion and connectedness are shown to be important for health. At the negative end, a number of studies illustrate the health risks of social isolation: The data show that the relative risks of mortality for the socially isolated range from 1.9 to 4 times greater than that for individuals who have greater social connections (Berkman and Glass, 2000; House et al., 1988).

The clearest example of the danger of social isolation comes from the 1995 heat wave in Chicago, in which 739 people died. The most vulnerable were poor elderly individuals living alone without air conditioning in neighborhoods that provided little social support. Afraid to leave their apartments, they succumbed to the extraordinary heat in their homes (Klinenberg, 2002).

Such events, although dramatic, do not account for the large relative risk of mortality associated with social isolation. Rather, the salutary effects of social connections may operate in a number of ways to affect health. For example, individuals with more social connections and social support may be better able to mobilize necessary resources to deal with problems and threats. This ability not only acts to buffer the effects of stress exposure (discussed below) but also can provide specific benefits that reduce health risk. These benefits include access to greater knowledge from others about health issues (ranging from information on health promotion to information about the skills of a doctor). Those living in areas of concentrated poverty (especially those in high-rise housing developments where social organization and community-building has been particularly challenging) or in sparsely populated rural areas have less opportunity to develop extended social networks that can provide such benefits.

Berkman and Glass (2000) provided a conceptual model of the various ways in which social networks affect health and suggested how these may mediate the association of race/ethnicity, gender, and SES on health. The mezzo level of social networks and social ties is shaped by macro social-structural conditions, which include racism and sexism, as well as socioeconomic factors. Various aspects of social networks and ties, in turn, affect psychosocial mechanisms, which then affect health through behavioral, psychological, and physiological pathways. Their model is consistent with those explaining social determinants of health or explaining how race/ethnicity and/or SES affect health (described in the next section).

At the community level, communities with greater social cohesion appear to be healthier places to live. Significant studies illustrate the health benefits of greater social capital in communities (Kawachi and Berkman, 2000). Those communities with greater social capital (generally defined as greater interpersonal trust and interaction) have lower morbidity and mortality. Greater social capital may foster health-promoting behaviors, provide support, reduce stress, and increase access to health-related goods and services. Communities with greater social capital may be more willing to invest in common goods (e.g., parks and other recreational facilities, community health care, and libraries) that will benefit everyone's health but that may be especially beneficial for the more disadvantaged, who would otherwise have more limited access to such facilities. However, social capital could be a two-edged sword in communities with concentrated poverty. The web of mutual social obligations, while beneficial to some, may place substantial demands on others. Nonetheless, those communities with greater social capital do appear overall to be healthier.

A related concept to social capital is collective efficacy (Cohen, Farley, and Mason, 2003; Cohen, Mason, et al., 2003; Kawachi and Berkman, 2000; Sampson et al., 1997). This is the sense of neighborhood residents that they can address social problems and threats (e.g., fight the closing of a fire house, look after lost children). The original research showing that neighborhoods with greater collective efficacy have lower rates of homicide (Sampson et al., 1997) has been extended. Lochner et al. (2003) showed that higher levels of neighborhood capital (reciprocity, trust, and civic participation) were associated with lower neighborhood death rates for total mortality, as well as death from heart disease and other causes for white men and women, and to a less consistent extent for African Americans (though no association was found with cancer deaths). Collective efficacy and social capital appear to contribute to health even when neighborhood SES is controlled for. However, more advantaged communities are also more likely to have greater social capital and collective efficacy, thus accounting for some part of health disparities.

Discrimination is a second aspect of the social environment relevant to health disparities associated with race and ethnicity. Racism and the history of discrimination in the United States have consequences in many domains of life that affect health for African Americans and may account for the findings that this group shows poorer health on nearly every indicator. One effect of racism and discrimination has been limited educational, occupational, and economic opportunities that contribute to the overrepresentation of African Americans in lower-SES categories. In addition, zoning and housing policies that have resulted in the development of predominantly poor African American neighborhoods bring a set of associated health problems (Williams and Collins, 2001). For example, the transmission of sexually transmitted diseases, including HIV/AIDS, is more rapid for individuals in high-risk sexual networks. Such networks are more common in areas of concentrated poverty. The same may be true for other communicable diseases.

In addition to the indirect effects on health of discrimination through social and economic pathways and associated exposures, some research suggests that the experience of discrimination may itself be detrimental to health (Guyll et al., 2001; Harrell et al., 2003; Krieger and Sidney, 1996). The associations are complex, however, suggesting that it is not just exposure, but also responses to that exposure, that have health consequences. One approach to understanding how experiences of discrimination affect health is to apply the theories and knowledge about more general stress exposure. The research on stress and health has shown that the ways in which individuals cope with the threat implicit in a stressor are key to determining the resultant health risk (Harrell et al., 2003). Current research on how best to measure experiences of discrimination should add to our understanding of this socially based risk factor for African Americans (Hill et al., 2004). Far less is known about the experiences of discrimination for other groups and the implications for their health.

Health Behaviors

According to the CDC's analysis, the single category of factors that contribute most to premature mortality is health behavior and lifestyle, estimated to account for 40 to 50 percent of premature mortality. On virtually every risk factor, one finds differences by SES and, to a lesser extent, by race/ethnicity.

The two greatest risk factors in this domain are tobacco use and obesity. Smoking is more common among those with less education and less income (Pierce et al., 1989), though it has not always been so. The most recent data from *Health, United States, 2004* (National Center for Health Statistics, 2004), shown in Table D-16, shows a marked effect of education. Rates of smoking are more than 3 times higher among those with less than a high school education, com-

TABLE D-16 Percentage Smokers, 2002

Level of Education	White Males	Black Males	White Females	Black Females
< HS	36.2	37.2	29.5	27.1
HS/GED	31.2	31.3	26.9	19.5
Some college	23.4	25.6	20.6	20.7
BA+	11.1	10.8*	9.7	7.7*
All	23.5	27.2	20.3	18.4

NOTE: HS, high school; GED, General Equivalency Diploma; BA, bachelor's degree.

*Estimates may be unreliable; relative standard error of 20–30%.

SOURCE: National Center for Health Statistics, 2004, Table 61.

pared with those who have graduated from college. The drop-off in rates of smoking is most marked between those with some college and those who graduate from college; the latter have smoking rates that are less than half those of the former. Smoking rates do not differ substantially between African Americans and whites; at most educational levels, rates are slightly higher for whites. Thus, although tobacco use may serve as an important mechanism in disparities associated with SES, it does not appear to be a major contributor to the relatively poorer health of African Americans.

Rates of obesity show a very different pattern, varying both by race/ethnicity, SES, and gender. As seen in Table D-17, in 2001, 31.1 percent of blacks and 23.7 percent of Hispanics were obese compared with 19.6 percent of non-Hispanic whites and 15.7 percent of "other" (which includes Asians). A comparable range is shown by education, where 15.7 percent of college graduates are obese compared with 27.4 percent of those who did not graduate from high school. Obesity is an outcome, not a behavior. The relevant behaviors for obesity are food consumption (nutrition) and amount of exercise. Lower SES is related to lower rates of exercise and lower consumption rates of fresh fruits and vegetables (Krebs-Smith et al., 1995; Pamuk et al., 1998). These behaviors are multidetermined. For example, those with less education and income may have less access to information about the hazards of smoking or the benefits of a low-fat diet and exercise, as well as information about potential methods for quitting smoking or reducing weight. At the same time, those with less education and income are more likely to be living in neighborhoods that provide less access to the resources needed to maintain their weight or quit smoking. As noted above, low-income neighborhoods have fewer resources for achieving good nutrition or undertaking exercise. In such neighborhoods, concerns about safety may inhibit outdoor exercise. These neighborhoods may also be differentially targeted for advertising and marketing for cigarettes, alcohol, and junk foods (Morland et al., 2002; Stoddard et al., 1998).

TABLE D-17 Percentage Obese, 2001, by Race/Ethnicity and Educational Level

Race/Ethnicity	Percent
Non-Hispanic white	19.6
Non-Hispanic black	31.1
Hispanic	23.7
Other	15.7
Educational Level	
Less than high school	27.4
High school degree	23.2
Some college	21.0
College or above	15.7

SOURCE: CDC, 1991–2001.

Exposure to stress. The contribution of the domains described above to premature mortality have all been quantified by the CDC. One domain was not part of their analysis, most likely because its effects on mortality are more difficult to quantify and overlap the other determinants. This domain is exposure to stress and the resultant behavioral and biological responses that put individuals at risk for a range of diseases (McEwen, 1998a). A number of studies document greater stress exposure for more disadvantaged groups, whether by race and ethnicity and/or by SES. Given this, differential stress exposure may be an important mechanism by which social disadvantage affects health. Stress can directly affect health through biological pathways as discussed below. It can also have indirect effects through its impact on health behaviors. One of the ways that individuals cope with stress is through the use of substances, including tobacco and alcohol, as well as through eating. Recent animal research (Dallman et al., 2003) has demonstrated that the ingestion of fat and sucrose may help to downregulate the biological cascade that occurs in response to stress. Chronic stress may thus foster weight gain and obesity. Moreover, in the presence of cortisol, which is part of the stress response, the resulting fat appears to be differentially deposited in the abdominal region. Abdominal adiposity is a risk factor for cardiovascular disease, stroke, and diabetes above and beyond the risk associated with overweight itself.

Much of the research on the physiological effects of stress exposure has examined responses to acute stress. This type of research is easier to model in laboratory settings because researchers can simulate an acute threat. However, the kind of stress associated with social disadvantage is more chronic. This includes the kinds of daily stressors that are more common for those with fewer resources. It also includes the chronic stress of experiences of discrimination. It is not simply the dramatic single events that signal discrimination but the day-to-day slights and ambiguities of unequal treatment (e.g., being stopped more often for routine traffic checks, being treated rudely by others, being followed by a store security guard, losing out on a promotion without explanation).

The concept of allostatic load was developed by McEwen and colleagues (McEwen, 1998b; McEwen and Stellar, 1993) to describe the biological processes involved in responses to chronic stress. This concept posits that over time, with repeated exposure to stress and engagement of the stress response systems, the affected systems may become dysregulated. Central to this process is the hypothalamic-pituitary-adrenal (HPA) axis and the regulation of cortisol. With repeated stress exposures, the HPA axis may become less flexible (McEwen and Seeman, 1999). Rather than showing the typical stress response (increased level of cortisol, which then downregulates the HPA axis to return cortisol to baseline), there may be either a prolonged response with a delayed return to baseline or a dampened initial response. The first pattern (delayed recovery) results in prolonged exposure to cortisol, which can increase visceral fat and raise the risk of diseases such as diabetes and cardiovascular disease. The second pattern (underresponse) is less effective in resolving the stress response and may increase vulnerability to autoimmune diseases, including rheumatoid arthritis. The concept of allostatic load provides a summative measure of the cumulative effects of stress and may reflect the multiple biological pathways by which social disadvantage can affect a range of health outcomes. Initial research testing this concept has shown that allostatic load is related, on the one hand, to race/ethnicity and SES and, on the other, to health. Among participants in the CARDIA sample, allostatic load scores are higher among African Americans than among whites and are greater among those with less education than among the more educated (Seeman, 2004). Allostatic load scores, in turn, have been shown in a sample of older adults to predict physical and cognitive decline, the onset of new cardiovascular disease, and mortality over a 7-year period (Karlamangla et al., 2002; Seeman et al., 2001).

PUTTING IT ALL TOGETHER—CONCEPTUAL APPROACHES TO MECHANISMS UNDERLYING DISPARITIES

The discussion has examined several categories of determinants of disease as candidates for pathways, from social disadvantage associated with race/ethnicity and with SES to health.[1] A number of conceptual models suggest some additional pathways and approaches to identifying the mechanisms by which health disparities occur. They also encompass some of the pathways presented above and provide unifying contexts in which the determinants are embedded. As stated at the beginning of this report, adequate understanding of health disparities will require measurement of the potential variables that shape differences in health.

[1]A similar analysis could be done for gender and rural residence, but this review focuses primarily on disparities associated with race/ethnicity and SES.

The choice of variables examined must be explicitly linked to models or theories of disparities.

A comprehensive framework of the determinants of health has been proposed by George Kaplan (see Kaplan, 1999). This framework, as shown in Figure D-4, ranges from microdeterminants (e.g., pathophysiologic pathways, genetic and constitutional factors, and individual risk factors) through interpersonal processes and local conditions (social relationships, living conditions, and neighborhoods and communities) to more macro factors (institutions and social and economic policies). Further, as the graphic portrays, these occur in an environmental context and across the life course. As Kaplan (2004) noted, models such as this one are "important metaphors, attempting to portray the component parts of complex processes, their interrelationships and the temporal relations between components" (p. 125). Because of their complexity, these models cannot be directly tested in their entirety but suggest factors that should be examined. Moreover, they "act as an important caution against the potentially misleading oversimplification that comes from focusing on one level of influence" (Kaplan, 2004, p. 125).

The model of social determinants portrayed in Figure D-4 does not explicitly include race/ethnicity, gender, or SES as variables. However, those who are less advantaged may experience greater health risks due to health-damaging factors at

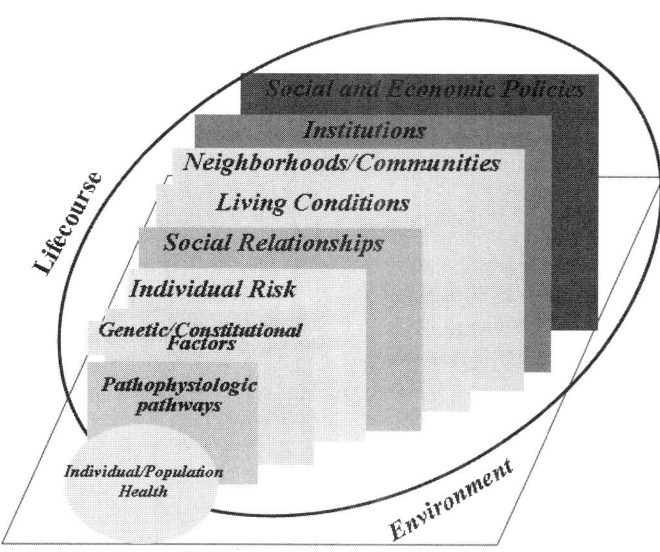

FIGURE D-4 Comprehensive framework of the determinants of health. SOURCE: Kaplan, 1999.

each level of determinants. Each level similarly provides opportunities for intervention to improve health and reduce disparities. This model also illustrates how social and economic policies that go beyond health care policies can impact on health care. This includes policies and legislation such as civil rights legislation, voting rights, zoning and housing policies, taxation and welfare policy, labor policies, and education policies. Such policies will have indirect effects on health as they influence the more proximal determinants of health. For example, housing policies affect the degree of concentrated poverty in urban centers. Such concentrated poverty, in turn, has implications for both physical and social environments that have health effects as described earlier.

Another model of the determinants of health, which puts somewhat more focus on the life course, was proposed by Hertzman (1999). This model, presented in Figure D-5, shows the lifecycle from birth to death as transversing the determinants of health that exist at three levels of aggregation. At the center are the social networks in which the individual is embedded and that have implications for their immediate social environment (e.g., social networks and social support as discussed earlier). These are embedded in the larger civil society that may be characterized both by its supportive characteristics (e.g., social capital) and by its challenges and stressors. The widest level of aggregation is the national context and policies that affect economic opportunities, among other factors. Both of these models include the life course and underline the importance of a developmental perspective in understanding how health disparities develop and are experienced over one's lifetime.

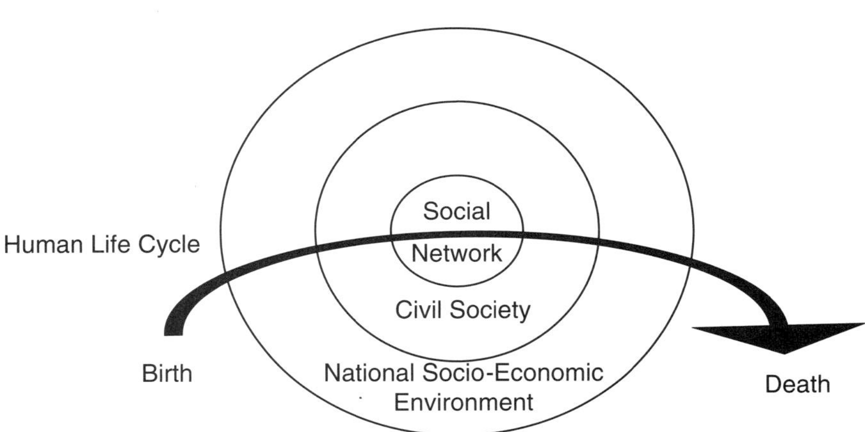

FIGURE D-5 Framework for human development and the social determinants of health.
SOURCE: Hertzman, 1999.

A third model, shown in Figure D-6, developed by Brunner and Marmot (1999), also depicts multilevel determinants of health. This model takes the social structure as the fundamental driver of health. This structure has direct effects on health through material factors and indirect effects through psychological and behavioral factors that are affected by work and social environments. The impact of these on pathophysiological processes and organ impairment is mediated in part through neuroendocrine and immune responses orchestrated by the brain. As shown by the arrows in the lower left, these processes are modified by early life, genes, and culture, although the specific effects of these are not specified.

Other conceptual frameworks highlight specific aspects of the complex processes represented in the three models discussed above, particularly the role of SES. House and Williams (2000; Figure D-7) provided a model that depicts the

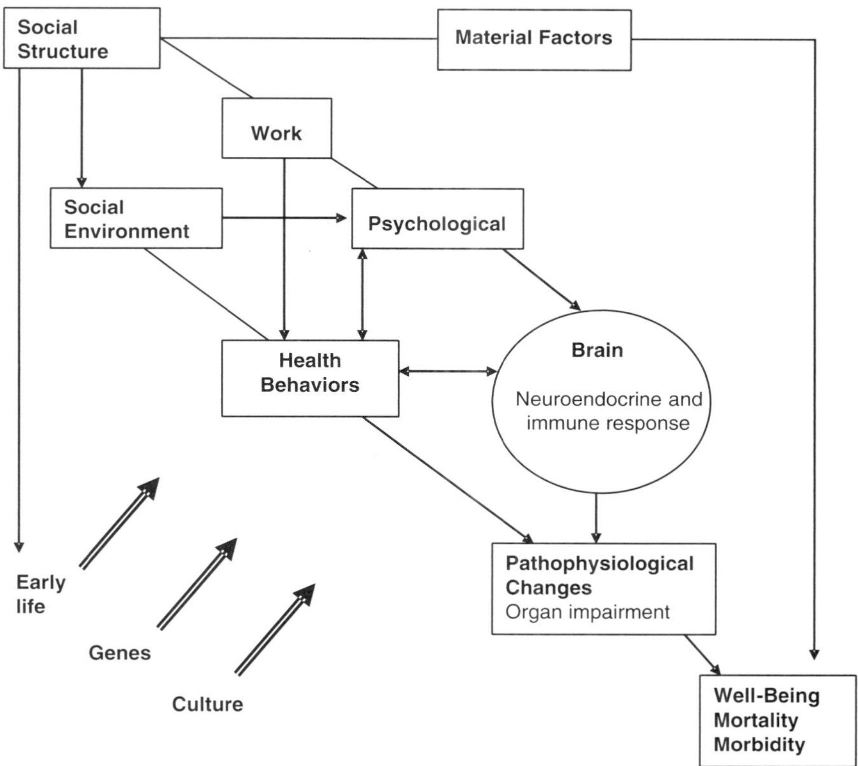

FIGURE D-6 Social determinants of health. The model links social structure to health and disease via material, psychosocial, and behavioral pathways. Genetic, early life, and cultural factors are additional important influences on population health. SOURCE: Brunner and Marmot, 1999.

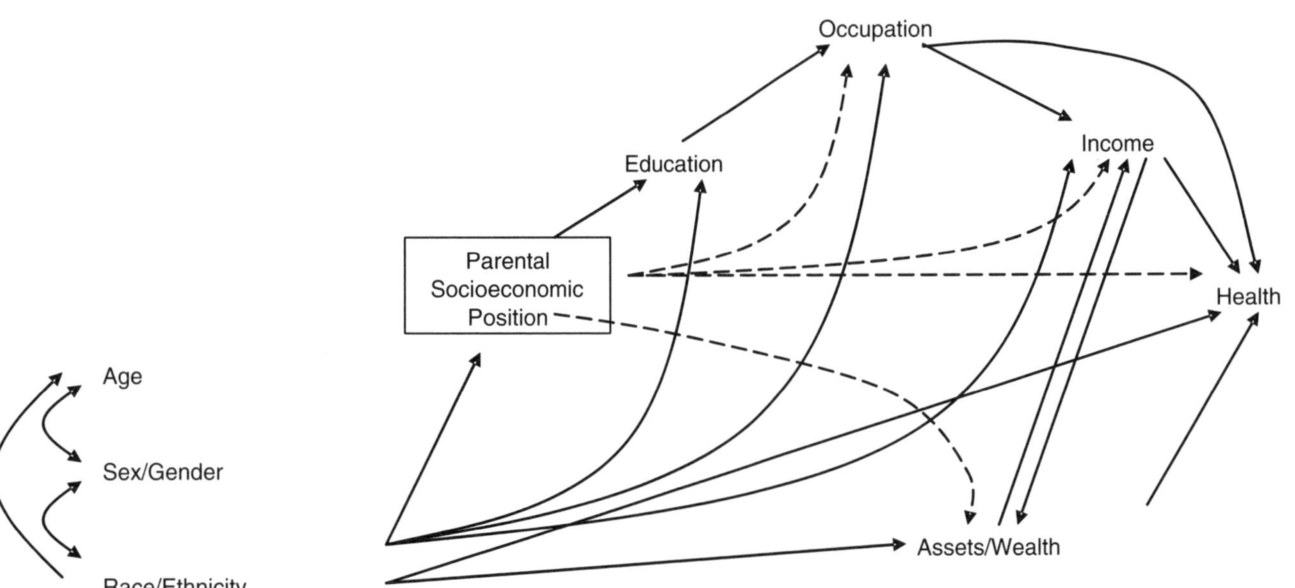

FIGURE D-7 Extended model of social determinants of health incorporating race/ethnicity, sex/gender, and age. NOTE: For clarity of presentation, no arrows are drawn from age and sex/gender to subsequent variables, but these would and should be exactly parallel to those for race/ethnicity. SOURCE: House and Williams, 2000.

association of race/ethnicity, as well as sex/gender and age, with health. Race and ethnicity play dual roles, first by affecting parental socioeconomic position and thus childhood SES and second by affecting the sequence of socioeconomic factors across the individual's life course, running from education to occupation to income and wealth and on to health. Although a major pathway from race/ethnicity to health runs through these socioeconomic contributors to health status, race and ethnicity also directly impact health. This is consistent with findings showing that socioeconomic disadvantage accounts for much of the association of race/ethnicity with health but that there is a residual effect of race/ethnicity on a number of health outcomes, even when SES is adjusted for.

It is worth noting that the model by House and Williams (2000) also includes a separate category for assets and wealth, apart from the usual SES indicators, and shows an interaction of wealth with income. This illustrates one complexity in the assessment of SES. SES is a multidimensional construct, encompassing education, occupation, and income. Each of these indicators themselves may have multiple aspects and associated complexities of measurements. This model points out two different aspects of economic resources and position. As discussed earlier, similar complexities affect the measurement of education. Although not discussed in this paper, varying aspects of occupational status also exist, including prestige, qualifications, relationship to capital, degree of autonomy and supervision, physical versus mental demands, and social relationships.

Another model by House (2002) elaborates on some of the explanatory variables between SES, race/ethnicity, and gender with health (Figure D-8). As with the prior model, race/ethnicity and gender are shown to operate both directly on mediating variables and health outcomes and indirectly through SES. These relationships are modified by more distal social, economic, and political policies and conditions. Three major classes of explanatory variables are included: (a) insurance and health care, (b) psychosocial factors, and (c) social and physical environmental exposures.

House's (2002) model is similar to that developed by the MacArthur Network on Socioeconomic Status and Health (Figure D-9), but some nuanced differences may be worth noting. Although the models by House (2002) and by House and Williams (2000) depict SES as being determined by race/ethnicity and gender, the MacArthur model depicts these factors as interacting to affect environmental exposures and psychosocial risk. Both processes are undoubtedly at play. SES is both determined by race/ethnicity and gender *and* interacts with them. As discussed earlier, the impact and even the meaning of socioeconomic factors may differ for men and women and for members of different racial/ethnic groups. The MacArthur Research Network model also makes explicit that there are different points in disease trajectories where SES (and its interaction with race/ethnicity and gender) may have an effect. Health outcomes encompass physical and cognitive functioning and decline, the onset of disease, recovery and relapse, and mortality. The models suggest the need for research that can describe

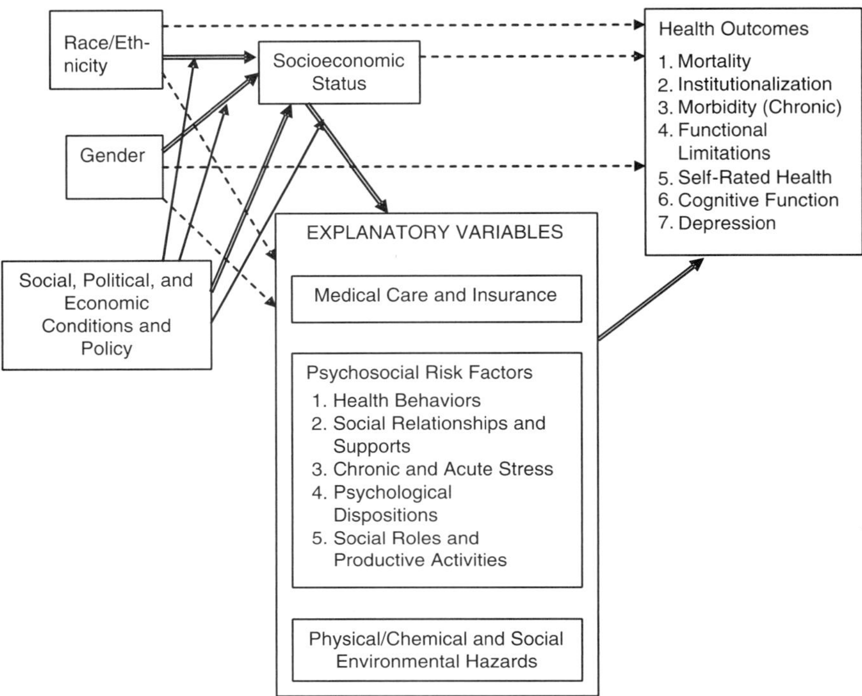

FIGURE D-8 Environmental, psychosocial, and biological pathways linking SES to diabetes mellitus, coronary heart disease, and well-being. SOURCE: House, 2002.

these associations more precisely. Such research will include studies on associations across domains as well as studies documenting the role of specific aspects of multidimensional variables, such as education, income and occupation, ethnicity, and health.

Implicit in several of the models described above is the notion that race/ethnicity, SES, and gender have implications for exposure to stress, including the stress of discrimination. Baum et al. (1999) presented a model that highlights the role of stress in the association between SES and health in adult life (Figure D-10). SES determines exposure to neighborhood or community hazards or supports as well as adverse social conditions, such as discrimination. Although race/ethnicity are not explicitly included in the model, it will shape these exposures. There is a placeholder for other aspects of SES that can affect health, which are not delineated, though examples include access to health care, role models, and nutrition. These operate directly on behavior and biology and indirectly through exposure to stress.

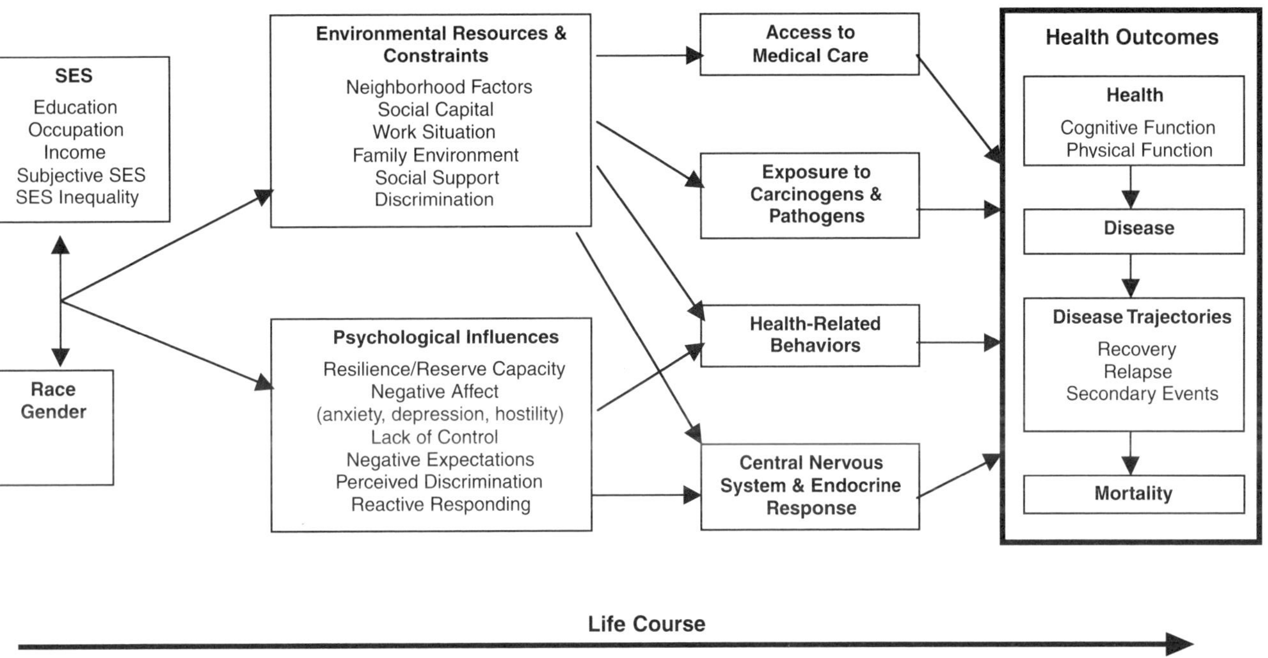

FIGURE D-9 MacArthur Foundation Research Network in Socioeconomic Status and Health model of pathways from SES to health.

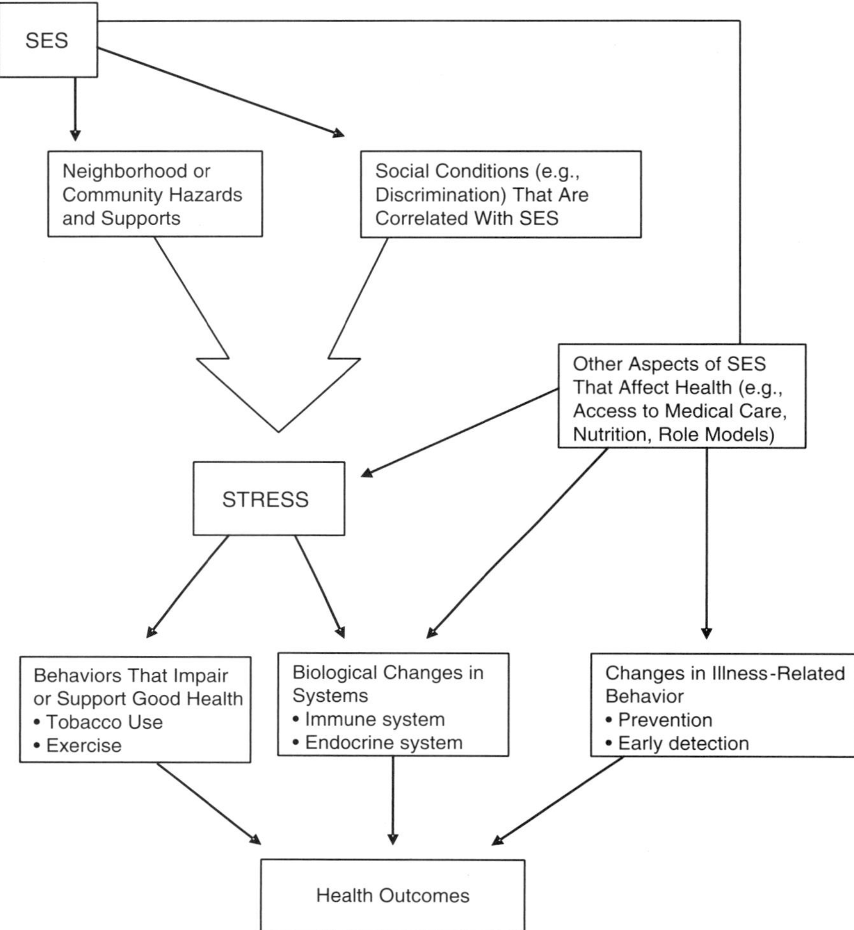

FIGURE D-10 Model for the pathways by which SES may affect health. SOURCE: Baum et al., 1999.

Stress exposure is at the heart of this model. Stress contributes to health outcomes both through its impact on health behaviors and through biological processes resulting from stress responses (see discussion earlier). Stress is implicit in some of the other models. Also depicted, with varying explicitness, are the developmental processes involved in the pathways linking sociodemographic factors to health. The arrow at the bottom of the MacArthur Network model in Figure D-9 indicates that these processes change over time and cumulate over the life course, but the model does not explicitly explain how this occurs. Other models depict pathways by which environments in childhood associated with socioeconomic factors affect health later in life and reflect data showing that socioeconomic factors throughout the life course affect adult health and disease risk (Kuh and Ben-Shlomo, 1997). Unlike biological programming, which is believed to occur during critical periods, the positive and adverse effects of socioeconomic environments on adult health are hypothesized to be due to cumulative exposure across the life course. However, it is an open question whether social conditions experienced during critical periods of development have a relatively greater impact on later health.

Kuh and colleagues (Kuh and Ben-Shlomo, 1997; Kuh and Wadsworth, 1991; Kuh et al., 1997) have developed three figures to illustrate the cumulative effects of childhood status. Figure D-11 is a simplified framework showing hypothesized major pathways whereby childhood socioeconomic factors affect adult health. There is substantial evidence (Britten, 1981; Goldthorpe, 1980; Halsey et al., 1980; Johnson and Reed, 1996; Kuh and Wadsworth, 1991) that family background (parental education, father's social class, and other parental or household characteristics) powerfully affects children's educational attainment and opportunity. Educational attainment, in turn, is a major determinant of adult income and occupation and also affects health behavior and the development of what researchers term *health capital*. Health capital is the accumulation of biological resources, inherited and acquired during earlier stages of life, that determine current health and future health potential including resilience to future environ-

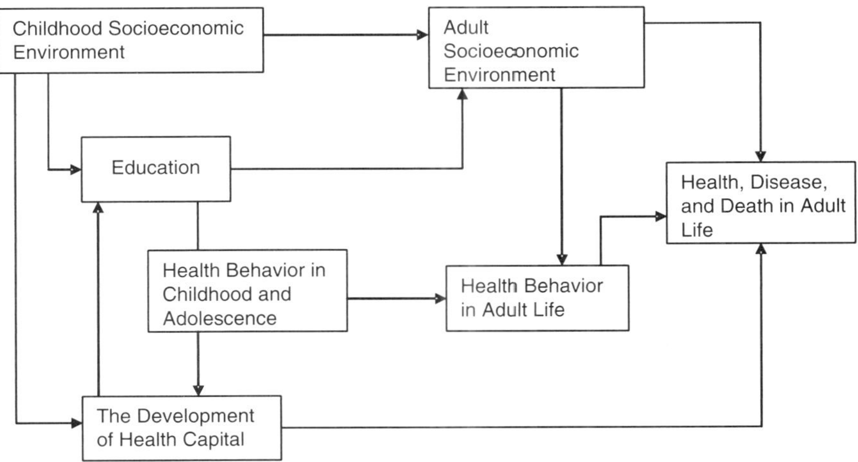

FIGURE D-11 Pathways between childhood and adult health: A simplified framework. SOURCE: Kuh and Ben-Shlomo, 1997.

mental insults. Having good stores of health capital affects one's ability to function optimally, for example, in educational settings. The feedback loop from health capital to educational attainment is worth noting. This paper focuses on social factors' impact on health because these factors provide opportunities for eliminating disparities, but the causal relationship between socioeconomic achievement and health is dynamic, with each influencing the other.

Figure D-12 expands the simplified framework presented above, adding psychosocial and behavioral explanations and the idea that an individual's health is affected by interactions with environments. One important influence on the individual in these interactions is the store of *social capital*. In this model, the term

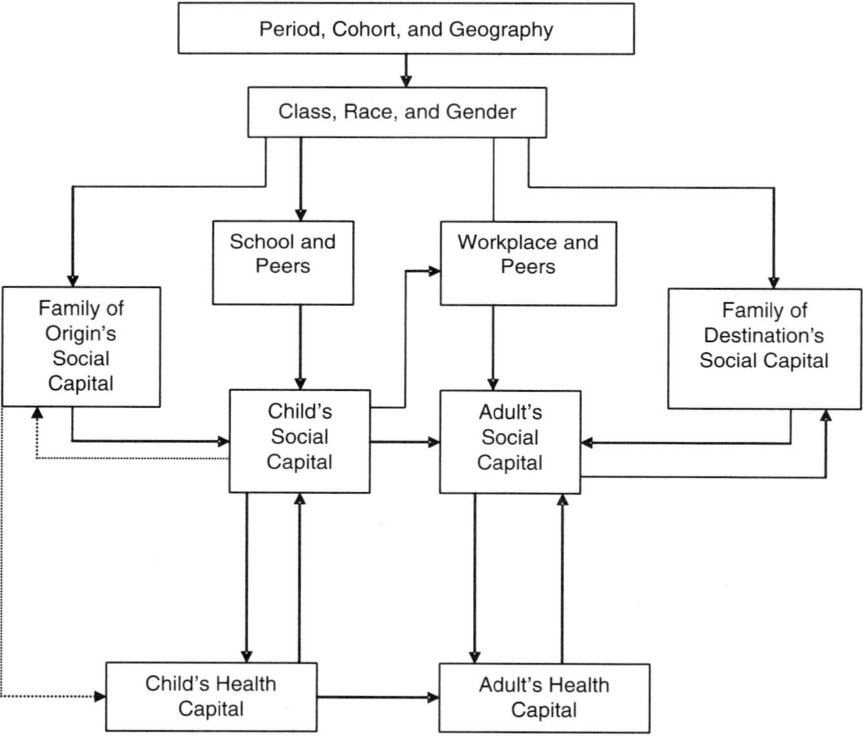

FIGURE D-12 The development of individual social capital over the life course and its relationship with individual health capital. Individual social capital comprises cognitive and social skills, coping strategies, self-esteem, attitudes, and values. A family's social capital also includes relationships between family members. SOURCE: Kuh and Ben-Shlomo, 1997.

does not refer to characteristics of communities or large social groups, which is the more recent usage. Rather, the term refers to the accumulation of social resources in the family that are reflected in social interactions among family members and an individual's resources, such as social and cognitive skills, self-esteem, coping strategies, attitudes, and values. The individual's social capital is thought to be determined primarily by the family and by two important social institutions: school and the workplace. All of these (family, school, and work) are shaped by class, race, and gender, and the ways in which these play out are determined by history, cohort, and geographical location.

Figure D-13 presents an example in which poor family functioning or other childhood stress associated with a poor socioeconomic environment sets in motion what Kuh and Ben-Shlomo (1997) labeled a *chain of risk* by inhibiting the acquisition of social capital (e.g., skills or self-esteem). This stunting of social capital may contribute to poor school functioning, health habits, and health outcomes (e.g., teenage pregnancy) that reverberate throughout life.

These models, along with the analyses of health determinants, can help direct us toward the selection principles for variables that have the highest payoff for

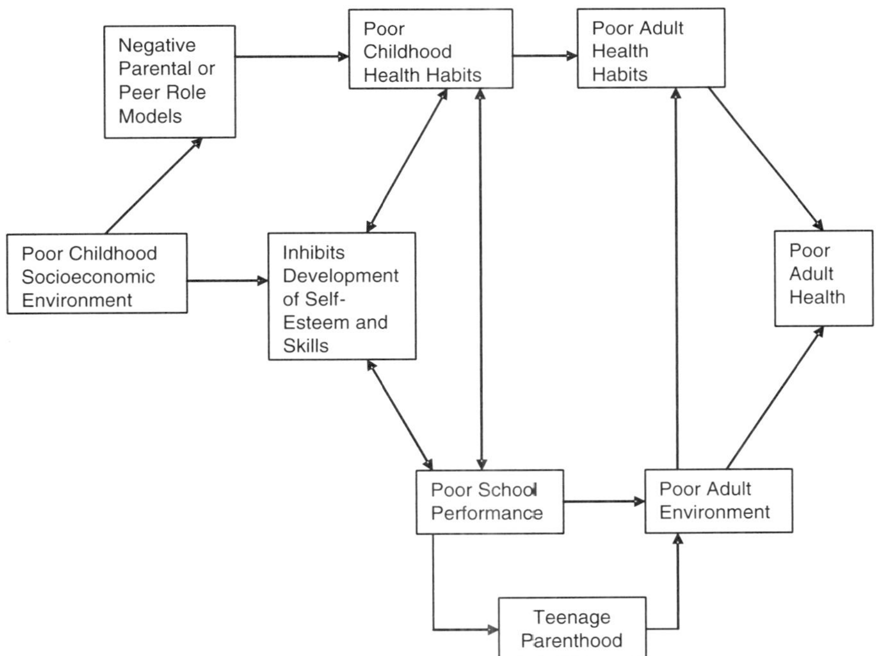

FIGURE D-13 Chains of risk associated with the socioeconomic environment.
SOURCE: Kuh et al., 1997.

research in reducing health disparities. They suggest at least five research considerations. First, each model depicts the importance of considering multiple levels of influence on health. Second, individuals, families, and communities are embedded in these multiple levels. This means that examination of only one level in isolation will be less successful in developing successful interventions and policies to eliminate disparities. Third, there is temporal continuity across levels and the life course. Fourth, there is intergenerational transmission of social and health capital. This means that individuals, communities, and populations carry the accumulated results of the balance of resources and stressors experienced at the multiple levels across time. Fifth, there are direct and indirect effects of variables (e.g., socioeconomic, racial/ethnic, gender, etc.), as well as interaction effects.

All the models described above, and the literature on which they are based, share a common perspective: health-enhancing opportunities and health-damaging exposures are socially patterned, with that patterning influenced by SES, race, class, and the roles associated with institutions such as the family, educational institutions, and occupational settings. The accumulated impact of multiple physical and social influences, starting during gestation, affects not only birth outcomes and childhood health but also adult morbidity and mortality. For example, most studies evaluating timing of exposure have found that childhood socioeconomic circumstances have an inverse relationship with cardiovascular morbidity or mortality, independent of subsequent adult social position, thus suggesting that some underlying causes of cardiovascular disease may strike early in life (Davey Smith et al., 1997; Gliksman et al., 1995; Hasle, 1990; Kaplan and Salonen, 1990; Lynch et al., 1994; Vagero and Leon, 1994; Wannamethee et al., 1996).

Remaining Issues

This review provides one overview of the vast data on health disparities. Different perspectives undoubtedly highlight different issues. This review demonstrated that the term *health disparities* is not being used in any single way. The papers on health disparities encompass research on socioeconomic factors, race and ethnicity, sex/gender, and rural health. The data point to the difficulty in specifying specific disparity groups. In examining a range of reports on overall mortality and on the prevalence of specific diseases, including the data used in the NIH Health Disparities Strategic Plan, Fiscal Years 2004–2008, the only racial/ethnic group that shows consistently poorer health across a range of indicators is African Americans. A caveat, however, is that the available data may not provide a full and accurate estimate of disparities. For some groups, for example, ethnicity may not be accurately captured in mortality data or in surveys, and this may lead to an undercounting of deaths or disease prevalence in these groups. There may be biases introduced for specific populations (e.g., a Mexican American health advantage may be due, in part, to the return of those who are ill or dying to Mexico). Also, as noted earlier, the identification of race and ethnicity into broad categories (e.g., Asian) may miss specific groups (e.g., Hmong) whose health status is markedly worse. This argues for greater attention paid to the nature of the data and the sampling being used to establish the degree of health disparities.

The data on disparities among other groups shows some consistency, although here, too, finer differentiations could yield more informative findings. Health in rural areas appears to be poorer than in more populated areas, though finer differentiators may be helpful in examining suburban versus urban areas. Health is also worse for those who are poorer and less educated, as well as those in low-SES occupations, and these factors account for much, but not all, of the health disadvantage experienced by different racial and ethnic groups and those in rural areas.

Policies to eliminate health disparities need to be informed by scientific understanding of their causes. The empirical and conceptual approaches to date have revealed that the poorer health of African Americans is largely, but not wholly, accounted for by socioeconomic disadvantage. This raises questions. What accounts for the remaining effect? One candidate is exposure to discrimination and racism, which may increase stress responses with their attendant health effects. Another candidate is inadequate measurement of socioeconomic disadvantage and the implications of SES for a range of environmental exposures. A second question: What aspects of socioeconomic disadvantage contribute to health disparities (for those that account for racial/ethnic disparities as well as those that operate for members of all racial and ethnic groups)? SES includes various aspects, each of which confers different resources and has different implications for health. In addition to individual-level factors (e.g., income, education, wealth/assets, occupation), both race/ethnicity and SES shape the area of residence and work environments, each of which has an additional effect on health. For example, residential segregation of African Americans has resulted in areas of concentrated poverty that have health-damaging effects. At the same time, recent research suggests that for Latinos, the barrio effect of greater ethnic density may be health-protective, despite the greater poverty in these areas (Eschbach et al., 2004). Within the work environment, physical conditions may contribute to the risk of injury or disease, as does the social organization of work and particularly the degree of control over demands (Bosma et al., 1997).

It should be noted that virtually all research on health disparities shows associations but does not establish causality. The challenges of establishing causality differ for various sociodemographic variables. Race/ethnicity and sex are determined at birth, and it is not plausible that these are affected by their own health status. With regard to socioeconomic factors, however, mutual causation between SES and health is possible, especially for income. When people become ill, they not only incur medical expenses but may also be less able to work. Smith (1999) demonstrated the adverse effect of poor health on income among participants in the Health and Retirement Study. In this sample of older adults, the most important factor in diminished income and wealth was early retirement due to health problems. Reverse causation is less plausible for education; disease later in life does not change earlier educational attainment. However, the life course models presented above suggest that health disparities early in life may, in turn, affect educational attainment that could both limit later SES and affect adult health. This suggests a reciprocal causal chain between SES and health, but one in which the socioeconomic factors are likely to be more fundamental (Link and Phelan, 1995).

There are some innovative approaches to establishing causal direction by forming links to experimental programs in which specific aspects of social disadvantage are reduced, and the health impact can be examined. For example, several Central and Latin American countries are embarking on anti-poverty programs that may yield health benefits. The PROGRESA project (now called OPORTUNIDADES) in Mexico has shown in a randomized social experiment that income supplementation tied to incentives for health-promoting behaviors—such as using prenatal care and pediatric check-ups and additional cash incentives to keep one's children in school—has resulted in improved growth and decreased anemia in children (Gertler, 2004). Programs in other countries may tease apart the beneficial effects of income supplementation versus income supplementation linked to behavioral incentives. In the United States, the Moving to Opportunity program called for randomized housing-project residents to receive a voucher to allow them to move elsewhere only to a low-poverty area, or to a control condition with no voucher. Both children and adults randomized to the low-poverty neighborhood condition subsequently showed better mental health outcomes but not other health outcomes; there were more favorable outcomes for girls than for boys (Kling et al., 2004).

Other social experiments have not explicitly examined health effects but could be used to do so. For example, a few early childhood education programs, such as the Perry Preschool, had a randomized design that showed economic and social benefits for the children randomized to the experimental condition (Barnett, 1996; Reynolds et al., 2001). However, long-term health effects of enriched early education have not yet been demonstrated.

Social experiments such as those described above require collaboration across sectors and links between health research and housing, education, labor, and so forth. With the exception of massive national programs like PROGRESA, these will necessarily be on a small scale because they are expensive to implement. In addition, there will be a continuing need for sophisticated and creative approaches to examining causal effects in the context of observational studies, which will likely comprise the bulk of research. In this work, longitudinal studies will be important to help establish temporal ordering, as well as cross-sectional studies to provide initial evidence of associations and identify possible mediators. If the National Children's Study is launched, it will be critical to have adequate measures of sociodemographic factors at each time point of data collection and measures of the psychosocial and environmental factors likely to shape health disparities in this population.

In such research, explicit models of health disparities should be specified. This will guide not only the selection of independent and mediating variables but also the health outcome to be studied. The latter may include mortality rates, life expectancy at birth or at different ages, the incidence or prevalence of specific diseases, functional status, and/or self-rated health. One of the questions in such research is whether to examine single diseases or multiple outcomes. Understanding disease-specific pathways is useful for delineating pathophysiological processes. However, data showing similar disparities across a range of diseases suggest that there may be some common pathways to multiple health outcomes. Some of the models and research reviewed above propose that exposure to stress is one such common pathway. Recent research linking greater stress to cell aging (Epel et al., 2004) provides some evidence that chronic stress may, indeed, lead to a type of accelerated aging that can increase risk for a number of diseases. Risk factors such as tobacco use and obesity (which are more common in more disadvantaged groups) may also serve as a common risk factor, as may environmental exposures. The linkage across diseases points to the need for greater cooperation across NIH institutes in supporting disparities research.

At the same time that research is needed on common pathways to multiple outcomes, some mechanisms may be unique to specific diseases. Not every disease shows the same associations with race/ethnicity, SES, etc. For some diseases, such as breast cancer and malignant melanoma, the usual SES gradient is reversed; these diseases are actually more common among more advantaged groups. One unexplained finding is why African Americans show more adverse outcomes in relation to physical health but often show lower rates of mental illness.

The pattern of associations with SES and race/ethnicity can also vary for different stages of disease. For example, higher-SES women are more likely to be diagnosed with breast cancer than women who are less well educated or affluent; this is a real difference in rates of onset and not simply due to better diagnosis. However, once diagnosed, higher-SES women have a greater length of survival, even when controlling for the stage of disease at diagnosis. Thus, it may be useful to look at predictors of different components of mortality associated with a given disease and take into account disparities in incidence and survival. More common than reversals in associations is the finding that the degree of disparities varies for different diseases. For example, the SES gradient is steeper for cardiovascular disease than for many cancers. Within cancer, the gradient is steeper for cervical cancer than for other types of cancer. As researchers identify disease-specific pathways that may account for disparities, they may also learn much by comparing the nature and degree of disparities across diseases. Finally, new approaches to measuring health outcomes also exist. Social disadvantage has a pervasive impact on a variety of risk factors and diseases. In addition to identifying common pathways, it would be helpful to have a valid measure of health capital, a summative measure of the overall health and functioning of individuals that could be aggregated to assess the health stock of groups. This would require operationalizing the World Health Organization (1948) definition of health. There are early efforts to do so, primarily by health services researchers who have developed instruments such as the 36-Item Short-Form Health Survey (SF-36). The next generation of measures should be done with an eye to their applicability to evaluating health disparities. Collaboration between NIH and the Agency for Healthcare Research and Quality (AHRQ), which uses such measures more frequently, may also prove beneficial.

Implications of This Analysis for the NIH Research Agenda

Researchers would find it difficult to implement the idea that the healthiest group be taken as the standard against which other groups could be evaluated, in terms of the extent of their health disparity. However, this strategy may be worth discussing. It shares common ground with that suggested by Murray et al. (1999), but it incorporates a focus on groups that may address the concern raised by Braveman et al. (2001) that the health status of disadvantaged groups could be overlooked. Such an approach may have the potential to stimulate novel research and provide information on the strengths of groups that could help inform others (e.g., understanding the Hispanic paradox may provide clues to health-protective social and cultural processes).

The data presented in this paper underline the importance of collaboration across NIH institutes, because health disparities cross-cut multiple diseases and populations. These data also suggest that a strategy based on disparity groups is not as likely to be fruitful as one based on disparity *processes*. Specifically, understanding the interrelationships and interactions among different sources of social disadvantage (which includes race/ethnicity, SES, gender, and area of residence) will provide a fuller explanation of the mechanisms by which disparities occur. The existing data suggest that socioeconomic disadvantage is a key pathway by which racial/ethnic disparities emerge. At the same time, African Americans show poorer health outcomes even when SES is adjusted for. There may be more impact from research on socioeconomic disadvantage because it is the more powerful effect and is more amenable to intervention. However, it is also important to understand what it is about the experiences of African Americans that places them at heightened risk above and beyond that associated with their socioeconomic position. This review makes clear the importance of encompassing the measurement of race/ethnicity, SES, and gender in research.

To achieve the dual goals of *Healthy People 2010* (U.S. Department of Health and Human Services, 2000), we will need more research—and, importantly, more sophisticated research—on understanding the pathways by which health disparities are created. This work will be facilitated by greater inclusion of appropriate measures of SES as well as race and ethnicity in national data sets and public health monitoring measures in addition to gender and area of residence. Additionally, to the extent possible, measures of psychosocial and behavioral variables that are likely to mediate these effects should be included. Strategies that involve the measurement of risk factors and preclinical indicators of disease states will be particularly important, as these may provide information on common underlying pathways to multiple diseases, as well as information on disease-specific risk states that can suggest strategies for earlier intervention. The examination of common pathways to multiple diseases underlines the importance of coordinating health disparities research across the NIH institutes, as well as the AHRQ.

REFERENCES

Backlund E, Sorlie PD, Johnson NJ. 1999. A comparison of the relationships of education and income with mortality: The national longitudinal mortality study. *Social Science and Medicine* 49:1373–1384.

Barnett S. 1996. *Lives in the Balance: Age-27 Benefit-Cost Analysis of the High/Scope Perry Preschool Program.* Monographs of the High/Scope Educational Research Foundation, Number 11, Ypsilanti, Michigan: High/Scope Press.

Baum A, Garofalo JP, Yali AM. 1999. Socioeconomic status and chronic stress: Does stress account for SES effects on health? In, Adler N, Marmot M, McEwen BS, Stewart J, eds. *Socioeconomic Status and Health in Industrial Nations.* Vol. 896. New York: Annals of the New York Academy of Sciences. Pp. 131–144.

Berkman LF, Glass TA. 2000. Social integration, social networks, social support, and health. In, Berkman LF, Kawachi I, eds. *Social Epidemiology.* New York: Oxford University Press. Pp. 137–173.

Bosma H, Marmot MG, Hemingway H, Nicholson AG, Brunner E, Stansfeld A. 1997. Low job control and risk of coronary heart disease in Whitehall II (prospective cohort) study. *British Medical Journal* 314:558–565.

Braveman P, Gruskin S. 2003. Defining equality in health. *Journal of Epidemiology and Community Health* 54:254–258.

Braveman P, Starfield B, Geiger HJ. 2001. World Health Report 2000: How it removes equity from the agenda for public health monitoring and policy. *British Medical Journal* 323(7314): 678–681.

Britten N. 1981. Models of intergenerational class mobility: Findings from the National Survey of Health and Development. *British Journal of Sociology* 32:224–238.

Brunner E, Marmot M. 1999. Social organization, stress and health. In, Marmot M, Wilkinson RG, eds. *Social Determinants of Health.* Oxford, UK: Oxford University Press. Pp. 17–43.

Carter-Pokras O, Baquet C. 2002. What is a "health disparity"? *Public Health Reports* 117:426–434.

CDC (Centers for Disease Control and Prevention). 2001. *Obesity Trends, 1991–2001. Prevalence of Obesity Among U.S. Adults, by Characteristics: Behavioral Risk Factor Surveillance System (1991–2001); Self Reported Data.* [Online]. Available: http://www.cdc.gov/nccdphp/dnpa/obesity/trend/prev_char.htm [accessed June 14, 2004].

Cho Y, Hummer RA. 2001. Disability status differentials across fifteen Asian and Pacific Islander groups and the effect of nativity and duration of residence in the U.S. *Social Biology* 48: 171–195.

Claudio L, Tulton L, Doucette J, Landrigan PJ. 1999. Socioeconomic factors and asthma hospitalization rates in New York City. *Journal of Asthma* 36:343–350.

Cohen DA, Farley TA, Mason K. 2003. Why is poverty unhealthy? Social and physical mediators. *Social Science and Medicine* 57:1631–1641.

Cohen DA, Mason K, Bedimo A, Scribner R, Basolo V, Farley TA. 2003. Neighborhood physical conditions and health. *American Journal of Public Health* 93(3):467–471.

Cooper R, Rotimi C, Ataman S, McGee D, Osotimehin B, Kadiri S, et al. 1997. The prevalence of hypertension in seven populations of West African origin. *American Journal of Public Health* 87:160–168.

Coughlin SS, Thompson TD, Seeff L, Richards T, Stallings F. 2002. Breast, cervical, and colorectal carcinoma screening in a demographically defined region of the southern U.S. *Cancer* 95:2211–2222.

Dallman MF, Pecoraro N, Akana SF, La Fleur SE, Gomez F, Houshyar H, et al. 2003. Chronic stress and obesity: A new view of "comfort food." *Proceedings of the National Academy of Sciences* 100:11696–11701.

Davey Smith G, Hart C, Blane D, Gillis C, Hawthorne V. 1997. Lifetime socioeconomic position and mortality: Prospective observational study. *British Medical Journal* 314:547–552.

DeNavas-Walt C, Proctor BD, Mills RJ. 2004. *U.S. Census Bureau, Current Population Reports Income, Poverty, and Health Insurance Coverage in the United States: 2003*. Washington, DC: U.S. Government Printing Office.

Eberhardt MS, Pamuk ER. 2004. The importance of place of residence: Examining health in rural and nonrural areas. *American Journal of Public Health* 94:1682–1686.

Epel ES, Blackburn EH, Lin, J, Dhabhar FS, Adler NE, Morrow J, et al. 2004. Accelerated telomere shortening in response to life stress. *Proceedings of the National Academy of Sciences* 101(49): 17312–17315.

Eschbach K, Ostir GV, Patel KV, Markides KS, Goodwin JS. 2004. Neighborhood context and mortality among older Mexican Americans: Is there a barrio advantage? *American Journal of Public Health* 94:1807–1812.

Evans GW. 2001. Environmental stress and health. In, Baum A, Revenson T, Singer JE, eds. *Handbook of Health Psychology*. Mahwah, NJ: Erlbaum. Pp. 365–385.

Evans GW, Lepore SJ. 1992. Conceptual and analytic issues in crowding research. *Journal of Environmental Psychology* 12:163–173.

Fang J, Madhaven S, Alderman MH. 1996. The association between birthplace and mortality from cardiovascular causes among black and white residents of New York City. *New England Journal of Medicine* 335:1545–1551.

Friedman HS, Tucker JS, Schwartz JE, Tomlinson-Keasey C, Martin LR, Wingard DL, et al. 1995. Psychosocial and behavioral predictors of longevity. *American Psychologist* 50:69–78.

Gertler PJ. 2004. Do conditional cash transfers improve child health? Evidence from PROGRESA's controlled randomized experiment. *American Economics Review* 94(2):331–336.

Gliksman MD, Kawachi I, Hunter D, Colditz GA, Manson JE, Stampfer MJ, et al. 1995. Childhood socioeconomic status and risk of cardiovascular disease in middle aged US women: A prospective study. *Journal of Epidemiology and Community Health* 49:10–15.

Goldthorpe JH. 1980. *Social Mobility and Class Structure in Modern Britain*. Oxford, UK: Clarendon Press.

Guyll M, Matthews KA, Bromberger JT. 2001. Discrimination and unfair treatment: Relationship to cardiovascular reactivity among African American and European American women. *Health Psychology* 20(5):315–325.

Haan M, Kaplan GA. 1985. *The Contribution of Socioeconomic Position to Minority Health. Report of the Secretary's Task Force on Black and Minority Health, Volume II: Crosscutting Issues in Minority Health*. Rockville, MD: U.S. Department of Health and Human Services.

Halsey AH, Heath AF, Ridge JM. 1980. *Origins and Destinations: Family, Class and Education in Modern Britain*. Oxford, UK: Clarendon Press.

Harrell JP, Hall S, Taliaferro J. 2003. Physiological responses to racism and discrimination: An assessment of the evidence. *American Journal of Public Health* 93(2):243–247.

Hartley D. 2004. Rural health disparities, population health, and rural culture. *American Journal of Public Health* 94:1675–1678.

Hasle H. 1990. Association between living conditions in childhood and myocardial infarction. *British Medical Journal* 300:512–513.

Healthy People 2010. (November 2000). *Understanding and Improving Health (Second Edition)*. Department of Health and Human Services.

Hertzman C. 1999. Population health and human development. In, Keating DP, Hertzman C, eds. *Developmental Health and the Wealth of Nations: Social, Biological, and Educational Dynamics*. New York: Guildford Press. Pp. 21–40.

Hill CV, Neighbors HW, Gayle HD. 2004. The relationship between racial discrimination and health for black Americans: Measurement challenges and the realities of coping. *African American Research Perspectives* 10(1):89–98.

House JS. 2002. Understanding social factors and inequalities in health: 20th century progress and 21st century prospects. *Journal of Health and Social Behavior* 43:125–142.

House JS, Williams D. 2000. Understanding and reducing socioeconomic and racial/ethnic disparities in health. In, Smedley, BD, Syme, SL, eds. *Promoting Health: Intervention Strategies from Social and Behavioral Research*. Washington, DC: National Academy Press. Pp. 81–124.

House JS, Landis KR, Umberson D. 1988. Social relationships and health. *Science* 241(4865): 540–545.

Johnson P, Reed H. 1996. *Two Nations? The Inheritance of Poverty and Affluence* [Institute for Fiscal Studies Commentary No 53]. London: Institute for Fiscal Studies.

Kaplan GA. 1999. Part III summary: What is the role of the social environment in understanding inequalities in health? In, Adler NE, Marmot M, McEwen B, Stewart J, eds. *Socioeconomic Status and Health in Industrialized Nations*. New York: Annals of the New York Academy of Sciences. Pp. 116–119.

Kaplan GA. 2004. What's wrong with social epidemiology, and how can we make it better? *Epidemiologic Reviews* 26:124–135.

Kaplan GA, Salonen JT. 1990. Socioeconomic conditions in childhood and ischaemic heart disease during middle age. *British Medical Journal* 301:1121–1123.

Kaplan GA, Pamuk ER, Lynch JW, Cohen RD, Balfour JL. 1996. Inequality in income and mortality in the United States: Analysis of mortality and potential pathways. *British Medical Journal* 312:999–1003.

Kawachi I, Berkman LF. 2000. Social cohesion, social capital and health. In, Berkman LF, Kawachi I, eds. *Social Epidemiology*. New York: Oxford University Press. Pp. 174–190.

Kennedy BP, Kawachi I, Prothrow-Smith D. 1996. Income distribution and mortality: Cross-sectional ecological study of the Robin Hood index in the United States. *British Medical Journal* 312:1004–1007. (Correction in *British Medical Journal* 312:1194.)

Klinenberg E. 2002. *Heat Wave: A Social Autopsy of Disaster in Chicago*. Chicago: University of Chicago Press.

Kling JR, Liebman, JB, Katz LF, Sanbonmatsu L. 2004. *Moving to opportunity and tranquility: Neighborhood effects on adult economic self-sufficiency and health from a randomized housing voucher experiment.* KSG Working Paper No. RWP04-035. [Online]. Available: http://ssrn.com/abstract=588942 [accessed June 14, 2004].

Krebs-Smith SM, Cook A, Subar AF, Cleveland L, Friday J. 1995. U.S. adults' fruit and vegetable intakes, 1989 to 1991: A revised baseline for the Healthy People 2000 objective. *American Journal of Public Health* 85:1623–1629.

Krieger N, Sidney S. 1996. Racial discrimination and blood pressure: The CARDIA study of young black and white adults. *American Journal of Public Health* 86:1370–1378.

Kuh D, Ben-Shlomo Y, eds. 1997. *A Life Course Approach to Chronic Disease Epidemiology.* Oxford, UK: Oxford University Press.

Kuh D, Wadsworth M. 1991. Childhood influences on adult male earnings in a longitudinal study. *British Journal of Sociology* 42:537–555.

Kuh D, Power C, Blane D, Bartley M. 1997. Social pathways between childhood and adult health. In, Kuh D, Ben-Shlomo Y, eds. *A Life Course Approach to Chronic Disease Epidemiology*. Oxford, UK: Oxford University Press. Pp. 169–200.

Lee P, Paxman D. 1997. Reinventing public health. *Annual Review of Public Health* 18:1–35.

Lin CC, Rogot E, Johnson NJ, Sorlie PD, Arias E. 2003. A further study of life expectancy by socioeconomic factors in the National Longitudinal Mortality Study. *Ethnicity and Disease* 13:240–247.

Link BG, Phelan J. 1995. Social conditions as fundamental causes of disease. *Journal of Health and Social Behavior* Spec. No:80–94.

Lochner KA, Kawachi I, Brennan RT, Buka SL. 2003. Social capital and neighborhood mortality rates in Chicago. *Social Science and Medicine* 56:1797–1805.

Lynch JW, Kaplan GA, Cohen RD, Kauhanen J, Wilson TW, Smith NL, et al. 1994. Childhood and adult socioeconomic status as predictor of mortality in Finland. *Lancet* 343:524–527.

Marmot MG, Rose G, Shipley M, Hamilton PJS. 1978. Employment grade and coronary heart disease in British civil servants. *Journal of Epidemiology and Community Health* 32:244–249.

McEwen BS. 1998a. Protective and damaging effects of stress mediators. *New England Journal of Medicine* 338(3):171–179.

McEwen BS. 1998b. Stress, adaptation, and disease: Allostasis and allostatic load. *Annals of the New York Academy of Sciences* 840:33–44.

McEwen B, Seeman T. 1999. Protective and damaging effects of mediators of stress: Elaborating and testing the concepts of allostasis and allostatic load. *Annals of the New York Academy of Sciences* 896:30–47.

McEwen BS, Stellar E. 1993. Stress and the individual: Mechanisms leading to disease. *Archives of Internal Medicine* 153:2093–2101.

McGinnis JM, Williams-Russo P, Knickman JR. 2002. The case for more active policy attention to health promotion. *Health Affairs* 21(2):78–93.

Morland K, Wing S, Diez Roux A, Poole C. 2002. Neighborhood characteristics associated with the location of food stores and food service places. *American Journal of Preventive Medicine* 22(1):23–29.

Murray CJL, Michaud CM, McKenna M, Marks J. 1998. *US Patterns of Mortality by County and Race: 1965–1994.* Boston: Harvard Center for Population and Development Studies.

Murray CJL, Gakidou EE, Frenk J. 1999. Health inequalities and social group differences: What should we measure? *Bulletin of the World Health Organization* 77:537–543.

National Center for Health Statistics. 2001. *Health, United States, 2001 with Urban and Rural Health Chartbook.* Hyattsville, MD: National Center for Health Statistics.

National Center for Health Statistics. 2004. *Health, United States, 2004 with Chartbook on Trends in the Health of Americans*. Hyattsville, MD: National Center for Health Statistics.

NIH (National Institutes of Health). 2002. *NIH Health Disparities Strategic Plan, Fiscal Years 2002–2006*. Vol. 1. Washington, DC: NIH, U.S. Dept. of Health and Human Services.

Palaniappan L, Wang Y, Fortmann SP. 2004. Coronary heart disease mortality for six ethnic groups in California, 1990–2000. *Annals of Epidemiology* 14:499–506.

Pamuk E, Makuc D, Heck K, Reuben C, Lochner K. 1998. *Socioeconomic Status and Health Chartbook: Health United States, 1998*. Hyattsville, MD: National Center for Health Statistics.

Peek-Asa C, Zwerling C, Stallones L. 2004. Acute traumatic injuries in rural populations. *American Journal of Public Health* 94:1689–1693.

Pierce JP, Fiore MC, Novotny TE, Hatziandreu EJ, Davis RM. 1989. Trends in cigarette smoking in the United States: Education differences are increasing. *Journal of the American Medical Association* 26:56–60.

Probst JC, Moore CG, Glover SH, Samuels ME. 2004. Person and place: The compounding effects of race/ethnicity and rurality on health. *American Journal of Public Health* 94:1695–1703.

Reynolds AJ, Temple JA, Robertson DL, Mann EA. 2001. Long-term effects of an early childhood intervention on educational achievement and juvenile arrest: A 15-year follow-up of low-income children in public schools. *Journal of the American Medical Association* 285:2339–2346.

Rumbaut RG. 1996. Origins and destinies: Immigration, race and ethnicity in contemporary America. In, Pedraza S, Rumbaut RG, eds. *Origins and Destinies; Immigration, Race, and Ethnicity in America*. Belmont, CA: Wadsworth Publishing Company. Pp. 21–42.

Sampson RJ, Raudenbush SW, Earls F. 1997. Neighborhoods and violent crime: A multilevel study of collective efficacy. *Science* 277:918–924.

Seeman TE, McEwen B, Rowe J, Singer B. 2001. Allostatic load as a marker of cumulative biological risk: MacArthur studies of successful aging. *Proceedings of the National Academy of Sciences* 98(8):4770–4775.

Singh GK, Miller BA. 2004. Health, life expectancy, and mortality patterns among immigrant populations in the United States. *Canadian Journal of Public Health* 95:114–121.

Smedley BD, Stith AY, Nelson AR, eds. 2003. *Unequal Treatment: Confronting Racial and Ethnic Disparities in Health Care*. Washington, DC: The National Academies Press.

Smith JP. 1999. Healthy bodies and thick wallets: The dual relationship between health and economic status. *Journal of Economic Perspectives* 13(2):145–166.

Stoddard JL, Johnson CA, Sussman S, Dent C, Boley-Cruz T. 1998. Tailoring outdoor tobacco advertising to minorities in Los Angeles County. *Journal of Health Communication* 3:137–146.

Thomas DB, Karagas MR. 1996. Migrant studies. In, Schottenfeld D, Fraumeni JF, eds. *Cancer Epidemiology and Prevention*. 2nd ed. New York: Oxford University Press. Pp. 236–254.

U.S. Census Bureau, American Fact Finder. 2000. *Sex by Age by Educational Attainment for the Population 18 Years and Over* [Census 2000 Summary File 4–Sample Data]. [Online]. Available: http://factfinder.census.gov [accessed January 19, 2005].

U.S. Department of Health and Human Services, Agency for Healthcare Research and Quality. 2003. *National Healthcare Disparities Report*. Rockville, MD: Agency for Healthcare Research and Quality.

Vagero D, Leon D. 1994. Effect of social class in childhood and adulthood on adult mortality. *Lancet* 343:1224–1225.

Wannamethee SG, Whincup PH, Shaper G, Walker M. 1996. Influence of father's social class on cardiovascular disease in middle-aged men. *Lancet* 348:1259–1263.

Weeks WB, Kazis LE, Shen Y, Cong Z, Ren XS, Miller D, et al. 2004. Differences in health-related quality of life in rural and urban veterans. *American Journal of Public Health* 94:1762–1767.

Wilkinson RG. 1996. *Unhealthy Societies: The Afflictions of Inequality*. London: Routledge.

Williams DR. 2005. The health of U.S. racial and ethnic populations. *Journal of Gerontology—Series B Psychological Sciences and Social Sciences* 60(Spec. Iss. Oct.): 53–62.

Williams DR, Collins C. 2001. Racial residential segregation: A fundamental cause of racial disparities in health. *Public Health Reports* 116:404–416.

Wolfson M, Kaplan G, Lynch J, Ross N, Backlund E. 1999. Relation between income inequality and mortality: Empirical demonstration. *British Medical Journal* 319:953–955.

World Health Organization. 1948. *Official Records of the World Health Organization, No. 2 (p. 100), Entered into Force on 7 April 1948. Preamble to the Constitution of the World Health Organization as Adopted by the International Health Conference, New York, 19–22 June, 1946; Signed on 22 July 1946 by the Representatives of 61 States.*

Yang RC, Mills PK, Riordan DG. 2004. Cervical cancer among Hmong women in California, 1988 to 2000. *American Journal of Preventive Medicine* 24:132–138.

Zsembik BA, Fennell D. 2005. Ethnic variation in health and the determinants of health among Latinos. *Social Science and Medicine* 61:53–63.

E

Schematic Diagram Showing Differences, Disparities, and Discrimination in Health Care

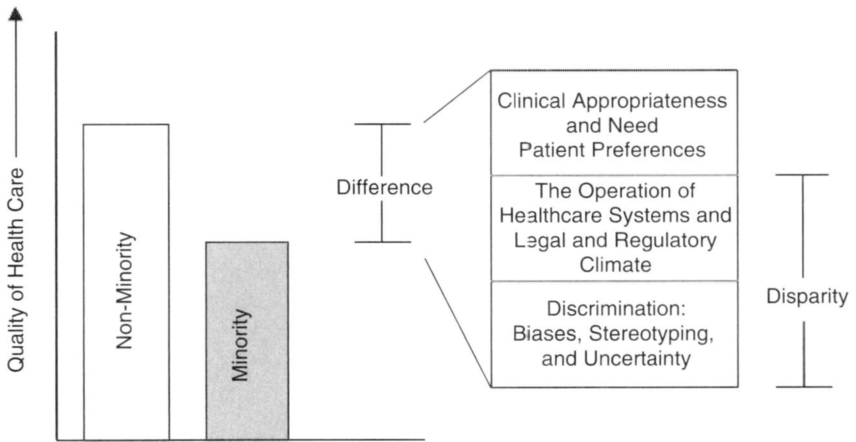

Differences, Disparities, and Discrimination: Populations with Equal Access to Health Care. SOURCE: Smedley et al., 2003.

F

National Institutes of Health NIH Health Strategic Plan Fiscal Years 2004–2008, Volume I

U.S. Department of Health
amd Human Services

VOLUME 1

VOLUME II

Foreword

Medical and scientific advances have introduced new opportunities for the continued improvement of health for all Americans. However, in spite of notable improvements gained as a result of the advancement of knowledge through basic and applied research, diagnostics and treatment, there continues to be an alarming disproportionate burden of illness among minority and medically underserved populations. NIH's mission of *"uncovering new knowledge that will lead to better health for everyone"* lays the foundation for the overall goal of understanding the causes of health disparities and for developing effective interventions to eliminate these disparities.

All of us who have been privileged to participate in this age of scientific discovery have a responsibility to ensure that the new knowledge generated in our laboratories and our clinics benefits all of our citizens and all of our communities. Our aim at the NIH is to promote the development and transfer of research-based information from the biomedical, behavioral, and social sciences for use by health professionals, communities, and others in working toward the elimination of health disparities.

In order to address the constant and confounding problem of health disparities experienced by the affected communities including the medically underserved population, the NIH is committed and remains vigilant in supporting research to understand biological, socioeconomic, cultural, environmental, institutional, and behavioral factors affecting health disparities. Research is but only one solution in a multifaceted effort. In addition to devoting resources toward the application of research programs, the NIH is also planning and conducting education and training programs and increasing outreach activities, to translate new knowledge from research into improved health outcomes for all Americans.

This updated version of the strategic plan, *NIH Health Disparities Strategic Plan, Fiscal Years 2004-2008,* continues the NIH commitment toward implementing Public Law (P.L.) 106-525, *The Minority Health and Health Disparities Research and Education Act of 2000.* The plan was developed through an open process with substantial input from the public, particularly from representatives of groups who disproportionately experience disparities in health, in addition to those in academia and health care professionals. It describes the activities underway and planned to bring the full strength of NIH's research, training and outreach programs to bear on the challenge of eliminating domestic health disparities, increasing participation by minorities in clinical research, and increasing the number of minority clinical and basic medical scientists who are essential to the success of our efforts.

While the diversity of the American population remains one of our Nation's greatest assets, the discrepancies in health status described here represent a challenge to better understand these disparities, and to reduce and ultimately eliminate them.

Public Law 106-525 required the NCMHD to report to the Congress by December 2003 recommendations for the methodology the NIH will use to determine the amount of NIH resources dedicated to the conduct and support of health disparities research.

In October 2003 the NIH Director and the Director, NCMHD, established an NIH Committee on Minority Health and Health Disparities Research Definitions and Application Methodology, which developed new definitions and a revised application methodology that were used by the NIH in developing this updated version of the NIH Strategic Plan. The Committee developed uniform NIH Guidelines that:

- Provide NIH operational definitions, based on Public Law 106-525, for minority health and health disparities research,
- Provide a consistent methodology for applying the definitions,
- Contain the criteria necessary to identify both minority health and health disparities population groups and diseases, and
- Serve as the foundation for identifying, coding, tracking, and reporting on NIH activities and resources.

Accordingly, the NIH budget figures based upon the NIH Guidelines and contained within this revised iteration of the NIH Strategic Plan are more precise. The NIH will continue to implement the plan and revise it based upon scientific opportunities and public input from affected communities.

Elias A. Zerhouni, M.D.
Director
National Institutes of Health

John Ruffin, Ph.D.
Director
National Center on Minority Health and Health Disparities, National Institutes of Health

Executive Summary

Over the last two decades the overall health of the Nation has improved significantly. Yet there continue to be striking disparities in the burden of illness and death experienced by African Americans, Hispanics, Native Americans, Alaska Natives, Asians, and Pacific Islanders. The most striking disparities include shorter life expectancy as well as higher rates of cardiovascular disease, cancer, infant mortality, birth defects, asthma, diabetes, stroke, sexually transmitted diseases, and mental illness. These disparities are believed to be the result of the complex interaction among biological factors, the environment, and specific health behaviors. Inequalities in income and education also appear to underlie many health disparities in the United States. Disparities in income and education levels are associated with differences in the occurrence of illness and death, including heart disease, diabetes, obesity, elevated blood lead level, and low birth weight.

MISSION
The NIH mission on minority health and health disparities is to support and promote biomedical and behavioral research, research training, research capacity, and research information dissemination, with the goal of improving the health status of racial and ethnic minorities and other health disparity populations.

Overcoming persistent health disparities and promoting health for all Americans rank as our Nation's foremost health challenge. To overcome this challenge, the National Institutes of Health (NIH) is supporting and conducting a wide range of research, and seeking new knowledge, strategies, and methodologies about disease and disabilities. This new knowledge has and will continue to lead to innovative diagnostics, treatments, and preventative strategies to reduce, and eventually eliminate, health disparities.

VISION
A time when all Americans have the opportunity for long, healthy, and productive lives regardless of race, ethnicity, or socioeconomic status.

Within the NIH, the National Center on Minority Health and Health Disparities (NCMHD) serves as the focal point for planning and coordinating minority health and other health disparities research. According to P.L. 106-525, the NCMHD was established by Congress to foster, coordinate, and assess the progress of all NIH- sponsored research activities involving minority health and other health disparities by working in collaboration with NIH's Institutes and Centers (ICs) and other program offices within the NIH Office of the Director (OD), and in consultation with the National Advisory Council on Minority Health and Health Disparities.

The initiatives described in this plan represent the major priorities and broad range of activities that the NIH will undertake to reduce and ultimately eliminate health disparities. The plan is not merely a compilation of all the activities of the NIH entities, but an aggregation of primary areas of emphasis and activities conducted across the NIH. An evolving process, the strategic plan has been and will continue to be revised based on public comments received, public health need, scientific opportunity, changes in available funds, and other factors. The plan will be posted on the NCMHD website on a continuing basis and public comments on the plan will be encouraged and considered at any time. The strategic plan follows a methodological planning model, which presents mission, vision, goals, objectives, and programs for reducing and eventually eliminating health disparities.

The Strategic Plan is focused on three major goals:

- **Research** - to advance the understanding of the development and progression of diseases and disabilities that contribute to health disparities in racial and ethnic minority populations and other health disparity populations, including the medically underserved, by increasing and diversifying biomedical, behavioral, social science, and health services research, as well as cultural, linguistic, and social epidemiology research conducted and supported by the NIH
- **Research Capacity** - to increase minority health and health disparity research training, career development, and institutional research capacity and infrastructure
- **Community Outreach, Information Dissemination, and Public Health Education** - to ensure the public, healthcare professionals, and research communities are informed and educated concerning the latest advances in minority health and health disparities research.

The objectives below, associated with each of these overarching goals, have been expanded in response to public comments received regarding the *NIH Strategic Research Plan and Budget to Reduce and Ultimately Eliminate Health Disparities, Fiscal Years 2002-2006.*

RESEARCH OBJECTIVES	RESEARCH CAPACITY OBJECTIVES	OUTREACH OBJECTIVES
■ Advance understanding of the development and progression of diseases and disabilities that contribute to health disparities ■ Develop new or improved approaches for detecting or diagnosing the onset or progression of diseases and disabilities that contribute to health disparities ■ Develop new or improved approaches for preventing or delaying the onset or progression of diseases and disabilities that contribute to health disparities ■ Develop new or improved approaches for treating diseases and disabilities that contribute to health disparities ■ In partnership with other agencies of DHHS, advance understanding of the multifactorial causes of health disparities, including non-biological bases of disease incidence and progression	■ Increase the number of participants in clinical trials from racial and ethnic minority populations and other health disparity populations ■ Expand opportunities in research training and career development for, and provide research supplements to, research investigators from racial and ethnic minority populations and other health disparity populations ■ Increase the number of researchers conducting health disparities research ■ Increase funding support for construction and renovation of research facilities across the Nation aimed at enhancing the ability of these institutions to conduct health disparities research ■ Provide increased funding at institutions across the country for resources, new equipment, and shared equipment programs for use in health disparities research ■ Increase representation in peer review from racial and ethnic minority populations and other health disparity populations ■ Promote the development of inter-institutional partnerships between historically research intensive and historically minority serving institutions that seek to build research infrastructure ■ Improve research data collection systems, and enhance data quality regarding health disparities, and develop uniform data systems that facilitate strategies for the elimination of health disparities ■ In collaboration with schools and programs of public health, state and local health departments, and academic health departments, support and promote community-based participatory research	■ Provide the latest research-based information to healthcare providers to enhance the care provided to individuals within racial and ethnic minority populations and other health disparity populations ■ Facilitate the incorporation of science-based information into the curricula of medical and allied health professions schools, theological education institutions, public health schools, and into continuing education activities of health professionals ■ Maintain ongoing communication linkages and partnerships with community-based and faith-based organizations, health care associations, foundations and academic institutions, and foster dialogue with racial and ethnic minority populations and other health disparity populations, including the underserved ■ Develop computer databases and internet resources to disseminate current information about scientific research and discoveries and other activities regarding health disparities ■ Develop targeted public health education programs focused on particular disease areas in order to reach those individuals within racial and ethnic minority populations and other health disparity populations who experience health disparities within these disease areas ■ Facilitate, document and disseminate practical strategies responsive to the health care needs, and appropriate to the cultural and linguistic needs, of communities throughout the United States ■ Collaborate with public health and other health oriented policy centers to translate research findings into policy documents that can be used by policy groups and other stakeholders to explain new discoveries from a policy perspective to decision makers

Specific initiatives to support these objectives are highlighted in Section IV, Volume I of the plan. The programs presented are a representative sampling, selected for their depth of activities and breadth of scope in addressing minority health and health disparities. They do not represent the totality of the NIH program. Further information about IC initiatives can be found in Volume II of this strategic plan.

All of these many initiatives cut across a variety of areas representing a myriad of diseases, disabilities, and organizational boundaries. These initiatives represent a trans-agency commitment to exploring and solving many of the health disparities problems our citizens and our Nation face. Much needs to be done, but we are confident that the medical research community working with, and informed by, the public, patients, health care providers, policymakers, and others will continue to develop new knowledge that will lead to improvements in the prevention, diagnosis, and treatment of diseases and disabilities that contribute to health disparities among minority and medically underserved populations.

Section I: Introduction

Despite notable improvements in the overall health of the Nation in the last two decades, there continue to be striking disparities in the burden of illness and death among African Americans, Hispanics, Native Americans, Alaska Natives, Asians, and Pacific Islanders and underserved groups such as disadvantaged rural Whites. Overcoming such persistent health disparities, and promoting health for all Americans ranks as one of our Nation's foremost challenges.

The findings section of P.L. 106-525, the Minority Health and Health Disparities Research and Education Act of 2000, notes the impact of health disparities upon minorities and upon the medically underserved across the nation:

> **Minority Health Disparities**
> Diseases, disorders, and conditions that disproportionately afflict individuals who are members of racial and ethnic minority groups
> **Other Health Disparity Populations**
> Population groups who suffer from health disparities when compared to the general population

(1) Despite notable progress in the overall health of the Nation, there are continuing disparities in the burden of illness and death experienced by African Americans, Hispanics, Native Americans, Alaska Natives and Asian Pacific Islanders, compared to the United States population as a whole.
(2) The largest number of the medically underserved are white individuals, and many of them have the same health care access problems as do members of minority groups.

Section 485(d)(2) of the law states that the Director, NCMHD, "shall give priority consideration to determining whether minority groups qualify as health disparity populations…."

The law defines the term "minority group" by reference to Section 1707 of the Public Health Service Act, which states at paragraph (g):

(1) The term "racial and ethnic minority group" means American Indians (including Alaska Natives, Eskimos, and Aleuts); Asian Americans; Native Hawaiians and other Pacific Islanders; Blacks; and Hispanics.
(2) The term "Hispanic" means individuals whose origin is Mexican, Puerto Rican, Cuban, Central or South American, or any other Spanish-speaking country."

Public Law 106-525 required the NCMHD to report to the Congress by December 2003 recommendations for the methodology the NIH will use to determine the amount of NIH resources dedicated to the conduct and support of health disparities research.

In October 2003 the NIH Director and the Director, NCMHD, established an NIH Committee on Minority Health and Health Disparities Research Definitions and Application Methodology, which developed new definitions and a revised application methodology that were used by the NIH in developing this updated version of the NIH Strategic Plan. In January 2004, the Committee provided uniform NIH Guidelines that:

- Provide NIH operational definitions, based on Public Law 106-525, for minority health and health disparities research,
- Provide a consistent methodology for applying the definitions,
- Contain the criteria necessary to identify both minority health and health disparities population groups and diseases, and
- Serve as the foundation for identifying, coding, tracking, and reporting on NIH activities and resources.

The health disparity populations included in the NIH Guidelines and covered by the *NIH Health Disparities Strategic Plan, Fiscal Years 2004-2008* are the minority groups delineated within Section 1707(g), PHS Act, above, as well as low socioeconomic status (low-SES) populations and rural populations.

The Congress recognized, however, that the *NIH Health Disparities Strategic Plan* should be an evolving document and required that the Plan be updated annually. In this way, the Congress also foresaw that additional health disparity populations may be identified and provided in Section 485(d)(1) of the law a vehicle for the designation of additional health disparity populations as follows:

"A population is a health disparity population if, as determined by the Director of the Center after consultation with the Director of the Agency for Healthcare Research and Quality, there is a significant disparity in the overall rate of disease incidence, prevalence, morbidity, mortality, or survival rates in the population as compared to the health status of the general population."

In the future as the *NIH Health Disparities Strategic Plan* is revised and updated over the years, and based upon the IOM Report described below, the NCMHD will work with the Agency for Healthcare Research and Quality to determine whether other populations meet this definition and should be designated as health disparity populations. Thus, future iterations of the plan will reflect the evolution of the development of health disparity populations.

It is imperative that the Nation make a concerted effort to reduce health disparities. The National Institutes of Health (NIH) has a unique and central role in this endeavor. By supporting and conducting a wide range of research, the NIH seeks new knowledge, strategies, and methodologies about disease and disabilities. This new knowledge has, and will continue to, lead to innovative diagnostics, treatments, and preventive strategies to reduce, and eventually eliminate, health disparities.

Public Comment

From late October 2003 to early January 2004, in order to receive public comment the NCMHD posted on its website the *NIH Strategic Research Plan and Budget to Reduce and Ultimately Eliminate Health Disparities, Fiscal Years 2002-2006*. Several major themes emerged from the public comments:

- Increase the number of health disparities populations studied by the NIH; in other words add additional populations, such as: lesbian, gay, bisexual and transgender communities; Haitians; individuals suffering from orphan diseases; underrepresented Asian subpopulations; the mentally ill; men; prisoners; and the disabled.
- Use racially and culturally sensitive and appropriate communication and ensure that all communications with health disparities populations and their sub-groups address their needs and perspectives.
- Expand the scope of scientific inquiry to include cultural, psychological, behavioral, social, racial, and gender-based influences on health and study access to health care. Produce accurate "health disparities" definitions and data.
- Improve research infrastructure at minority academic institutions.
- Strengthen the capacity of minority communities by broadening partnerships and leveraging resources available from professional associations, health care organizations, academic institutions, and other community members that serve minority communities.
- Distribute NIH resources equitably across all population groups by increasing research regarding men, Native Americans, Hispanics, and groups from southeast Asia.

The public comments received were provided by the NCMHD to each of the NIH Institutes and Centers and involved offices of the NIH Office of the Director (OD) for their consideration in developing their updated submissions contained within Volume II of the *NIH Health Disparities Strategic Plan, Fiscal Years 2004-2008*. Each IC and OD Office was asked specifically to address how they applied the public comments in developing their revised submission.

As indicated above, the NCMHD received a number of public comments recommending that additional groups be designated as health disparity populations. The NCMHD is sensitive to these comments and will follow the process described above to determine whether additional groups should be so designated. The thorough consideration of public comment will continue to be a fundamental component of the development of each future iteration of the *NIH Health Disparities Strategic Plan*.

NIH Organizational Structure

The mission of the NIH is to improve the Nation's health by uncovering new knowledge about the prevention, detection, diagnosis, and treatment of diseases and disabilities. NIH's mission is, thus, central to expanding national efforts to address differences in incidence, prevalence, morbidity, mortality and burden of diseases and other adverse health conditions that exist among specific population groups in the United States.

The NIH, comprised of twenty-seven Institutes and Centers (ICs) and other program offices in the Office of the Director (OD), has long been committed to addressing and eliminating health disparities. The National Center on Minority Health and Health Disparities (NCMHD) serves as the focal point for planning and coordinating minority health and other health disparities research across the NIH.

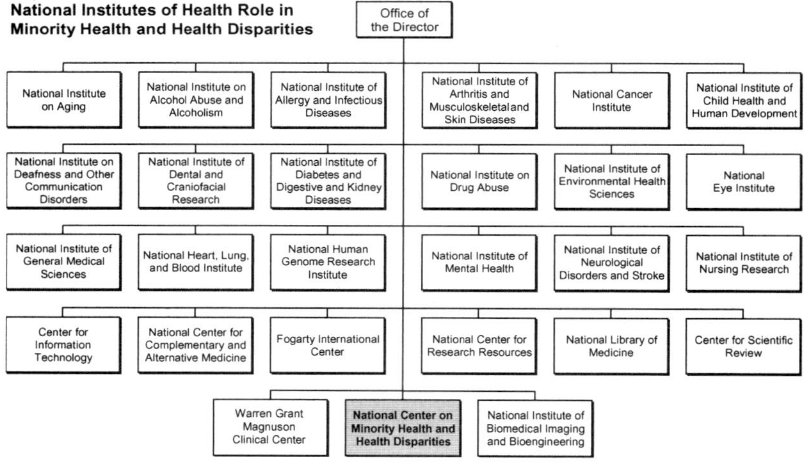

NCMHD Role

According to P.L. 106-525, the NCMHD was established by Congress to work in collaboration with other NIH IC's to foster, coordinate, and assess the progress of all NIH-sponsored research activities involving minority health and other health disparities.

The NCMHD leads the federal effort at the National Institutes of Health to stimulate new research, improve the health status of minority Americans and other underserved groups across their lifespan and promote programs aimed at expanding the participation of underrepresented minorities in all aspects of biomedical and behavioral research.

Specific priorities for the Center include:

- Developing an integrated, cross-disciplinary national research agenda on health disparities
- Promoting and supporting research capacity-building activities in the minority and medically underserved communities
- Establishing broad aspects of two-way communication and outreach with the Center's many stakeholders
- Collaborating with NIH research partners to sponsor activities involving minority health and health disparities
- Assessing, tracking, and monitoring the results of NIH minority health and health disparities research progress

NCMHD's effort cuts across disease areas and organizational boundaries and involves a trans-agency commitment. It coordinates and augments the efforts of each Institute, Center, and program office in the NIH Office of the Director. Furthermore, the Center functions as the central repository for minority health and health disparity research information and fosters knowledge sharing among the IC's. More information regarding NCMHD's mission, vision, and strategic objectives can be found in the NCMHD's section in Volume II.

Objectives of the Strategic Plan

In response to P.L. 106-525, the five-year Trans-NIH Strategic Plan describes an ambitious approach to reduce and ultimately eliminate health disparities among racial and ethnic minorities and other health disparity groups. The scope of the problem of health disparities among minorities and other populations, the specific objectives for solving the problem, and the means for advancing those objectives are the substance of this strategic plan. The initiatives described here represent the major priorities and the broad range of activities that the NIH will undertake to reduce and ultimately eliminate health disparities. This plan allows for the evaluation of NIH's progress and the extent to which NIH meets its projected goals. The plan is not merely a compilation of all the activities

Objectives of the Trans-NIH Strategic Plan

- Present NIH's role in minority health and health disparities, including the function of the NCMHD
- Discuss the methodology used to develop the Trans-NIH Strategic Plan
- Examine factors that contribute to minority health and health disparities
- Outline Department of Health and Human Services (HHS) and NIH efforts to reduce and ultimately eliminate health disparities
- Present the structured planning model used to support minority health and other health disparities activities; including the mission, vision, goals, objectives and sample programs that support reducing and eliminating minority health and other health disparities

of the relevant NIH entities, it aggregates the primary areas of emphasis and activities conducted across the agency and provides the reader with an understanding of the cross-cutting nature of disease and scientific discovery.

This plan is an evolving document. It will be updated and revised on a yearly basis based on public comments received, public health need, scientific opportunity, changes in available funds, and other factors.

Organization of the Strategic Plan

This strategic plan sets forth NIH's goals for reducing and, ultimately, eliminating health disparities among racial and ethnic minorities and other populations and describes some of the many initiatives that will be expanded or created to meet these goals. Volume I contains background on minority health and health disparities, future initiatives to address these issues, and NIH long-term goals and objectives. Volume II includes strategic plan submissions from all the IC's, as well as from NIH's Office of Research on Women's Health (ORWH), Office of Disease Prevention (ODP), Office of Rare Diseases Research (ORD), Office of Intramural Research (OIR), Office of AIDS Research (OAR) and Office of Behavioral and Social Sciences Research (OBSSR).

SECTION	TOPICS
VOLUME I	
I. Introduction	Describes the NIH organizational structure, the objectives of the Trans-NIH Strategic Plan, the organization of the plan, and the methodology used to develop the strategic plan.
II. Background on Minority Health and Health Disparities	Presents the factors that contribute to the problem of minority health and other health disparities
III. Department of Health and Human Services (HHS) and NIH Efforts to Reduce and Ultimately Eliminate Health Disparities	Describes HHS, and NIH efforts to address minority health and other health disparities and the coordination of the interdisciplinary approach
IV. Strategic Planning Model	Presents the strategic planning model; including the mission, vision, goals, objectives, and sample programs established to support reducing and eventually eliminating health disparities among minorities and other populations. In addition, the NIH Minority Health and Health Disparities Budget and the conclusion are presented in this section.
VOLUME II	
Individual IC, ORWH, ODP, ORD, OIR, OAR, and OBSSR Strategic Plan Submissions	Provides IC, ORWH, ODP, ORD, OIR, OAR, and OBSSR strategic areas of emphasis, objectives, action plans, timelines and performance measures to reduce and ultimately eliminate health disparities in the United States.

Development of the Strategic Plan

The NIH followed a structured strategic planning model in developing this strategic plan. The initial draft five-year Trans-NIH Strategic Plan incorporated the efforts of a Trans-NIH working group, which consisted of each NIH Institute and Center Director. The draft was published on October 6, 2000 for technical and public review. The plan was developed through an open process with substantial public input, particularly from representatives of groups who disproportionately experience disparities in health. Comments were received and archived up until February 23, 2001. Next, each IC, the OBSSR, and the OAR developed a mission-specific submission for the strategic plan that sets forth in greater detail ongoing and future efforts to reduce health disparities among minority and other health disparity populations. The NCMHD synthesized and analyzed all IC submissions to develop the Trans-NIH Strategic Plan.

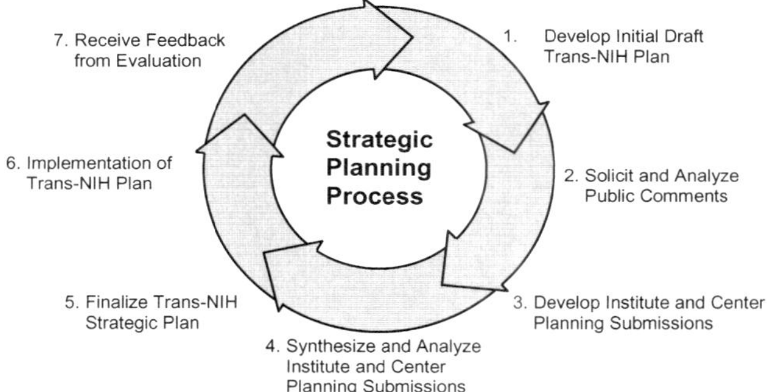

The first iteration of the *NIH Strategic Research Plan and Budget to Reduce and Ultimately Eliminate Health Disparities, Fiscal Years 2002-2006*, was submitted to the Congress in March 2003. The Plan was posted on the NCMHD website for a 60 day public comment period from October 30, 2003 to January 5, 2004.

Accordingly, this revised and updated version of the strategic plan incorporates input from the public, professional and patient advocacy groups, health care organizations, academic institutions, ethnic/minority groups, federal agencies, and the scientific community. The input from these stakeholders is reflected throughout the plan.

During the implementation of the Strategic Plan, the NCMHD will continue to seek additional public comment to aide in revising the plan. The Center also will continue to provide support to the other ICs to assist them in convening workshops that will include outside experts to assess their health disparities agendas, progress and outcomes in health disparities research. This process will enable further refinement of the IC submissions to the Trans-NIH Strategic Plan in future years.

In addition, the NCMHD has asked the National Academy of Sciences/Institute of Medicine to conduct a study that will review the NIH Strategic Research Plan. This review will assess the adequacy of the plan in achieving the NIH's goals and objectives regarding research, research infrastructure, and public information and community outreach. The study also will assess the adequacy of coordination across NIH ICs in helping to develop and carry out the elements of the strategic plan.

To conduct an independent analysis of the strategic plan, the IOM will assemble a 15-member study committee. Because of the interdisciplinary nature of health disparities research, the study committee will include individuals with expertise in scientific areas ranging from population-based genetic variation to social and socioeconomic influences on health. The IOM committee will be composed of individuals with expertise in health disparities research, public health, health services research, and will reflect relevant health research disciplines, such as biology, sociology, genetics, medicine, anthropology, and other fields. The study committee will meet five times over the course of the study at 2-3 month intervals. Study committee meetings will be publicly announced via the IOM's website at www.iom.edu.

A critically important part of this process will be to ensure that the NCMHD and NIH officials, as well as interested advocacy and scientific groups, can discuss the strategic plan with the study committee in an open forum. The study committee will therefore host three public workshops at which the NCMHD Director and the NIH IC Directors will be asked to comment on the strategic plan, followed by input from scientific and advocacy groups. In addition, the study committee will invite written comments from interested scientific and advocacy groups. The public workshops will be planned and convened in conjunction with the committee's meetings, to ensure that the committee hears the perspectives of community leaders, academic health professions leaders, and other relevant stakeholders.

The primary product of this study will be a technical report, reviewed in accordance with National Research Council procedures. The report, due to be completed in fiscal year 2005, will be widely disseminated to stakeholders, including the NCMHD, NIH ICs, scientific leaders, health policymakers (including the Congress and relevant Federal agencies), advocacy groups, major health care provider professional organizations, foundations, and relevant individuals and organizations. Copies of the report summary will be produced for broader distribution, and made available on the Internet through the National Academy Press (www.nap.edu).

Section II: Background on Minority Health and Health Disparities

The health disparities that afflict racial and ethnic minorities as well as other underserved populations are not limited to one or two disease categories. They apply to a broad spectrum of disease types that encompass infectious diseases, vascular diseases, endocrine diseases, arthritic diseases, connective tissue diseases, malignancies, mental illness and others. Health disparities also exist within different geographic regions of the United States. Consequently, "health disparity" is an issue that is relevant to the work of every NIH Institute and Center, and certain offices within the NIH Office of the Director. A brief sample of relevant diseases follows:

- **Infant Mortality** – Over the last decade, the infant mortality rate remains twice as high among African Americans as compared to Whites, even when controlling for socioeconomic factors. Native American and Alaska Native infants also have a death rate almost double that of Whites.

- **Heart Disease and Stroke** Cardiovascular disease takes a heavy toll on certain populations. Heart disease rates have been consistently higher in the African American population than in whites. Data on stroke risk factors are sparse for most racial and ethnic populations, except for African Americans whose stroke deaths, when adjusted for age, are almost 80 percent higher than in whites. Stroke death rates for people aged >35 years from 1991 to 1998 show that African American men (182 per 100,000 population) and women (153 per 100,000 population) have the highest stroke death rate than any other race or ethnic group.

- **Cancer** – Cancer deaths vary by gender, race, and ethnicity. Certain racial and ethnic groups have lower survival rates than whites for most cancers. Colorectal cancer rates among Alaska Natives are higher than the national average and Asian Americans suffer disproportionately from stomach and liver cancers. African American men have the highest rates of colon, rectum, prostate, and lung cancers.

  Specifically, colorectal cancer incidence and death rates were higher among men than among women and were higher among African American men and women than among white men and women. Five-year trends in death rates in all states were stable or declined for both men and women, with the exception of African American men in Louisiana and Oklahoma.

- **Mental Health** – Disease burden associated with mental disorders falls disproportionately on ethnic minority populations. Native American and

Alaska Natives not only suffer disproportionately from depression, but this population also experiences a higher rate of suicide.

- **Type 2 Diabetes** – The prevalence of diabetes in African Americans is nearly 70 percent higher than in whites. Native Americans, Hispanics, African Americans, and some Asian Americans and Pacific Islanders, including Japanese Americans, Samoans, and Native Hawaiians are at particularly high risk for development of type 2 diabetes.

- **HIV and AIDS** – The disproportionate impact of HIV/AIDs on certain populations underscores the importance of sustained research and prevention efforts. In 2002, the AIDS diagnosis rate among African Americans was almost 11 times the rate among whites. African American women had a 23 times greater diagnoses rate than white women. African American men had almost a 9 times greater rate of AIDS diagnosis than white men. In addition, the AIDS incidence per 100,00 population among Hispanics in 2000 was 22.5, more then 3 times the rate for whites.

The table that follows further describes, in quantitative terms, health disparities of certain conditions in selected populations. It is clear from this overview that the nature of the disparity may vary significantly from group to group, and that for certain groups there is a paucity of data to adequately assess the problem. This data was compiled from the following resources: *"Health, United States 2002"; "Trends in Racial and Ethnic-Specific Rates for the Health Status Indicators: United States, 1990-98";"Healthy People 2010: Understanding and Improving Health";* and National Vital Statistics Reports, *"Deaths: Leading Causes for 2000"; "The Burden of Chronic Disease and Their Risk Factors: National and State Perspectives"; "A Public Health Action Plan to Prevent Health Disease and Stroke: Executive Summary and Overview"; "HIV/AIDS among African Americans"; "HIV /AIDS among Hispanics in the United States"; and "Annual Report to the Nation of the Status of Cancer 1975—2000, Featuring the Uses of Surveillance Data for Cancer Prevention and Control".*

HEALTH DISPARITIES OF CERTAIN CONDITIONS IN SELECTED POPULATIONS

HEALTH CONDITION AND SPECIFIC EXAMPLE	INDEX IN SELECTED POPULATIONS				
	WHITE	AFRICAN AMERICAN	HISPANIC or LATINO	ASIAN or PACIFIC ISLANDER	AMERICAN INDIAN or ALASKA NATIVE
Infant mortality rate per 1000 live births[1]	5.9	13.9	5.8	5.1	9.1
Cancer mortality rate per 100,000[2]	199.3	255.1	123.7	124.2	129.3
Lung Cancer - age adjusted death rate[3]	38.3	46.0	13.6	17.2	25.1

Female Breast Cancer age adjusted death rate	18.7	26.1	12.1	9.8	10.3
Coronary Heart Disease mortality rate per 100,000[2]	206	252	145	123	126
Stroke mortality rate per 100,000	58	80	39	51	38
Diabetes diagnosed rate per 100,000	36	74	61	DSU	DSU
End-Stage Renal Disease rate per million[2]	218	873	DNA	344	589
AIDS – percentage of persons with AIDS [4]	34	44.9	19.7	0.8	0.4

DSU = Data are statistically unreliable

DNA = Data have not been analyzed

[1] *Chartbook on Trends in the Health of Americans.* Excerpted from Health, United States 2002. Department of Health and Human Services. National Center for Health Statistics. DHHS Publication No. 1232-1. August 2002.

[2] *Healthy People 2010. Understanding and Improving Health (Second Edition).* Department of Health and Human Services. November 2000.

[3] Keppel, Kenneth, Jeffrey Pearcy and Diane Wagener. *Trends in Racial and Ethnic-Specific Rates for the Health Status Indicators: United States, 1990-98.* Statistical Notes. Number 23. January 2002, pgs. 1-16.

[4] Morbidity and Mortality Weekly Report. *HIV and AIDS – United States, 1981-2000.* June 1,2001. Vol. 50:21:430-433.

[5] *National Vital Statistics Reports.* 2002 Deaths: Leading Causes for 2000. *Vol. 50:16:1-41.*

Multifactorial Basis of Health Disparities

The genesis of health disparities is multifactorial and hence requires a coordinated and interdisciplinary approach to eliminate them. Below we present one author's perspective of the various factors contributing to the disproportionate burden of morbidity and mortality suffered by racial and ethnic minorities. Other schema and classifications could be created as well, however they would have in common many of the factors cited below. With the exception of race, many of these factors apply to non-ethnic underserved populations as well. The common denominator in the latter case is related to low socio-economic status and the protean effects of poverty on health.

A Framework for Understanding the Relationship Between Race and Health[1]

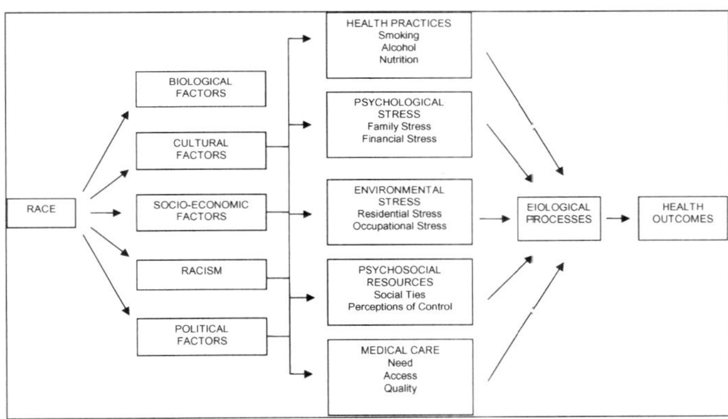

Not only are there multiple factors, there is great overlap between them that produces a destructive synergy. We describe several of these factors in greater detail below:

Socioeconomic Status/Education Level. An extensive body of literature has demonstrated a strong association between health and socioeconomic status. (The highest educational level achieved is often considered one of the best measures of socio-economic status.) For instance Marmot and colleagues have shown that illness and mortality decreased in British civil servants as measures of socioeconomic status rose. Low socioeconomic status and poor health were most closely correlated with a perception of reward imbalance and lack of control in

[1] *King G. and William D.R., 1995. Race and Health: A multidimensional approach to African American Health. In: Amick BC, Levine S, Tarlov AR, Walsh DC, eds. Society and Health: New York: Oxford University Press (Taken from Workshop Summary: Pharmacokinetics and Drug Interactions in the Elderly, National Academy Press*

the work place. This also correlated with an increase in fibrinogen, a biological marker of inflammation and certain chronic disease states. The negative health effects of depressed socioeconomic status are relevant to many racial and ethnic minorities, as well as to underserved white populations.

Biology. Even after controlling for socioeconomic status there seem to be factors that further influence disease states in racial and ethnic populations. Some of this residual effect may be biological in nature. For instance differences in socio-economic status do not completely explain the higher rates of hypertension, glaucoma and lupus in African Americans. "Thrifty genes" and other predisposing genetic factors have been proposed to explain the epidemic of obesity and diabetes in Pima Indians. Biological differences seem responsible for different rates of drug metabolism in various populations. This may help explain why immunosuppressive agents may not be as effective in African Americans.

Access and Quality of Health Care. Health care access and quality are often substandard in the same populations that suffer from health disparities. Lack of access may result in failure to prevent disease, delayed detection and inadequate treatment of disease. In the United States racial minorities and other health disparity groups suffer from barriers to medical care for multiple reasons i.e., lack of insurance, which is in turn related to unemployment or employment in the small business sector; language barriers; travel barriers; immigration status; and issues related to culture, trust and discrimination. Among racial and ethnic minorities Hispanics seem to face particularly high barriers to access, though disadvantaged whites who are unemployed or work in the small business sector are frequently uninsured and face many of the same issues. However, equalizing access will not be sufficient to eliminate health disparities. Even in countries that have optimized and equalized access, for example Britain and Finland, health disparities persist and closely track socioeconomic status.

Racial and Ethnic Discrimination. Racial and ethnic discrimination creates additional barriers to care. Even if discrimination is not overt, perceived discrimination that occurs as a consequence of insensitivity or a lack of cultural competence can create further barriers to care and an ineffective therapeutic relationship. The struggle to "advance and achieve" in the face of discrimination creates stress that may manifest itself in disease. This phenomenon, known as John Henryism, has been thought to contribute to the disproportionate degree of hypertension in African Americans. Hypertension is a major risk factor for stroke, which is also disproportionately elevated in African Americans.

Cultural Issues. Culture may be interpreted in the traditional sense as applying to a racial or ethnic group, or more broadly to include socioeconomic status, urban, rural or suburban lifestyles, as well as geographic location and other factors. Cultural practices may influence diets and other behaviors that influence health status. In addition cultural factors may include alternative methods of healing that may conflict with mainstream medicine. Many racial and ethnic minority patients who employ traditional methods of healing often feel uncomfortable informing non-ethnic caregivers of these modalities, which may include pharmacologically active herbs.

Coordination of an Interdisciplinary Approach

While this list of factors is not meant to be exhaustive, it is illustrative of the complexity of the problem and points to the need for a coordinated interdisciplinary approach if we are to reduce and ultimately eliminate the "health gap". The coordination must occur within the NIH as well as among the other federal agencies devoted to this objective. The goal of the coordinated interdisciplinary approach is to promote synergies and reduce redundancy in this formidable effort. This has implications for the trans-NIH plan on multiple levels:

- Many of the disease complexes that afflict health disparity groups cut across boundaries of several Institutes and Centers (IC's). Examples include coronary artery disease, diabetes, obesity, anger and depression, and behavioral factors that contribute to all these. This suggests a need for enhanced collaboration among the Institutes and Centers in conducting health disparity research. In addition, IC's that are traditionally biological must develop an increased awareness of, and an integration with, the non-biological factors contributing to disease. For instance establishing more extensive correlation between disease states and educational status, or using surveys and other instruments that are more tailored to minority populations.

- It is important to build infrastructure for health disparity research by supporting minority-serving institutions that may not have adequate resources, increasing the number of minority researchers, and increasing the scope and depth of research that focuses on health disparities. Sharing "best practices" in attracting minority researchers is an obvious way different IC's can collaborate.

- It is essential that the IC's develop new and innovative ways to reach health disparity populations so that the fruits of research can benefit the target populations. This outreach must go beyond mere information dissemination. It must strive to influence behaviors that are relevant to health. Collaboration between biologically focused and behaviorally focused IC's and offices is important in this effort. Once again establishing and sharing best practices in this regard would be highly beneficial.

- Finally, in order to achieve the Congressionally mandated goal of reducing and ultimately eliminating health disparities, it is important that we establish interim goals and objectives with outcomes that are, where possible, quantifiable. This is a challenging task and IC's can learn from each other in establishing best practices in measuring outcomes related to the reduction of health disparities.

Congress established the NCMHD to play the central role in leading, coordinating and monitoring this effort. One of the first steps was to produce and continue to update this trans-NIH plan to reduce and ultimately eliminate health disparities in the United States.

Section III: Department of Health and Human Services (HHS) and NIH Efforts to Reduce and Ultimately Eliminate Health Disparities

HHS Efforts

In developing the NIH Strategic Plan, a review of existing Department of Health and Human Services (HHS) activities to address minority health and other health disparities was undertaken to ensure the NIH Strategic Plan is aligned with similar HHS efforts and to ensure that the NIH is leveraging the full breadth and depth of programs and activities directed toward minority health and other health disparity populations. Two key cross cutting initiatives, the HHS *Initiative to Eliminate Racial and Ethnic Disparities in Health* and *Healthy People 2010,* were considered given that aspects of their goals and objectives are related directly to this Plan.

- The *Initiative to Eliminate Racial and Ethnic Disparities in Health* was initiated by the HHS to eliminate the disparities in six areas of health status experienced by racial and ethnic minority populations.

Initiative to Eliminate Racial and Ethnic Disparities In Health
- Infant Mortality
- Cancer Screening and Management
- Cardiovascular Disease and Stroke
- Diabetes
- HIV/AIDS Rates
- Child and Adult Immunization Levels

- Complementing the *Initiative to Eliminate Racial and Ethnic Disparities in Health* is another HHS initiative, *Healthy People 2010*, a national health promotion and disease prevention initiative involving several federal agencies such as the U.S. Department of Agriculture and the U.S. Department of Education. *Healthy People 2010* sets forth the Nation's health objectives for the next decade, which include a major goal for eliminating health disparities among different segments of the population.

Healthy People 2010
- Conduct New Outreach Campaign
- Develop New Approaches to Build on Existing Successes to Address Racial and Ethnic Health Disparities
- Major New Foundation/Public Sector Collaboration to Address Disparities
- Develop more Effective Ways to Target Existing Federal Programs to Address Health Disparities
- Involve Communities, Foundations, Advocacy Organizations, and Businesses to Develop Ways to Target Racial and Ethnic Health Disparities

The NIH Strategic Plan is consistent with these HHS-wide efforts and furthers the objectives of HHS to prevent disease, promote health, and deliver care to the U.S. population, especially racial and ethnic minority and other health disparity populations.

The coordination of HHS health disparities research activities will be further enhanced by NIH participation in the activities of the HHS Health Disparities Council and the HHS Research Coordination Council.

NCMHD Efforts

The NCMHD has accomplished much since its creation. Today, the NCMHD has 60 Health Disparities Centers of Excellence spread across the nation. These Centers of Excellence, now located in 23 states, the District of Columbia, and Puerto Rico, support health disparities research, research training and community involvement to identify factors that contribute to health disparities and to develop and implement new diagnostic, treatment, and prevention strategies.

The NCMHD addresses the national need to develop a diverse, strong, and culturally competent scientific workforce by eliminating barriers that prevent racial and ethnic minority students and students from disadvantaged backgrounds from pursuing research careers. Currently, the NCMHD supports about 300 researchers from 38 states through its two Loan Repayment Programs, which help to level the playing field and make it possible for under represented individuals to enter the scientific, technological, and engineering workforce. These Health Disparities Ambassadors are key to creating the culturally competent scientific and clinical research workforce of the future.

The NCMHD also has created a one-of-a-kind Research Endowment Program. Unique at the NIH, this program addresses the national need to build research and training capacity in institutions that make significant investments in the education and training of minority and disadvantaged individuals. This program is making it possible for 13 institutions located in 11 states and Puerto Rico to establish health disparities endowed chairs and programs; enhance student recruitment efforts; provide merit-based scholarships; recruit and retain faculty; develop innovative instruction delivery systems in minority and health disparities research areas; and access emerging technologies.

The NCMHD Research Infrastructure in Minority Institutions Program, born out of a partnership between the NIH National Center for Research Resources and the former NIH Office of Research on Minority Health (the predecessor to the NCMHD), is making it possible for institutions to target research efforts on health disparities that exist in the Southwest Border States; in rural communities, such as the Appalachia Region, the Mississippi Delta, and the Frontier States; and in urban centers of the nation. Currently, 11 institutions in eight states benefit from this program.

In addition to using its core programs, the NCMHD strategy to eliminate health disparities also includes leveraging NIH dollars and expertise by creating partnerships with the NIH ICs and other agencies within the Department of Health and Human Services (DHHS) to fund health disparities research, training, and outreach programs. Over the past two years alone, the NCMHD forged many new partnerships, supporting more than 400 research projects to combat health disparities in our nation.

For example, the Center provides support to increase the number of funded meritorious programs through the Centers for Disease Control and Prevention's *Racial and Ethnic Approaches to Community Health (REACH 2010)*, the Agency for Healthcare Research Quality's *Excellence Centers to Eliminate Racial and Ethnic Health Disparities (EXCEED)* programs, and the Indian Health Service's *Tribal Epidemiology Centers* program.

In addition, the Center and the DHHS Office of Minority Health, Office of Public Health and Science, co-fund several projects to support other organizations, including:

Interamerican College of Physicians and Surgeons (ICPS) - The National Hispanic Youth Initiative in Health, Biomedical Research and Policy Development includes a rigorous curriculum and comprehensive approach to increasing Hispanic manpower in health care and biomedical research. It comprises a series of lectures and round table/group discussions on health care issues and scientific research, academic preparation, and opportunities in the health sciences and research, health legislation and public policy, the health status of Hispanic communities, and clinical and scientific preceptor ships. This program contributes to retaining students in the academic pipeline and serves as a pre-college program to increasing the number of Hispanic youth pursuing careers in the health sciences and/or scientific research arenas.

National Medical Association (NMA) - The National African American Youth Initiative in Health and Policy Development Scholars Program increases the awareness of African American youth on national health issues, scientific research, public policy and the role and impact of the Federal Government in the development of health policy. The Youth Initiative prepares, motivates, and encourages young African Americans to pursue careers in the health and scientific fields.

American Indian Youth Initiative - This project recruits promising high school students into biomedical careers and further expands the Indian Health Network, an on-line electronic service designed to link isolated tribes and urban organizations with physicians and other providers, health facilities, and educational institutions to enhance the health of all Indian communities.

The Asian and Pacific Island American Health Forum - This project will establish and maintain a national on-line Asian and Pacific Islander (A/PI) *Health Information Network* to expand and enhance health promotion and disease prevention, health advocacy, mental health and substance abuse, education, health services research opportunities, and cultural competency. NIH can use this information network to target information about research opportunities and clinical trials to A/PI communities.

NIH Efforts

The NIH occupies a unique place in the federal effort to eliminate health disparities among minorities and the medically underserved. The NIH works with the public, health care providers, scientists, and policymakers to identify the relevant issues; develop the research plans to address these issues; and support and conduct a broad range of studies in this area. These studies include epidemiological; biological, behavioral, and social science research; as well as health services research. In addition, the NIH provides support for the infrastructure that underpins the research enterprise, such as training, instrumentation, and research facilities. The NIH carries out public information and community outreach programs to communicate research findings to individuals, organizations, and other entities that can put the research results into practice.

While NIH-funded research yields information important to addressing the complex problems among racial and ethnic minorities and other underserved populations, it is only a part of a multi-faceted effort to prevent disease, promote health, and deliver appropriate care to these communities.

Section IV: Strategic Planning Model for Reducing and Ultimately Eliminating Health Disparities

The strategic plan follows a methodical planning model, which presents the mission, vision, goals, objectives, and programs for reducing and eventually eliminating health disparities among minorities and other populations - elements of the model that will guide the remainder of this volume.

Strategic Planning Model

Mission — Captures the enduring focus of the organization – the organization's grand purpose; why it exists and what needs it fulfills.

Vision — Captures the desired end state of the organization and describes future direction. Provides unity of direction and long-term focus.

Goals — Identifies how the vision will be realized. Goals are longer term in nature, and are broad statements describing a desired future condition or achievement.

Objectives — Provides additional specificity about how the goals will be accomplished. Objectives are more near term and measurable, and clearly describe an intended outcome.

Programs — Identifies programs to support meeting the objectives.

Mission to Reduce and Ultimately Eliminate Health Disparities

The mission is to promote minority health and to lead, coordinate, support, and assess the NIH effort to reduce and ultimately eliminate health disparities. In this effort the NCMHD conducts and supports basic, clinical, social, and behavioral research; promotes research infrastructure and training; fosters emerging programs; disseminates information; and reaches out to minority and other health disparity communities.

Vision to Reduce and Ultimately Eliminate Health Disparities

The vision to support minority health and health disparities is to envision an America in which all populations will have an equal opportunity to live long, healthy and productive lives.

Goals and Objectives to Reduce and Ultimately Eliminate Health Disparities

The Strategic Plan is focused on three major goals:

- Research
- Research Capacity; and
- Community Outreach, Information Dissemination, and Public Health Education

Each goal area has multiple objectives on how each goal will be accomplished.

Research. Research to advance our understanding of the development and progression of diseases and disabilities that contribute to health disparities in minority populations is central to this effort. Research includes developing new and improved approaches for detecting, diagnosing, preventing, treating or delaying onset or progression of diseases and disabilities that contribute to health disparities. It also includes advancing understanding of the multifactorial causes of health disparities.

GOAL	OBJECTIVES
Research	■ Advance understanding of the development and progression of diseases and disabilities that contribute to health disparities ■ Develop new or improved approaches for detecting or diagnosing the onset or progression of diseases and disabilities that contribute to health disparities ■ Develop new or improved approaches for preventing or delaying the onset or progression of diseases and disabilities that contribute to health disparities ■ Develop new or improved approaches for treating diseases and disabilities that contribute to health disparities ■ In partnership with other agencies of DHHS, advance understanding of the multifactorial causes of health disparities, including non-biological bases of disease incidence and progression

Research Capacity. Just as a building is only as solid as its foundation, the success of the biomedical research enterprise depends on a solid infrastructure. Broadly defined, research capacity includes biomedical researchers and personnel and the means and resources for supporting and training them, as well as research facilities, equipment, and supportive services. The NIH recognizes that our ability to reduce health disparities through the research proposed in this plan requires a strong commitment to training and supporting investigators in these areas. Our ability to sustain and even increase the momentum of recent scientific progress and our international leadership in medical research depends upon recruitment, training, support, and retention of biomedical investigators from diverse population groups. To ensure this, the NIH has identified nine research capacity objectives:

GOAL	OBJECTIVES
Research Capacity	▪ Increase the number of participants in clinical trials from racial and ethnic minority populations and other health disparity populations ▪ Expand opportunities in research training and career development for, and provide research supplements to, research investigators from racial and ethnic minority populations and other health disparity populations ▪ Increase the number of researchers conducting health disparities research ▪ Increase funding support for construction and renovation of research facilities across the nation aimed at enhancing the ability of these institutions to conduct health disparities research ▪ Provide increased funding at institutions across the country for resources, new equipment and shared equipment programs for use in health disparities research ▪ Increase representation in peer review from racial and ethnic minority populations and other health disparity populations ▪ Promote the development of inter-institutional partnerships between historically research intensive and historically minority serving institutions that seek to build research infrastructure ▪ Improve research data collection systems, and enhance data quality regarding health disparities, and develop uniform data systems that facilitate strategies for the elimination of health disparities ▪ In collaboration with schools and programs of public health, state and local health departments, and academic health departments, support and promote community-based participatory research

Community Outreach, Information Dissemination, and Public Health Education. Communicating the scientific and health information gained from research into health disparities is of paramount importance. These efforts extend beyond dissemination of the results of research to other scientists, and include the transmission of all information that may improve the health of racial and ethnic minorities and other health disparity populations to the general public, patients, advocacy groups, health care providers, media, and policymakers. Additionally, this includes a comprehensive and aggressive outreach to those groups whom the research is intended to help and their health care providers. These messages must be tailored to the communities at highest risk for the adverse consequences of the health disparity in question. The efforts must also include producing health information that is culturally applicable, ensuring that it is disseminated to the appropriate communities, and assessing the effectiveness of these communication efforts. In the arena of community outreach, information dissemination, and public health education our objectives include the following:

GOAL	OBJECTIVES
Outreach	■ Provide the latest research-based information to healthcare providers to enhance the care provided to individuals within racial and ethnic minority populations and other health disparity populations ■ Facilitate the incorporation of science-based information into the curricula of medical and allied health professions schools, theological education institutions, public health schools, and into continuing education activities of health professionals ■ Maintain ongoing communication linkages and partnerships with community-based and faith-based organizations, health care associations, foundations and academic institutions, and foster dialogue with racial and ethnic minority populations and other health disparity populations, including the underserved ■ Develop computer databases and internet resources to disseminate current information about scientific research and discoveries and other activities regarding health disparities ■ Develop targeted public health education programs focused on particular disease areas in order to reach those individuals within racial and ethnic minority populations and other health disparity populations who experience health disparities within these disease areas ■ Facilitate, document and disseminate practical strategies responsive to the health care needs, and appropriate to the cultural and linguistic needs, of communities throughout the United States ■ Collaborate with public health and other health oriented policy centers to translate research findings into policy documents that can be used by policy groups and other stakeholders to explain new discoveries from a policy perspective to decision makers

Overview of NIH Programs to Reduce and Ultimately Eliminate Health Disparities

This section highlights a number of the NIH programs related to minority health and health disparities research, research capacity, and public information and community outreach. The specific programs presented in this section are a representative sampling, selected for their depth of activities and breadth of scope in addressing minority health and health disparities. They do not represent the totality of the NIH program.

Each program outlines how objectives will be accomplished and identifies specific examples of how program performance will be measured through performance measures and/or outcome measures. Further information about IC initiatives and corresponding performance/outcome measures, can be found in Volume II of this strategic plan.

Sample Programs – Research. The research programs listed below are a representative example of the variety of research studies that NIH supports as part of its strategic plan for understanding and reducing health disparities among ethnic and racial minorities and other populations. The ultimate goal of these research efforts is to develop improved means for prevention, diagnosis, and treatment of diseases and disabilities that disproportionately affect specific populations. The table below outlines sample research programs and provides selected examples of program performance measures:

Selected Examples of Programs: Research

IC RESEARCH OBJECTIVES	IC PROGRAMS
NHBLI Support research to increase understanding of the development and progression of heart, lung, and blood diseases and sleep disorders that contribute to health disparities	■ Multi-Ethnic Study of Atherosclerosis, ■ Specialized Centers of Research (SCOR) on Ischemic Heart Disease in Blacks ■ Glucose Tolerance and Risk for Cardiovascular Disease in the Elderly
NHGRI Study genetic factors that contribute to diseases disproportionately affecting minority populations	■ African America Diabetes Mellitus Study (AADM) ■ African American Hereditary Prostate Cancer Study Network (AAHPC), ■ Barbados Prostate and Breast Cancer Study ■ Study of Hereditary Hemochromatosis and Iron Overload Disease in Diverse Populations
NIAID Reduce disparities in the incidence and prevalence of asthma	■ Inner-City Asthma Study
NIDA Epidemiology of Drug Abuse, Health Consequences and Infectious Diseases among Minority Populations Addressing Disparities in Treatment and Health Services Research	■ National Household Survey on Drug Abuse ■ Behavioral Therapy Development Program ■ National Drug Abuse Treatment Clinical Trials Network (CTN)
NIDDK Combine genetic linkage data from collaborating research groups and identifies regions of the human genome that show evidence for linkage in type 2 diabetes.	■ Diabetes Prevention Program (DPP)
NIMH Identify Factors that Overcome Health Disparities Related to Health Service Delivery and Use by Ethnic Populations	■ National Institute of Mental Health's Child and Adolescent Research Consortium, the American Psychological Association, and Fordham University's Center for Ethics Education
NINR Demonstrated community partnerships to reduce health disparities in racial and ethnically diverse minority populations Identify and address the disparities in health and health outcomes among racial and ethnic minority males	■ Interventions to Reduce Health Disparities ■ Health Promotion Among Racial & Ethnic Minority Males

Selected Examples of Measuring Program Performance

- Track the number of articles published in scientific journals
- Percentage increase mechanisms for healthcare providers to better diagnose, prevent, and treat minority health and health disparities
- Percent of studies which are "targeted studies"
- Percent of studies that are "Inclusion studies"
- Percent of total research budget spent on addressing minority health and health disparities
- Percentage research that influence policy
- Track rates of health disparity indicators and project a percent reduction of the those rates over a set period of time

Sample Programs – Research Capacity. Research capacity programs provide selected examples of the variety of activities that the NIH supports as part of its strategic plan for understanding and reducing health disparities among ethnic and racial minorities. The ultimate goal of these efforts is to support research, expand opportunities in training, foster career development, and increase research funding for health disparities research. The table below outlines sample research capacity programs in this area and provides selected examples of program performance measures:

Selected Examples of Programs: Research Capacity

IC RESEARCH CAPACITY OBJECTIVES	IC PROGRAMS
NIAID Provide training opportunities for minority scientists	■ Introduction to Biomedical Research Program ■ Bridging the Gap Program ■ Training Grants Program
NHLBI Expand the opportunities in research training and career development for underrepresented minorities.	■ Historically Black Colleges and Universities (HBCU) ■ Research Scientist Award ■ NHLBI Mentored Development Award for Minority Faculty ■ Biomedical Research Training Program for Underrepresented Minorities ■ NHLBI Minority Institution Research Scientist Development Award
NIDDK Expand the genetic/familial studies of diabetic nephropathy to include more minority patients	■ FIND Study – Family Investigation in Nephropathy of Diabetes
NINR Enhance research infrastructure allowing for an increased emphasis on projects relating to health disparities Enhance mentorship, training and research opportunities for minority students and researchers	■ Nursing Partnership Centers on Health Disparities ■ Mentored Research Scientist Development Award for Minority Investigators (RFA: NR-00-002) ■ Research Supplements for Underrepresented Minorities (RSUM)
NCI Increase the number of minority scientists in biomedical research and enhance the careers of those already in the field	■ Center to Reduce Cancer Health Disparities (CRCHD) ■ Comprehensive Minority Biomedical Program (CMBP) ■ Continuing Umbrella of Research Experiences (CURE)
NCRR Increase research competitiveness through Institutional Development	■ Institutional Development Award (IDeA) ■ Biomedical Research Infrastructure Networks (BRIN) ■ Centers of Biomedical Research Excellence (COBRE)
NICHD Promote the entry and participation of underrepresented minority institutions into biomedical and behavioral research and research training Improve the research capacity and infrastructure at minority institutions	■ Extramural Associates Program (EA) ■ Extramural Associates Research Development Award Program (EARDA)

Selected Examples of Measuring Program Performance

- Monitor number and progress of minorities entering training programs (% increase in minorities entering training programs over previous years and number completing training programs)
- Increase and track the number of minority scientists engaged in research (establish targets)
- Increase and track minority subjects enrolled in research and clinical trails
- Percentage increase in partnerships with minority institutions
- Increase number of research projects addressing minority health and health disparities
- Track the number of articles published in scientific journals by minority investigators
- Number of minority faculty, post doctoral fellows, and graduate students trained while conducting research
- Number of competitive grants issued to minority researchers

Sample Programs – Community Outreach, Information Dissemination, and Public Health Education. NIH is continuing its efforts to translate highly technical research advances into clear, culturally relevant explanations of the steps individuals can take to improve their health. The matrix below describes sample programs for enhancing communications and outreach related to the goal of reducing health disparities and provides selected examples of program performance measures:

Selected Examples of Programs: Outreach

IC OUTREACH OBJECTIVES	IC PROGRAMS
NIDCR Ensure the development, collection, and distribution of proven oral health communication and education methods/materials for populations associated with health disparities, to oral health education program planners	■ Health Communication and Information Dissemination Research: Opportunities in Oral Health ■ Health Information National Trends Survey (HINTS)
Ensure the integration of science-based oral health messages and materials into existing federal health communication and education programs for racial/ethnic minorities and the underserved	■ Administration for Children and Families' Head Start program ■ USDA's Women, Infants, and Children program (WIC)
NHLBI Expand and strengthen our programs of outreach and education for minority populations.	■ Asian American and Pacific Islander (AAPI) ASPIRE Project ■ Strengthening the Heartbeat of American Indian/Alaska Native Communities
NIDA Put research into practice in minority communities by providing science-based prevention and treatment information to service providers serving these populations	■ NIDA Toolkit Program
NLM Explore the use of new information technologies to enable diabetes patients, especially patients from minority and medically underserved populations, to manage their disease and avoid or delay the onset of costly and debilitating complications	■ Naomi Berrie Diabetes Center at Columbia/Presbyterian Hospital in New York City to study Type 1 diabetes ■ Children's Hospital in Los Angeles Project

Selected Examples of Measuring Program Performance

- The number of materials developed or adapted for minority and underserved populations
- Linkages with minority organizations
- Collaborative relationships with federal, state and local agencies to improve communication to minority and underserved populations
- Research on communication methods that are effective for minority and underserved populations
- Utilization of published materials by schools and institutions
- Greater participation in, and awareness of, health disparity studies

NIH Minority Health and Health Disparities Budget

The tables below, based upon the new NIH Guidelines, provide total minority health and health disparities research budget figures for each NIH Institute and Center. These financial resources demonstrate the commitment of the NIH to help close the health disparity gap among ethnic minority populations and those living in rural areas. In order to make notable progress in the overall health of the nation, this funding will be used for conducting and supporting research, addressing the national need for minority scientists and health professionals and providing information to the relevant communities for improving health conditions.

Budget Table To Be Provided

NOTE: No budget table was provided in the original draft document received by the committee.

Conclusion

This document describes an ambitious and evolving plan being undertaken by the NIH for reducing and ultimately eliminating the increased burden or disease and premature mortality suffered by racial and ethnic minority and other health disparity populations. This effort cuts across disease areas and organizational boundaries and involves a trans-agency commitment. It augments the efforts of each Institute and Center, and relevant program offices in the NIH Office of the Director in this important arena. As in many areas of research, more remains to be done. The medical research community working with, and informed by, the public, patients, health care providers, policymakers, and others has and will continue to develop new knowledge that leads to improvements in the prevention, diagnosis, and treatment of diseases and disabilities that contribute to health disparities.

In fiscal year 2003, the NIH spent over $2 billion on research, research infrastructure, and public information and community outreach efforts to reduce health disparities. This provided a strong basis for further investments over the longer term – investments that promise substantial progress in reducing the incidence, prevalence, severity, and social and economic burdens of diseases and disabilities that affect racial and ethnic minorities and other health disparity populations.

G

Public Communications and Its Role in Reducing and Eliminating Health Disparities

Kasisomayajula Viswanath, Ph.D.
Harvard University

An amazing feature of the waning years of the 20th century and the beginning of the 21st century is the stunning transformation in both the generation and delivery of information of all kinds—a development that few of us have yet come to grips with. Combined with revolutionary developments in the biomedical sciences and telecommunications, plenty of health information and delivery channels now exist. The number of health-related news stories on television and in both the mainstream and ethnic printed news media has been steadily increasing over the last 25 years (Figures G-1 to G-3).[1] The increase is evident in major disease areas such as cardiovascular disease, tobacco/smoking, HIV/AIDS, and

---

Background paper prepared for the Institute of Medicine's Committee on the Review and Assessment of the National Institute of Health's (NIH) Strategic Research Plan to Reduce and Ultimately Eliminate Health Disparities.

[1]Media attention to leading health issues from 1980 to 2004 was assessed as the number of stories published/broadcast that mentioned four major health topics: cardiovascular disease, tobacco-related cancer, obesity, and HIV/AIDS. The print, television, and online media environment was assessed using LexisNexis, Vanderbilt University's TV News Archive, Ethnic NewsWatch, and Google. The following search terms were entered into each of these databases/archives: *cardiovascular disease* or *heart disease*, *tobacco* or *smoking and cancer*, *obesity*, and *HIV* or *human immunodeficiency virus* or *acquired immune deficiency syndrome*. Using LexisNexis, almost 300 publications under the U.S. News category were searched. Vanderbilt University's TV News Archive was used to search news coverage of the health issues on the four major U.S. national broadcast networks (ABC, CBS, NBC, and CNN). Ethnic NewsWatch provided information on coverage of health issues in almost 300 English- and Spanish-language ethnic newspapers, magazines, and journals. The search terms were also entered into Google to assess the number of Internet web pages that mention the four major health issues.

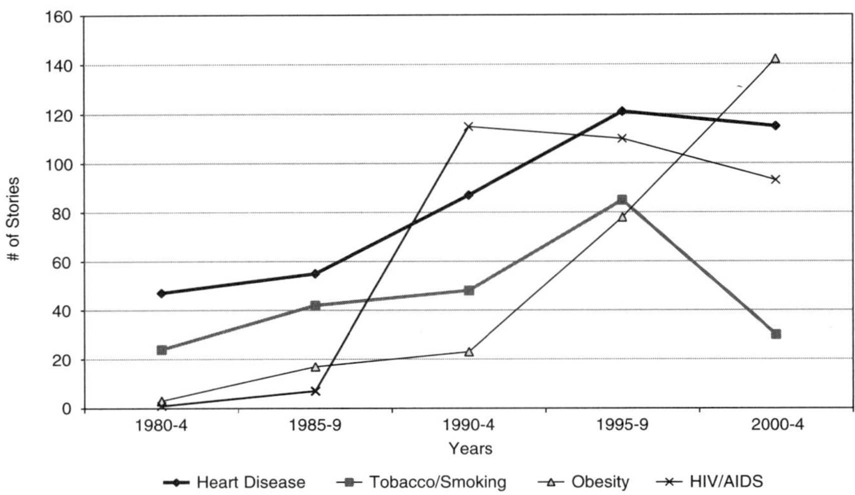

FIGURE G-1 National TV news coverage of leading health issues. SOURCE: See Footnote 1.

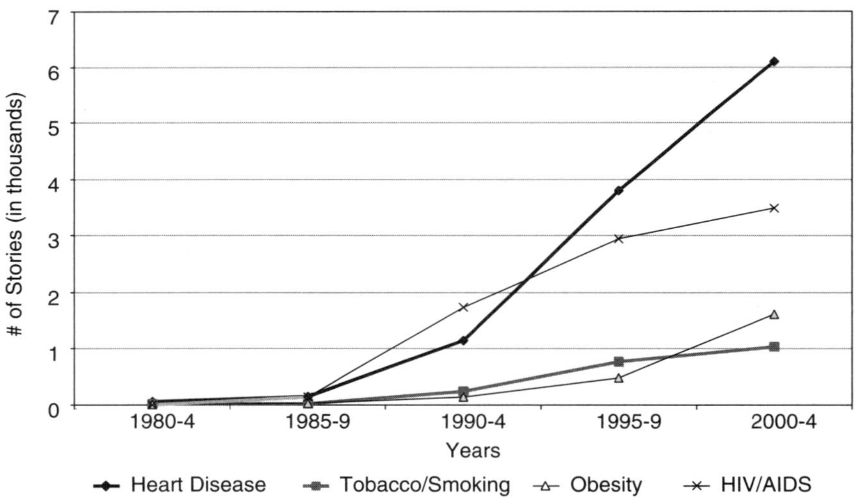

FIGURE G-2 Ethnic print media coverage of leading health issues. SOURCE: See Footnote 1.

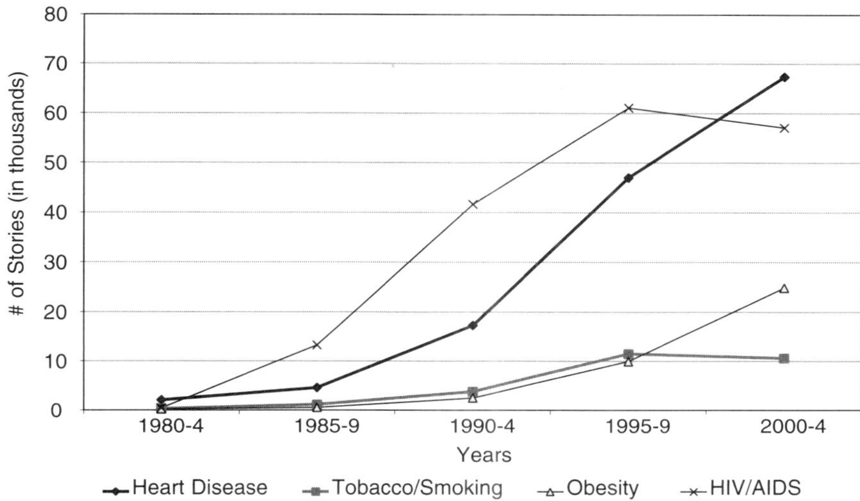

FIGURE G-3 Print news coverage of leading health issues. SOURCE: See Footnote 1.

obesity.[2] In addition, the number of Internet sites offering health information of varying quality is increasing rapidly. This strong secular trend in the information explosion in health is matched only by the public's increasing hunger for such information. For example, the proportion of Internet users looking for health information has risen from 55 percent in 2000 to almost 79 percent in 2005 (Pew Internet & American Life Project, 2000, 2005).

This explosion in health information poses two fundamental challenges. One is a need to translate scientific information in a usable format and language that can be understood and used by different audiences through appropriate channels. Such a translation would require attention to the dissemination of evidence-based and timely information to different publics—a role that the National Institutes of Health (NIH) is uniquely qualified for. This challenge is compounded by the large number of channels and actors, which make it difficult to control the interpretation of biomedical information as it cascades through different segments of society.

A second and equally, if not more, important challenge is that we need to ensure that the information is available to all of those who need it, regardless of

[2]In the absence of a denominator, it is difficult to argue that media attention to health news is increasing in relation to other topics. It is equally conceivable that the increase may also be related to more channels of information. What the numbers do suggest is a change in the information environment where more information on health is available on organized communication channels such as the news media.

their social class, cultural, geographic, and individual backgrounds. This latter need is a particular challenge, given the profound information inequalities that characterize our society. While the number of channels through which information, particularly through subscription telecommunication services, increases, it also comes at a price that requires recurring expenditures and investment to obtain those services.

Such challenges are compounded by the reality of profound disparities in disease burden among different social classes, possibly partly attributed to lack of information. For example, even as the overall burden of cancer is steadily falling, the decline varies for groups of different racial/ethnic and socioeconomic backgrounds (Kawachi and Kroenke, in press; Krieger, 2001; Lynch and Kaplan, 2000). African American males are much more likely to develop any type of cancer than white males. The incidence rate among African American males for developing any type of cancer is 689.2 per 100,000 compared with 556.5 among white males (Ries et al., 2004). A similar trend has been noted among American Indians and Alaskan Natives in which the incidences of leukemia and colorectal, stomach, and pancreatic cancers continue to increase (Paltoo and Chu, 2004). In addition to higher cancer incidences, minorities and lower socioeconomic groups also tend to have high rates of death due to cancer. Incidence rates of developing breast cancer are higher among white women than African American women (141.7 compared with 119.9); however, African Americans are more likely to die from breast cancer (mortality rate of 35.4 compared with 26.4) (Ries et al., 2004). Similarly, African Americans are 2.0 times more likely, Hispanics/Latinos are 1.9 times more likely, and American Indians and Alaska natives are 2.6 times more likely to have type 2 diabetes than whites of similar age (CDC and NCCDPHP, 2000). African American childhood and adolescent obesity rates are more than 2 times higher than all other American racial and ethnic groups combined (Story et al., 1999). Minority and low-income populations have higher rates of death and disability from cardiovascular disease. The rate of death due to cardiovascular disease among African Americans was 321.3 per 100,000, compared with 245.6 among whites (CDC, 2004).

Another consideration is the evidence that a majority of health problems are attributable to lifestyles and behaviors that are modifiable given the right opportunity structure, access to health care, and, above all, information (Emmons, 2000). Most major chronic illnesses are preventable through appropriate health strategies such as avoiding or quitting tobacco use, pursuing an active lifestyle, proper diet and nutrition, and timely health screening (IOM, 2002). Communication plays a central role in promoting preventive behaviors and influencing patient-provider interactions (Hornik, 2002; IOM, 2002; Smedley et al., 2003).

What are some of the major challenges to disseminating evidence-based health information to different stakeholders, particularly in bridging health disparities? How is the dissemination constrained by the differential capacity of the community and the American publics to access, interpret, and use the information in their day-to-day health? The focus of this essay is to address these twin challenges of the dissemination of health information and communication inequality through a delineation, clarification, and amplification of their dimensions insofar as they are relevant to reducing and eliminating health disparities. This assessment will be followed by a discussion of how the objectives of NIH's National Center on Minority Health and Health Disparities (NCMHD) could be achieved by a delineation of components of public communication.

THE NCMHD STRATEGIC PLAN: PUBLIC INFORMATION AND OUTREACH OBJECTIVES

NCMHD's Strategic Plan (2002-2006) outlined the following public information and outreach objectives:

1. Provide the latest research-based information to health care providers to enhance the care provided to individuals within populations experiencing health disparities.
2. Facilitate the incorporation of science-based information into the curricula of medical and allied health professions schools and into continuing education activities of health professionals.
3. Maintain ongoing communication linkages and dialogues with minority, ethnic, and other special populations, including the underserved, who experience health disparities.
4. Develop computer databases and Internet resources to disseminate current information about scientific research and discoveries and other activities regarding health disparities.
5. Develop targeted public health education programs focused on particular disease areas in order to reach those individuals within minority, ethnic, and other special populations who experience health disparities within these disease areas.

NCMHD's objectives focus on two broad strategies and groups of audiences to reduce and eliminate health disparities. One strategy is to disseminate information on health to different individuals or groups that face a disproportionate burden of disease with regard to health. Such diffusion of information involves a primarily nonprofessional audience with limited resources, skills, and training. A second broad strategy is to disseminate research-based information to trained professionals in medicine and public health or to organizations and groups that deal primarily with the medically underserved. We will briefly discuss the distinction between the two in the next section, which will then be followed by a more careful delineation.

KNOWLEDGE TRANSFER: RESEARCH DISSEMINATION, DIFFUSION, AND PUBLIC INFORMATION[3]

The nation's massive investment in the biomedical enterprise over the past few decades has resulted not only in advances in basic sciences, technology, and drug development but also in a fundamental understanding of how lifestyle changes can prevent some diseases and how evidence-based treatment can be effective (Hiatt and Rimer, 1999; IOM, 2002). Yet despite these advances, there are significant gaps in translation of this knowledge from the lab or research setting to clinical and community settings, thus limiting the advantages that might accrue from our investments. What is needed is a deeper understanding of: (a) how communication can accelerate the process of knowledge transfer from research settings to the community—from "bench to the bedside and bench to trench"—a process that demands a careful delineation in audience; (b) the publics involved; (c) communication processes; and (d) channels. Equally critical is a *feedback loop* between the *audience*, the consumers of research-based knowledge, and those who produce that knowledge.

Two related communication strategies are worth considering in accelerating knowledge transfer: public health communication and research dissemination.

Public health communication may be defined as the strategic communication of evidence-based health information on primary and secondary prevention, detection, diagnosis, and treatment to lay or nonprofessional audiences. The public here may include citizen individuals or groups such as community activists, workers unions, and civil and social service organizations. Some have characterized this phenomenon as *research diffusion*, a passive movement of health information through a social system. We will use the term *public health communication*, implying that it includes both purposeful (campaigns) and secular communications.

Research dissemination is an effort to close the gap between discovery and program delivery through the promotion of adoption, reach, and impact of evidence-based interventions across primary prevention to end-of-life care (NIH and NCI, 2005). Dissemination is particularly targeted to health care settings, practitioners, policy makers, and community groups. Although reporters are seldom mentioned, it is also critical to add news media as a group that could serve as a significant mediator in translating evidence-based information to the public.

---

[3]I want to thank Dr. Jon Kerner, Deputy Director of Research Dissemination and Diffusion at the National Cancer Institute, for clarification of the terms *diffusion* and *dissemination*. The conceptual distinction between them has been muddy, and these terms have often been used interchangeably. Dr. Kerner and colleagues in his office have been engaged in the conceptual explication of diffusion and dissemination as well in promoting the science of dissemination in cancer control.

Research dissemination stands in sharp contrast to *research diffusion*, which is a passive process that leaves the translation of scientific information to different publics to chance. In this process, scientific information is likely to spread only if the social actors, such as providers or the public health community, happen to come across the research results in a scientific publication or some other forum or if the news media picks up the article from a press release.

According to some scholars, successful dissemination involves a *push-pull process*, thus explicitly suggesting the feedback loop mentioned earlier (Kerner et al., 2005). That is, those pushing the dissemination should help the audience adopt and use the scientific information, but those pushing the information should also be sensitive to the needs and wants of the ultimate end-users of that knowledge.

We will briefly discuss the opportunities and challenges in public health communications and research dissemination and their relevance to health disparities.

PUBLIC COMMUNICATION, OUTREACH, AND COMMUNICATION INEQUALITIES

Functions of Health Communication

Communication in health may serve several functions: informational, instrumental, social control, and communal. The *informational* function is what we commonly describe as learning from media and other channels by acquiring knowledge on issues along a disease continuum, including prevention, detection, diagnoses, treatment, and end-of-life issues. Medical advice may also fall under this function. Several studies have noted the importance of communication in learning about health from either public health campaigns or incidental learning, and the threat of differential learning across social classes has also been noted (Hornik, 2002; IOM, 2002; Viswanath and Finnegan, 2002). The *instrumental* function is the provision of information that is useful, enabling practical action. It may include calling for a refill of prescriptions, verification of drug regimens on the Internet, clarification of questions with providers, learning of a time and place for preventive screening or vaccination, and skills in following certain health behaviors, among others. Communication performs the vital *social control* function in defining social norms, reinforcing or inducing beliefs, and defining the limits of what is acceptable and unacceptable in health (Tichenor et al., 1980; Viswanath and Demers, 1999). Campaigns to change social norms around binge drinking (Wechsler et al., 2003) or tobacco use (Gilpin et al., 2003) are, in essence, serving the social control function. The *communal function* may include building a sense of community, social connectedness, norms of reciprocity, and access to social capital (Berkman, 1986; Demers, 1996; Friedland and McLeod, 1999; Kawachi, 1999; Kawachi and Berkman, 2000; Kawachi et al., 1999; Putnam, 2000; Stamm, 1985; Viswanath et al., in press). Social and emotional support during treatment is another example of the communal function of health communication.

Communication, therefore, is central to learning about health, defining the norms of acceptable health behavior, and providing information to make appropriate decisions regarding treatment.

Communication Inequality

Two more principles of communication are worth noting. First, communication is always controlled as it spreads through the system. Second, more germane to the discussion here, communication or, more precisely, information is always unequally distributed. Inequalities in communication offer one potent explanation for inequalities in health. *Communication inequality* is defined as the differences among social groups in their ability to generate, disseminate, and use information at the macro level and to access, process, and act on information at the individual level. Although much of the discussion on communication inequality is focused at the individual level, the macro level of inequality will be briefly addressed in the next section on dissemination, as there has been limited research in that area.

In general, three common indicators of socioeconomic status (SES) often used in the literature are education, income, and, less often, occupation and employment (for a thoughtful discussion on SES and its association with cancer as an example, see Kawachi and Kroenke, in press). More recently, a number of scholars have argued for more refined measures of social class at multiple levels including individual, household, neighborhood, regional, and even national levels in addition to commonly used measures of education, income, and occupation. These include indicators such as poverty, material and social deprivation, wealth, and macro determinants of health including poverty and the distribution of income and wealth among others (Krieger et al., 1997; Subramanian et al., 2002).

Often, race and ethnicity are used synonymously with lower SES—a highly questionable premise given the large variation among different ethnic and racial groups as well as within the ethnic groups. The differences are manifest both within and across groups on such dimensions as income, education, occupation, and language. Any temptation to use race and ethnicity as synonymous with SES must therefore be resisted in the interest of more nuanced sensitivity to the differences within and across groups as will be evident from examples discussed in this chapter.

Lastly, the interactive and multiplicative effects of different indicators of SES and the complex pathways through which they are related to health outcomes is yet another subject that is beginning to attract attention (Lahelma et al., 2004).

There are several dimensions to communication inequality: (a) access to and use of information channels and services, (b) attention to and processing of health information, and (c) capacity and ability to act on information provided.

SES, Race, and Ethnicity and Their Relation to Inequalities in Access to and Use of Information

Education is the most common indicator often used as a proxy for social class. Education enables one to cultivate certain tastes and interests for different media content, provides skills in processing information, and offers the ability to apply information for day-to-day use. For example, education may provide the necessary confidence, sense of efficacy, and knowledge in enabling someone to navigate complex health systems. Income provides the tangible resources to access and subscribe to media services. Discretionary income may allow one to invest in recurring expenditures such as cable TV, the Internet, newspapers, and magazines. One may hypothesize that the greater the discretionary income, the greater the opportunity to obtain a variety of information services to improve one's well-being and derive intellectual nourishment and entertainment. Less investigated is the role of occupation and employment, though it is reasonable to speculate on occupation's influence on communication choices. Apart from wages, occupation provides opportunities for social networks, particularly in providing exposure to heterogeneous networks that are helpful in spreading new information. Employment and occupation are likely to be related to the use of, and exposure to, local community media and information channels (Viswanath et al., 1990), which, in turn, are related to knowledge and social capital, the roles of which in health and politics are acknowledged to be critical (Berkman, 1986; Kawachi and Berkman, 2000; Viswanath et al., 2000; Viswanath et al., in press). One may speculate that the effects of income, education, and occupation are not necessarily exclusive but potentially complementary and interactive.

Differences in access to communication services may include such dimensions as the ease of availability of information, the use of different media channels, and the affordability in subscription to communications services among different SES groups. The data from National Cancer Institute's (NCI's) Health Information National Trends Survey (HINTS) tellingly demonstrate differential access and exposure to information services among different social groups.[4] Income, education, and employment are positively associated with subscription to cable or satellite TV and the Internet—services that allow for access to diverse information sources (Table G-1). Similarly, income and education are associated with daily readership of newspapers (Figures G-4 and G-5). Television is one medium where the association with income and education is negative or nonexistent (data not shown).

Although different patterns of media use among different racial/ethnic groups do not necessarily indicate inequality, they deserve consideration. For example, African Americans spend more time with television but less with newspapers

[4]HINTS is a national survey of cancer communication behaviors of American adults conducted by the National Cancer Institute. The first survey was fielded in 2002/2003 through a random-digit-dialing sample of almost 6,400 adults with oversampling of African Americans and Hispanics.

(Figure G-6). They also have lower access to the Internet and cable and satellite TV (Table G-1).

In addition, almost 18 percent of the U.S. population that is 5 years or older speaks a language other than English at home. The proportion of non-English speakers varies from state to state, from roughly 3 percent in West Virginia to

TABLE G-1 Access to Information Services Among Different Socioeconomic Status and Racial/Ethnic Groups

	Percent Reporting Access to:	
	Cable/Satellite TV %	Internet %
Education (n = 6,149)		
High school or less	77.17	38.17
Some college plus	83.25	80.64
Income (n = 6,149)		
< $24,999	70.91	35.52
$25,000–$49,999	79.20	62.69
$50,000+	89.53	87.64
Employment status (n = 6,131)		
Employed	82.03	73.52
Not employed	78.70	47.36
Race (n = 5,372)		
White	82.56	66.02
African American	77.30	55.81
Ethnicity (n = 5,666)		
Non-Hispanic	81.72	66.42
Hispanic	77.08	44.94

NOTE: For all ethnicity assessments, multiracial persons were excluded from the analysis.

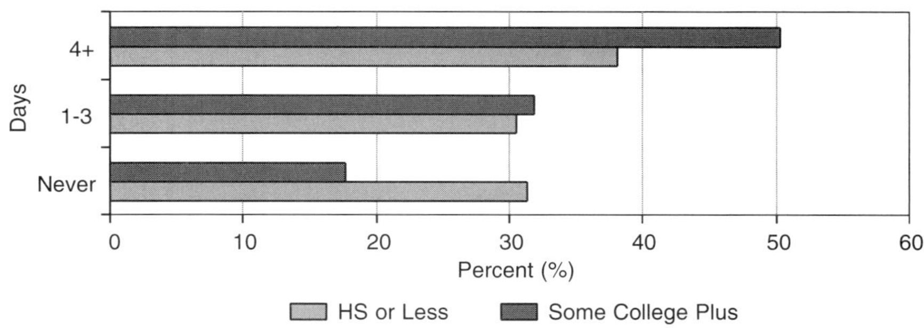

NOTE: HS, high school.

FIGURE G-4 Days read newspaper in last week, by education. SOURCE: See Footnote 4.

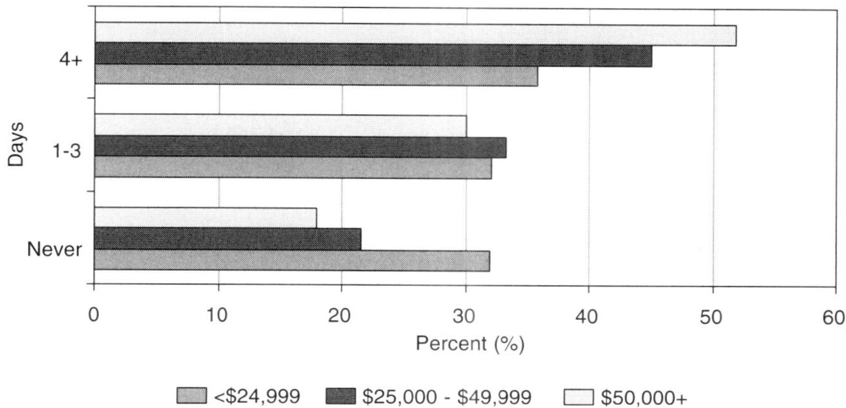

FIGURE G-5 Days read newspaper in last week, by income. SOURCE: See Footnote 4.

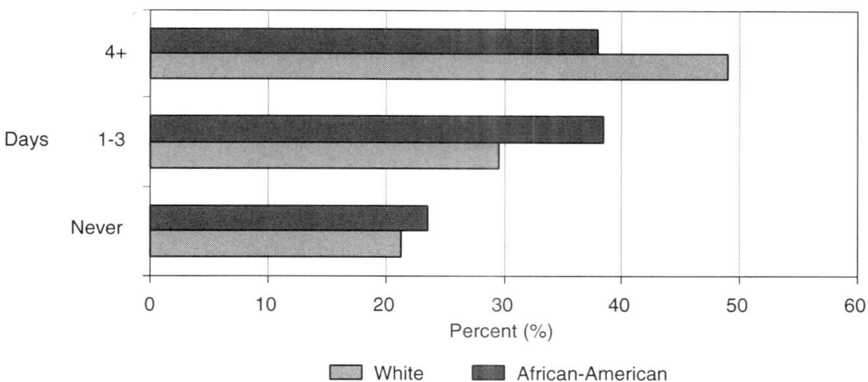

FIGURE G-6 Days read newspaper in last week, by race. SOURCE: See Footnote 4.

almost 40 percent in California. In fact, roughly 20–33 percent of the population 5 years or older in California, Florida, Arizona, Hawaii, Nevada, New Jersey, New York, and Texas speak a language other than English. Their exposure, use, and access to English-language mass media are likely limited and perhaps nonexistent. Media access, in the case of non-English-speaking minority groups, must take into account ethnic media that are widely prevalent both in print and online versions (Viswanath and Lee, in press).

Despite such long-standing evidence in inequalities in access at the individual level, some have suggested that these differences will disappear, due to technological advances (Compaine, 1986). This is a reasonable speculation, given the saturation-level diffusion of such technologies as electricity and the telephone and the widening use of cell phones. This proposition of eventual equalization and the amelioration of the invidious effects of inequality, however, is questionable for two reasons.

First, it may be argued that as information technologies grow cheaper, access becomes a less important issue. The communication environment, however, is dynamic, with constant improvements in the technology and services being offered. With improvement comes greater demand for more high-end equipment (e.g., high-speed computers or high-definition television). For example, the creation of websites with sophisticated multimedia software places a greater demand to upgrade equipment periodically, which places a disproportionate burden on lower-SES groups. Moreover, unlike the investment in equipment that is a one-time expenditure, subscription to information services demands recurring investment. The question is whether the recurring monthly fee will rise or fall over time, thereby improving or deterring access. In essence, forces outside their control—such as the telecommunication industry, corporate consumers, and national communication policies—shape the communication choices of individuals and families.

Second, it may also be argued that people make conscious choices as to how they allocate money to different communication services, including entertainment, telephones, and the Internet. Yet, communication is a social function. One's tastes, interests, and needs are shaped and influenced by an individual's immediate orbit, including social networks, significant peers, class interests, group norms, and perceptions about leadership roles. Moreover, choices are made within certain constraints of availability, the degree of discretion, and calculations about relative costs. For example, spending on cable TV is relatively cheap, compared with admission prices to so-called high-culture events such as the theater or the opera. That is, choices in both subscriptions to media services and exposure to content are still influenced by SES and social networks.

SES, Race, and Ethnicity and Their Relation to Inequalities in Attention to and Processing of Health Information

To a large extent, SES influences attention to health information and one's ability to process that information. For example, there are differences in the degree of attention people pay to health—or any content, for that matter—among different groups, with education and income positively influencing media attention (Figures G-7 and G-8). At the same time, different racial and ethnic groups report a similar amount of attention to health information in different media. (We do not have an idea of how those groups with limited proficiency in English pay attention to health content, either in English or ethnic media.) This suggests a strong interest in health information among all racial and ethnic groups despite their differential access.

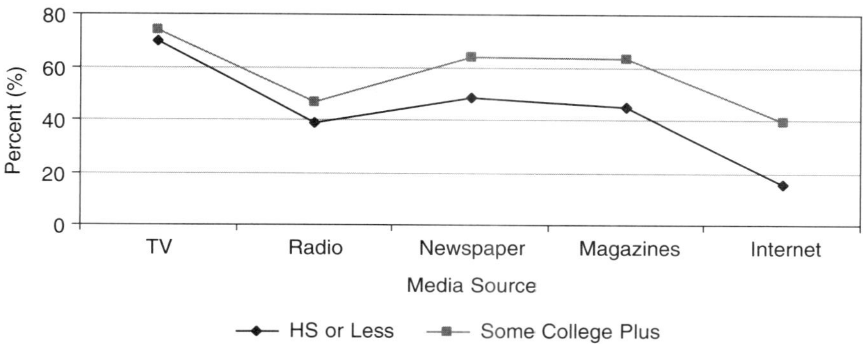

FIGURE G-7 Percent paying "a lot/some" attention to health information on various media, by education. SOURCE: See Footnote 4.
NOTE: HS, high school.

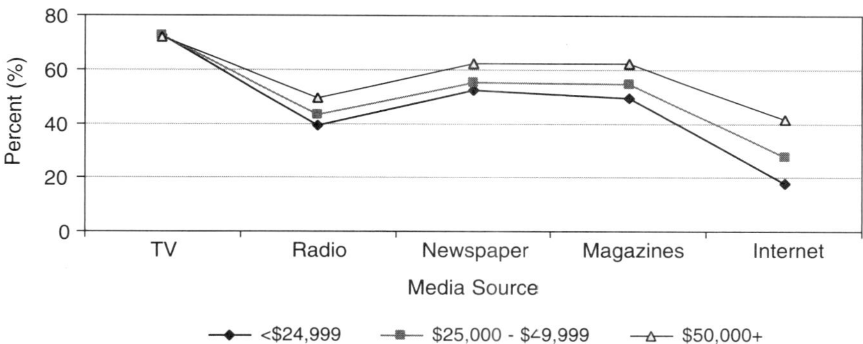

FIGURE G-8 Percent paying "a lot/some" attention to health information on various media, by income. SOURCE: See Footnote 4.

SES, Race, and Ethnicity and Their Relation to Inequalities in the Comprehension of and Action on Health Information

A significant dimension of health inequality is the ability of the individual or the capacity of a community group to process and act on health information.

At the individual level, the sheer complexity of the subject matter of health poses a significant challenge to those trying to learn, understand, and act on information. For example, information on prevention for different chronic diseases may overlap, such as tobacco use or cessation for cardiovascular disease or cancer, but information may differ in recommendations for consumption of different foods and nutrients. Recommendations for fighting infectious disease are different from recommendations for cardiovascular disease or cancer. In fact, cancer comprises many diseases with different causes, and prevention and treatment recommendations vary by the type of cancer. Diagnosis and treatment stages become even more complicated. The recommendations for diagnoses and treatment are disease- and stage-specific. For example, recommendations for breast cancer screening may vary, depending on age and family history. They are different from recommendations for cardiovascular disease, such as blood pressure and cholesterol screening. The navigation of the health system and the organization of medical care place an unfair burden on low-SES groups. Such issues as language, culture, and social status may interfere with having a more positive experience with the system (Cooper and Roter, 2003). Issues in treatment require adherence to complex drug regimens and compliance with recommendations. Lastly, the recommendations and instructions are dynamic and change over time depending on one's age and life course.

Acting on obtained health information is subject to opportunity structure, particularly the built environment. For example, it is difficult to act on prevention information on obesity, when one does not have decent grocery stores in the neighborhood, an availability of fruits and vegetables at reasonable prices, and safe neighborhoods to engage in physical activity. Lack of this insurance may deter people from acting on screening recommendations. Any effort to bridge this inequality requires efforts to offer information on possible resources that allow people to act.

There are differences in what people learn from the mass media and differences in the advantages that accrue from public health communication campaigns. The success and failure of campaigns has been of considerable interest to scholars and practitioners, given the mixed record of major public health education efforts over the past several decades (Hornik, 2002; Snyder and Hamilton, 2002). Yet, one type of failure (or unintended effect) is often observed: absent some conditions, the information flow on a given topic in a community is likely to lead to differential learning among members of different SES groups, thereby widening the existing knowledge gaps instead of bridging them, ultimately perpetuating inequalities in information (Tichenor et al., 1980; Viswanath and Finnegan, 1996). The HINTS study, cited above, illustrates the argument about learning from the general information environment about cancer risk factors. Members of higher-SES groups often know more than those from lower-SES groups, even on such widely publicized risk factors such as smoking and its link to cancer (Figures G-9 and G-10).

Conditions that may deter information gaps include inducing or increasing relevance for that information, extensive coverage in mass media, wide diffusion of information leading to saturation on that topic (e.g., the Columbia disaster or SARS crisis), the controversial nature of the topic (e.g., anthrax or bioterrorism), extensive social ties, participation and involvement in community groups, and use of appropriate information channels, among others (Gaziano, 1983; Viswanath and Finnegan, 1996; Viswanath et al., 2000).

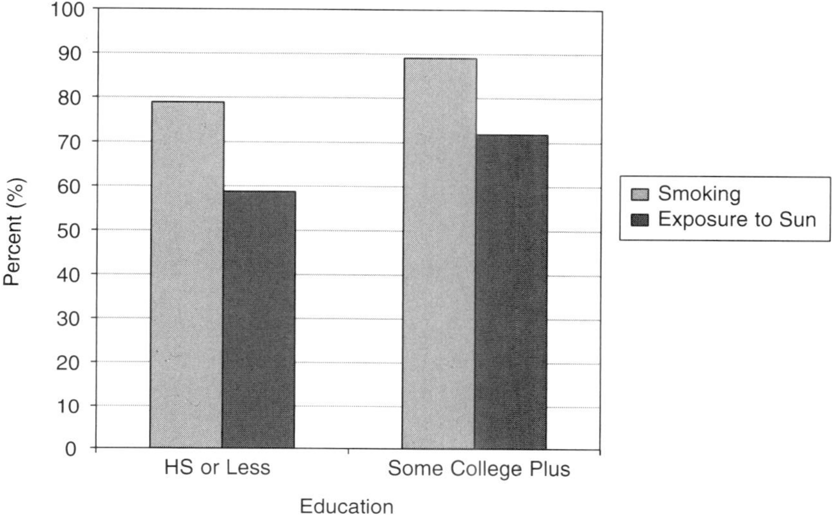

FIGURE G-9 Percent saying risk of cancer increases by "a lot/some" with exposure, by education. SOURCE: See Footnote 4.
NOTE: HS, high school.

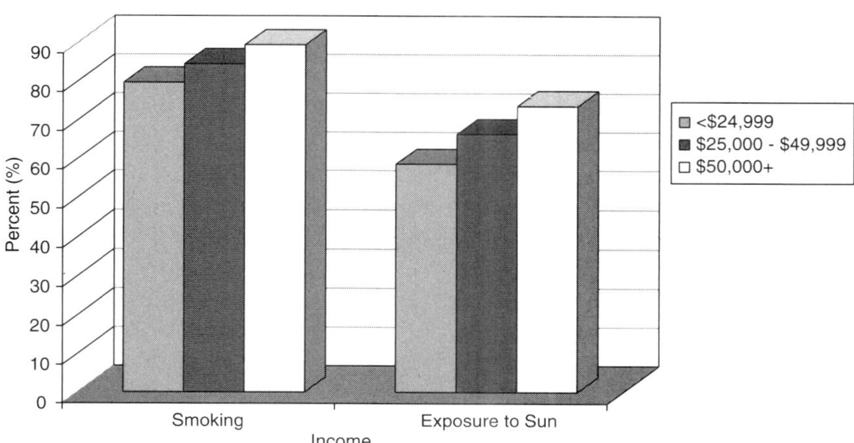

FIGURE G-10 Percent saying that their chances of cancer increase by "a lot/some" with exposure, by income. SOURCE: See Footnote 4.

On the other hand, carefully designed public health communication campaigns have successfully reduced smoking among adults and teens, increased seat belt use, reduced Sudden Infant Death Syndrome, and increased mammogram use (Hornik, 2002; Rimer, 1997).

Yet another type of knowledge gap may also deter mobilization for social action. There is a lack of awareness among both providers and patients on the existence of disparities or the extent to which disparities pose a significant problem in health care. Moreover, these perceptions vary by the racial/ethnic background of the citizens and providers (Henry J. Kaiser Family Foundation, 1999, 2002).

In short, learning from and acting on health communications is a complex, challenging process. It is little wonder that students of public health and medicine are now discussing how to improve *health literacy*, the capacity of people to obtain health information and make informed decisions about their health (Nielsen-Bolhman et al., 2004). Much discussion on health literacy is based on its potential; more systematic and empirical evidence of its effectiveness still remains to be found. In addition, the fact that almost 48 million Americans older than 5 years speak a language other than English at home may warrant a closer look at not only health literacy, but also the importance of providing services and information in different languages.

In summary, the recent developments in (a) information delivery services, (b) the generation of information as a result of biomedical research, and (c) the interest in health information among different publics offer tremendous potential in changing public health through the provision of information, thereby contributing to a reduction if not elimination of health disparities. Yet, in line with existing disparities in health, inequalities in communication can act as significant deterrents to bridging disparities, unless concerted efforts are made to reduce them. In the so-called information age, a fair and equitable distribution of relevant information may be considered a critical need.

RESEARCH DISSEMINATION AND HEALTH DISPARITIES: OPPORTUNITIES AND CHALLENGES[5]

The objectives of NCMHD's Strategic Plan (2002–2006) include: providing research-based information to health care providers; influencing the curricula of medical schools, allied health professionals, and continuing medical education; and maintaining a dialogue with community groups that serve medically underserved populations. In addition, although the target audience is not clear, one objective explicitly identifies the establishment of an informatics infrastructure to disseminate scientific information regarding health disparities. Such an infra-

[5]A part of the discussion in this section draws from the author's testimony to the President's Cancer Panel (Viswanath, 2004).

structure is more likely to be used by trained, professional public health stakeholders than ordinary citizens.

NIH is uniquely qualified to disseminate research-based information to health professionals and community stakeholders involved in public health. The richness of NIH's research portfolio and the proximity of NIH to the work of its grantees may, in theory, allow for a more efficient dissemination of evidence-based information than may be possible by other groups, agencies, and professional journals.

NCMHD's objectives for research dissemination raise several questions. What are the barriers in disseminating evidence-based information on health disparities to different stakeholders? What kind of infrastructure exists to facilitate knowledge dissemination to groups working with medically underserved groups? How can there be more coordination and collaboration among both federal and nonfederal partners on public outreach and communications to reduce, if not eliminate, health disparities? This section will attempt to address some of these questions.

Health Disparities and Research Dissemination: Some Issues for Consideration

It was recently commented that findings from clinical research take as long as 17 years before they find their way into practice (Balas et al., 2000; Isaacson, 2004). There is no reason to suspect that dissemination of information on prevention should be any faster, though news media routinely cover major developments published in medical journals. There are many reasons why translation of evidence-based information to the clinic, as well as to the community, is slow or even absent:

- The academic setting and reward system encourage publications in peer-reviewed journals, and few incentives, if any, encourage work on dissemination (Jacobson et al., 2004). Health care systems are unlikely to adopt innovations unless there are incentives in place that will support dissemination, as it will incur costs in production, personnel, and technical support. Individual scholars need incentives to promote dissemination as well as study dissemination. The entire incentive structure around the adoption of evidenced-based information in practice must be closely examined.
- By nature, most academic research is abstract and not in a format immediately usable by practitioners. NCMHD's goal of developing appropriate informatics systems might take into account how research from their grantees can be translated into formats that can be used by practitioners, decision makers, and policy makers (Donatiello et al., 2004). The importance of knowledge brokers who can move in both knowledge-generating (research) and practice (community) settings has often been cited as useful in a speedier dissemination of labora-

tory research into practice, as is evident in the case of AIDS treatment in sub-Saharan Africa (Philpott et al., 2002). There are models that could serve as sound exemplars of knowledge transfer, such as the NCI's Cancer Control Planet. For the last 4 years, NCI's Division of Cancer Control and Population Sciences has attempted to build coalitions with federal agencies, such as the Centers for Disease Control and Prevention (CDC), the Agency for Healthcare Research and Quality (AHRQ), and other organizations, such as the American Cancer Society (ACS), in promoting evidence-based dissemination and the use of successful behavioral interventions. The culmination of those efforts is Cancer PLANET (Plan, Link, Act Network with Evidence-based Tools). The idea behind Cancer PLANET is to promote evidence-based cancer control efforts on the part of community groups. Cancer PLANET is a website that (a) provides information on behavioral interventions in cancer control, (b) rates different behavioral interventions in cancer on their effectiveness, and (c) provides links to grantees who developed those interventions. By linking community groups that plan on doing interventions with their target community and the people who developed the successful interventions, Cancer PLANET obviates the need for the "reinvention of the wheel" and makes the process more efficient. The success of Cancer PLANET over the long term may provide a good model for other institutes and disease realms.

- It is still the case that institutions take the "if you build it, they will come" approach to knowledge transfer. Within academic medical centers and federal and state agencies, research dissemination often is an afterthought—and not a very systematic one at that. For example, as was observed in another context, it is a matter of some irony that considerable time, money, and intellectual capital is exerted in ensuring rigor in day-to-day health research, but somehow the same intensity is lacking when translating that research into the community (Viswanath, 2004). What are the ideal systems and processes to ensure speedy translation of rapid medical advances to the bedside and the community? What roles do different organizations, federal and state agencies, scientific associations, and commercial and civil sectors play in the speedy delivery of services? More important, how do we ensure that the benefits of translation accrue equally to all groups that need the most appropriate and up-to-date treatments? Addressing these questions requires partnerships between researchers, academic medical centers, and federal funding agencies.

- The science of dissemination in general, and our knowledge about dissemination to reduce health disparities in particular, is still underdeveloped (Kerner et al., 2005). At the federal level, agencies such as NIH can contribute to the science of dissemination by working with NIH study sections to be sensitive to the challenges of studying dissemination. The challenges include review criteria that value innovativeness, the risk-aversive nature of the reviewers, and discomfort with research designs that are not conventional randomized controlled trials, among others (Glasgow et al., 2004; Kerner et al.,2005). NCMHD could play a crucial role in promoting more systematic inquiries into studying research dissemination to professionals dealing with health disparities.

• Systems and people vary in their capacity to learn and use information related to both well-established and emerging innovations. These communication inequalities at the system level are one of the least investigated areas in public health communication research. We have not yet successfully designed systems and processes to cater to the so-called hard-to-reach groups. Some have advocated and argued for a push-pull approach in accelerating knowledge transfer (Kerner, 2004). On the push side, we need information on the existing capacity among academic medical centers to disseminate appropriate information to the clinicians, community groups, and the people. Some questions to ask on the push side include: (a) What kind of organizational structure, personnel, processes, and policies currently exist within the academic medical centers to pursue dissemination? (b) What is the extent of resources that are committed to research dissemination and diffusion? (c) What are the skills of the people involved in promoting research translation? and (d) What are the optimal organizational structures and processes that can accelerate knowledge transfer under different conditions for different groups? The pull side is a major challenge in translation. There is a differential capacity among different community and social groups and publics in accessing, processing, and using health-related information. Such differential capacity coincides rather inconveniently with profound inequities in disease prevalence, treatment, and mortality along racial, ethnic, and social class lines. We know little about the kind of community groups and networks that could be helpful in accelerating knowledge transfer. For example, several community groups engage in health promotion programs on a voluntary basis. The health promotion efforts may or may not be evidence-based, and often the groups reinvent the wheel by creating programs from scratch. NCI's Cancer PLANET is precisely aimed at such groups so that they have access to programs that have been found to be effective. At the same time, several groups in the community may conceivably lack the resources to use Cancer PLANET and other such resources, as they survive on volunteer time and efforts. We need more information on how academic medical centers, in collaboration with other groups, can enhance community capacity to use existing resources such as Cancer PLANET. Here is one place where academic medical centers can build linkages with community groups and networks by offering information, training, and modest resources.

• Moreover, what kind of systems and services are available to different ethnic groups and non-English speakers? The cultural and ethnic fabric of the nation is changing rapidly, with increasing migration into the United States from other countries. About 11.5 percent of the population is foreign-born, and almost half these individuals are from Latin America. About 47 million people in the United States speak a language other than English. Any effort to promote dissemination and adoption of evidence-based practice cannot ignore the needs of different ethnic and linguistic groups.

- The organization of the health care systems that tend to the medically underserved also remains to be explored. What are the training and resources needs of such organizations? What constraints do the practitioners working in these organizations face in adopting the latest innovations (and how can we build this into intervention development)? How do they keep up with the latest advances in biomedical science, and how do they translate it to treat population groups suffering from a disproportionate disease burden?
- Currently, the state of the science allows us to identify interventions that are effective in reaching groups that bear the brunt of the most preventable diseases. The translation of the interventions to more real-world settings, however, faces at least two challenges: scalability and sustainability. Interventions and trials work well in controlled settings, given the careful oversight, nurturing, and funding provided by the scientists and the funding agencies. A successful transfer of knowledge requires that we understand how real-world conditions influence the integration of new treatments and technologies from the lab to the clinic and the field. The uncertainty resulting from new variables and the larger scale can dilute the effectiveness and adoption of innovation unless scalability is taken into account. Similarly, how do we ensure successful ownership and incorporation of clinical innovations and preventive practices from the research centers by practitioners and groups in the community? Successful integration demands resources that either exist somewhere or need to be raised. Unless we take the issues of sustainability more seriously, we will be stuck in the vicious cycle of bench-to-peer-review-journals and back to the bench. If so, whatever information reaches the bedside and the community is more due to adventitious circumstances than to deliberate efforts.
- The institutional and social context in adopting evidence-based information for prevention and treatment must be closely examined to ensure successful adoption. Some suggest that health disparities could be reduced by promoting environmental change (systems as opposed to the individual) and building community capacity at the local level (Lavis et al., 2003). Although it is correct that building community capacity to adopt evidence-based information is critical, it is also worth noting that the focus in examining the adoption of innovations should not be exclusive to either the system or the individual, but at the intersection of individual and the system. Patients, for example, draw support from their providers, family and friends, and mass media. In addition, they are also likely to be members of social groups, community networks, and faith-based and secular organizations. Similarly, clinicians are influenced by their organizational structures, incentive and payment systems, and the legal and regulatory environment. Understanding these diverse sources of influence on individual behaviors and practices—whether a clinician or a community group or an individual—is critical in enabling knowledge transfer.

• The adoption of evidence-based information by groups and practitioners representing underserved groups faces the additional challenge of mistrust due to previous experiences, a lack of awareness about medical innovations such as clinical trials, and a disconnection with the established medical system. It is unlikely to change unless there is more sustained interaction between those promoting evidence-based information and the consumers that use the information—an interaction that may repair trust and confidence. NCMHD should actively engage existing community groups, organizations, and social movements to accelerate the transfer of research knowledge. One effective way is to build relationships with community groups, including voluntary associations, civic organizations, faith-based organizations, and community practices, among others (Farquhar et al., 2005). Outreach efforts could be made by careful needs assessment and active programs to satisfy those needs. Sustained efforts could potentially be fruitful over the long term and may also result in reaching groups that are traditionally difficult to reach.

A PLANNING MATRIX TO ADVANCE PUBLIC COMMUNICATION AND OUTREACH

Public communication to a general audience or research dissemination to health professionals, community groups, or policy and decision makers can be effective, if preceded by systematic and strategic planning, careful execution, and rigorous evaluation. The elements of such strategic communications are outlined in Table G-2, a planning matrix that could guide outreach efforts. The matrix is not meant to replace a plethora of other such matrices/frameworks that are routinely offered in literatures in social marketing and communication campaigns. A good discussion about campaigns can be found in such works as the Institute of Medicine's *Speaking of Health* (IOM, 2002). The matrix to be discussed here is only meant to be a practical, heuristic tool that could be used once the marketing research has been done and a decision has been made on the product, service, or information to be disseminated. We will next discuss each element of the matrix briefly.

Sponsors

In theory, NIH, or one of its Institutes and Centers (ICs), is the primary sponsor for the public information or outreach effort on health disparities. Other agencies of the U.S. Department of Health and Human Services, such as AHRQ, CDC, and the Centers for Medicare and Medicaid Services (CMS), are also likely to play an active and lead role in outreach to diverse audiences on different health subjects. Several federal agencies have overlapping roles in health promotion and sometimes partner with each other. Such a partnership is strongly encouraged, so that each agency can bring its unique strengths and expertise to the table. The strength of the

TABLE G-2 A Suggested Matrix for Campaign Planning, Using Cervical Cancer Screening as an Exemplar

Primary Sponsor	Audiences	Message	Partners	Strategy	Tactics	Channels	Impact Sought	Time Line	Tracking / Evaluation
NIH Institutes and Centers	Health care providers Primary care providers Clinics	Promote screening for cervical cancer	Local chapter of the American Cancer Society	Target providers of the usual source of care	Training of local providers Frequent contacts with members of local professional associations	Targeted mailings and news-letters Meetings with local professional associations One-on-one meetings	Change in clinical practice	16 months	Adoption of screening Track screening rates

NIH's ICs is their proximity to the scientific expertise of its grantees. This closeness enables NIH to tap into the most up-to-date science on health disparities and translate the science for the consumption of different stakeholders to bridge those disparities.

The NIH's ICs may want to capitalize on existing investments in infrastructure, such as research networks and patient advocacy groups. For example, NCI's Special Populations Networks are funded to provide cancer education, research, and training to underserved communities and groups. Lessons learned from such experiences could come in handy to develop and study outreach programs to eliminate health disparities.

The Audience

Any information outreach must start with a close identification, definition, and characterization of the target audience, and the same principle applies to the information outreach objectives of NCMHD. Some questions to guide the selection and profiling of the audience include:

- What is the degree of understanding about the needs of the audience and the extent to which the product being disseminated meets those needs?
- How well is the audience profiled or characterized? and
- What kind of advanced information through formative research informs audience selection and characterization?

It is important that the product or information selected for outreach meets the needs of the audience and addresses a particular problem or threat that they face. For example, it could be a recommendation to the general public to increase one's physical activity or improve one's diet. For physicians, it could be a recommendation on treatment, such as when an intervention is warranted to reduce cholesterol. It could be a consensus statement on screening guidelines, to address uncertainty or lack of consensus. In all cases, information outreach efforts are assumed to follow formative research that, in addition to messages and channels, identifies and profiles the audience.

Audiences for NCMHD's efforts could include: racial and ethnic minorities; medically underserved groups; people who bear the disproportionate burden of morbidity and mortality for a certain disease; or providers, such as practitioners, decision makers and policy makers, businesses managers, and community leaders whose clients include citizens experiencing health disparities (Lavis et al., 2003).

Audience characterization is also commonly termed *audience segmentation,* an effort to define groups that share certain characteristics. A number of variables are used to segment the audience:

- Demographics such as age, gender, race/ethnicity, and SES (Albrecht and Bryant, 1996);
- Psychographics such as personal values, lifestyles, preferences, orientations, and religiosity (Albrecht and Bryant, 1996; Slater and Flora, 1991);
- Beliefs such as a sense of perceived risk (Lemon et al., 2003; Snyder and Rouse, 1992; Trenkner et al., 1990) or religiosity (Parrott et al., 2004);
- Personality traits such as innovativeness (Rogers, 1995) or sensation seeking (Stephenson et al., 2003);
- Health behaviors and health status (Boslaugh et al., 2004; Williams and Flora, 1995);
- Product use or consumption, for example, the number of drinks consumed or contraceptive usage (El-Zanaty, 1994; Lintonen and Konu, 2004); and
- A combination of all or some of the above factors.

A number of statistical techniques such as factor analyses (Trenkner et al., 1990), cluster analysis (Slater and Flora, 1991), automatic interaction detection and logistic regression (Albrecht and Bryant, 1996), classification and regression tree analysis (Lemon et al., 2003), and signal detection analysis (Williams and Flora, 1995), among others, are used to group the audience.

The idea behind segmentation is that homogeneity within segments will allow campaign sponsors to design messages that are compatible with the cultural, structural, and attitudinal status of the segments, thereby enhancing the probability of campaign success. Segmentation is also useful in channel selection, and, in fact, many commercial providers of audience measurement and market research services offer information on different audience segments that a given channel could potentially reach.

Despite the apparently successful track record of segmentation strategies, certain caveats are warranted and worthy of future investigations:

- The segmentation philosophy sometimes makes the naïve assumption that segments are mutually exclusive. Second, it sometimes also takes a static view of membership in the segments as if people do not change. Both are questionable and empirically untenable. People often enjoy a web of affiliations by often simultaneously belonging to several groups and playing multiple roles. They concomitantly draw from and contribute to the collective experiences of those groups and affiliations. Their views, status, values, and preferences may change with changes in either group norms or group affiliations.
- Another pitfall in this assumption of homogeneity could be when one variable may or may not be appropriate for segmentation. It is now widely agreed, for example, that Hispanics are extremely heterogeneous in SES and political and cultural beliefs, despite their common language. In fact, one recent analysis showed that Spanish-speaking Hispanics are considerably different from English-

speaking Hispanics in their SES, media use, and media credibility (Clayman et al., 2004).

• Lastly, segmentation strategies are based on the premise that individuals can change given the appropriate messages through appropriate channels when sometimes the systems and the social context in which health behaviors occur may warrant more attention.

The Message

The first assumption here is that the sponsors have already made a decision about what product, service, or idea should be disseminated. The message specifically refers to what is being disseminated and how it is being disseminated. A product or a service could be a set of treatment recommendations on hypertension in a minority group or vaccination against influenza in the elderly. It could be a synthesis of knowledge about a treatment of a particular disease or disorder, or it could be a national campaign to reach minorities on AIDS education.

The challenge is: How should an agency go about deciding what areas, topics, diseases, or products are likely to be subjects of outreach? A set of criteria may be developed to decide on the (a) target audience, (b) documented level of disparities that trigger action, and (c) selection of the subject or product for outreach (e.g., evidence review, knowledge synthesis, or information campaign) that reduces if not eliminates disparities.

If a product or service is a broad public information campaign—say, a campaign on obesity that is aimed at African Americans who suffer disproportionately from its consequences—there is first a need to understand the behavioral and environmental determinants that may reduce the barriers to physical activity. Both individual-level and structural-level factors are likely to mediate the effect of public communication efforts on different groups of people. Within communication science, a body of work on *message theories* and their impact on public health has begun to emerge to better inform the work of public health practitioners.

The assumption behind message-effects theories is that certain features of messages—their format, structure, and construction—interact with individual attributes of the audience, thus influencing information processing and leading to changes in audience knowledge, attitudes, and behaviors. Several types of message formats have been studied: fear appeals, sensation seeking, narratives, exemplars, and framing, among others.

Theories of *fear appeals* posit that audiences, when exposed to information, make a calculated appraisal of the threat of the topic or the issue to the self; evaluate the efficacy of the recommended action, if it is accompanied with action; and may react accordingly (Witte and Allen, 2000). *Sensation seeking* is a personality type where the individual seeks adventure and novelty to reduce boredom (Donohew et al., 2002). Sensation seekers are likely to seek out intense experiences or stimulations and often are spontaneous in their actions while ignoring the consequences. Several studies have found an association between sensation seeking and risky behaviors, such as drug and alcohol use, sex with multiple partners, and even unprotected sex. Health campaigns have successfully used messages with high-sensation value to change attitudes and behaviors about illicit drug use and risky sex among teenagers (Donohew et al., 2002).

One of the more intriguing message effects is *exemplification*. Exemplification is the extent to which selected events or cases in a news story are illustrated as representative of a general class of events typifying those events (Zillmann, 2002). The contention of proponents of this message effect is that recipients of campaign messages often ignore quantitative information, such as the risk of contracting an infection or sexually transmitted disease from unsafe sex, for example, but will be more attentive to exemplars that discuss the very same issue. Exemplars are successful when they are concrete, vivid, simple, consequential, and emotional.

Evidence shows that people learn about health—or any knowledge topic, for that matter—through purposeful campaigns and through incidental exposure to media messages, such as when watching a sitcom on a television. This ability of stories to engender deeper involvement and learning has been used to study the message effects of *narratives*. Narrative messages are stories with persuasive health content (Slater, 2002). Narratives work though positive or negative reinforcement of behaviors through modeling (Bandura, 2002). The positive effects of narratives have been touted with examples from teaching health and social issues in Latin America and Africa (Rogers, 1995). On the negative side, some have argued that exposure to televised violence can have negative effects of aggressive behavior among children and distorted worldviews among adults (Gerbner et al., 2002). Intuitively, it should make sense that stories are powerful and have both positive and negative effects. The empirical evidence on narratives so far has been less than rigorously gathered and requires more study.

Framing is yet another message effect that has been studied and has two meanings, based on its intellectual origins. Drawing from the psychology of communication, framing refers to the construction of messages that highlights either the benefit in performing a health behavior (gain-framed) or the costs of not performing a behavior (loss-framed) (Salovey et al., 2002). It has been argued that loss-framed messages are more persuasive when the audience member is facing uncertainty or risk such as infection, and gain-framed messages are more persuasive when outcomes are certain, such as treatment. Yet another meaning of framing draws from the sociology of communication and is defined as a "central organizing principle that holds together a diverse array of symbols and idea elements," thus giving a coherent structure to one's worldviews (Gamson, 2001). For example, the recent debate over mammography was framed in the news media as either leading to false positives, thereby resulting in unnecessary treatment and distress, or as a prevention tool that has saved lives through early detection. Studies have shown that such debates in the media have differential effects on the audience, depending on their SES.

This brief overview of message effects offers some interesting possibilities in reaching different target audiences in bridging disparities. Much of the work on message effects has been done at the individual level by taking into account the audience's individual psychological characteristics. Yet, an alternative structural view suggests that audiences attend and react to mediated content based on their structural location in the environment and the social roles they play (McLeod et al., 1991; Viswanath and Demers, 1999). Structural determinants such as social class, occupational structure, race and ethnicity, and gender mediate the impact of messages through such factors as collective experiences, group membership, access, preferences, appeals, attention, and processing and capacity to act on the information. We have, however, little scientific knowledge of how such structural determinants interact with personality variables to mediate different message effects. Even less is known about how these determinants are mediated in different racial and ethnic groups. Lastly, more work is needed on the influence of message effects on health among groups suffering with differential disease burdens.

Partners

The reach and effectiveness of NCMHD's public communication is likely to be enhanced by identifying and then working with partners who can supplement and complement its strengths. Such partnerships will obviate duplication among different governmental and nongovernmental organizations, facilitate coordination, and rationalize outreach expenditures. Depending on the nature of the outreach, one can imagine a variety of partners working with NCMHD.

For example, campaigns to reduce HIV among African Americans could be done through federal partners such as the National Institute of Allergy and Infectious Diseases, CDC, and state health departments. A number of community groups that work with minority audiences and that are sensitive to the culture of the minority community may lend credibility to the program.

In fact, several such examples in public communication exist. The National Youth Anti-Drug Campaign is primarily based on mass media but also uses a variety of partners including "civic, community, educational, faith-based, government, nonprofit, public health, workplace and other youth-serving organizations and coalitions" (Office of National Drug Control Policy, 2005).

The dissemination of evidence-based medicine and guidelines can be promoted through AHRQ's Evidence-based Practice Centers (EPC) Program. EPCs have been designed to perform systematic reviews of scientific literature on clinical, behavioral, organizational, and financing issues related to treatment and then produce reports.

Other nonfederal partners may include such organizations as the ACS and the American Heart Association. Professional organizations such as the National Medical Association could serve the twin purposes of providing forums for disseminating evidence-based medicine and also bringing the necessary credibility to the campaigns within the target audience community.

NIH and various ICs are funding several networks that already have an infrastructure to educate and conduct research. For example, NCI's Special Population Networks are funded to conduct cancer education, research, and training among minority and low-SES citizens. Such networks could be good vehicles to translate knowledge speedily.

In summary, a partnership approach could go a long way in stretching the limited budget for outreach, bringing credibility to the programs, and broadening reach.

Strategy and Tactics

A strategy may structure the actions one might take to achieve broad communication goals. A tactic is the specification of execution of the strategy—that is, an operationalization of it. It lays out the specific actions the sponsor might take to achieve the campaign or outreach goal. For example, to draw from Table G-2, the goal of promoting the most current understanding of cervical cancer screening guidelines may involve the strategy to target health care providers that provide the usual source of care for the medically underserved. It could involve such tactics as training, providing continuing medical education credits, and following up with frequent meetings.

A national campaign to promote physical activity among Hispanic audiences may involve a broader strategy of reaching Hispanic children and specific tactics of promoting organized community physical activity programs. Although the distinction between strategy and tactics often seems academic, the exercise of identification and delineation will help clarify this distinction.

Channels

Channels are the means through which health information is disseminated to target audiences, which may include citizens, providers, or community leaders. Optimal channel selection is a critical and essential factor in the dissemination of health information to different publics, as it will make the difference between reaching the right target audience and missing them completely. Channel selection is done by careful formative research, either through custom research done by individual sponsors or by subscription to commercial providers of information such as Nielsen Media Research.

There are a variety of channels, including interpersonal, organizational, and mass media channels. Campaign sponsors may use one channel at a time or multiple channels that complement one another. Using a variety of channels that complement and supplement each other is usually more effective (Hornik, 2002; IOM, 2002). For example, the National Youth Anti-Drug Media Campaign is an integrated social marketing effort that uses advertising, mass media, and the Internet with outreach efforts to different partners, including Hollywood and racial ethnic organizations.

The decision to select one or more channels depends on factors such as reach, control over the message, intensity, and costs. Mass media can provide a wide reach with a lower cost per person, but it is also difficult to exert control over how the message is disseminated and to collect immediate feedback from the audience. On the other hand, one might be able to exert greater control over the message and obtain immediate feedback when using interpersonal or organizational channels, but these offer limited reach and may be more expensive. Given the complexity and intractability of the problem of health disparities, it is desirable to use both mass media as well as interpersonal and organizational channels.

Channel selection is based on the principle that the information provided through those channels draws distinct groups of people who are interested in that information and who share some common characteristics. Often, the audience characteristics that are considered in channel selection include:

- *Demographics* such as age, gender, income, and residence. For example, local newspapers are optimal for reaching a variety of people and are usually consumed by adults who are enjoy strong social ties to the local media (Viswanath et al., 1990). Magazines and radio provide ideal vehicles for careful segmentation given the specialized content they offer. There are varieties of magazines that cater to different age and gender groups.
- *Race or ethnicity*, while often included in demographics, are unique factors given the nature of the media that reaches different racial and ethnic groups and the heterogeneity among different racial and ethnic groups. American society is becoming increasingly diverse with more than 32.5 million Americans identifying themselves as foreign-born. Hispanics constitute about 13 percent of the population and African Americans another 13 percent. Asian Americans account for about 4 percent of the U.S. population. The U.S. Census Bureau projects that between 2000 and 2050, the U.S. population will likely increase from the current 282 million to roughly 419 million when almost 1 out of 2 Americans is likely to be non-White. That is, factors that usually drive the establishment and maintenance of ethnic media, such as audience size, general consumption expenditures, and SES, are already in place. In fact, there is already a tremendous diversity in American mass media catering to different ethnic and racial groups: African and African American, Arab, Chinese, Filipino, Hispanic, Asian Indian, Japanese, Korean, and Vietnamese, among many others. These media play a variety of roles such as community boosters, transmitting culture, assimilation into the mainstream of American culture, and

watching out for the community (Viswanath and Lee, in press). The ethnic media offers an ideal and optimal set of vehicles in addition to the mainstream channels in providing health information to audiences of diverse racial and ethnic backgrounds. Yet, we know little about how widely these vehicles are being used to provide health information and how successful those efforts have been—both areas worthy of future investigation.

- *Lifestyle and orientation* refer to factors that go beyond demographics to interests and orientations. These may include media catering to audiences with subject interests including travel, news, recreation, sports, sexuality, health, movies, and shopping, among many others.

In contrast to reaching general audiences, research dissemination to provider organizations may be done through professional and civic organizations such as medical societies, nursing organizations, and national civic organizations. These organizations are optimal vehicles for the release of state-of-the-art information on prevention, screening, diagnoses, and treatment through their professional meetings, newsletters, and workshops. Some professional organizations are fruitful avenues for national research dissemination, including the Association of American Indian Physicians, the National Medical Association (African Americans), the National Hispanic Medical Association, the Association of Black Cardiologists, the Association of Physicians of Indian Origin, the National Association of Hispanic Nurses, the National Black Nurses Association, and the National Council of La Raza Institute for Hispanic Health, among many others.

A significant challenge is reaching nonprofessional audiences and community groups; this warrants creativity in the form of using existing structures or in funding the creation of new ones. For example, cancer education, training, and research could be conducted through NCI's Community Networks to Reduce Cancer Health Disparities through Education, Research and Training Program. EXCEED (Excellence Centers to Eliminate Ethnic/Racial Disparities), funded by AHRQ, has centers that focus on health communication in medical settings. NIH's Hispanic Communications Initiative includes an aim to address communication strategies with Hispanic/Latino community-based organizations. National nongovernmental organizations and their local chapters, including the ACS, the American Lung Association, the AHA, the National Association for the Advancement of Colored People, and the National Council of La Raza, are some potential avenues in reaching hardly reached groups.

Despite the opportunities and the availability of organizations, researchers lack a systematic body of evidence on the appropriate dissemination vehicles for groups suffering from a disproportionate burden of disease and ill health. We have little idea of the effectiveness, receptivity, resources, barriers, and capacity of these community groups to carry out dissemination and the conditions under which they could be effective. NCMHD may do well to promote research in this important area.

IMPACT SOUGHT AND TIMETABLE

This element is included to compel clarity in specifying communication goals. NCMHD's broad objectives are fine, such as incorporation of science-based information into the curricula of medical and other professions schools or maintenance of communication and dialogue with minority, ethnic, and other special populations. The development of programs and measurement of their success in achieving those objectives, however, requires greater specificity and operationalization.

For example, one specific goal under the objective of incorporation of science-based information into the medical curriculum could be the treatment guidelines for diabetes among African Americans. Yet another example is incorporating cultural competence into medical school curricula. The objective of maintaining a dialogue with ethnic groups also requires greater specificity to assess the impact. One possible goal could be a periodic survey of specific groups to do needs assessment surveys to understand the barriers in obtaining access to, and the use of, health information.

Such specificity will help to clarify exactly what objectives are being pursued and will aid in developing appropriate products, target audiences, and message strategies. It will also help to identify the necessary incentives that will facilitate the adoption of the innovation.

Specification of a timeline will provide an idea of requirements in staffing, resources, and budget. A timeline will minimize the danger of setting unrealistic goals, a common feature of public health education. Moreover, specifying the timeline for translation could narrow the long period between research discovery and delivery.

TRACKING AND EVALUATION

It is essential that there be mechanisms in place to track the success of the outreach programs and products. Tracking and evaluation offers several advantages:

- Mid-course correction of current outreach efforts,
- Lessons learned for future outreach efforts, and
- The refinement and redefinition of current outreach objectives and the development of new goals.

It is important that the evaluation distinguish between hard and soft outcomes. Soft measures include, for example, how many brochures have been distributed to provider groups on treatment. Another soft measure is how many linkages have been created with community organizations. The soft outcomes are intermediate process measures, outcomes of process evaluation that could be helpful in serving as markers of outreach efforts. Yet more important is the development of hard measures that actually assess change in the provider practice or health behaviors as a result of the outreach efforts. This will also provide the necessary feedback loop discussed earlier so that NIH can ascertain and incorporate the needs of different publics into programming.

SOME RECOMMENDATIONS TO HELP NCMHD ACHIEVE ITS OUTREACH OBJECTIVES

The current NCMHD objectives for public information and outreach appropriately identify challenges in identifying target audiences that may help in bridging the deep chasm between research discovery and delivery, when it comes to health disparities. As NCMHD refines its strategic plan in subsequent years, some additional considerations will be necessary for success.

Surveillance System for Public Communications

There is currently no comprehensive system in place for communication and outreach surveillance that will help NCMHD systematically assess the needs of academic, professional, and community groups working with the underserved groups and use that information in program planning. Similarly, we know little about the information needs, media use, and information-seeking patterns of citizens suffering from disproportionate disease burdens. It is unclear what systems are in place to do such surveillance and how they are being fed back in program planning.

There is a need for more information that addresses the following questions:

- What is the priority assigned in studying health disparities in the medical and allied health school curricula?
- What barriers exist to integrating health disparities issues within the health professions schools?

Some questions pertaining to providers working with underserved groups include:

- What are the sources of information on health disparities among providers? Where do they go to seek information on health disparities in general? What can be done to increase awareness among providers that disparities exist? For example, a recent article in the journal *Circulation* showed that only 34 percent of the cardiologists surveyed agreed that there are disparities in health care in the U.S. system, and 5 percent felt that these might exist in their practices (Lurie et al., 2005).

- To what extent do the NIH ICs serve as guidance for providing the latest scientific information related to health disparities?
- What are the barriers faced by the providers working with underserved groups in adopting the latest evidence-based information in their day-to-day practice? What incentive structures will encourage them to incorporate innovations in their practice?
- What are the organizational factors—structures, culture, and hierarchies—that deter providers from using the most up-to-date information to treat patients?

On community groups and citizens, some questions that a surveillance program may address include the following:

- The Internet has the potential to provide detailed medical information tailored to the specific needs of different groups in formats that they can use. Yet, how helpful are the NIH IC websites in communicating with groups that are suffering from disparities in health information, access to health care, and use? To what extent does the digital divide between social classes discussed earlier deter the use of the Internet-based health information? Is it only likely to exacerbate the disparities?
- How can NCMHD assist target audience groups with the incorporation of the latest evidence-based information into their practice and day-to-day health behaviors?
- How can investment in Internet-based resources be designed to yield a maximum dividend in reducing and eliminating disparities given the challenges of digital divide or communication inequality discussed earlier?

These are only some examples of questions that are worth exploring in future research on dissemination, and they have strong implications for practice. It is strongly recommended that NCMHD develop a surveillance system that will track the health information needs, sources, and information-seeking patterns of different audience subgroups, as well address the needs of providers and institutions working with medically underserved groups. The NCI's HINTS study could serve as one model in developing a surveillance system on information needs of health disparities groups.

Developing the Science of Communication and Dissemination

Currently, a number of NIH ICs are supporting research on public health communication and provider-patient communication and developing an infrastructure to promote dissemination. It is unclear what proportion of the ICs' budget is set aside for doing research on studying public communication. There is a significant gap in our understanding of public information when it comes to minority and low-SES audiences, as well as the appropriate models of dissemination to transfer the latest medical knowledge to academia and providers dealing with health disparities groups. In short, there is a need to develop and accelerate work on the science of health communication and research dissemination, with a particular focus on minorities and low-SES groups.

A strong program of research on communication and dissemination could address the following issues:

- How does inequality in communication contribute to and exacerbate existing health disparities?
- How do daily hassles of racism, discrimination, and poverty affect information seeking and processing?
- What are the intervention and policy options that could bridge information inequities to reduce and eliminate health disparities?
- What is the capacity of community groups in accessing and using evidence-based information to communicate with their membership?
- What are the barriers faced by health care providers in obtaining and using the latest scientific information on health disparities?
- How can medical establishments be prepared for translating knowledge and accelerating information dissemination to groups and providers working on health disparities?
- What are the training needs of providers to improve communication with patients facing a disproportionate disease burden?
- How can NCMHD develop the training of future scientists who can contribute to the study of public communication to bridge health disparities?

These questions are only suggestive and are not meant to be exhaustive. They do give an idea of the need for a more evidence-based and scientific approach to public information outreach on health disparities.

SOME CONCLUDING REMARKS

With the development of a strategic plan, NCMHD made a sound start by clearly identifying the objectives for research, research infrastructure, and public information and community outreach. The objectives for public information and community outreach suggest two broad strategies to reduce health disparities: (a) ensuring the dissemination of health information to individuals and community groups that are suffering from health disparities and (b) disseminating research-based information to trained medical and public health professionals working with groups that are traditionally underserved to ensure access as well as quality health care.

This essay provided some broad outlines that can enable NCMHD to achieve its objectives by taking the following steps:

- Continue to refine and operationalize the objectives by the greater specification of intended outcomes and the development of specific measures.
- Be aware of, and sensitive to, the issue of *communication inequities* in developing any programs of public information and outreach.
- Develop strategic research dissemination plans that address professional groups that work with groups suffering from an unfair disease burden.
- Systematize outreach efforts by clearly identifying sponsors, audiences, messages, partners, channels, and tracking systems. Such systematic efforts can draw from communication science using the suggested planning matrix.
- Work deliberately and proactively in developing programs and initiatives that contribute to the development of science of communication and research dissemination with a particular focus on health disparities.
- Develop a surveillance system for public health communication with a focus on groups that suffer from health disparities. Currently, little information is available on the information needs of the underserved, and what is available is in disparate locations in the federal government or in the private sector. A well-developed system can track health information needs, media use, seeking behaviors, and knowledge of low-SES and minority groups and can contribute to both the science of surveillance as well as program planning.
- To be successful, NCMHD should set aside a budget for both doing and studying public information efforts.
- NCMHD can play a lead role in coordinating the disparate communication and outreach efforts by various NIH ICs in their attempts to reduce and eliminate health disparities. Relevant expertise and resources often reside within the ICs, but NCMHD's coordination may bring synergy to individual IC efforts. Equally desirable is a partnership with other federal agencies, such as CDC, CMS, the Health Resources Services Administration, and AHRQ, among others, and nonfederal and private-sector partners.

The unprecedented advances in engineering and biomedical sciences offer a tremendous opportunity to prevent and treat diseases that have long plagued humans. These advances, coupled with the communications revolution in telecommunications and informatics, offer the potential to intervene along the different stages of the disease control continuum—from prevention to survivorship and end of life—thereby reducing mortality and morbidity due to disease. Yet the persistent inequities in health and the corresponding inequality in communications among different social groups could disrupt the revolution, resulting in the rich getting richer and the poor poorer, in terms of health and information. A national action plan involving careful, systematic, scientific, strategic, and deliberate efforts to address the twin disparities in communication and health could potentially help to fulfill the promise of the revolution to all instead of a few.

ACKNOWLEDGEMENTS

The author is grateful to the assistance and suggestions from a number of people in writing the manuscript. Specific thanks are due to Karen Lee, Shoba Ramanadhan, Stacy Petta, Ichiro Kawachi, Faith Mitchell, Gerald Thomson, Monique Williams, members of the Committee and the Institute of Medicine staff.

REFERENCES

Albrecht TL, Bryant C. 1996. Advances in segmentation modeling for health communication and social marketing campaigns. *Journal of Health Communication* 1(1):65–80.

Balas EA, Weingarten S, Garb CT, Blumenthal D, Boren SA, Brown GD. 2000. Improving preventive care by prompting physicians. *Archives of Internal Medicine* 160(3):301–308.

Bandura A. 2002. Social cognitive theory of mass communication. In, Zillman D, Bryant J, eds. *Media Effects: Advances in Theory and Research*. Hillsdale, NJ: Lawrence Erlbaum. Pp. 61–90.

Berkman LF. 1986. Social networks, support, and health: Taking the next step forward. *American Journal of Epidemiology* 123(4):559–562.

Boslaugh SE, Luke DA, Brownson RC, Naleid KS, Kreuter MW. 2004. Perceptions of neighborhood environment for physical activity: Is it "who you are" or "where you live"? *Journal of Urban Health-Bulletin of the New York Academy of Medicine* 81(4):671–681.

CDC (Centers for Disease Control and Prevention). 2004. *The Burden of Chronic Diseases and Their Risk Factors: National and State Perspectives 2004*. Atlanta, GA: U.S. Department of Health and Human Services.

CDC & NCCDPHP (National Center for Chronic Disease Prevention & Health Promotion). 2000. *National Diabetes Fact Sheet*. [Online]. Available: http://www.cdc.gov/diabetes/pubs/estimates.htm#prev4 [accessed July 5, 2005].

Clayman M, Viswanath K, Arora NK. 2004 (November 9). *Differences in mass media source credibility ratings for cancer information among Spanish responding and English responding Hispanics/Latinos to the HINTS survey*. Paper presented at the American Public Health Association, Washington, DC.

Compaine BM. 1986. Information gaps—Myth or reality. *Telecommunications Policy* 10(1):5–12.

Cooper L, Roter D. 2003. Patient-provider communication: The effect of race and ethnicity on process and outcomes of healthcare. In, Smedley B, Stith A, Nelson A, eds. *Unequal Treatment: Confronting Racial and Ethnic Disparities in Healthcare*. Washington, DC: The National Academies Press. Pp. 552–593.

Demers D. 1996. *The Menace of Corporate Newspaper: Fact or Fiction*. Ames, IA: Iowa State University Press.

Donatiello JE, Droese PW, Kim SH. 2004. A selected, annotated list of materials that support the development of policies designed to reduce racial and ethnic health disparities. *Journal of the Medical Library Association* 92(2):257–265.

Donohew L, Palmgreen P, Lorch EP, Zimmerman R, Harrington N. 2002. Attention, persuasive communication, and prevention. In, Crano WD, Burgoon M, eds. *Mass Media and Drug Prevention: Classic and Contemporary Theories and Research*. Mahwah, NJ: Lawrence Erlbaum. Pp. 119–144.

El-Zanaty FH. 1994. Women segmentation based on contraceptive use. *Egypt Population and Family Planning Review* 28(1):19–54.

Emmons KM. 2000. Behavioral and social science contributions to the health of adults in the United States. In, Smedley BD, Syme SL, eds. *Promoting Health: Intervention Strategies from Social and Behavioral Research*. Washington, DC: National Academy Press. Pp. 254–321.

Farquhar SA, Michael YL, Wiggins N. 2005. Building on leadership and social capital to create change in 2 urban communities. *American Journal of Public Health* 95(4):596–601.

Friedland LA, McLeod JM. 1999. Community integration and mass media: A reconsideration. In, Demers D, Viswanath K, eds. *Mass Media, Social Control & Social Change: A Macrosocial Perspective*. Ames, IA: Iowa State University Press. Pp. 197–226.

Gamson WA. 2001. Foreword. In, Reese SD, Gandy JR, Grant AE, eds. *Framing Public Life: Perspectives on Our Understanding of the Social World*. Mahwah, NJ: Lawrence Erlbaum.

Gaziano C. 1983. The knowledge gap—An analytical review of media effects. *Communication Research* 10(4):447–486.

Gerbner G, Gross L, Morgan M, Signorielli N, Shanahan J. 2002. Growing up with television: Cultivation processes. In, Bryant J, Zillman D, eds. *Media Effects: Advances in Theory and Research*. 2nd ed. Mahwah, NJ: Lawrence Erlbaum.

Gilpin EA, Emery S, White MM, Pierce JP. 2003. Changes in youth smoking participation in California in the 1990s. *Cancer Causes & Control* 14(10):985–993.

Glasgow RE, Marcus AC, Bull SS, Wilson KM. 2004. Disseminating effective cancer screening interventions. *Cancer* 101(5):1239–1250.

Hiatt RA, Rimer BK. 1999. A new strategy for cancer control research. *Cancer Epidemiology Biomarkers Prevention* 8(11):957–964.

Hornik R, ed. 2002. *Public Health Communication: Evidence for Behavior Change*. New York: Lawrence Erlbaum.

IOM (Institute of Medicine). 2002. *Speaking of Health: Assessing Health Communication Strategies for Diverse Populations*. Washington, DC: The National Academies Press.

Isaacson SD. 2004 (October 28). *Translating Research into Practice*. Paper presented at the Therapeutic Environments Forum, Washington, DC.

Jacobson N, Butterill D, Goering P. 2004. Organizational factors that influence university-based researchers' engagement in knowledge transfer activities. *Science Communication* 25(3): 246–259.

Kaiser Family Foundation. 1999. *Race, Ethnicity and Medical Care: A Survey of Public Perceptions and Experiences*. [Online]. Available: http://www.kff.org/minorityhealth/loader.cfm?url=/commonspot/security/getfile.cfm&PageID=32574 [accessed July 3, 2005].

Kaiser Family Foundation. 2002. *National Survey of Physicians. Part 1: Doctors on Disparities in Medical Care*. [Online]. Available: http://www.kff.org/minorityhealth/loader.cfm?url=/commonspot/security/getfile.cfm&PageID=13955 [accessed July 3, 2005].

Kawachi I. 1999. Social capital and community effects on population and individual health. *Annals of the New York Academy of Science* 896:120–130.

Kawachi I, Berkman L. 2000. Social cohesion, social capital, and health. In, Berkman L, Kawachi I, eds. *Social Epidemiology*. New York: Oxford University Press. Pp. 174–190.

Kawachi I, Kroenke C. In press. Socioeconomic disparities in cancer incidence and mortality. In, Schottenfeld D, Fraumeni JFJ, eds. *Cancer Epidemiology and Prevention*. 3rd ed. Oxford, UK: Oxford University Press.

Kawachi I, Kennedy BP, Glass R. 1999. Social capital and self-rated health: a contextual analysis. *American Journal of Public Health* 89(8):187–1193.

Kerner J. 2004 (August 30). *Testimony to the President's Cancer Panel*. Translating Research into Clinical Practice, San Francisco, CA.

Kerner J, Rimer B, Emmons KM. 2005. Dissemination research and research dissemination: How can we close the gap? *Health Psychology* 24(5):443–446.

Krieger N. 2001. Historical roots of social epidemiology: Socioeconomic gradients in health and contextual analysis. *International Journal of Epidemiology* 30(4):899–900.

Krieger N, Williams DR, Moss NE. 1997. Measuring social class in U.S. public health research: Concepts, methodologies, and guidelines. *Annual Review of Public Health* 18:341–378.

Lahelma E, Martikainen P, Laaksonen M, Aittomaki A. 2004. Pathways between socioeconomic determinants of health. *Journal of Epidemiology and Community Health* 58(4):327–332.

Lavis JN, Robertson D, Woodside JM, McLeod CB, Abelson J. 2003. How can research organizations more effectively transfer research knowledge to decision makers? *Milbank Quarterly* 81(2):221–248.

Lemon SC, Roy J, Clark MA, Friedmann PD, Rakowski W. 2003. Classification and regression tree analysis in public health: Methodological review and comparison with logistic regression. *Annals of Behavioral Medicine* 26(3):172–181.

Lintonen TP, Konu AI. 2004. The misperceived social norm of drunkenness among early adolescents in Finland. *Health Education and Research* 19(1):64–70.

Lurie N, Fremont A, Jain AK, et al. 2005. Racial and ethnic disparities in care: The perspectives of cardiologists. *Circulation* 111(10):1264–1269.

Lynch J, Kaplan G. 2000. In, Berkman L, Kawachi I, eds. *Social Epidemiology*. New York: Oxford University Press. Pp. 13–35.

McLeod JM, Kosicki GM, Pan Z. 1991. On understanding and misunderstanding media effects. In, Curran J, Gurevitch M, eds. *Mass Media and Society*. New York: Edward Arnold. Pp. 235–266.

Nielsen-Bohlman L, Panzer AM, Kindig DA, eds. 2004. *Health Literacy: A Prescription to End Confusion*. Washington, DC: The National Academies Press.

NIH and NCI (National Institutes of Health and National Cancer Institute). 2005. *Cancer Control & Population Sciences, Research Diffusion & Dissemination*. [Online]. Available: http://www.cancercontrol.cancer.gov/d4d/index.html [accessed July 5, 2005].

Office of National Drug Control Policy. 2005. *National Youth Anti-Drug Media Campaign*. [Online]. Available: http://www.mediacampaign.org/newsroom/factsheets/overview.html [accessed December 6, 2005].

Paltoo DN, Chu KC. 2004. Patterns in cancer incidence among American Indians/Alaska natives, United States, 1992-1999. *Public Health Reports* 119(4):443–451.

Parrott R, Silk K, Krieger JR, Harris T, Condit C. 2004. Behavioral health outcomes associated with religious faith and media exposure about human genetics. *Health Communication* 16(1): 29–45.

Pew Internet and American Life Project. 2000. *The Online Health Care Revolution: How the Web Helps Americans Take Better Care of Themselves*. [Online]. Available: http://www.pewinternet.org/pdfs/PIP_Health_Report.pdf [accessed July 5, 2005].

Pew Internet and American Life Project. 2005. *Health Information Online*. [Online]. Available: http://www.pewinternet.org/pdfs/PIP_Healthtopics_May05.pdf [accessed July 5, 2005].

Philpott A, Maher D, Grosskurth H. 2002. Translating HIV/AIDS research findings into policy: Lessons from a case study of 'the Mwanza trial'. *Health Policy Plan* 17(2):196–201.

Putnam R. 2000. *Bowling Alone: The Collapse and Revival of the American Community*. New York: Simon & Schuster.

Ries LAG, Eisner MP, Kosary CL, Hankey BF, Miller BA, Clegg L, et al., eds. 2004. *SEER Cancer Statistics Review, 1975–2001*. Bethesda, MD: National Cancer Institute.

Rimer BK. 1997. Current use and how to increase mammography screening in women. *Surgical Oncology Clinics of North America* 6(2):203–211.

Rogers E. 1995. *Diffusion of Innovations*. 4th ed. New York: The Free Press.

Salovey P, Schneider TR, Apanovitch AM. 2002. Message framing in the prevention and early detection of illness. In, Dillard JP, Pfau M, eds. *The Persuasion Handbook: Theory and Practice*. Thousand Oaks, CA: Sage Publications. Pp. 391–406.

Slater MD. 2002. Entertainment education and the persuasive impact of narratives. In, Green MC, Strange JF, Brock TC, eds. *Narrative Impact: Social and Cognitive Foundations*. Mahwah, NJ: Lawrence Erlbaum. Pp. 157–181.

Slater MD, Flora JA. 1991. Health lifestyles: Audience segmentation analysis for public health interventions. *Health Education Quarterly* 18(2):221–233.

Smedley B, Stith A, Nelson A, eds. 2003. *Unequal Treatment: Confronting Racial and Ethnic Disparities in Health*. Washington, DC: The National Academies Press.

Snyder LB, Hamilton MA. 2002. *A Meta-Analysis of U.S. Health Campaign Effects on Behavior: Emphasize Enforcement, Exposure, and New Information, and Beware of Secular Trends*. In Hornik R, ed. *Public Health Communication: Evidence for Behavior Change*. New York: Lawrence Erlbaum. Pp. 357-383.

Snyder LB, Rouse RA. 1992. Targeting the audience for AIDS messages by actual and perceived risk. *AIDS Education and Prevention* 4(2):143–159.

Stamm KR. 1985. *Newspaper Use and Community Ties: Toward a Dynamic Theory*. Norwood, NJ: Ablex Publishing.

Stephenson MT, Hoyle RH, Palmgreen P, Slater MD. 2003. Brief measures of sensation seeking for screening and large-scale surveys. *Drug and Alcohol Dependence* 72(3):279–286.

Story M, Evans M, Fabsitz R, Clay T, Holy Rock B, Broussard B. 1999. The epidemic of obesity in American Indian communities and the need for childhood obesity prevention programs. *American Journal of Clinical Nutrition* 69:747S–754S.

Subramanian SV, Belli P, Kawachi I. 2002. The macroeconomic determinants of health. *Annual Review of Public Health* 23:287–302.

Tichenor PJ, Donohue GA, Olien CN. 1980. *Community Conflict and the Press*. Newbury Park, CA: Sage Publications.

Trenkner L, Rooney B, Viswanath K, et al. 1990. Development of a scale using nutrition attitudes for audience segmentation. *Health Education Research* 5:479–487.

Viswanath K. 2004 (September 27). *Best Mechanisms for Moving Research into the Communities*. Paper presented at the President's Cancer Panel: Translating Research into Clinical Practice, The Novice G. Fawcett Conference Center, Ohio State University.

Viswanath K, Demers D. 1999. Mass media from a macrosocial perspective. In Demers D, Viswanath K, eds. *Mass Media, Social Control and Social Change: A Macrosocial Perspective*. Ames, IA: Iowa State University Press. Pp. 3–28.

Viswanath K, Finnegan JR. 1996. The knowledge gap hypothesis: Twenty five years later. In Burleson B, ed. *Communication Yearbook 19*. Thousand Oaks: Sage Publications. Pp. 187–227.

Viswanath K, Finnegan JR. 2002. Community health campaigns and secular trends: Insights from the Minnesota Heart Health Program and Community Trials in Heart Disease Prevention. In, Hornik R, ed. *Public Health Communication: Evidence for Behavior Change*. New York: Lawrence Erlbaum. Pp. 289–312.

Viswanath K, Lee KK. In press. Ethnic media in the United States. In, Waters M, Ueda R, eds. *The New Americans*. Cambridge, MA: Harvard University Press.

Viswanath K, Finnegan JR, Rooney B, Potter J. 1990. Community ties and the use of newspapers and cable TV in a rural Midwestern community. *Journalism Quarterly* 67:899–911.

Viswanath K, Kosicki GM, Fredin E, Park E. 2000. Community ties, community boundedness, and local public affairs knowledge gaps. *Communication Research* 27(1):27–50.

Viswanath K, Randolph W, Finnegan JR. In press. Connecting the dots between social capital and public health outcomes: The role of communication and community pluralism. *American Journal of Public Health*.

Wechsler H, Nelson TF, Lee JE, Seibring M, Lewis C, Keeling RP. 2003. Perception and reality: A national evaluation of social norms marketing interventions to reduce college students' heavy alcohol use. *Journal of Studies on Alcohol* 64(4):484–494.

Williams JE, Flora JA. 1995. Health behavior segmentation and campaign planning to reduce cardiovascular disease risk among Hispanics. *Health Education Quarterly* 22(1):36–48.

Witte K, Allen M. 2000. A meta-analysis of fear appeals: Implications for effective public health campaigns. *Health Education and Behavior* 27(5):591–615.

Zillmann D. 2002. Exemplification theory of media influence. In, Bryant J, Zillmann D, eds. *Media Effects: Advances in Theory and Research*. Mahwah, NJ: Lawrence Erlbaum. Pp. 19–42.

H

NIH Committee on Minority Health and Health Disparities Research Definitions and Application Methodology

FINAL REPORT (REVISED JANUARY 2004)

The NIH Committee on Minority Health and Health Disparities Research Definitions and Application Methodology (see Attachment A, Committee) was established in the Fall of 2002 at the request of Dr. Elias Zerhouni (Director, NIH) and Dr. John Ruffin (Director, NCMHD) to determine operational definitions and a methodology to form the basis for future reporting on all NIH activities related to minority health and health disparities. Given the inconsistencies in the manner in which Institutes/Centers (ICs) have previously reported on their minority health-related activities (see Attachment B, Minority Direct), the Committee focused on developing a methodology that could be applied uniformly by all ICs and in as automated a way as possible.

Guidance for two reports—the Minority Health Report and the Health Disparities Report—was developed (see Attachment C, Guidelines). In both reports, activities are reported in each of five categories: basic research; clinical research; infrastructure; research training and career development; and outreach. The Health Disparities Report builds upon the Minority Health Report, adding to it those activities directed at low socioeconomic status (low-SES) and rural populations that are not included in the Minority Health Report. The process followed by the Committee to develop the Guidelines is outlined in Attachment D (Activities).

The Committee believes that limiting reporting according to the recommendation made by the Institute of Medicine (IOM) in its 1999 report (Recommendation 3-3, page 140, *The Unequal Burden of Cancer*) would severely under-report and misrepresent the NIH commitment to minority health and health disparities research. The IOM report asserts that percent relevancy accounting methods, such as the one used at the NIH, that calculate minority health research funding based on the percentage of minority individuals in the study population, "overstate the relevance of research for addressing ethnic minority health issues." The Committee believes, however, that restricting NIH reporting to "studies whose purpose is to address a priori research questions uniquely affecting ethnic minority and medically underserved groups" (as the IOM recommends) would do a disservice to NIH efforts to foster attention to minority health issues. In fact, most of the major NIH-supported clinical studies are now designed with the statistical power to detect racial/ethnic differences in incidence, prevalence, or efficacy of treatment even when the study is not focused primarily on minority health issues. They provide valuable results applicable to minority groups, as well as to the majority population.

With this in mind, the Committee established the following criteria for inclusion in the minority health and health disparities reports:

- For *basic research, infrastructure, and outreach* activities, include only projects targeted to minority health and health disparity issues.
- For *clinical research*, include non-targeted as well as targeted studies. For clinical research related to minority health, report a percentage of the award based on the ratio of minority participants to total participants (subject to a 25 percent minority participation minimum); for clinical research related to low-SES and rural populations, report a percentage of the award based on the emphasis level assigned by CRISP.
- For *research training and career development*, include non-targeted as well as targeted activities. For non-targeted activities, include only dollars received by under-represented minority individuals.

Minority Health Report

For the Minority Health Report, the following operational definitions were developed:

Targeted research (report at 100 percent) includes:

- basic research on a disease, condition, or biological process that affects **exclusively or almost exclusively** one or more minority populations
- basic research on a behavior that is found **exclusively or almost exclusively** in one or more minority populations
- basic research on whether and/or how the mechanisms of disease or basic biological processes differ in minority populations; or how behaviors differ in minority populations
- clinical research conducted **exclusively or almost exclusively** in one or more minority populations

- clinical research investigating whether and/or how the manifestations, consequences, or responses to treatment of diseases or other conditions differ in minority populations
- clinical research investigating how behaviors differ in minority populations.

Non-targeted research (report at the percent minority participation, as long as it exceeds the threshold of 25 percent) is clinical research focused on prevention, diagnosis, or treatment of diseases or other conditions that affect minority populations.

Targeted infrastructure (report at 100 percent) includes solicited programs that are focused exclusively on developing the research capabilities of historically black colleges and universities (HBCUs) and minority medical schools, as well as solicited programs designed to enhance the research resources available specifically to under-represented minorities at other institutions educating or training high numbers of one or more minority populations that are under-represented in biomedical or behavioral research.

Targeted research training and career development (report at 100 percent) includes programs that focus **exclusively** on supporting research training or career development of under-represented minorities.

Non-targeted research training and career development (report only dollars received by under-represented minority individuals) includes activities that support research training or career development of under-represented minority investigators, but that are not focused exclusively on these population groups.

Targeted outreach (report at 100 percent) includes:
- programs that focus **exclusively** on providing health-related information to minority populations
- programs that focus **exclusively** on providing information to health care providers about preventing, diagnosing, or treating diseases or other conditions in minority populations.

Health Disparities Report

Minority health issues are considered to be a subset of health disparities issues. The Health Disparities Report includes all activities in the Minority Health Report plus activities related to low-SES and rural populations. An activity that addresses minority health **as well as** low-SES or rural health is included in the Health Disparities Report based on either its percent relevance to minority health or its percent relevance to low-SES and rural health—whichever is higher.

For the low-SES and rural component of the Health Disparities Report, the following operational definitions were developed:

Targeted research (report at 100 percent) includes:

- basic research on a disease, condition, or biological process that affects **exclusively or almost exclusively** low-SES or rural populations
- basic research on a behavior that is found **exclusively or almost exclusively** in low-SES or rural populations
- basic research on whether and/or how the mechanisms of disease or basic biological processes differ in low-SES or rural populations; or how behaviors differ in minority populations
- clinical research on whether and/or how the manifestations, consequences, or responses to treatment of diseases or other conditions differ in low-SES or rural populations
- clinical research conducted **exclusively or almost exclusively** in low-SES or rural populations.

Non-targeted research (report at 50/25 percent if coded in CRISP as Secondary/Tertiary for low-SES or rural health—or at the minority participation percent, if higher) includes:

- clinical research related to the manifestations, consequences, or responses to treatment of diseases or other conditions in low-SES or rural populations
- clinical research conducted in populations that include low-SES or rural populations.

Infrastructure is equal to the minority health figure for this category (due to difficulties in identifying institutions that educate large numbers of people from low-SES or rural populations).

Research training and career development is equal to the minority health figure for this category (due to difficulties in identifying trainees of low-SES or rural backgrounds and institutions that educate large numbers of people from low-SES or rural populations).

Targeted outreach (report at 100 percent) includes:

- programs that focus **exclusively** on providing health-related information to low-SES or rural populations
- programs that focus **exclusively** on providing information to health care providers about preventing, diagnosing, or treating diseases or other conditions in low-SES or rural populations.

The Committee recommends that the attached Guidelines (Attachment C) be used to report on NIH activities in FY 2003 related to minority health and health disparities, but that a system be developed and implemented by FY 2006 that will accommodate more automated (perhaps even fully automated) and consistent reporting of these activities.

ATTACHMENT A

COMMITTEE ON MINORITY HEALTH AND HEALTH DISPARITIES DEFINITIONS AND APPLICATION METHODOLOGY

Membership

Andrew von Eschenbach, NIH/NCI (co-chair)
Claude Lenfant/Barbara Alving, NIH/NHLBI (co-chair)

Tommy Broadwater, NIH/NCMHD
Harold Freeman, NIH/NCI
Ann Hagan, NIH/NIGMS
Milton Hernandez, NIH/NIAID
Raynard Kington, NIH/OD
Donald Poppke, NIH/OD
Carl Roth, NIH/NHLBI
Nathan Stinson, DHHS/OMH

ATTACHMENT B

MINORITY DIRECT, TOTAL IC BUDGETS, AND MINORITY DIRECT AS PERCENT OF TOTAL IC BUDGETS

Based on Old Definition

	Minority Health and Assistance Direct/Specifically Targeted Programs (Dollars in millions)			FY 2004 President's Budget Request from 2004 Congressional Justification (Dollars in millions)			Minority Direct as % of Budget
IC	FY 2002 Actual	FY 2003 Estimate	FY 2004 Estimate	FY 2002 Actual	FY 2003 Amend PB	FY 2004 Estimate	FY 2002
NCI	$121.9	$128.0	$131.9	$4,177.3	$4,609.0	$4,770.5	2.9
NHLBI	241.7	256.0	262.5	2,569.3	2,762.4	2,868.0	9.4
NIDCR	19.1	20.8	21.3	342.3	369.3	382.4	5.6
NIDDK	133.2	144.0	150.0	1,560.0	1,703.1	1,820.0	8.5
NINDS	49.2	53.9	57.0	1,325.2	1,416.4	1,468.9	3.7
NIAID	331.3	375.4	392.6	2,339.8	3,981.1	4,335.3	14.2
NIGMS	141.7	154.0	154.0	1,722.9	1,849.0	1,923.1	8.2
NICHD	277.2	298.6	310.8	1,110.5	1,194.9	1,245.4	25.0
NEI	23.2	25.0	25.9	580.0	625.1	648.3	4.0
NIEHS	23.4	25.3	26.1	644.7	608.9	630.8	3.6
NIA	75.9	81.6	84.7	891.3	957.6	994.4	8.5
NIAMS	49.1	53.3	55.2	447.7	485.5	502.8	11.0
NIDCD	5.8	6.3	6.5	341.3	365.7	380.4	1.7
NIMH	26.7	28.8	29.9	1,245.3	1,332.5	1,382.1	2.1
NIDA	74.7	81.0	84.0	892.6	960.0	995.6	8.4
NIAAA	35.9	37.7	39.3	383.2	414.9	430.1	9.4
NINR	28.1	29.8	30.7	120.2	129.7	134.6	23.4
NHGRI	10.8	13.1	13.8	428.2	457.8	478.1	2.5
NIBIB	0.3	1.0	1.0	111.7	270.5	282.1	0.3
NCRR	48.7	52.6	55.3	1,010.2	1,065.1	1,053.9	4.8
NCCAM	7.4	8.0	8.2	104.3	112.4	116.2	7.1
NCMHD	147.2	173.9	180.3	157.4	185.8	192.7	93.5
FIC	1.0	1.1	1.1	56.8	61.8	64.3	1.8
NLM	8.8	9.6	9.6	275.4	305.9	316.0	3.2
OD	5.9	5.9	5.3	234.8	274.0	318.0	2.5
Total*	1,888.4	2,064.4	2,137.1	23,073.4	26,498.4	27,734.0	

*May not add due to rounding.

SOURCE: Budget Office, OD, NIH; Budget Office, NHLBI, NIH.

ATTACHMENT C

GUIDELINES FOR MINORITY HEALTH AND HEALTH DISPARITIES REPORTING (REVISED DECEMBER 2003)

The Guidelines for Minority Health and Health Disparities Reporting describe reporting requirements for two reports—the Minority Health Report and the Health Disparities Report.

Minority Health Report: This report should include all funding for minority health research as defined by PL 106-525 (i.e., basic, clinical, and behavioral research on minority health conditions, including research to prevent, diagnose, and treat them.) Minorities are defined by statute as American Indians/Alaskan Natives (including Eskimos and Aleuts); Asian Americans; Native Hawaiians and other Pacific Islanders; Blacks; and Hispanics (i.e., individuals whose origin is Mexican, Puerto Rican, Cuban, Central or South American, or any other Spanish-speaking country).

Health Disparities Report: For the purposes of this report, health disparities populations are minority populations, low socioeconomic status (low-SES) populations, and rural populations. Therefore, this report will include all funding included in the Minority Health Report plus funding for activities that address health issues affecting low-SES and rural populations.

General Reporting Principles:

- Any distinction between "targeted research" and "non-targeted research" is for internal methodological and computational purposes only. Only the aggregate (i.e., sum of targeted and non-targeted research) will be reported outside the NIH.
- For co-funded grants, each IC should report its own dollar contribution only.
- All reporting should be done at the **subproject** level (consistent with the decision of the Director, NIH, in his memo dated October 18, 2002, to report clinical research at the subproject level starting with FY 2003).
- Starting with FY 2003 reporting, ICs are required to report costs attributable to clinical research at either 0, 25, 50, 75, or 100% of the total award amount for all projects and subprojects (see memo from Director, NIH, dated October 18, 2002, referenced above). Consistent with this decision, when calculating clinical research dollars for minority health and health disparities, each IC should first multiply each award amount by the percent relevance assigned for clinical research.
- For FY 2003, ICs should report intramural minority health and health disparities research consistent with their procedures in past years. It is the inten-

tion of the NIH to develop a standardized trans-NIH reporting procedure for this area in the future.

MINORITY HEALTH REPORT

Each IC will develop its own list of activities and corresponding dollars based on the guidelines below. **Only the total is to be reported**, but separate guidance is provided for each of five categories: basic research, clinical research, infrastructure, research training and career development, and outreach.

- For **extramural research**, dollar estimates should be generated for each of the areas.
- For **intramural research**, dollar estimates should only be developed only for basic research and clinical research.

Basic Research

Report only targeted research projects. This would include research on:

- A disease, condition, or biological process that affects **exclusively or almost exclusively** one or more minority populations
- A behavior that is found **exclusively or almost exclusively** in one or more minority populations
- Whether and/or how the mechanisms of disease or basic biological processes differ in minority populations; or how behaviors differ in minority populations.

All targeted projects should be included in the report at 100% of the funded amount. For multi-project grants, ICs may include a percentage of the funding for their core(s), based on the number of subprojects in the grant that perform targeted basic minority health research. Note that for this report, career development awards (K series awards) should be considered "research training and career development," rather than "research."

Non-targeted basic research (i.e., basic research focused on diseases, conditions, or processes that affect minority populations but that does not satisfy the requirements of the definition of targeted research) should be **excluded** from the report.

Clinical Research

All targeted and non-targeted minority clinical research should be reported. However, funding for clinical research studies conducted on foreign populations should be omitted. Note that for this report, career development awards (K series awards) should be considered "research training and career development", rather than "research."

Targeted Clinical Research

Targeted clinical research should be reported at 100% of the funded amount. (Remember to adjust the award amount to reflect the clinical percent relevance—25, 50, 75, or 100%—assigned by your IC for each clinical research project. See "General Reporting Principles" on page 260 of this book.) This category would include clinical research:

- Conducted **exclusively or almost exclusively** in one or more minority populations
- Investigating whether and/or how the manifestations, consequences, or responses to treatment of diseases or other conditions differ in minority populations. (Studying one minority group exclusively is sufficient to qualify as targeted minority research; i.e., no comparison group is necessary.)
- Investigating how behaviors differ in minority populations.

Non-Targeted Clinical Research

Non-targeted clinical research is clinical research focused on prevention, diagnosis, or treatment of diseases or other conditions that affect minority populations.

Reporting non-targeted clinical research The dollar amount for each non-targeted clinical project should be multiplied by the percent minority participation in that study. (Remember to adjust the award amount to reflect the clinical percent relevance—25, 50, 75, or 100%—assigned by your IC for each clinical research project. See "General Reporting Principles" on page 260 of this book.) **Note however that only non-targeted clinical projects with aggregate minority participation of 25 percent or more should be included.**

Determining Percent Minority Participation ICs have several options for determining percent minority participation to use for this report. The IMPAC II Population Tracking database (POP Tracking) should be the "starting point." *Minority participation* represents the aggregate of ethnic and racial minority participation. If recruitment is not complete, projected numbers for minority recruitment should be used. If projected numbers do not exist, the actual recruitment should be used.

ICs may:

- use the percent minority participation contained in POP Tracking.

• override the percent minority participation in POP Tracking if they determine that the study should be considered "targeted" clinical research (by the definition provided above). In this case, ICs should report the project at 100% of its award amount.

• try to obtain participation data from other sources when data are missing from POP Tracking. For example, recruitment data (projected or actual) might be contained in the original applications or progress reports, even when they have not been entered into POP Tracking. In addition, not all projects in POP Tracking are *required* to have participation data; examples of such "exceptions" are studies with fewer than 10 participants and studies performing secondary analysis of data. In these cases, ICs should obtain participation data from other sources when possible. For example, project officers might have data on the original study population for studies performing secondary analysis of data.

Infrastructure

Report only targeted infrastructure activities. This would include solicited programs that are focused exclusively on developing the research capabilities of historically black colleges and universities (HBCUs) and minority medical schools, as well as solicited programs designed to enhance the research resources available specifically to under-represented minorities at other institutions educating or training high numbers of one or more minority populations that are under-represented in biomedical or behavioral research. Examples of targeted infrastructure activities include the Extramural Associates Research Development Award (EARDA) and the HBCU Research Scientist Award. All targeted infrastructure activities should be reported at 100% of the funded amount.

Research Training and Career Development

All targeted and non-targeted activities should be reported. Training and career development activities include career development awards (K series awards), fellowships (F series awards), institutional training awards (T series awards), and minority supplements. ICs may support other training and career development activities, as well. Note that for this report, a research grant (e.g., R01) awarded to a minority investigator, or to an investigator at a minority serving institution, should not be included in the Training and Career Development category.

Targeted Activities

Report all targeted activities at 100%. Targeted activities are programs that focus **exclusively** on supporting research training or career development of under-represented minorities (e.g., Mentored Research Scientist Development

Award for Minority Faculty-K01; Minority Predoctoral Fellowship-F31; Minority Research Supplements).

Note regarding Minority Research Supplements: IMPAC II does not include separate records (type 3 records) for the minority supplements after their first year of funding. (i.e., After the first year, minority supplement dollars are included in the total award amount of the parent grant.) To avoid double counting, only new minority research supplements should be reported separately.

Non-Targeted Activities

Non-targeted activities are ones that, although not focused exclusively on minority groups, support research training or career development of under-represented minority investigators. For non-targeted activities, report only the dollars know to be received by under-represented minority individuals.

For example:

- A fellowship (F32) awarded to an under-represented minority individual would be included at 100%.
- A T32 that supports 6 graduate students, only 2 of whom are under-represented minorities, would be reported at 33%.

Outreach

Report only targeted outreach activities. Targeted outreach activities are those that focus **exclusively** on providing health-related information to minority populations or information to health care providers about preventing, diagnosing, or treating diseases or other conditions in minority populations.

All targeted activities should be included in the report at 100% of the funded amount. In general, non-targeted activities that provide education applicable to both minorities and non-minorities should be **excluded**. However, if a non-targeted outreach project has identifiable costs associated with specific activities targeted toward minorities (e.g., translating brochures into Spanish), those costs should be included in this report. On the other hand, simply taking a percentage of an outreach project for "general" minority-related activities is not appropriate.

Note: For this report, conference grants (R13s) should be reported under the "outreach" category.

HEALTH DISPARITIES REPORT

The report will include all activities that address issues with low socioeconomic status (low-SES) and rural populations **plus** those that are included in the minority health report. The basis for the low-SES and rural component of the report is to be a list of activities identified by a CRISP search. (See page 9 for the list of CRISP search terms used to generate the list.)

For each grant, the percent relevance should be determined as follows. If any of the CRISP search terms is designated as "primary" for a particular grant, then its relevance is 100%; if no term is "primary," but at least one of the terms is "secondary," then its relevance is 50%; and if no terms are "primary" or "secondary," but at least one term is "tertiary," then its relevance is 25%. For example, if an activity is coded as "primary" for **low income** and **rural area** and "secondary" for **Medicaid**, then its percent relevance should be 100%. Similarly, if a grant does not have any of the health disparity terms coded as "primary", but **medically under-served population** is coded as "secondary" and **homeless** is coded as "tertiary", its percent relevance should be 50%.

Once the list of grants is generated:

- Sort it into the same five categories used in the Minority Report—basic research, clinical research, infrastructure, research training and career development, and outreach—and process according to the guidance below (presented under each category heading).
- For each category, add the activities compiled for the Minority Health Report, being careful not to double-count. For any grant that included in both the Minority Health Report **and** the health disparities CRISP search, count the grant only once and at the **higher** of the two percent relevances. (For example, if the CRISP list shows a grant at 50% relevance due to a low-SES search term, but the percent minority participation in the study is 63%, 63% relevance should be used for the health disparities report. Likewise, if a grant is considered 100% relevant for rural health but is reported at only 50% for minority research, it should be included at 100% in the health disparities report. (However, a higher percent relevance for an activity in the health disparities list **should not** be transferred back to the minority health report.)
- Add activities funded by any mechanisms not coded in CRISP (e.g., contracts). Assign each a percent relevance (100%, 50%, or 25%) based on whether the CRISP terms that would be appropriate would be of "primary," "secondary," or "tertiary" importance to that activity. (Use only those terms listed on page 9. See page 10 for a short description of how CRISP coders determine relevance for a particular term.)
- Delete activities from the CRISP-generated list that do not address low-SES or rural health issues. However, if a grant should be included that is not on the list (or should be included at a relevance different from that assigned by CRISP), the CRISP office (CRISP contact person: Ms. Dorrette Finch, 435-0656) should be contacted to work together to resolve any concerns about how the study is coded in CRISP.
- Multiply the corresponding dollar amount for each activity by the associated (disparities) percent relevance to calculate the amount to include in this

report for each activity. (Remember to adjust award amount to reflect the clinical percent relevance—25, 50, 75, or 100%—assigned by your IC for each clinical research project. See "General Reporting Principles" on page 260 of this book.)

Basic Research

Report only targeted research projects. For the low-SES and rural component, this would include research on:

- A disease, condition, or biological process that affects **exclusively or almost exclusively** low-SES or rural populations
- A behavior that is found **exclusively or almost exclusively** in low-SES or rural populations
- Whether and/or how the mechanisms of disease or basic biological processes differ in low-SES or rural populations; or how behaviors differ in minority populations.

All targeted projects should be included in the report at 100% of the funded amount.

Leave in all **non-duplicate** basic research activities from the Minority Report.

Clinical Research

Report the sum of all targeted and non-targeted research activities.

For the low-SES and rural component:

- **targeted** research is:
  - research on whether and/or how the manifestations, consequences, or responses to treatment of diseases or other conditions differ in low-SES or rural populations
  - research conducted **exclusively or almost exclusively** in low-SES or rural populations.
- **non-targeted** research is:
  - research related to the manifestations, consequences, or responses to treatment of diseases or other conditions in low-SES or rural populations
  - research conducted in populations that include low-SES or rural populations.

For calculating the low-SES and rural component, use the CRISP relevance (100%, 50%, 25%) assigned to each activity. However, for those activities that appear in the CRISP low-SES and rural list **and** in the Minority Report, use the larger of: (1) the CRISP relevance or (2) the percent minority population used for the Minority Report. Be careful not to double-count.

Remember to add any research contracts with an IC-specified relevance of 100%, 50%, or 25% to low-SES or rural health.

Leave in all **non-duplicate** research activities (targeted and non-targeted) from the Minority Report. They should be reported just as they were in the Minority Report—at 100% for the targeted activities; at the percent of minority participation for the non-targeted activities.

Infrastructure

Report the same total here as that reported for Infrastructure in the Minority Health Report (due to difficulties in identifying institutions that educate large numbers of people from low-SES and rural populations).

Research Training and Career Development

Report the same total here as that reported for Research Training and Career Development in the Minority Health Report (due to difficulties in identifying trainees of low-SES or rural backgrounds and institutions that educate large numbers of people from low-SES and rural populations).

Outreach

Report only targeted outreach activities. For the low-SES and rural health component, include:

- programs that focus **exclusively** on providing health-related information to low-SES or rural populations
- programs that focus **exclusively** on providing information to health care providers about preventing, diagnosing, or treating diseases or other conditions in low-SES or rural populations.

These would include outreach activities in the CRISP-generated list with a relevance of 100%. In addition, any targeted outreach activities addressing low-SES or rural health disparities issues that are not in the CRISP list (e.g., contracts) must be added. Report these activities at 100% of their funded amount.

Leave in all **non-duplicate** Outreach activities from the Minority Report (reported at 100%).

Activities providing education that is applicable to health disparity populations, but that is also applicable to all populations, should be **excluded**. However, if a non-targeted outreach project has identifiable costs associated with specific activities targeted toward low-SES or rural populations (e.g., partnering with community-based organizations in low-income communities), those costs should be included in this report. On the other hand, simply taking a percentage of an outreach project for "general" health disparity activities is not appropriate.

Note: For this report, conference grants (R13s) should be reported under the "outreach" category.

CRISP THESAURUS TERMS TO IDENTIFY LOW-SES AND RURAL HEALTH DISPARITIES ACTIVITIES

health disparities
homeless
income
income maintenance
low income
Medicaid
medical indigency
medically underserved population
migrant
public assistance
rural area
social class
social mobility
social status
socioeconomics
urban poverty area

HOW CRISP CODERS DETERMINE RELEVANCE FOR A TERM

CRISP EMPHASIS CODES: P, S, T

An emphasis code:

1) is assigned to every indexing term selected for a research project;
2) reflects the relevancy of the indexing term to the aims and objectives of the project;
3) may have one of three values -
   P = primary
   S = secondary
   T = tertiary

Primary Emphasis

The primary emphasis code, "P", should be used to indicate the main aspects of a single project or subproject. Assigning "P" emphasis should be reserved for those terms with major significance to the project or subproject. A good common sense rule to follow would be to ask the question "would this project be wanted as primary on a subject search by the user or requestor?"

It will always require judgment on the part of the indexer to determine how many "P" terms as well as which ones are assigned "P" emphasis. There will usually be 1-5 primary concepts per project or subproject. Many times it will require more than one P term to "cover" one of the major areas of a project.

EXAMPLE:
A project may be studying obesity as a risk factor for stroke.
The following terms should all be assigned a P:
disease /disorder proneness /risk
stroke
obesity

If the example above were modified to emphasize, instead, the many different risk factors for stroke, the following terms should be assigned a P:
disease /disorder proneness /risk
stroke

The specific risk factors, which are of less importance in this example, should also be indexed but with an "S" emphasis.
obesity
exercise
diet

Secondary emphasis

"S" is the emphasis code for indexing terms lacking primary significance but of greater importance to the research than routine tools, subjects, methods, etc. Some specific terms are required to be indexed only at this level (i.e., cooperative study).

Tertiary emphasis

"T" is the emphasis code for indexing terms representing materials and methods such as instruments and routine methodology, research subjects, including animals, and tag terms, etc.

ATTACHMENT D

ACTIVITIES OF THE NIH COMMITTEE ON MINORITY HEALTH AND HEALTH DISPARITIES RESEARCH DEFINITIONS AND APPLICATION METHODOLOGY

NOVEMBER 2002–OCTOBER 2003

As a first step, the Committee surveyed the Institutes/Centers (ICs) to determine how each currently reports on activities related to minority health and health disparities. ICs were asked whether they report at the project or sub-project level and how they determine the percent relevance for activities in each of four categories: basic research, clinical research, infrastructure and training, and outreach. They were also asked which populations they include in health disparities reporting: minorities, low socioeconomic, rural, and other. Based on the data reported, the Committee discussed the pros and cons of the different methods used and decided upon some basic standards, such as requiring all reporting at the sub-project level.

Members of the Committee reviewed definitions and reporting requirements in PL 106-525 (the Minority Health and Health Disparities Research and Education Act of 2000), and drafted a range of suggestions (including operational definitions) on how to report each of the four categories—basic research, clinical research, infrastructure and training, and outreach—for minority health and health disparities. The suggestions were used for discussion among the full Committee to determine the rules upon which each of the two new reports—the minority health report and the health disparities report—should be based. The rules for reporting on minority health include, for example, for basic research, reporting only targeted activities, and for clinical studies reporting a percentage of the total dollars based on the ratio of minority to non-minority participants in the study. The rules also specify that only racial/ethnic minorities, low socioeconomic status (low-SES) populations, and rural populations should be included in the health disparities report at this time.

Draft guidelines were developed to aid the ICs in preparing their reports. Two different methodologies were proposed for producing each report. One methodology for the minority health report allowed the ICs to develop their own lists of minority activities, while incorporating the definitions and rules agreed upon by the Committee; the other methodology relied upon the NIH CRISP database for the lists of minority research activities. Both methodologies for the health disparities report relied upon the same CRISP-generated list for the low-SES and rural health component; the only difference was the methodology used to develop the minority health component of the report.

The Committee then decided to conduct a pilot using the draft guidelines to determine whether they enabled easy and consistent reporting. Six Institutes (two large, two mid-size, two small) were asked to participate in the trial: NCI, NHLBI, NINDS, NICHD, NIAAA, NIDCR. The ICs were provided the requisite instructions and data files, and were invited to a training session that was held early in the trial for representatives from each IC. NHLBI staff were available for questions and provided technical help throughout the trial. Upon completion of the pilot, a meeting was held at the request of the participating ICs to provide them an opportunity to share their experiences.

Several collaborations were created to produce basic data required by all ICs in the pilot:

- CRISP coders worked closely with a sub-committee of the larger group to devise a way for the reporting to be based on the existing NIH-wide system. Lists of grants, created using a standard set of search terms, were provided to each of the ICs as their starting point for one of the minority health reports and for the low-SES and rural health component of the health disparities reports.
- The Information Resources and Technology Program at the NHLBI developed a program for all the ICs to use to pull clinical data from the Population Tracking database, a subset of the NIH IMPAC II system. Again, this will allow all ICs to generate a list of qualifying activities that will be based on the same criteria.
- The Office of Extramural Research, Office of the Director, NIH worked out a way for participating institutes to report funding awarded to minority individuals who have received NIH training grants and fellowships that were not specifically targeted to minority individuals or minority institutions.

Results of the pilot were presented to the Committee in early September 2003. Most of the ICs participating in the pilot expressed reservations about the adequacy of CRISP as the basis for an automated reporting system for minority health and health disparities, noting that in their view it would seriously underestimate the NIH commitment to health disparities. Therefore, after reviewing the pilot results and hearing the opinions of the pilot ICs, the Committee selected the methodology that allows the ICs to develop their own lists of minority activities (within the rules agreed upon by the Committee and described in the revised Guidelines) for the Minority Health Report in FY 2003. Consequently, the methodology selected for the Health Disparities Report is the one that incorporates this selected methodology for the minority health component and that uses CRISP only to generate lists of activities for the low-SES and rural health component.

A sub-group of the Committee then conducted a final review and refinement of the definitions and review of the CRISP terms for health disparities. The Guidelines were revised to reflect the Committee decisions and final definitions.

Looking ahead, the Committee recommended that a group be selected to develop and implement a more automated and perhaps fully automated system by FY 2006, possibly involving the CRISP database, for reporting minority health and health disparities activities.

I

Acronyms

CC	NIH Clinical Center
CIT	Center for Information Technology
CSR	Center for Scientific Review
FIC	John E. Fogarty International Center
NCCAM	National Center for Complementary and Alternative Medicine
NCI	National Cancer Institute
NCMHD	National Center on Minority Health and Health Disparities
NCRR	National Center for Research Resources
NEI	National Eye Institute
NHGRI	National Human Genome Research Institute
NHLBI	National Heart, Lung, and Blood Institute
NIA	National Institute on Aging
NIAA	National Institute on Alcohol Abuse and Alcoholism
NIAID	National Institute of Allergy and Infectious Diseases
NIAMS	National Institute of Arthritis and Musculoskeletal and Skin Diseases
NIBIB	National Institute of Biomedical Imaging and Bioengineering
NICHD	National Institute of Child Health and Human Development
NIDA	National Institute on Drug Abuse
NIDCD	National Institute on Deafness and Other Communication Disorders
NIDCR	National Institute of Dental and Craniofacial Research

NIDDK	National Institute of Diabetes and Digestive and Kidney Diseases
NIEHS	National Institute of Environmental Health Sciences
NIGMS	National Institute of General Medical Sciences
NIH	National Institutes of Health
NIMH	National Institute of Mental Health
NINDS	National Institute of Neurological Disorders and Stroke
NINR	National Institute of Nursing Research
NLM	National Library of Medicine
OAR	Office of AIDS Research
OBSSR	Office of Behavioral and Social Sciences Research
OIR	Office of Intramural Research
ORWH	Office of Research on Women's Health

J

Centers of Excellence Funded by the National Center on Minority Health and Health Disparities, 2005

Institution	City	State	Mech-anism
Alabama State University	Montgomery	Alabama	R24
Albert Einstein College of Medicine/Yeshiva Univ.	Bronx	New York	P60
Black Hills State University	Spearfish	South Dakota	R24
Bluefield State College	Bluefield	West Virginia	R24
Carlos Albizu University	San Juan	Puerto Rico	R24
Charles R. Drew University of Medicine and Science	Los Angeles	California	P20
Children's National Medical Center	Washington	District of Columbia	P20
Clemson University	Clemson	South Carolina	P20
Columbia University Health Sciences	New York	New York	P60
East Tennessee State University	Johnson City	Tennessee	R24
Emory University	Atlanta	Georgia	P60
Florida A&M University	Tallahassee	Florida	P20
Florida International University	Miami	Florida	R24
Governors State University	University Park	Illinois	R24
Hampton University	Hampton	Virginia	R24
Henry M. Jackson Foundation for the Advancement of Military Medicine, Inc.	Rockville	Maryland	P20
Howard University	Washington	District of Columbia	P20
Jackson State University	Jackson	Mississippi	P20
Johns Hopkins University	Baltimore	Maryland	P60
Loma Linda University	Loma Linda	California	P20
Medical University of South Carolina	Charleston	South Carolina	P60

Institution	City	State	Mech-anism
Medstar Research Institute	Washington	District of Columbia	P20
Meharry Medical College	Nashville	Tennessee	P20
Morehouse College	Atlanta	Georgia	R24
Morehouse School of Medicine	Atlanta	Georgia	P20
Morgan State University	Baltimore	Maryland	P60
Mount Sinai School of Medicine of New York University	New York	New York	P60
New York University School of Medicine	New York	New York	P60
North Carolina Central University	Durham	North Carolina	P20
San Diego State University	San Diego	California	P60
Shaw University	Raleigh	North Carolina	R24/ P60
South Carolina State University	Orangeburg	South Carolina	P60
State University of New York at Albany	Albany	New York	R24
SUNY Downstate Medical Center	Brooklyn	New York	R24
Temple University	Philadelphia	Pennsylvania	R24
Texas A&M Research Foundation	College Station	Texas	R24
Texas College	Tyler	Texas	R24
Texas Southern University	Houston	Texas	R24
Texas Tech University Health Sciences Center	Lubbock	Texas	R24
The Robert Wood Johnson Medical School	Camden	New Jersey	R24
The University of Medicine and Dentistry	Newark	New Jersey	R24
Tuskegee University	Tuskegee	Alabama	P20
University of Alabama in Tuscaloosa	Tuscaloosa	Alabama	P20
University of Alabama, Birmingham	Birmingham	Alabama	R24
University of Alabama, Birmingham	Birmingham	Alabama	P60
University of Alaska, Anchorage	Anchorage	Alaska	R24
University of Arizona	Tucson	Arizona	P60
University of California–Los Angeles	Los Angeles	California	P20/ P60
University of California–San Diego	La Jolla	California	P60
University of California, Davis	Davis	California	P60
University of Colorado Health Sciences Center	Aurora	Colorado	P60
University of Connecticut, Storrs	Storrs	Connecticut	P20
University of Hawaii at Manoa	Honolulu	Hawaii	P20
University of Illinois at Chicago	Chicago	Illinois	P20
University of Maryland Baltimore Professional School	Baltimore	Maryland	P60
University of Michigan at Flint	Ann Arbor	Michigan	R24
University of Nevada Las Vegas	Las Vegas	Nevada	R24
University of North Carolina	Chapel Hill	North Carolina	P60
University of North Carolina, Greensboro	Greensboro	North Carolina	R24

Institution	City	State	Mech- anism
University of Northern Iowa	Cedar Falls	Iowa	R24
University of North Texas Health Science Center	Fort Worth	Texas	P20
University of Oklahoma Health Sciences Center	Oklahoma City	Oklahoma	P20
University of Pennsylvania	Philadelphia	Pennsylvania	P60
University of Pittsburgh	Pittsburgh	Pennsylvania	P60
University of Puerto Rico Medical Sciences Campus	San Juan	Puerto Rico	P20
University of South Alabama	Mobile	Alabama	R24
University of South Carolina, Columbia	Columbia	South Carolina	P20
University of South Dakota	Vermillion	South Dakota	P20
University of Texas at Brownsville	Brownsville	Texas	P20
University of Texas Health Science Center, Houston	Houston	Texas	P20
University of Texas MD Anderson Cancer Center	Houston	Texas	P60
University of Texas, El Paso	El Paso	Texas	R24
University of the Virgin Islands	Charlotte Amalie	Virgin Islands	R24
University of Wisconsin, Madison	Madison	Wisconsin	P60

K

NCMHD Endowment Program Awardees

Institution	State	Award Amount
FY2004 Awardees		
Tuskegee University	AL	$5.00 million
California, University of, San Diego	CA	0.63
Charles R Drew University of Medicine	CA	5.00
Howard University	DC	0.94
Florida A&M University	FL	5.00
Morehouse School of Medicine	GA	5.00
Hawaii University	HI	1.56
Kansas University Medical Center	KS	1.88
Xavier University of Louisiana	LA	5.00
Montana University	MT	1.56
Creighton University	NE	0.63
Puerto Rico University, Medical	PR	5.00
Meharry Medical College	TN	5.00
Texas, University of, San Antonio	TX	0.31
14 Awards		*$42.50 million*
FY2005 Awardees		
Tuskegee University	AL	$5.00 million
Charles R Drew University of Medicine	CA	5.00
Howard University	DC	0.94
Morehouse School of Medicine	GA	5.00
Kansas University Medical Center	KS	1.88
Xavier University of Louisiana	LA	5.00
Montana University	MT	1.56
Creighton University	NE	0.63
New Mexico University	NM	0.94
Puerto Rico University, Medical	PR	5.00
Meharry Medical College	TN	5.00
11 Awards		*$35.94 million*

L

Summary of Recommendations

1. The National Institutes of Health (NIH), through the National Center on Minority Health and Health Disparities (NCMHD) and the Institutes and Centers (ICs) and, when appropriate, collaborating agencies, should undertake research to further refine and develop the conceptual, definitional, and methodological issues involved in health disparities research and to further the understanding of the causes of disparities.

2. The NIH director should assure that the Strategic Plan is reviewed and revised annually using an established, trans-NIH process subject to timely review, approval, and dissemination.

3. The Strategic Plan research objectives should promote more integration of research on the multifactorial nature of health disparities, including non-biological factors; population research to further the understanding of the presence, prevalence, trends, and other elements of health disparity conditions; and when opportunity exists, an understanding of the causes of disparities in health care.

4. The Strategic Plan should include measurable targets and time periods for the research capacity objectives. NIH, through NCMHD's oversight, should develop methods of measuring, analyzing and monitoring the results of programs that address research capacity, including workforce, institutional, infrastructure, and community-based participatory health disparity research objectives.

5. The Strategic Plan's communication programs should be organized as a specific trans-NIH effort with centralized coordination with particular attention to the strategic planning, design, prioritization, implementation, and evaluation of efforts across NIH. The initiative should: be informed by advisory expertise; develop a surveillance system to identify information needs and availability,

sources, behaviors, and use patterns; and promote attention to the issue of inequalities in health communication.

6. The development of updated Strategic Plans should include assessments of the appropriateness of the individual strategic plans of the ICs, including whether they adequately reflect the overall goals and objectives of the NIH Strategic Plan.

- Objectives should be time-based and targeted with measurable outcomes.

7. NCMHD should consider the designation of additional health disparity groups based on an informed process and developed criteria. It should promote development of, and access to, a registry of diseases and conditions for which disparities exist with regard to race, ethnicity, socioeconomic status, geographic locale, and other designated health disparity populations.

8. Within NIH, a clear and timely budget process should be linked to the Strategic Plan, and it should be updated in a timely manner. Annual budgets should include information for NIH as a whole, and for each involved IC and office, and should detail allocations for the Strategic Plan goal areas and each objective. Trans-NIH budget information on efforts made in the major categories of research, research capacity, and communication also should be made available.

9. The NIH director should review and assess the administrative staffing of NCMHD to assure that it is sufficient to attend to the Center's responsibilities.

- Increasing the science leadership and presence within NCMHD should be pursued by the NIH and NCMHD directors. This entails the appointment of additional eminent scientists, recognized in the areas of minority health and health disparities, and the establishment by NCMHD of committees and panels with relevant expertise from within and outside NIH.

10. The NIH director, through the established authority of the NCMHD director, should assure continuous, effective coordination of the health disparities research program across the NIH including:

- Timely development of Strategic Plan revisions;
- Effective, ongoing participation of the ICs in the Strategic Plan and the health disparities research program.
- Establishing appropriate committees involving the directors of the ICs and others to facilitate collaboration and coordinated approaches to health disparities research and the setting of priorities;
- Fostering of conferences and the use of committees and panels involving the NIH, extramural scientific communities, and others to inform and advise on initiatives and directions; and
- Monitoring of the execution of the Strategic Plan to ensure that its elements are implemented.

M

Committee and Staff Biographies

Gerald E. Thomson, M.D. ***(Chair)***, is Professor of Medicine Emeritus and Senior Associate Dean Emeritus at the Columbia University College of Physicians and Surgeons. A graduate of Queens College and the Howard University College of Medicine, he was director of a dialysis unit at the State University of New York—Kings County Hospital Center from 1965 to 1968, Director of Medicine at Harlem Hospital from 1970 to 1985, Executive Vice President and Chief of Staff at the Columbia-Presbyterian Medical Center from 1985 to 1990, and Senior Associate Dean from 1990 to 2003. From 1972 to 1985 he served on numerous advisory committees and panels on hypertension at the National Institutes of Health (NIH) as well as on the NIH Clinical Trials Review Committee. More recently, he has served with efforts addressing delivery of primary medical care, professionalism in medicine, and racial and ethnic disparities in medical care. Dr. Thomson is past President of the American College of Physicians and former Chairman of the American Board of Internal Medicine. He has been a member of the Institute of Medicine (IOM) since 1996.

John F. Alderete, Ph.D., is Professor of Microbiology at the University of Texas (UT) Health Science Center at San Antonio. He received two B.S. degrees (mathematics and biology) as an undergraduate student at New Mexico Institute of Mining and Technology at Socorro. He received his Ph.D. in microbiology in 1978 from the University of Kansas-Lawrence. He did postdoctoral work at UNC-Chapel Hill prior to a faculty position at the UT Health Science Center at San Antonio. He has over 110 publications in peer-review journals and is the author of 54 book chapters and invited OP-ED editorials. His research on the number one, nonviral sexually transmitted agent, *Trichomonas vaginalis*, has been presented as abstracts published in 138 proceedings of national and international scientific meetings, where he has also participated in, chaired, and organized scientific symposia. His research has resulted in 5 patents and 2 patents-pending. He serves on three editorial boards and has been an ad hoc reviewer of 46 scientific journals. He is asked to speak on issues involving minorities, higher education, and the scientific workforce by government agencies. These include the President's National Science Board, the NIH, the Federal Food and Drug Administration (FDA), the White House Office for Science and Technology Policy, and White House "One Nation" on race and health disparities. He has received many honors and awards, most notably the Premio Encuentro Award for Science and Technology in 1992, the single highest honor given to a Hispanic in America. Dr. Alderete is the past president of the Society for the Advancement of Chicanos and Native Americans in the Sciences (SACNAS), and SACNAS has honored him with the 2003 Distinguished Scientist Award presented at the annual conference. He is an ASM Academy of Microbiology Fellow and was elected a member of the Mexican Academy of Sciences. He is co-founder of a biotechnology company, Xenotope Diagnostics, Inc., that has FDA approval for two products for the diagnosis of Trichomonas vaginitis.

Moon S. Chen, Jr., Ph.D., M.P.H., is a Professor, Department of Public Health Sciences and the Associate Director for Cancer Disparities and Research at the University of California, Davis Cancer Center in Sacramento. He previously served as Chair, Division of Health Behavior and Health Promotion, School of Public Health at The Ohio State University's College of Medicine and Public Health. He has authored or co-authored over 90 refereed articles or abstracts that have appeared in various medical and scientific journals. Dr. Chen is frequently being sought for his expertise in public health and has served as a consultant to the Ministry of Public Health of the People's Republic of China, the U.S. Centers for Disease Control, NIH, Susan G. Komen Breast Cancer Foundation, University of South Florida, University of Hawaii, and the University of California-San Diego, as well as state public health departments in California, Ohio, Michigan, Virginia, and Hawaii. He is perhaps best known as being a preeminent scholar/researcher in public health issues affecting Asian Americans. In 2002 President George W. Bush named him to the National Cancer Advisory Board for a six-year term; he is the only Asian American on that Board. In 2003, he was one of two non-Federal Co-Chairs of the first-ever Trans-HHS (U.S. Health and Human Services) Cancer Health Disparities Progress Review Group charged with overseeing and leading a national effort to reduce cancer health disparities. Later that year, Dr. Chen received the American Cancer Society's Humanitarian Award for his "unfailing commitment and considerable contributions to the field of public health..." his "dedication to addressing and improving the health of Asian Americans and Pacific Islanders..." and his "leadership in investigating and securing funds for continued research on the health disparities within minority populations."

Harvey R. Colten, M.D., Vice President and Senior Associate Dean for Academic Affairs at Columbia University Medical Center, was the Chief Medical Officer, *i*Metrikus, Inc. and Clinical Professor Pediatrics at UCSF between 2000 and 2002. Previously, he served as Dean of the Medical School and VP for Medical Affairs at Northwestern University from 1997–1999 and was the Harriet B. Spoehrer Professor and Chair of the Department of Pediatrics at Washington University School of Medicine, St. Louis, MO from 1986–1997. Dr. Colten earned a B.A. at Cornell in 1959, an M.D. from Western Reserve University in 1963, and an M.A. (Honorary) from Harvard in 1978. Following his clinical training in 1965, he was an investigator at NIH until 1970. In 1970, he was appointed to the faculty at the Harvard Medical School, where he was named Professor of Pediatrics in 1979 and Chief of the Division of Cell Biology, Pulmonary Medicine, and Director of the Cystic Fibrosis Program at Children's Hospital Medical Center, Boston. Dr. Colten's research interests include the regulation of acute phase gene expression and genetic deficiencies of proteins that play a major role in pulmonary diseases, autoimmunity and inflammation, on which he has published more than 270 original articles, book chapters and invited reviews. He is a member of Alpha Omega Alpha and a recipient of other honors, including a Special Faculty Research Award from Western Reserve University, the E. Mead Johnson Award for Pediatric Research, a MERIT Award from NIH, Distinguished Service Award from the American Association of Immunologists, and Honorary Membership in the Hungarian Society of Immunology. He has been listed in Who's Who in America since 1982. He has trained more than 60 investigators in pediatric allergy/immunology, pulmonology and related scientific disciplines, many of whom have achieved leadership positions in academic medicine both nationally and internationally. He served on and was Vice Chairman of the Council of the Institute of Medicine. He is also a member of the American Society for Clinical Investigation, the Society for Pediatric Research, the Association of American Physicians, the American Pediatric Society, the American Association of Immunologists (former secretary and treasurer), and the American Society for Biochemistry and Molecular Biology. He is also a Fellow of the American Association for the Advancement of Science, the American Academy of Allergy and Immunology and the American Academy of Pediatrics. Dr. Colten is a Diplomat of the American Board of Pediatrics and the American Board of Allergy and Immunology (former Board member and chair Examination Committee), and was a member of the National Heart, Lung, and Blood Institute Advisory Council and the Board of Managers Central Institute for the Deaf. He currently serves on the Boards of Immtech, International, Inc., Parents as Teachers and the March of Dimes Scientific Advisory Council. Dr. Colten has been on editorial boards and advisory committees of several leading scientific and medical journals, including the *New England Journal of Medicine*, *Journal of Clinical Investigation*, *Journal of Pediatrics*, *Journal of Immunology*, and the *Annual Review of Immunology*. Dr. Colten is a member of the IOM and former member and Vice Chair of the IOM Council.

Robert A. Hiatt, M.D., Ph.D., is the Director of Population Science and Deputy Director of the UCSF Comprehensive Cancer Center. He is a Professor of Epidemiology and Biostatistics at UCSF and also a Senior Scientist for the national Kaiser Permanente Medical Care Program in Oakland. From 1998 to early 2003 he was the Deputy Director of the Division of Cancer Control and Population Sciences at the National Cancer Institute (NCI), where he oversaw cancer research in epidemiology and genetics, surveillance, and health services research. Before that he was the Director of Prevention Sciences at the Northern California Cancer Center and also Assistant Director for Epidemiology at the Division of Research, Kaiser Permanente Medical Care Program in Northern California. He was trained in medicine at the University of Michigan and in epidemiology at the University of California at Berkeley. He is Board Certified in Preventive Medicine and, until taking his NCI position, practiced general internal medicine. After an early career in international health and tropical disease research, his research interests have included cancer epidemiology, especially breast cancer, cancer prevention and screening. He is a past president of the American College of Epidemiology and is now President of the American Society for Preventive Oncology. His central focus at UCSF is building a strong, interdisciplinary program in cancer population sciences that includes epidemiology and genetics, behavior and health services research, surveillance, and survivorship research.

Sherman A. James, Ph.D., is the inaugural Susan B. King Professor of Public Policy Studies in the Terry Sanford Institute of Public Policy, Duke University. Prior to joining Duke University, he taught at the University of North Carolina-Chapel Hill (1973–1989) and at the University of Michigan (1989–2003). At Michigan, he was the John P. Kirscht Collegiate Professor of Public Health with joint appointments in the Departments of Epidemiology and Health Behavior & Health Education in the School of Public Health. He was also a Senior Research Scientist in the Survey Research Center at the Institute for Social Research. Dr. James' research focuses on the social determinants of racial and ethnic health inequalities and community-based and public policy interventions designed to minimize these inequalities. Dr. James was elected to the IOM of the National Academy of Sciences (NAS) in 2000. In 2001, he received the Abraham Lilienfeld Award from the Epidemiology section of the American Public Health Association for career excellence in the teaching of epidemiology. He is a fellow of the American Epidemiological Society, the American College of Epidemiology, the American Heart Association, and the Academy of Behavioral Medicine Research. Currently, he serves as an Associate Editor of the *American Journal of Public*

Health. A social epidemiologist, Dr. James received his Ph.D. (Social Psychology) from Washington University, in St. Louis (1973).

Ichiro Kawachi, M.D., Ph.D., is Professor of Social Epidemiology and the Director of the Harvard Center for Society and Health, both at the Harvard School of Public Health. Kawachi received his M.D. and Ph.D. (epidemiology), both from the University of Otago, New Zealand. Kawachi's research is focused on the social and economic determinants of population health. He has published over 300 peer-reviewed articles and reviews in scientific journals on health disparities. He was the co-editor (with Lisa Berkman) of the first textbook on *Social Epidemiology*, published by Oxford University Press in 2000, and currently in its 6th printing. His most recent books include *The Health of Nations* with Bruce Kennedy (The New Press, 2002) and *Neighborhoods and Health* with Lisa Berkman (Oxford University Press, 2003). A textbook on Globalization and Health (Oxford University Press), co-edited with Sarah Wamala of the Swedish National Institute of Public Health, is forthcoming in June 2006. Kawachi is the Co-Director of the Harvard site of the national Robert Wood Johnson Scholars Program in Health and Society, as well as the site director of the national Kellogg Foundation Fellows in Minority Health Disparities. Kawachi is also the Senior Editor (Social Epidemiology) of the international journal *Social Science & Medicine*, as well as an Editor of the *American Journal of Epidemiology.* He has served as a consultant/special advisor to the Pan-American Health Organization, the World Health Organization, and the World Bank.

Claude Lenfant, M.D., is the former director of the National Heart Lung and Blood Institute (NHLBI). He received his B.S. degree in 1948 from the University of Rennes, France, and his M.D. in 1956 from the University of Paris. In 1960, he joined the University of Washington in Seattle where he rose to the rank of Professor of Medicine, Physiology and Biophysics. In 1970, Dr. Lenfant was appointed the first associate director for lung programs of the then NHLI. This program evolved into the Division of Lung Diseases, formed in 1972, with Dr. Lenfant as its director. For his accomplishments he was awarded the HEW Superior Service Honor Award in 1974. The Division of Lung Diseases continued to grow and to coordinate a strong and diverse program of research into the prevention, diagnosis and treatment of lung diseases. He became NIH associate director for international research and director of the Fogarty International Center in 1980, positions he held until his appointment as director of NHLBI in 1982. In 1983 he was elected member of the IOM, NAS. He was named Distinguished Executive of the Senior Executive Service in 1991 and Federal Executive of the Year in 1992 by the Federal Executive Alumni Association. Dr. Lenfant received the Surgeon General's Exemplary Award in 1993, the Laura Graves Award—National Marrow Donor Program and the Consortium of Southeastern Hypertension Centers' Excellence in Leadership Award in 1995, and the Honorary Fellowship Award from the American College of Cardiology in 1997. In 1992 he received the Golden Heart Award of the American Heart Association. He holds honorary degrees from the University of New York at Buffalo; Wake Forest University, Winston Salem; University of Medona, Italy; University of Montpellier, France; and the Medical University of Toledo, Ohio. His memberships include the Soviet Union's Academy of Medical Sciences and of the National French Academy of Medicine. He is a fellow of the Royal College of Physicians (London), an honorary member of the Royal Society of Medicine, and an honorary fellow in the Polish Society of Hypertension. Dr. Lenfant is a member of the American Society for Clinical Investigation, and the Association of American Physicians. He has served on the editorial boards of the *Journal of Applied Physiology*, *American Review of Respiratory Disease*, and the *American Journal of Medicine*. He is the chief editor of a series of monographs, Lung Biology in Health and Disease, that includes 212 volumes. He has published 308 papers in his areas of research interest.

Spero M. Manson, Ph.D., is Professor of Psychiatry, and Head, American Indian and Alaska Native Programs at the University of Colorado Health Sciences Center. Over the last 19 years, Dr. Manson and his colleagues have acquired a research portfolio currently in excess of $62 million, drawing upon federal, state, private, and tribal sources, and involving collaboration with 102 Indian and Native communities. He has published over 160 articles on the assessment, epidemiology, and prevention of alcohol, drug, mental and physical health problems across the developmental life span of Indian and Native people. Dr. Manson is the founding editor of *American Indian and Alaska Native Mental Health Research*, a professionally refereed journal dedicated to this area of concern. He also serves on a wide range of boards and panels, including the National Institute of Mental Health, Office of the Surgeon General, Department of Veterans Affairs, Office of Technology Assessment, IOM, State of Oregon Governor's Commission on Alcohol and Drugs, American Association of Retired Persons, Gerontological Society of America, and Denver Community Mental Health Commission. Dr. Manson has received numerous awards for his work, including the Colorado Public Health Association Researcher of the Year (1994), Beverly Visiting Professorship at the Clarke Institute of Psychiatry, University of Toronto (1995), the Indian Health Service's Distinguished Service Award (1996, 2004), the prestigious Rema Lapouse Mental Health Epidemiology Award from the American Public Health Association (1998), Walker-Ames Professorship at the University of Washington (1999–2000), the Hammer Award from former Vice President Gore (1999), being named among the 10 Best TeleHealth Programs in the US by *TeleHealth Magazine*, and election to the IOM (2002).

Jeanne Miranda, Ph.D., is a Professor in the Department of Psychiatry and Biobehavioral Sciences at UCLA. She is a mental health services researcher who has focused her work on providing mental health care to low-income and minority communities. She holds a Ph.D. in Clinical Psychology from University of Kansas and completed post-doctoral training at University of California, San Francisco. Dr. Miranda's major research contributions have been in evaluating the impact of mental health care for ethnic minority communities. She conducted a trial of treatment of depression in impoverished minority patients at San Francisco General Hospital. Traditional care for depression was contrasted with traditional care supplemented by case management. Case management offered additional benefits for Latino patients but was not beneficial for African American and white participants. She has also studied the impact of care for depression in low-income, minority women screened through county entitlement programs. This study found that short-term care for depression is effective for impoverished women, but outreach is necessary to engage these women in care. Dr. Miranda is an investigator in two UCLA centers focusing on improving disparities in health care for ethnic minorities. She directs community cores and an innovative research core focusing on translating lifestyle interventions (diet and exercise) for low-income and minority communities. She was the Senior Scientific Editor of Mental Health: Culture, Race and Ethnicity, A Supplement to Mental Health: A Report of the Surgeon General, published August 2001. She is a member of the IOM of the NAS.

Kyu Bak Louis Rhee, M.D., M.P.P., serves as a primary care physician and medical director at the Upper Cardozo Community Health Center in Washington, DC. He is board-certified in both Internal Medicine and Pediatrics and he is an active member of the National Health Service Corps. As medical director of the largest community health center serving the underserved in Washington, DC, he manages and leads a staff of over 40 full- and part-time clinicians. He also has a joint appointment at the George Washington University School of Public Health in the Departments of Prevention and Community Health and Health Policy. He teaches a course on Health Disparities and Community Health Management and Leadership. In addition, Dr. Rhee is the immediate Past President of the Board of the Association of Clinicians for the Underserved (ACU). ACU is a national, nonprofit, transdisciplinary organization of clinicians, advocates, and health care organizations united in a common mission to improve the health of America's underserved populations by enhancing the development and support of the health care clinicians serving these populations. Prior to coming to Washington, DC, Kyu did his residency and served as a Chief Resident in Internal Medicine and Pediatrics at Cedars-Sinai Medical Center in Los Angeles, California. His medical school training occurred at the University of Southern California in Los Angeles. He also finished a Master's degree in Public Policy with a concentration in Health Policy at the John F. Kennedy School of Government at Harvard University. His undergraduate education was at Yale University where he received a Bachelor's degree in Science in Molecular Biophysics and Biochemistry and also served as President of the 5,100-member student body.

Lynne D. Richardson, M.D., F.A.C.E.P., is Associate Professor of Emergency Medicine and Vice Chair for Academic, Research and Community Programs of the Department of Emergency Medicine at the Mount Sinai School of Medicine in New York City. She holds Bachelor of Science degrees from the Massachusetts Institute of Technology in Life Sciences and Management; and an M.D. degree from the Albert Einstein College of Medicine (AECOM). Her postdoctoral training included the Emergency Medicine Residency at Jacobi Hospital/AECOM, and a research fellowship with the AAMC Health Services Research Institute. Dr. Richardson is a nationally recognized expert in health services research; her areas of interest are access to care, ED utilization and ED crowding. She was the Principal Investigator of the Emergency Medicine Patients' Access to Healthcare (EMPATH) Study and the New York City Site Principal Investigator for the PAD Trial, an NHLBI-funded, randomized trial of public access defibrillation. She is currently Principal Investigator of "*Community VOICES*" (Views On Informed Consent In Emergency Situations), an NHLBI-funded project to study community perspectives on the ethics of research without consent in emergency conditions. She has served on the Agency for Healthcare Research and Quality's Research Training study section, and review panels for the National Institute for Alcohol Abuse and Alcoholism and NHLBI. Dr. Richardson serves on the American College of Emergency Physicians (ACEP) Public Health Committee and for the past three years has been national ACEP liaison to the Healthy People 2010 Consortium. Dr. Richardson's other current memberships include the Society for Academic Emergency Medicine (SAEM) HP 2010 Task Force, the joint SAEM/CORD (Council of Residency Directors) Diversity Curriculum Task Force, the New York City Board of Health and the New York City Advisory Committee on Weapons of Mass Destruction.

Antonia M. Villarruel, Ph.D., is Professor and The Nola J. Pender Collegiate Chair in Health Promotion at The University of Michigan. She has an extensive background in health promotion and health disparities research and practice. Her research focuses on the development and testing interventions to reduce HIV sexual risk among Mexican and Latino youth. Dr. Villarruel is also the Director of a National Institute of Nursing Research P20, which is a partnership with the University of Texas Health Sciences Center in San Antonio, designed to increase the capacity of minority nurse researchers. Dr. Villarruel has assumed leadership roles in many national and local organizations. She is the Vice President and founding member of the National Coalition of Ethnic Minority Nursing Associations and past president of the National Association of Hispanic Nurses. She was appointed by Secretary Thompson to the HRSA/CDC HIV/STD Advisory Council and also served as a charter member of the Secretary of the Department of Health and Human Services' Advisory Council on Minority Health and Health Disparities.

David R. Williams, Ph.D., is at the University of Michigan where he serves as the Harold W. Cruse Collegiate Professor of Sociology, a Senior Research Scientist at the Institute for Social Research, a Professor of Epidemiology in the School of Public Health, and a Faculty Associate in the Center for AfroAmerican and African Studies and the Program of Research on Black Americans. Previously, he was an Associate Professor of Sociology, Yale University, and Associate Professor of Public Health, Yale School of Medicine. He holds a master's degree in public health from Loma Linda University and a Ph.D. in Sociology from the University of Michigan. His research has focused on social influences on health and he is centrally interested in the trends and determinants of socioeconomic and racial differences in mental and physical health. He is the author of more than 125 papers in scientific journals and edited collections. He has served as a member of the editorial board of 8 scientific journals and as a reviewer for some 45 others. In 1995, he received an Investigator Award in Health Policy Research from the Robert Wood Johnson Foundation. In 2001, he was elected as a member of the Institute of Medicine of the National Academy of Sciences. He has served on the Department of Health and Human Services' National Committee on Vital and Health Statistics (and chair of its subcommittee on Minority and Other Special Populations), and on five panels for the IOM/NAS. He has also held elected and appointed positions in professional organizations, such as the American Sociological Association and the American Public Health Association. Currently, he is a member of the board of directors for Academy Health and is a member of the MacArthur Foundation's Research Network on Socioeconomic Status and Health.

HEALTH SCIENCES POLICY BOARD LIAISON

Martha N. Hill, R.N., Ph.D., FAAN, is Dean and Professor at the Johns Hopkins University School of Nursing. Dr. Hill has been a faculty member of the School of Nursing since it opened in 1983 and holds academic appointments in The Johns Hopkins University Bloomberg School of Public Health and The Johns Hopkins University School of Medicine. From 1994 to 2001, she directed the School of Nursing Center for Nursing Research. Dr. Hill received a doctorate in behavioral sciences from The Johns Hopkins University School of Hygiene and Public Health, a Master of Science degree in nursing from the University of Pennsylvania, and a Bachelor of Science degree in nursing from The Johns Hopkins University. Dr. Hill is a Fellow in the American Academy of Nursing and a member of the IOM of the NAS. She served as the co-Vice Chair of the IOM Committee which produced the 2002 publication "Unequal Treatment: Confronting Ethical and Racial Disparities in Health Care." She also served on the IOM/National Research Council committee which produced the report "Enhancing the Vitality of the National Institutes of Health: Organizational Change to Meet New Challenges." Currently she serves on the IOM Board on Health Sciences Policy. Dr. Hill also is a past president of the American Heart Association (1997–1998), the only nonphysician to serve in that role. Internationally known for her research, Dr. Hill's studies have focused on preventing and treating hypertension and its complications, particularly among young, urban African American men. She currently is an active investigator on several NIH-funded projects, including "Comprehensive HBP Care for Young Urban Black Men," "Barriers to HBP Care and Control in Black South Africans," and "Research Training in Health Disparities in Underserved Populations." Dr. Hill has also consulted on hypertension and other cardiovascular-related issues among populations outside the United States, including those in Australia, Israel, Scotland, South Africa, and China. Dr. Hill has over 150 publications, including journal articles and book chapters on hypertension care and control, nurse led clinics, and community outreach. She currently serves on several review panels, editorial boards, and advisory committees including the Board of Directors of Research!America.

IOM PROJECT STAFF

Faith Mitchell, Ph.D., is a Senior Program Officer at The National Academies, where she has been on the staff since 1995. Her professional experience includes ethnographic research, academic appointments, philanthropy, and government service. She is co-editor of several National Research Council reports, including *Multiple Origins, Uncertain Destinies: Hispanics and the American Future; Hispanics and the Future of America; Terrorism: Perspectives from the Behavioral and Social Sciences*; *Discouraging Terrorism: Some Implications of 9/11*; *America Becoming: Racial Trends and Their Consequences*; *Governance and Opportunity in Metropolitan America*; and *Premature Death in the New Independent States*. Her doctorate is in medical anthropology from the University of California, Berkeley.

Monique B. Williams, Ph.D., is a Program Officer at The National Academies. Dr. Williams received her B.A. in Urban Studies from Vanderbilt University in 1997. After receiving her Ph.D. in Demography from the University of Pennsylvania in 2001, she worked as a demographic statistician at the U.S. Census Bureau. She joined the IOM staff for the Committee on the Review and Assessment of the NIH's Strategic Research Plan to Reduce and Ultimately Eliminate Health Disparities in 2004 after serving as a research analyst on the National Institute of Alcohol Abuse and Alcoholism-sponsored Alcohol Epidemiology Database Surveillance project at CSR, Incorporated.

Thelma Cox is a Senior Program Assistant in the Board on Health Sciences Policy. During her years at the IOM, she has also provided assistance to the Division of Health Care Services and the Division of Biobehavioral Sciences and Mental Disorders. Ms. Cox has worked on several IOM reports, including *In the Nation's Compelling Interest: Ensuring Diversity in the Health-Care Workforce; Unequal Treatment: Confronting Racial and Ethnic Disparities in Health Care;* and *Ethical Issues Relating to the Inclusion of Women in Clinical Studies.* She has received the National Research Council Recognition Award and two IOM Staff Achievement Awards.

Index

C

I

N

O

P

Q

R

S

T

U

V

W